PROUST, A JEWISH WAY

EUROPEAN PERSPECTIVES

Proust *"Jéru-salem! Jéru-salem!"* (title page)

Illustration © Coll. Reiner Speck, Cologne.

PROUST, A JEWISH WAY

ANTOINE COMPAGNON

Translated by Jody Gladding

Columbia University Press
New York

Columbia University Press wishes to express its appreciation for assistance given by the government of France through the Ministère de la Culture in the preparation of this translation.

Columbia University Press
Publishers Since 1893
New York   Chichester, West Sussex
Copyright © 2022 Editions Gallimard
Translation copyright © 2024 Columbia University Press

Library of Congress Cataloging-in-Publication Data
Names: Compagnon, Antoine, 1950- author. | Gladding, Jody, 1955- translator.
Title: Proust, a Jewish way / Antoine Compagnon ; translated by Jody Gladding.
Other titles: Proust du côté juif. English
Description: New York : Columbia University Press, 2024. | Series: European
    perspectives : a series in social thought and cultural criticism | Includes
bibliographical references and index.
Identifiers: LCCN 2024023474 (print) | LCCN 2024023475 (ebook) | ISBN 9780231211345
    (hardback) | ISBN 9780231211352 (trade paperback) | ISBN 9780231558860 (ebook)
Subjects:LCSH:Proust,Marcel,1871- 1922—Appreciation—France—History—
    20th century. | Proust, Marcel, 1871-1922—Relations with Jews. | Judaism and
literature—France—History—20th century. | LCGFT: Literary criticism. Classification:
LCC PQ2631.R63 Z545984713 2024 (print) | LCC PQ2631.R63 (ebook) |
    DDC 843/.912—dc23/eng/20240528

Cover design and illustration: Henry Sene Yee

EUROPEAN PERSPECTIVES

A SERIES IN SOCIAL THOUGHT AND CULTURAL CRITICISM

Lawrence D. Kritzman, Editor

European Perspectives presents outstanding books by leading European thinkers. With both classic and contemporary works, the series aims to shape the major intellectual controversies of our day and to facilitate the tasks of historical understanding.

For a complete list of books in the series, please see the Columbia University Press website.

Columbia University Press gratefully acknowledges the generous contribution to this book provided by the Florence Gould Foundation Endowment Fund for French Translation.

Swann belonged to that strong Jewish race, in whose vital energy and resistance to death its individuals themselves seem to share.

Contents

Introduction

During the decade that followed Marcel Proust's untimely death in 1922, how was his novel received in the Jewish community by those who were called the "French Israelites?" And how did the rising generation read *À la recherche du temps perdu*, in particular the "few young Jews and half-Jews" who would promptly discuss it? I am quoting the title of the volume published by André Spire in 1928, *Quelques juifs et demi-juifs*, a collection that, not surprisingly, included a chapter entitled "Marcel Proust."[1] The earliest reception of Proust's work in those circles and those years could shed light on some questions we are asking ourselves today.

In relation to Proust, these men, plus a few women, represented the next generation, the one discovering *À la recherche du temps perdu* with the publication of its first volume, *Du côté de chez Swann*, in 1913, on the eve of World War I, or more likely, the second volume, *À l'ombre des jeunes filles en fleur*, after it was awarded the Prix Goncourt in 1919 and thanks to the publicity that followed. Having cast aside the assimilationist illusion that had characterized Israelitism and Franco-Judaism in the decades between the Restoration and July Monarchy and the Dreyfus affair, many members of this younger generation were attracted to political Zionism after the November 1917 Balfour Declaration in favor of establishing a Jewish homeland in Palestine. What was their attitude toward their elders, and toward Proust especially? Were they suspicious of him? Were they captivated by him? Did they reject him, embrace him, or not even know about him?

Proust is sometimes described as "anti-Semitic," even "anti-Jewish."[2] The treatment of Bloch, Swann, Nissim Bernard, and Rachel in his work shocks present-day sensibilities. The discourse on the *"race maudite"* in *Sodome et Gomorrhe I*, linking homosexuals and Jews, is increasingly perceived in the twenty-first century as "a classic form of self-hatred."[3] In one recent work, a strange, generous, and slightly mad mix of erudition and fabrication, we can read this: "The reader cannot help but breathe in the odor of anti-Semitism enveloping Combray. It will never stop emanating from the novel."[4]

Except that the young Proustian Zionists of the 1920s were in no way alerted to this stench. How did they judge Proust and his novel? Does it really make sense to call one or the other, the man or the work, or both of them, anti-Semitic? Or does that judgment rest on an anachronism, the projection onto the past of our present sensitivities and our good conscience, instructed by the Holocaust? Those are some of the questions I will try to answer in the following pages.[5]

This book was written during the COVID confinement of spring 2020. With time on my hands, I decided to revive and carry through to completion a research project I had begun many years earlier. I wanted to examine the way in which Proust's work was read by the French Jewish community during the 1920s, and by young Zionists in particular.

The strange circumstances under which we were living led me to consider presenting this work in the form of "research notes" or a "work in progress," or simply a series of posts I would publish on the Collège de France website to entertain Proust lovers. Their comments would be taken into account in the book that might perhaps result from this new writing experiment.

The bet was on. I submitted my materials over the following ten weeks. When confinement ended, I was able to go to libraries and archives to complete my research, and especially to the Père-Lachaise cemetery, which became both the point of departure and the last stop on the itinerary, as we will see. From Père-Lachaise to Père-Lachaise, in short. After a book of ragpicking with *Les chiffonniers de Paris*, here is a book of grave digging, or rather of unearthing the tomb of the Weils, Proust's maternal family, in the Jewish section of the east Paris cemetery.

Along the way, this series was given boosts several times through sudden new developments and dramatic turns of events, thanks to documents that were sent to me and memories that were reawakened. The notebook form allows a research project to become collective. Readers awaited the regular appearance of entries, responded, sent comments, approved or disputed the development, enriched the discourse, and transformed a solitary inquiry into a close collaboration. This book is dedicated to them.

CHAPTER 1

Ultima Verba

The point of departure for this inquiry is a sentence by Proust, often cited as the last word on the Jewish question. In his final years Proust supposedly confided to a correspondent whose identity remains unknown to us (at least for the moment): "There is no longer anybody, not even myself, since I cannot leave my bed, who will go along the Rue du Repos to visit the little Jewish cemetery where my grandfather, following a custom that he never understood, went for so many years to lay a stone on his parents' grave."

During the First Empire, through a decree issued 15 June 1809, the Seine prefect, Nicolas Frochot, made available to the Jewish consistory of Paris a part of the capital's east cemetery, called Mont-Louis or Père-Lachaise, and opened by Frochot in March 1804. The central consistory of France and the departmental consistories had just been established in 1808 by Napoleon I, following the Grand Sanhédrin convened in 1807. That part of the east cemetery located along Rue Saint-André, renamed Rue du Repos in 1873, was surrounded by walls paid for by the consistory (figure 1).[1] "In Père-Lachaise, as in all other cemeteries, the Jews had a burial ground enclosed by walls, absolutely isolated, before which was a chamber where prescribed purifications were performed and where all religious rituals could be carried out far from the eyes of nonbelievers," wrote Maxime Du Camp in his monumental monograph of Paris in the early 1870s.[2] The consistory kept the burial registry until 1828, at which time they provided the cemetery commissioner with a map identifying the grave sites. Baruch Weil, Proust's great-grandfather, grandfather of Madame Proust, née Jeanne Weil, was born about 1780 in Niederenheim in Alsace (Niedernai, Bas-Rhin). Founder of the Weil dynasty, he was buried in the Jewish section of Père-Lachaise in 1828. It was at his tomb that Proust's grandfather, Nathé Weil, led his grandson in the annual ritual.

Figure 1. Père-Lachaise Cemetery, seventh division.

Photo © Collection particulière / private collection.

THE PATRIARCH

Baruch Weil spent part of his childhood in Germany, near Frankfurt, where his father, Lazare Weil, or Leyser Weyl (c. 1742–1815) was said to have trained in the porcelain trade. During the Directory, the family settled in Fontainebleau, where a porcelain factory had been established in 1795 by Alsatian Jews. The enterprising young Weil took over the business in 1799 and rapidly grew rich, between the Fontainebleau factory, which his father turned over to his brother Cerf Weil (c. 1788–1836), and the decoration workshops and warehouse established in Paris in 1802.[3] Considered a Paris manufacturer, he soon became a distinguished member of the capital's Jewish community. He was the collector for and then a member of the charity committee created by the Paris consistory in 1809; he was president of that committee from 1816 to 1820, at which time he was elected to the Paris consistory where he served as vice-president from 1824 until his death; he also served on the education committee from the time of its creation by the consistory in 1819.[4] Charity and education were the two social missions of highest priority to the Jewish community.

As a wise businessman and Paris notable, Baruch Weil's first establishment was on Rue du Temple, under the sign "Au vase d'or."[5] Then the business moved to Rue Chapon and Rue Boucherat, present-day Rue de Turenne, while in the 1820s, his warehouse was on Rue de Bondy, present-day Rue René-Boulanger, between the Saint-Martin gate and the Château-d'Eau fountain, near the present-day Place de la République. He also opened a shop in an elegant neighborhood, at 10–12 Galerie de l'Horloge, in the Passage de l'Opéra, inaugurated in 1822 near the new Le Peletier opera house (figure 2). The Duchess of Berry was a faithful client;[6] *Le guide des acheteurs ou Almanach des passages de l'Opéra* compared Baruch

Figure 2. Charles Marville *Passage de l'Opéra, Galerie de l'Horloge*, 1865–1868. Photo © CC0 Paris Musées / Musée Carnavalet.

and Cerf Weil to Bernard Palissy, whose methods they credited with "the highest degree of perfection." The king granted them his royal warrant and "one of them has just been decorated."[7]

Baruch Weil was indeed named knight of the Legion of Honor, symbolizing his success as "founder of the great porcelain factory established in Fontainebleau" on the occasion of the coronation of Charles X in May 1825 in a royal decree of 13 May 1825.[8] He had just presented to the king a portrait "remarkable for its finish and its resemblance."[9] During the Exhibition of Industrial Products at the Louvre in August 1827, his porcelain pieces won praise: "M. Baruch-Weil, 16 Rue de Bondy, exhibited, among other remarkable pieces, a lilac-colored tea service in the most exquisite taste," read one review of the exhibition.[10] "M. Baruch-Weil, manufacturer in Fontainebleau, whose porcelain store is in the Passage de l'Opéra, exhibited several remarkable pieces, especially a dish of great size and perfect whiteness," added *Le Constitutionnel*.[11] Too bad if *Le Figaro*, then a small newspaper, poked fun, "That is the work of M. Baruch-Weil. What soft shades! What great size!"[12] As the exhibit was held in a temporary structure erected in the courtyard of the Louvre, Baruch Weil argued for the construction of a permanent hall for industrial exhibitions.[13]

At the time of his death less than a year later, on 8 April 1828, at a very young age—forty-eight according to the newspapers, forty-six according to the registry—he left eleven living children, nine of whom were minors, out of at least thirteen children whom his two wives had born to him.[14] "The entire Jewish population of Paris and a crowd of distinguished people of other religions accompanied the mortal remains of this good man to the final resting place."[15] His assets were estimated at about 280,000 francs, a large fortune to amass in twenty years (in Paris, a male worker's daily earnings were two to three francs at that time). But his estate was complicated, between the factory, warehouse, and shop, and his heirs soon abandoned the porcelain business.[16]

THE DYNASTY

Two family vaults existed in the Jewish section of Père-Lachaise. Not long after the definitive opening of the Jewish enclosure in February 1810, one of the first tombs was destined for Hélène Schoubach (1787–1811).[17] She was Baruch Weil's first wife, the daughter of Moÿse Schoubach, a prominent member of the Paris Jewish community, head of one of the mutual aid societies (*hevra kadicha*) active before the consistory was established.[18] That tomb is no longer to be found.

Seven of Hélène Schoubach's children were alive when their mother died in 1811.[19] But only five were still alive when their father died in 1828): Merline, Godecheaux, Benjamin, Moyse, and Joseph Pinckhas (Mayer and Jules had died by that time).

Merline (1804–1873), called Mélanie, married Benoist Léon Cohen (1798–1856), born in Amsterdam, and employed in his father-in-law's business.[20] He came into the warehouse on Rue de Bondy by auction in January 1829. Once the Fontainebleau factory was sold in 1833, he worked in insurance. Also very active in Jewish organizations, he became a member of the charity committee, and then its vice president, president, honorary president, member of the consistory, and finally the first director of the Rothschild hospital.[21]

Godchaux (1806–1878), Godecheaux for the registry office, the oldest of Baruch's surviving sons, inherited a share of his father's business in partnership with his uncle Cerf Weil and his brother-in-law Benoist Cohen, before leaving the porcelain business for law.[22] In 1841 he became Paris's first Jewish bailiff.[23] He also took on responsibilities in the community, including secretary for the consistory, member of the school committee, and member of the charity committee. A strong personality and energetic writer, he became a faithful contributor to the *Archives isréalites de France*, a new periodical for Reformed Judaism, created in 1840 (known as the *Archives isréalites* beginning in 1848). Throughout the 1840s, under the pseudonym of Ben Lévi for his news articles, and under the Initial W. for his columns on religion or current events, he argued for the social and civic assimilation of Jews even while opposing their cultural absorption.[24] Before Marcel Proust he was the first writer of note in the family. His publications are important, and we will return to him.

Benjamin (1807–1866) was a building contractor.[25] He went bankrupt in Paris in 1837.[26] He then settled in Algeria as head of colonial operations.[27] Finally he became an architect.[28] He married Rachel Crémieux (1825–1901) in Algiers in 1842.[29] He worked as an architect in Lyon and then in Marseille, where he died and where his children remained.[30] His oldest son, Alfred Weil (1843–1926), was a naturalist and director of the Marseille Zoological Garden beginning in 1880, and then director of technical services for the Paris Zoological Garden, the setting for the public exchange between Madame Blatin and a Sinhalese reported by Swann in *À l'ombre des jeunes filles en fleur*: " 'Me blackie,' he bellowed at Mme Blatin, 'you camel!' "[31] It was also a regular destination for the hero who accompanies Madame Swann there.[32] Another of his sons, Félix Weil (1852–1932), attended the funeral of his cousin Georges Weil, Madame Proust's brother, in 1906, proof that relations had not broken off between the cousins.[33]

Moïse (1809–1874), Moyse for the registry office, became an architect for the state in the département of Oise.[34] He was in charge of building a Catholic seminary in Beauvais, hailed by the *Archives israélites de France* in 1845 as proof of the beginning of "the era of true tolerance."[35] He married Amélie Berncastell (1821–1911), elder sister of Proust's grandmother, Adèle Berncastell, and he never left Beauvais.[36] A member of the Société Française pour la Conservation des Monuments, the Société des Antiquaires de Picardie, and other scholarly organizations, he was the author of a study on church crypts and undergrounds in the département of Oise.[37] These crypts prefigure the depths of Saint-Hilaire in Combray, where Théodore guides the hero "into a Merovingian night."[38]

And finally, Joseph Pinckhas, born in Paris on 10 July 1811, was the last child of the first marriage.[39] We know almost nothing about him, not even the date of his death, but he is named in his father's will in 1828, as heir to an eleventh of his father's estate, and much later, in the will of his half-brother Lazard, called Louis, in 1886, which lists his residence as Rue des Jardins in Koléa, twenty-five kilometers southwest of Algiers, Algeria. We do not know if he was married or had children; the bequest was removed in a codicil in 1895, either because Joseph had died in the interim or because Louis had decided to leave him nothing (as with the children of his half-brothers Godchaux and Benjamin).[40]

Baruch Weil believed in the benefits of learning and he had greatly invested in the education of his sons.[41] He entrusted this to David Drach, a rabbi employed by the central consistory, whose conversion to Catholicism in 1823 left a lasting mark on the Paris Jewish community.[42]

The name Baruch-Weil, beside that of Jeramec-Raphaël, appears at the bottom of a lithograph representing the consistorial temple on Rue Notre-Dame-de-Nazareth, the Ashkenazi synagogue that opened in 1822 (figure 3). Along with Raphaël Jeramec (1807–1870), the Baruch-Weil who contributed to the production of this print was Moïse, educated in architectural design.[43]

Baruch Weil was president of the charity committee in 1818 when the consistory asked the committee to advance the funds necessary to purchase land on

Figure 3. The Temple Israélite of Paris in 1830.
Photo © MAHJ / Christophe Fouin.

which the new synagogue was to be built. The minutes show his signature, very elaborate and assured, at the center of the page.[44]

THE SECOND MARRIAGE

At the death of Baruch Weil in 1828, a plot held in perpetuity was acquired in the Jewish section of Père-Lachaise, separate from the vault where his first wife had been buried in 1811.[45] His second wife, Marguerite Sarah Nathan (1785-1854), whom he married in 1812, joined him there at death.[46] We can find information on six children whom she raised following the death of her husband, all minors at the time.

Nathé (1814-1896) was the oldest and the grandfather of Proust.[47] He was a silent partner or associate stockbroker, working for Albert Ramel and then for his successor Alexandre Blin. That situation ended badly, with a lawsuit that Nathé Weil lost in 1893.[48] He married Adèle Berncastell (1824-1890), and they had two children, Georges (1847-1906), a magistrate—Georges Baruch Denis for the registry office, Georges-Denis on the cover of his works—and Jeanne (1849–1905), who married the doctor Adrien Proust.

Lazard (1816–1896), called Louis, became a manufacturer, a button maker from 1844 to 1865, notably of Trelon-Weldon-Weil (TWW) metal buttons for uniforms.[49] His factory on Rue Bercy-Saint-Antoine, which employed more than four hundred workers, welcomed the president of the Republic on a visit there in October 1849.[50] Lazard Weil was made a member of the Legion of Honor in August 1870.[51] A person of independent means, honorary member of the customs authority commission, former member of the Comptoir National d'Escompte, widower of Émilie Oppenheim (1821–1870) and childless, Uncle Louis provided a home to the family of his brother Nathé, his niece Jeanne, and his Proust grand-nephews at his residence in Auteuil. Marcel Proust was born there. Jeanne Weil and her brother Georges were his sole legatees.[52]

Adélaïde (1818–1892), called Adèle, married Joseph Lazarus (1815–1850).[53] He was a clock merchant at the time of their marriage in 1845.[54] She was the mother of Laure Lazarus Neuburger and the grandmother of Louise Neuburger, who married Henri Bergson.

Of Salomon we know little more than we do of his half-brother Joseph, only that he was born in Paris in 1820 and that he is also listed for an eleventh of his father's estate in 1828.[55] He does not appear in Louis's will of 1886, and must therefore have died in the interim. Are these two unknown half-brothers, Joseph and Salomon (in addition to Mayer and Jules, dead between 1811 and 1828) the cloth merchants Salomon and Joseph Weil whose company, the Weil Brothers, went bankrupt in Paris in 1859?[56] Did Salomon try his luck in Algeria like his older half-brothers Benjamin and Joseph?

Abraham Alphonse (1822–1886), a military officer, fought in the African campaign and was part of the expeditionary corps in Rome. A prisoner of war briefly following the siege of Strasbourg, he received the Legion of Honor in October 1870.[57] Unmarried, he retired in 1872 as captain and paymaster of the Eighty-Seventh Heavy Infantry Regiment.[58]

And last, Flora (1824–1867), who married Edmond Alcan (1824–1893) in 1850, a merchant and sometime maker of caps.[59] She lived on Rue de l'Echiquier at the time of her death, not far from her brothers and especially 40a Rue de Faubourg-Poissonière, home of Proust's grandparents.[60] In the marble tomb of the Jewish section of Montmartre, the dates are inscribed in Hebrew, evidence of her fidelity to her religion. Baruch Weil was undoubtedly a remarkable man of many talents, a dazzling career, and exceptional accomplishments. He faithfully adhered to the Torah's precept: "Be fruitful and multiply." His first wife gave him a daughter and six sons in seven years, before dying at the age of twenty-four; his second wife, more moderate, gave him four sons and two daughters in ten years and lived to be almost seventy.

One of Baruch's cardinal responsibilities among his fellow believers deserves to be noted: for a long time he was the *mohel* for the Paris Jewish community, its appointed circumciser. According to custom, the circumciser himself practiced on his sons: "My respectable father performed circumcisions at least six hundred times, and always, thank God, without the slightest accident," wrote Godchaux Weil in 1821. "He himself circumcised his eight sons."[61] Godchaux was then a young man of fifteen, and his pamphlet in defense of Jewish traditions was clearly inspired by his father, proud of his circumcising feats. The *Archives israélites de France* evoked them in 1844, well after his death: "For the twenty-five years that the now deceased Baruch Weil practiced in Paris with so much zeal, piety, and selflessness, no one, from the richest to the poorest, would allow a child to be circumcised by an outside *mohel*."[62]

His sons retained a lasting admiration for him, especially Nathé, who was not yet fourteen when he lost his father. The four sons of the first marriage, Godchaux, Benjamin, Moïse, and Joseph, were called Baruch-Weil long after their father's death. Thus honoring his memory and distinguishing themselves from other Parisian Weils, they made early use of the hyphen as "the democratic particle," according to Proust's estimable phrase.[63]

Raised in a large tribe, orphaned at a young age (only Merline and Godchaux were of age when their father died in 1828), Baruch's progeny did not follow their father's lead: they had either one child (Godchaux), two children (Merline, Nathé, Adélaïde), three children (Moïse, Flora), or none (Louis, Alphonse, and, it seems, Joseph and Salomon). Only Benjamin took a more traditional path: in 1842 in Algiers he married Rachel Crémieux, a seventeen-year-old originally from Avignon, with whom he had six children. There is no better evidence of the Paris Jewish community's social evolution in the nineteenth century than these small statistics.

Finally, as a last tribute to the patriarch, many of his children, Godchaux, Nathé, Louis, Adèle, and Alphonse, as well as their spouses, were buried in the Baruch Weil tomb, that tomb where Proust's grandfather Nathé brought his grandson, in the little Jewish cemetery on Rue du Repos.

THE FIRST WRITER

Ben Lévi was a pen name of Godchaux Weil, the oldest son of Baruch Weil and great-uncle of Proust, who paid visits to his widow, née Frédérique Zunz (1823–1897), who seems to figure allusively, under the name "Aunt Friedel," in *Jean Santeuil*.[64] Ben Lévi published a long piece in the *Archives israélites de France* in 1841 to set the record straight on the "Jewish Cemeteries of Paris," from Père-Lachaise to Montmartre. He noted there that from time immemorial, "respect for the dead has been kept pure" among the Jews.[65]

The walls surrounding the Jewish cemeteries in France, including the Jewish portion of the east Paris cemetery where the vault of Proust's great-grandparents, grandparents, uncles, and aunts is located, were pulled down following the passage of the law of 14 November 1881. That law repealed the imperial decree of 23 Prairial in year 12 of the French Republican calendar (12 June 1804) that had required towns to assign a part of a cemetery or create a cemetery especially for each religion. Fought against in vain by the Jewish press, the new law forbade any grouping by faith in the form of a physical separation from the rest of the cemetery. Called the law on the neutrality of cemeteries, it was one of the first republican laws of secularization, and it abolished Protestant and Jewish enclosures adjacent to Catholic cemeteries.[66]

As for the small stone left on the tomb during cemetery visits, especially on the eve of Rosh Hashanah or Yom Kippur, various explanations of the age-old rite have been put forward. It might have honored the site of archaic burials mounds simply marked by a pile of stones. Whatever its origin and variants (sometimes the stone is removed after the prayer, before leaving the cemetery), this custom symbolizes remembrance of the dead, the perpetuation of their memory.

If we are to believe Proust, Nathé Weil, his grandfather, placed a stone on the tombstone of his father Baruch and his mother Marguerite; this gesture was most likely accompanied by the recitation of the Kaddish, the prayer of the dead, but he no longer understood its meaning. It seems inconceivable that the tradition had been so entirely lost in the Weil family by the generation of Nathé, son of Baruch and half-brother of Godchaux, called Ben Lévi, both benefactors of the Jewish community, moderate reformists, partisans of the civic integration of French Jews but not of total assimilation or the absorption of their culture, attentive to the preservation of ancient religious customs in modern France.

Godchaux became known at a very young age, under the name of Godecheaux Baruch-Weil, for his refutation in 1821 of the radical reforms, beginning with the shifting of the Sabbath to Sunday (or at least the Sunday repetition in French of the Sabbath services in Hebrew) and the replacement of circumcision with a "symbolic solemnity," advocated by the polytechnician and mathematician Olry Terquem (1782–1862). Under the pseudonym of Tsarphati, Olry Terquem challenged Baruch Weil's activities both as manufacturer, defending the Sabbath but opening his workshops and shops on Saturdays, and as circumciser.[67] "The insult to religion and the aggressions against my virtuous father make it my duty to pick up my pen," replied Godchaux.[68] Because he was only fifteen years old, his father and his preceptor David Drach no doubt contributed to these "Reflections of a Young French Jew on the Two Pamphlets by M. Tsarphati," which served as the consistory's response to Tsarphati during the early part of the debate over reforming Judaism. Godchaux Weil would remain faithful to the position he took in 1821 in his contributions in the 1840s to the *Archives israélites de France*. For example, in the story "Les poissons et les miettes de pain" he defends the custom of Tashlikh (for Rosh Hashanah, throwing pieces of bread from one's pockets into a water source, symbolizing the casting away of one's sins).[69]

Godchaux Weil, secretary of the consistory from 1825 to 1831, member of the boys' school committee beginning in 1829, member of the charity committee beginning in 1835, never deviated from his moderate reformism, which he called "Israelitism."[70] But he also never advanced as happily as his father and his brother-in-law, Benoist Cohen, in the consistory hierarchy and its committees, and he distanced himself from those institutions in the 1850s.

He long remained alive in the memory of the Jewish community as author of a children's handbook, *Les matinées de samedi: Livre d'éducation morale et religieuse à l'usage de la jeunesse israélite*, published by the *Archives israélites de France* in 1842, with a preface by Samuel Cahen (1796–1862), the founder of that publication in 1840 and its longtime editor (his sons and three grandsons succeeded him), as well as the director of the consistory school in Paris and translator of the Bible into French.[71] Widely distributed, the handbook went through at least four editions by the end of the nineteenth century, the fourth appearing in 1897 with a foreword by Isidore Cahen (1826–1902), son of Samuel Cahen and his successor as editor of the *Archives israélites*.[72] How to imagine that Proust had not leafed through it in his youth, when visiting either his grandparents or Godchaux Weil's widow?

The *Archives israélites* still ran an advertisement for *Les matinées du samedi* in 1907 (figure 4).[73] At that time Proust was beginning to write again after two years of mourning the death of his mother; it was then he first conceived the rudiments of *À la recherche du temps perdu*. The symbolism of the stone left on the tombstone

Figure 4. Ben Lévi's *Les matinées du samedi* advertisement and funeral-home advertisements, *Archives israélites de France*, 15 August 1907.

Photo © Bibliothèque de l'Alliance israélite universelle, Paris.

could not have been unknown to Proust's grandfather, and it is highly unlikely that he had not explained it to his grandson, and that his grandson, in turn, had not performed this ritual gesture when they went together to Baruch Weil's grave in the Jewish section of Père-Lachaise.

IN THE LANGUAGE OF SHAKESPEARE

To sum up Proust's perspective on his Jewishness, his supposed *ultima verba* on his visits to the cemetery with Nathé Weil are cited almost everywhere in reputable books: by André Maurois, who places it "near the end of his life," in *À la recherche de Marcel Proust*; by Jean-Yves Tadié, who inferred from it in his Proust biography that Proust "did not consider himself Jewish;" by Évelyn Bloch-Dano in *Madame Proust*.[74] But curiously, no one gives a footnote for it or cites a source or reference. Hence these winged words have been passed along for decades without anyone knowing where they come from. Nevertheless, they are important, even essential, and could just as well indicate a nostalgic attachment on the writer's part for his Jewish origins as the indifference imagined by certain interpreters. Alice Kaplan, who translated *Madame Proust* into English, adds a note indicating that Maurois was the first to cite the words in question.[75]

In search of earlier occurrences and going back years, I soon came upon the same words in Georges Cattaui, in a note to the chapter "Proust and the Jews" in his book *L'amitié de Proust*, published in 1935 in Gallimard's "Les Cahiers Marcel Proust" series, but written in 1930, according to a note appearing on the volume's last page. The sentence is preceded there by a precise piece of information: "See André Spire: 'Marcel Proust' (*Jewish Chronicle*, May 1923) and *Quelques juifs et demi-juifs* (Grasset)."[76] Because of Cattaui's fame and his long contribution to Proust studies, spanning more than half a century, from the 1920s to the 1970s, Cattaui's book does indeed seem to be the source for subsequent appearances of the quote in the works of Maurois, Tadié, Block-Dano, and others. In fact, before 1935 (or even 1930, if his book really was composed in that year), Cattaui cited the sentence in an article, one of the first on the subject, already entitled "Proust et les juifs" and published in a French Zionist periodical, *Palestine*, in July 1928.[77] I will have reason to come back to this publication.

Yet Cattaui was not the first, it turns out. Before him, the citation seems to have appeared in a work by André Spire, in the chapter, "Marcel Proust" of his

Quelques juifs et demi-juifs, which was also published in 1928: "'There is no longer anybody,' he wrote not long ago to a friend, 'not even myself, since I cannot leave my bed, who will go along the Rue du Repos...'"[78]

There is a slight variation nevertheless between Spire's text ("*puisque je ne* peux *me lever*") and the one traditionally repeated by Maurois, Tadié, Bloch-Dano, and others ("*puisque je ne* puis *me lever*"). The transmission is complicated, since Cattaui wrote "*puisque je ne* peux *me lever*" in 1928 in the *Palestine* article, and again in 1930 (or 1935) in *L'amitié de Proust*, as did Spire, and since it was only in 1952, in *Marcel Proust: Marcel Proust et son temps, Proust et le temps*, that he began to write "*puisque je ne* puis *me lever*," as Maurois had in 1949.[79] Why, in 1952, did Cattaui substitute Spire's 1928 *peux* for Maurois's 1949 *puis*? How to explain this variant? Was it a correction made after returning to the document, or was it a misprint, a whim? Impossible to resolve this for the moment.

But let us go back still further. In *Quelques juifs et demi-juifs*, Spire dates his "Marcel Proust" chapter as 4 December 1922, barely two weeks after Proust's death on 18 November 1922; another striking detail: this chapter is dedicated to Georges Cattaui. A few pages from the middle of that chapter appeared in the Paris press some months after Proust's death, on the first page of *Nouvelles littéraires*, 28 July 1923, under the title "Marcel Proust et les Juifs," creating quite a stir (figure 5).[80] There we find the same sentence as in the 1928 book, only missing a couple commas.[81]

Now this chapter of *Quelques juifs et demi-juifs*, containing the piece from the July 1923 *Nouvelles littéraires*, was itself, as Georges Cattaui's note would suggest, the original French version of an article by Spire that appeared in English translation, under the title "Marcel Proust," in May 1923 in *The Jewish Chronicle* (figure 6).[82] Thus Proust's final word on his Jewishness appeared for the first time in the language of Shakespeare on 25 May 1923: "'There is no longer anybody,' he wrote not long ago to a friend, 'not even myself, since I cannot leave my bed, who will go along the Rue du Répos [sic] to visit the little Jewish cemetery where my grandfather, following a custom that he never understood, went for so many years to lay a stone on his parents' grave.'"[83]

The Jewish Chronicle, a weekly newspaper founded in London in 1841, is the oldest Jewish periodical published continuously to this day.[84] In 1907 it was bought by supporters of the Zionist Organization and henceforth found itself in conflict with a part of the local Jewish community and official Judaism, including the Board of Deputies of British Jews. The weekly newspaper was very influential at

LES NOUVELLES LITTÉRAIRES

ARTISTIQUES ET SCIENTIFIQUES

HEBDOMADAIRE D'INFORMATION, DE CRITIQUE ET DE BIBLIOGRAPHIE

DU COTE DE CHEZ SWANN

MARCEL PROUST et les JUIFS

JEAN AJALBERT

A TRAVERS NOS PROVINCES

LES NORMANDS

Alexandre Dumas intime

ERRATA

Du document en littérature

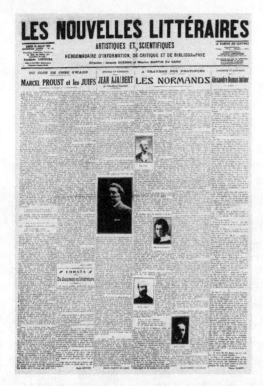

Figure 5. André Spire, "Marcel Proust et les juifs," *Les nouvelles littéraires*, 28 July 1923.

Photo © BnF, Paris.

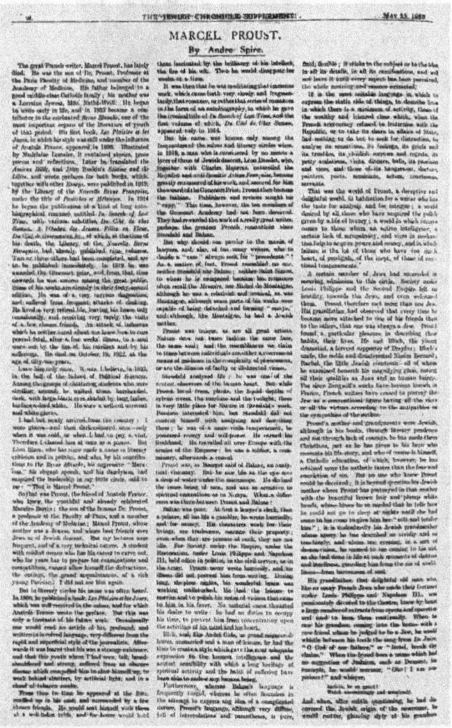
THE JEWISH CHRONICLE SUPPLEMENT. MAY 25, 1923

MARCEL PROUST.

By André Spire.

Figure 6. André Spire, "Marcel Proust," *The Jewish Chronicle*, 25 May 1923.

Photo © The Jewish Chronicle/Hartley Library, Archives & Manuscripts, University of Southampton.

the time. In 1917 the British government, which had close ties to *The Jewish Chronicle*, delayed the announcement of the Balfour Declaration so that news could be broken in its 9 November 1917 edition. Subsequently the weekly was critical of Chaim Weizmann, president of the Zionist Organization beginning in 1921, for his slowness in establishing a national Jewish homeland in Palestine.[85]

André Spire, who had declared himself a Zionist as early as 1904 and who attended the tenth Zionist Congress in Basel in 1911, wrote to his mother at the time: "It is not by assimilation that I expect us to be regenerated. Assimilation is death. Zionism is life."[86] Having served as liaison officer for the directors of the Zionist Organization during the 1919 Peace Conference in Paris, Spire was very well known to the *Jewish Chronicle*. They noted the presence of "André Spire, the well-known Jewish writer" at the funeral in Montparnasse Cemetery of Max Nordau, who died in Paris, 22 January 1923.[87] And they noted that Israel Zangwill, in his opening remarks to the American Jewish Congress in New York in October 1923 had praised "the young poets of the Diaspora, arraigning the so-called civilisation of Christendom. You can hear it in Paris from Fleg and Spire and Cohen."[88] That explains the presence, albeit disconcerting, of a long obituary of the author of *À la recherche du temps perdu* in the most influential organ of political Zionism in the English language as early as May 1923.

Given this visibility, the piece was immediately picked up by various weekly newspapers of the diaspora Jewish community in almost all of the United States, from Chicago to Philadelphia, Pittsburgh, Saint Paul, and Minneapolis.[89] Recognizing that Spire could further its cause, the Jewish Correspondence Bureau, the news service for the Zionist Organization, spread that writer's good word.

André Spire was thus apprised of these *ultima verba* as early as Proust's death in November 1922. But who was the addressee of the letter, the friend to whom Proust had written "not long ago?" Spire himself? He would have had no reason whatsoever to hide in anonymity. Or Cattaui, to whom Spire dedicated his chapter on Proust in 1928? Except, how would Spire have had access to that letter to cite these words for the first time? A young Egyptian Jew born to a prominent family in Cairo, Georges Cattaui was only twenty-six years old at the time of Proust's death, whereas André Spire, born in Nancy to a Jewish family long established in Lorraine, and a senior French official, was Proust's contemporary. The two of them will be discussed in depth further on and relevant details of their biographies will be provided. But according to Louis Gautier-Vignal in his obituary of Cattaui, Proust and Cattaui did not know each other, and Cattaui regretted it.[90] Although why title a book *L'amitié de Proust* if you had never met him? In his preface to Cattaui's book Paul Morand calls the author "one of the latecomers to Proust's friendship," thus maintaining the ambiguity.[91] It is true that Cattaui himself never claimed to have kept company with Proust, and the "unpublished letter," which he included in his book and announced on the cover to attract readers, is not addressed to him, since there is an inscription to a doctor Abel Desjardins (1870–1951), a high school friend of the Proust brothers at Condorcet and the younger brother of Paul Desjardins.[92] The Cattaui archives in Geneva contains a letter to Proust, written during a stay in Egypt and dated 10 August 1922.[93] Was it sent? We do not know and there are no letters from Proust to Cattaui or to Spire available to us. Thus the mystery regarding the addressee of Proust's *ultima verba* on his Jewishness remains unresolved for the moment.

A letter from Spire to one of his friends, the poet and translator Ludmila Savitzky, dated 30 July 1923, offers very interesting details on the article in *Nouvelles littéraires* published two days earlier: "You must have seen in the *Nlles litt* an excerpt from my 'Proust.' M d G did it himself, and could have done better, in my opinion. Of course the "flashy" title was chosen and somehow imposed by them."[94] Thus Maurice Martin du Gard, editor of *Nouvelles littéraires*, an ambitious new weekly launched less than a year earlier, in October 1922, seems to have been responsible not only for excerpting ("not the best") Spire's article but also for the title, "*Du côté de chez Swann*: Marcel Proust et les juifs," which seems to have annoyed or offended Spire. He considered it flashy, eye-catching, maybe scandalous, although he recognized its effectiveness, since he immediately conceded, "But there it is, the idea of Proust's Jewishness has now been launched in public in France. That seems necessary to me. And everyone will know that the Proust promoted by Daudet and Barrès had Jewish blood. And how will the literary public take that? Fortunately they are on vacation and thinking more about bathing in the sea than literature!"[95] Spire did not feel completely comfortable with all this, as the conflicts and convolutions of his reasoning show. He considered it useful or even indispensable for Proust's readers to know of his Jewishness, if only to discomfit those who lay claim to him, like the disciples of Barrès (who died later that year) and Léon Daudet (who sponsored Proust for the Prix Goncourt), that is, the French nationalists and far-right Action Française. In revealing their usurpation, was it possible that he himself had designs on Proust and wanted to appropriate him as well? Nevertheless, he worried about the harm his article might cause, and he ended with a clever deflection, hoping not to be read during the high summer holidays, yet not without a hint of denial. As for Ludmila Savitzky, she did not rush out to her newsstand (as Joyce's translator she was not an ardent Proustian, as we will see), and she answered Spire two days later, "I have not yet read the *Nlles littéraires* and the article on Proust."[96]

Thus André Spire seems have been first to publish a study directly addressing the question of Proust's Jewishness, first to "launch" the idea of the writer's "Jewish blood," certainly, to some degree, despite himself and not without anxiety, since the showy title must be attributed to Maurice Martine de Gard. But until there is proof to the contrary, it is very much Spire—and first in English, in the very same Zionist weekly that broke the news of the Balfour Declaration in 1917—whom we find at the origin of the tradition that has propagated Proust's remark on the Jewish cemetery on Rue du Repos, even though Spire himself was not the addressee of the letter in question.

CHAPTER 2

Menorah

Even as the *Jewish Chronicle* in London published a long obituary for
Proust, widely reprinted throughout the diaspora, his death was not
announced in either *L'univers israélite* or the *Archives israélites*, the two
major news outlets for the French Jewish community. His mother's death was the
subject of a short notice in *L'univers israélite* in 1905: "28 September. Mme Proust
(Adrien), née Weil (Jeanne), 56 years old, Rue de Courcelles, 45," sharing the page
with Charles Ephrussi (1849-1905), an art collector and editor of the *Gazette des
beaux-arts*, the review where Proust published his articles on Ruskin after Ruskin's
death.[1] Jeanne Weil had never converted, and at the request of her sons the Paris
consistory delegated a rabbi for her funeral.

Founded in 1844, *L'univers israélite*, subtitled *Journal conservateurs du judaïsme*,
was the organ of the central consistory and the Paris consistory, while the *Archives
israélites*, established four years earlier by Samuel Cahen, would long represent
reform Judaism. A bitter rivalry set these two publications against each other:
L'univers israélite was created to combat the influence of the *Archives israélites*, and
it was certainly due to positions taken by his alter ego Ben Lévi in the *Archives
israélites* that Godchaux Weil, Proust's great-uncle, lost his August 1850 election
bid for the Paris consistory, of which his father, Baruch Weil, had been a member and vice-president: "168 votes paid tribute to the skills of our witty columnist. The Paris consistory seems not yet ready to welcome literary talents,"
bemoaned the *Archives israélites*.[2] Nissim Sciama (1783-1856), a Sephardic Jew born
in Aleppo, an ostrich feather merchant, defeated Godchaux Weil. Merging
the two traditions, Portuguese and German, was the order of the day at that
time, and the opportunity for an evolving worship service divided the Jewish

community, for example, over the introduction of an organ into the synagogue. This defeat coincided with the 16 July 1850 law forbidding the use of pseudonyms in the press and followed shortly after Godchaux Weil's marriage.[3] It would temper his involvement in Jewish community institutions and bring to an end his regular contributions to the *Archives israélites*, thus curtailing Proust's great-uncle's literary career. Explaining himself in an article entitled "Défunt Ben-Lévi!" (The Late Ben-Lévi!), Godchaux Weil reconsidered the battles he had fought under this pseudonym: "With what devotion he always defended the holy cause of Judaism! With what courage he struggled ceaselessly against our adversaries from within, against our enemies from without! He began by paying his debt to Jewish youth by writing *Les matinées du samedi* and ended with contributions to the *Archives* in every register, regarding all subjects and more besides."[4] After a decade of obsessive writing, Godchaux Weil, using the new law as pretext, retired and published almost nothing more.

In January 1854 Isidore Cahen announced with great fanfare Ben Lévi's return, under the signature of W., in the *Archives israélites*:

> Hosannah! The phoenix has risen from its ashes! Ben Lévi has returned to the *Archives*, and we are not, dear reader, the first to bring you this good news, since this very issue contains visible proof in two little gems of articles that only this fine writer could produce and that need no other signature than the style in which they are written: with such a trademark, all the rules imagined by the illustrious M. Biétry become useless.[5] The recent law forbidding anonymity and use of pseudonyms in the press appears to be respected here with regard to its most important precepts. . . . Achilles shut up in his tent has finally come out; woe to the poor Hectors![6]

This proved to be a false start however, and Godchaux Weil would contribute only a few rare pieces attesting to his new activities as lawyer.[7] In 1858 two columns addressed religious freedom.[8] These were followed by a critical review in 1859.[9] He then took up his pen again in 1865, under the signature "Ben Lévi (G. Weil)" in this particular instance, to denounce the constraint of Roman Jews by Pope Pius IX and to demand their release from the ghetto, which Monseigneur de Bonnechose, archbishop of Rouen, cardinal and senator, had just depicted to the Senate in benevolent terms.[10] This intervention by Godchaux Weil won him congratulations from the Alliance Israélite Universelle.[11]

Nevertheless, in the aftermath of World War I and facing the rise of political Zionism, and under the long supervision of editor-in-chief (1891–1935) Hippolyte Prague, who opposed liberal Judaism, the *Archives israélites* hardly distinguished itself anymore from *L'univers israélite* in matters of religious orthodoxy.[12] Unlike international Zionist publications, these French papers thus took no interest in Proust, never laying claim to him (with the exceptions of a few paragraphs in the *Archives israélites*, as we will see). It was a different story with a new bimonthly Paris review, just launched in August 1922, that first went by the name *L'illustration juive*, and then, following protest from the venerable weekly *L'illustration*, took the name *Menorah* (figure 7), the candelabra with seven branches that adorns the temple of Jerusalem and symbolizes the Jewish people. Aimed at an enlightened audience, banking on the exhaustion of Franco-Judaism, and arguing for a return to Israel, *Menorah* attested to the curiosity of young Zionists regarding the Jewish presence in contemporary French literature, with Proust front and center.[13]

Figure 7. *Menorah*, 22 December 1922.

Photo © Bibliothèque de l'Alliance Israélite Universelle, Paris.

There, precisely in November 1922, we find an important article by André Spire that extends over issues 5 and 6, from 10 November to 24 November, framing the date of Proust's death, 18 November. His study, despite its title, "Romans judéo-français," essentially addresses a single work, the short novel by Jacques de Lacretelle, *Silbermann*, which had just been previewed in *La nouvelle revue français* on 1 August and 1 September 1922.[14] Published as a single volume already in October 1922 by Éditions de la NRF, this novel moved the reading public, Jews and non-Jews alike, and was awarded the Prix Femina-Vie Heureuse in December 1922.

Lacretelle knew Proust and saw him frequently beginning in 1917, and subsequently *Silbermann* would be mentioned routinely with *À la recherche du temps perdu* when the question of Jewish representations in contemporary literature arose. The hero, David Silbermann, a gifted but frail adolescent, is the victim of anti-Semitic schoolmates in Paris at an elegant Sixteenth Arrondissement lycée that resembles Janson-de-Sailly where Lacretelle had been a student. Silbermann brings to mind both Bloch for his arrogance and Swann for his endurance. Passionate about French literature but proud of his Jewishness (one of his models might have been Henri Franck, one of Lacratelle's classmates), he keeps in his library, hidden behind the works of Ronsard, Chateaubriand, Hugo, and Courier, his collection of *La Sion future*.[15] This title might call up *La Palestine nouvelle*, a bulletin published in 1918 by the Ligue des Amis du Sionisme, for which André Spire served as secretary general (and was in fact its founder).

In view of the stir created by *Silbermann* in the press, Émile Cahen, editor of the *Archives israélites* since 1902, son of Isidore Cahen and grandson of Samuel Cahen, believed that the moment had come to step in. On 30 November 1922, a few days after Proust's death, he wrote that while he considered the portrait of the "Jewish mindset" presented by Lacretelle to be one of "absolute impartiality" he held that "this book certainly had to have been written before the war, because, thank God, the fierce anti-Semitism in schools that it portrays no longer exists anywhere in our great establishments."[16]

This observation of the apparent abatement of anti-Semitism, including in the "most notoriously nationalist Paris papers" (Émile Cahen was undoubtedly thinking of *L'action française*), seems representative of the general frame of mind immediately following World War I, and it helps us to understand how Proust was read in the years following his death. The conclusion of Spire's article in *Menorah* on "Judeo-French novels" and on *Silbermann* bears the same mark. Spire reports an anti-Semitic incident that had just taken place in the Besançon lycée and that, according to him, was dealt with promptly and honorably. A month later *Menorah* reconsidered that affair and provided more details. By noteworthy coincidence, the article, entitled "Un grave incident," framed a Proust obituary written, as we will see, by Cattaui.[17] The lycée students had spit at the feet of a schoolmate named Weill after having learned from their Catholic chaplain that Muslims had treated Jews that way in the Middle Ages. The headmaster had immediately contacted the victim's parents and arranged a meeting between the rabbi and chaplain, who went to the Weills' home to apologize. Taking this information from *Menorah*, *L'univers israélite* concluded similarly that a new Silbermann affair no longer seemed possible after the "sacred union":

> The *Menorah* relates an incident that took place recently at Besançon. A Jewish student there was insulted one day by his schoolmates who filed past him spitting at his feet. Upon inquiry, it was learned that this was the result of a lesson by the Catholic chaplain of the lycée who had taught his students that Muslims had treated Jews this way in the Middle Ages. The chaplain, dismayed by the effect of his words, apologized to the Jewish family and a public explanation and very "sacred union" took place between him and the head rabbi, the school's Jewish chaplain.
>
> We do not want to dwell on this painful incident, since it was handled in a satisfactory manner; but we cannot keep from asking a few questions. Where had the Father seen that Muslims had a ritual or rule involving filing past Jews and spitting on them? Does he believe that Muslims held Christians in higher esteem? And finally, even if this lesson was historical and impartial, what place does it have in a catechism course?[18]

Nevertheless, *La vieille France*, edited by Urbain Gohier, violently denounced the way in which the school's administration had resolved the affair, the headmaster and chaplain having "humiliated the French race and patrimony before a nest of *Youddis*."[19] Thus the leniency of the three Jewish community publications, the *Archives israélites*, *Menorah*, and *L'univers israélite*, may surprise us.

At the heart of the incident, the school chaplain Father Jean Flory (1886–1949) had certainly committed a blunder, but it seems as though his catechism students' interpretation of his medieval apologue ran counter to his intentions, because he himself was never suspected of anti-Semitism. Moreover, he was later recognized as one of the "Righteous Among the Nations." In 1939, France's chief rabbi paid tribute to this social militant priest, a member of the Action Catholique de la Jeunesse Française (ACJF), for having saved and put in safekeeping the three Torahs and the shofar from the Seppois-le-Bas synagogue in Alsace that was destroyed by bombing.[20] Then, in 1942, as Montbéliard parish priest and member of the Resistance, he memorably adorned the Holy Family in a Christmas Nativity scene with a yellow star to protest the anti-Jewish policies of Vichy.[21]

After having reported this "little Silbermann affair" at Besançon, *L'univers israélite*, in its next issue, showed similar restraint in its opinion of Lucretelle's novel, since that satire spares no one, neither Jew nor gentile. The review's conclusion absolved Lacretelle because his hatred was so ecumenical: "If the author is anti-Semitic, he is also anti-Catholic, anti-Protestant, anti-academic, anti-parliamentarian, and so on."[22]

Thus *Silbermann* was discussed in the *Archives israélites* and *L'univers israélite*, but nothing could compare to the stir created by Spire's article in *Menorah*; the Jewish Correspondence Bureau had it translated into English, like his Proust obituary a few months earlier, as we have noted. Under the title "The Jew in French Literature," it appeared in many Jewish newspapers on the other side of the Atlantic.[23]

GEORGES CATTAUI, 1922

In the 22 December 1922 *Menorah*, two issues after the one featuring Spire's *Silbermann* article, the opening piece on Henri Bergson was written by Paul Allard and included a beautiful photograph because the review never gave up its ambition to become *L'illustration juive*. An obituary of Proust was also published, also accompanied by an excellent photographic portrait (figure 8).[24]

The article was unsigned, but the name of Georges Cattaui, a regular contributor to *Menorah*, appears on the cover. This glowing tribute begins with two epigraphs. The first comes from Virgil: "*Tu Marcellus eris . . . ,*" an allusion to *puer* Marcellus, son of Octavia, nephew and son-in-law of Augustus, and his heir apparent. Marcellus died at twenty years old, too soon to achieve his promise. He is celebrated in Book 6 of the Aeneid (lines 882–883) in the prophetic words of Anchises showing Aeneid, who has descended to the Underworld, the glorious descendants of his race:

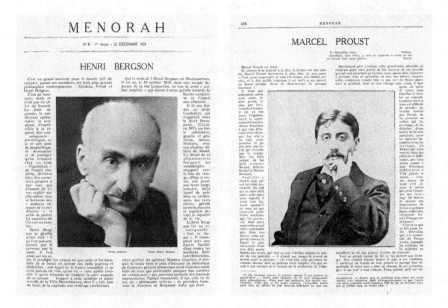

Figure 8. "Henri Bergson" and "Marcel Proust," *Menorah*, 22 December 1922.
Photo © Bibliothèque de l'Alliance Israélite Universelle, Paris.

Heu, miserande puer, si qua fata aspera rumpas!
Tu Marcellus eris. Manibus date lilia plenis . . .

Alas, boy to be pitied! If only you could shatter harsh fate!
You will be a Marcellus. Give me handfuls of lilies . . .

According to legend, Virgil read these lines to Augustus and Octavia, who fainted at hearing her son's name, withheld until the end of the account, and Virgil was paid ten thousand sesterces for each verse. The phrase *Tu Marcellus eris* widely used in the nineteenth century and appearing in the *Petit Larousse* in its pink pages of Latin and Greek sayings, expresses both regret at the premature death of a prince and the consecration of a poet, the birth of a writer. During the war, these lines, which all high-school students had translated, were often evoked to pay tribute to young men, writers in particular, killed in action without having been able to fulfill their potential.

Cattaui could have found no better line to cite, because Proust, whose work had been slow in coming, was able to identify with Marcellus. Having been awarded the Prix Goncourt and finally sure of himself, he quipped in a January 1921 note sent to Paul Souday with his book *Les plaisirs et les jours*: "A kindly oracle might have said to me, '*Tu Marcellus eris.*' But the '*aspera fata*' came."[25] This early book by the young Marcel had long remained an unfulfilled promise. Proust's lycée classmates surely used Virgil's lines to make fun of his literary ambitions. Robert Dreyfus reported that the "friends in [their] small Condorcet clan" never failed to cite this verse to him as a check against his snobbery: "we used to say to him, laughing, '*Tu Marcellus eris! . . .*' as an affectionate warning that he was just as threatened by the blows dealt by fate, and much more foolhardy than the innocent adolescent mourned by Virgil, and that he would risk wasting his divine gifts if he persisted in pursuing the perilous appeal of worldly elegance."[26]

The second of Cattaui's epigraphs evokes the words of David in the Book of Samuel: "Jonathan, my brother, I am distressed for you; you have given me the greatest pleasure."[27] The combination of Virgil and Samuel, of classical culture and the Jewish Bible, perfectly summarizes what Proust represented for Cattaui and suggests the passion he felt for the writer.

The opening words of the article touch on friendship: "If, as he liked to say, reading is friendship, then Marcel Proust will remain the dearest of my friends." Nevertheless, Cattaui omits the beginning of his Proust quote, drawn from "Sur la lecture," the 1906 preface to *Sésame et le lys*, and reprinted in *Pastiches et mélange* under the title "Journées de lecture" in 1919. Now the first part of the sentence greatly alters its meaning: "Without a doubt, friendship, friendship with respect to individuals, is a frivolous thing, and reading is friendship."[28] Comparing reading to friendship, Proust disparages rather than glorifies it. But the emphasis that Cattaui immediately puts on friendship shows that he has already identified his theme, since he would give his 1935 book the title *L'amitié de Proust*, a formulation, as we have seen, that could mislead hasty readers unless they recall how the friendship of a writer is primarily the one that results from reading that writer's work.

Proust's Jewishness was openly debated as soon as Cattaui's obituary of him appeared in December 1922, even before the one by Spire in the *Jewish Chronicle*. As a new Zionist review, *Menorah*, in league with the *Jewish Chronicle*, did not distance itself at all from Proust, and expressed not the least reservation with regard to his Jewish characters. Quite the contrary: "He alone knew how to see, understand, and judge, with an accuracy that did not exclude sympathy, those Jews around him whom he named Swann, Bloch, Rachel, and Nissim Bernard.

Perhaps he was aided in this by his maternal heritage." Or again, "She was Jewish as well, that maternal grandmother who, in his work, appears to us as the most moving figure." And the Proust novel is a miracle based on "the gift of sympathy." Even the treatment of Bloch finds favor with the obituarist of *Menorah*: "Thus Bloch, the most unbearable, the most vain of Proust's companions, is presented to us with such genuine indulgence that we are sometimes tempted to excuse him, to take pity on him, to blush for him and his blunders—a bit like Saint-Loup does." In short, all the Jewish characters in *À la recherche du temps perdu* are saved, and "if they have all the faults of certain Jews, they are at least truer, more vibrant, more recognizable than those Jewish entities that unflaggingly, for over fifty years, have been trotted out for us in plays and novels." Swann, "the most human of them," "seems to symbolize the Jewish soul itself," removed from Judaism, "suddenly [he] finds himself profoundly Jewish" and he "is not afraid to discredit himself by expressing his support of Dreyfus in anti-Semitic circles where he has been so favorably received until now."[29] He "only remembers that he is Jewish on the day when the Jew is persecuted," thus preparing the way for Zionism.

This militant Zionist periodical expresses not the least suspicion of malevolence or even ambiguity in Proust's representation of Jews in his novel. Just the opposite: "That Proust conveyed all this: his maternal heritage can undoubtedly explain it." Even the comparison with Montaigne and allusion to Bergson are already present; they would become commonplace following the article by Albert Thibaudet that appeared a month later, in January 1923, in the "Homage to Marcel Proust" issue of *La nouvelle revue française*. "He is very Jewish as well," writes Cattaui, "through the feeling he gives us of a continuous flow, a constant mobility; and in that, as in many other things, it is Montaigne, more than any other French writer, whom he calls to mind." A footnote on that page reports that the obituarist met Thibaudet a few days after writing these lines, and that they were both in agreement on this point. "Proust was born of a French father and Jewish mother," Cattaui reminds us. The statement may sound shocking today because of its exclusivity, but in *Menorah* it served to claim Proust as a Jew, *juif*, a term greatly preferred to *israélite*, the euphemism that partisans of assimilation had promoted since the emancipation. "Such marriages are often rich and fertile," the obituary continues, "It seems that crossing the strong, clear logic of the French with the nervous sensitivity of the Jews produces the most precious fruits." With regard to Montaigne, Cattaui recalls a remark by Barrès who, in *Greco ou le secret de Tolède*, after noting that Montaigne's mother belonged to a family of Marrano

refugees in France, thus infers: "This Montaigne is a bit of a foreigner who does not have our prejudices," and goes on to compare him to the poet Heinrich Heine.[30] As a great admirer of Barrès, Cattaui quotes this claim about Montaigne without comment or reservation, but as we will see, he did not accept it, which was one of the reasons he preferred Proust. Perhaps Proust was even more sensitive than Montaigne; perhaps Proust was the true humanist who united masculine will and feminine sensitivity, in the way of George Sand, Marguerite Audoux, or Anna de Noailles. "Proust is Montaigne, but Montaigne corrected by Pascal, his skepticism tempered by such ardent love for humans."[31]

Thus Proust joins a great line of prophets ("Like Pascal, Marcel Proust is all love") and before Pascal and Francis of Assisi, the prophets and mystics of Israel, including—and this is no small paradox in *Menorah*—"the greatest among them, the one who, on Golgotha, wanted to suffer and bleed for men."[32] Cattaui makes Proust a messianic and even Christlike figure, a conclusion indicating the confusion of these young Zionists whose messianic mysticism sometimes led to baptism (Jean de Menasce, Cattaui's cousin, secretary for the Zionist Organization in Geneva and assistant editor of *La revue juive* in 1925, converted in 1926, subsequently becoming a Dominican priest, and Georges Cattaui himself would be baptized in 1928).

So what did *Menorah* represent? The editorial board was introduced in the following issue, numbers 9-10, in January 1923. A mix of French Jews and immigrants, the board included, notably, Georges Cattaui, Henri Hertz, and André Spire, as well as Ludmila Bloch-Savitsky, Spire's friend, who was not Jewish. By the March 1923 issue, number 13, the board had expanded to include Edmond Fleg, Aimé Pallière, and the symbolist poet Gustave Kahn. Kahn became the editor-in-chief of *Menorah* in June 1924. The review remained faithful to Proust, and the issue on the first anniversary of his death, in December 1923, ran an article by André Spire entitled "Marcel Proust."[33] This was not simply his obituary from the May 1923 *Jewish Chronicle*, nor the shorter version from the July 1923 *Nouvelles littéraires*, which is not mentioned. An explanatory note reads: "We are publishing here the complete text, in French, of the article by André Spire written a few days after the death of Marcel Proust for the *Jewish Chronicle*, which published the English translation in its literary supplement, May 1923."[34] This time the article is dated 4-9 December 1922, immediately following Proust's death, and the famous quote on the cemetery on Rue du Repos again finds a place there.[35] Thus Spire cited it at least four times: in the

Jewish Chronicle, Les nouvelles littéraires, and *Menorah* in 1923 and in *Quelques juifs et demi-juifs* in 1928.

It is noteworthy that within the circles of political Zionism in the early 1920s there was no perceived contradiction between a commitment to Israel and a passion for Proust. André Spire and Georges Cattaui did not belong to the same generation, but they were close friends and saw each other frequently in 1922 and 1923.[36] Cattaui was still a young man of twenty-six whereas Spire was more than twice that age, but their Proust obituaries were written at the same time and resembled each other, and they were the first to report the anecdote regarding the Jewish section of Père-Lachaise. They provide the ideal entry into the world that interest us, thanks to this series of landmarks: the Proust obituary by Cattaui in *Menorah* in December 1922; the Proust obituary by Spire in the *Jewish Chronicle* in May 1923, partially reprinted in *Les nouvelles littéraires* in July 1923, and then in its entirety in *Menorah* in December 1923; Cattaui's article in *Palestine* in July 1928; Spire's chapter in *Quelques juifs et demi-juifs,* also in 1928; Cattaui's pages, which he dates to 1930, in *L'amitié de Proust* in 1935; then those by Maurois in 1949, and again those by Cattaui in 1952 and 1963, adopting Maurois's version of Proust's *ultima verba,* and finally the appearance of those last words everywhere. The fate of Proust's *ultima verba* on his Jewishness passed indisputably through Spire and Cattaui, two major intermediaries for Jewish culture, Zionism, and the Proust readership between the wars, but not only through them. A throng of young Jews (and some not so young), in fact, figure among the first champions of *À la recherche du temps perdu* in the 1920s. I will review them more or less quickly, and only some, not all of them. In the series of conferences on "Proust and his Friends," begun about ten years ago by Jean-Yves Tadié at the Fondation Singer-Polignac, it would be good to consider this little troop of scouts.[37]

ANDRÉ SPIRE, 1923

It is easy to experience a kind of optical illusion when attempting to assign André Spire (1868–1966) to an intellectual generation. That is the case as well with Julien Benda (1867–1956), another not-so-young Jewish reader of Proust between the wars and, in his case, a frankly hostile one. In fact, they both were Proust's contemporaries or even slightly older than he was (as well as a whole magnificent generation that included—in addition to Proust—Claudel, Gide, Valéry, Péguy, and Colette). But they survived him by decades (thirty-four years for Benda, forty-four years for Spire who lived for almost a century and whose daughter, the current editor of his letters, is roughly our contemporary and our friend). Thus the tendency is to identify them with the following generation, to think of them as the same age as the young readers who were discovering *Du côté de chez Swann* in 1913 or *À l'ombre des jeunes filles en fleur* in 1919, like François Mauriac, Paul Morand, Jean Cocteau, Jacques de Lacretelle, Bernard Faÿ, Philippe Soupault and so many more. They both endured World War II (Spire in America, Benda in Carcassonne and Toulouse), to emerge unscathed and rejoin Paris literary life. They lived long enough to discover *Jean Santeuil* and *Contre Sainte-Beuve*, appearing in 1952 and 1954, which reinvigorated the understanding of Proust's work by shedding light on its genesis; they witnessed the creation of the State of Israel; they learned, following the Holocaust, of definitions of Jewishness and anti-Semitism different from those current in Proust's time and the 1920s. All that explains the false impression of a great gap between them and Proust.

Born in Nancy, writer and poet, pioneer in free verse and poetic theory, Spire (figure 9) was a lawyer who went through the École Libre des Sciences Politique at the same time as Proust, whom he recalled passing in the hall in 1893.[38] He became an auditor for the Council of State in 1894, as did Léon Blum, and was involved in the Dreyfus affair. As a senior official, he worked in the Labor Ministry, participated in the movement for working-class universities, and contributed to the *Cahiers de la quinzaine* before declaring himself a Zionist in 1904, an advocate for territorialist Zionism, in the model of Israel Zangwill, and for the creation of a Jewish homeland outside of Palestine.[39] He published numerous essays and poetry collections, among them *Poèmes juifs* (1908),[40] *Le secret* (1919), and *Poèmes de Loire* (1929). Following the defeat of France in 1940 and the anti-Semitic measures taken by the Vichy, he went into exile in the United States, where he taught the history of French poetry at the New School for Social Research in New York. Returning to France after the war, he again published many works, including *Plaisir poétique et plaisir musculaire: Essai sur l'évolution des techniques poétiques* (1949), from which I benefited as a student.

Spire fought a duel in January 1895 with a journalist from *La libre parole* who had denounced the overrepresentation of Jews in the Council of State.[41] It could not have escaped him that Éduoard Drumont's daily newspaper

Figure 9. André Spire, the distinguished man of letters, at his desk, 1927.
Photo © BnF, Paris.

identified Proust as a Jew in a February 1898 article, at the height of the Dreyfus affair, among the contributors to *La revue blanche* characterized as "Dreyfus intellectuals:"

> This little society led by two Polish Jews, the Nathanson [*sic*] brothers, and composed of young Jewish literary hacks Gustave Kahn, Romain Coolus, Lucien Muhlfeld, Fernand Gregh, Marcel Proust, Tristan Bernard, Léon Blum, has just conveyed its categorical rebuke to Maurice Barrès through an article by Lucien Herr speaking for the review as a whole.... This is what a handful of Jews, newly arrived in this country, has the audacity to say to an elder, a writer of the French race like Barrès.... So they insist on introducing anti-Semitism into every soul and every corporation?[42]

No doubt this notoriety did not overjoy Professor Adrien Proust, indifferent to Alfred Dreyfus's condemnation, unlike his wife and sons. Nor was this the only mention of Proust in *La libre parole* at the time of the Dreyfus affair. On

24 April 1899, Proust gave an elegant dinner at his parents' home. The whole press talked of it, including Drumont's newspaper:

> Noble gentlemen, intellectuals, and great Yids continue to flirt with more gusto than ever.
>
> Last Monday, an illustrious unknown poet by the name of Marcel Proust hosted a delightful soirée that gathered together the Cahens of Anvers, the Foulds, the Strausses [sic], Edmond de Rothschild, and Charles Ephrusi [sic]. Also present was Anatole France and his brilliant friend, the boring poet Robert de Montesquiou.[43]

Spire is mentioned in a letter from Proust to Daniel Halévy from December 1913, shortly after the publication of *Du côté de chez Swann*: "Dear friend, if among the young or old intelligentsia whom you know, there are some (who knows, the Spires, the Porchés, the Bendas, or Péguy, I name at random) whom you think would like my book, I would be happy to send you a few copies to give to them."[44] All those Proust named belonged to the circle of the *Cahiers de la quinzaine*, including François Porché (1877–1944), the future husband of Pauline Benda (1877–1985), the famous Madame Simone, who even survived her cousin Julien Benda and was well over a hundred years old when she died. The uncertainty regarding age for this ever pugnacious *Quinzaine* band was already present, since Proust, a contemporary who nevertheless always behaved like the youthful old man, hesitated to call them all "young."

Following this exchange, Halévy seems to have seen to it that Spire received a copy of *Du côté de chez Swann*. Moreover, Spire dined with the Halévys at the end of January 1914.[45] And Halévy conveyed Spire's reaction to Proust, as Proust alludes to it in a letter to Halévy from February 1914: "M. Spire might have been wrong to be annoyed by people who try to see into themselves without caring about others. When one does that in a disinterested way in order to discover objective realities (as in my case) one is doing the only thing that has ever served others. People who, in order to reach others, write by thinking of others are like people who think they are writing *for* children."[46] Proust expresses clearly here, and well before *Le temps retrouvé*, his distrust of militant literature, after Spire, a politically engaged senior official, sensitive to the poverty of the working classes and concerned with improving their conditions, had apparently disapproved of the lack of social considerations and altruistic concerns in Proust's novel. In any case, Spire refrained from reviewing *Du côté de chez Swann* in 1914. But his 1923 obituary of Proust proves that, despite his moral and political disapproval, he had read it thoughtfully and attentively.

In the same period, Spire published *Quelques juifs* (1913), on Israel Zangwill, Otto Weininger, and James Darmesteter, presented as three variations of modern Jewish identity. Through them, Spire retraces his own progression, beginning from denial or even hatred for this identity (Weininger), followed by the pursuit of assimilation, even absorption, according to the doctrine of Franco-Judaism (Darmesteter), then coming around to acceptance, and finally arriving at pride in Zionism. *Chad Gadya!* by Israel Zangwill (1864–1926), the story published in Péguy's *Cahiers de la quinzaine* in 1904, translated by Mathilde Salomon, marked Spire forever. A prodigal son living in Vienna, a lover of French novels and opera, far removed from Judaism, "indifferent to traditions," returns by chance to his father's home in Venice the evening of Passover, in a palace along the Grand Canal, just as the ritual song *Chad Gadya!* is being recited at the end of the family Seder. Overcome, "the most modern of moderns,"[47] the dejudaized Jew, flees the house in despair and throws himself into a canal. Zangwill's story, which Spire first commented on in *Cahiers de la quinzaine* in 1909, made the death of its hero an allegory for Israel's suicide through assimilation and abandoning rites: "Israel that is erased in us, Israel that dies absorbed in a world that does not value it."[48] Of course Spire was not indifferent to the stone left on the tomb, the ritual lost on Proust.

An early Zionist, at first attracted by Zangwill's "territorialism," that is, by the creation of a Jewish political entity somewhere other than Zion, but immediately win over by the Balfour Declaration in November 1917, Spire at once launched the Ligue des Amis du Sionisme, and then the bulletin *La Palestine nouvelle*. The league brought together academics and writers, as he recalled in his *Souvenirs*:

> With the tireless collaboration of Robert Lévy, a relative of Bergson and cousin of Henri Franck, the poet of *La danse devant l'arche*, a young assistant at the Centre du Documentation de l'Histoire de la Guerre, working under professor Maurice Vernes, chair of the Religious Studies Department at the École des Hautes Études de la Sorbonne, the Ligue des Amis de Sionisme was founded at the end of 1917, composed of French Jews and non-Jews, among them former ministers like Albert Thomas, important academics like professors Seignobos, Gabriel Séailles, and Ferdinand Brunot, Zionists and pro-Zionists like poets Gustave Kahn, Henri Hertz, Edmond Fleg, doctor Léon

Zadoc-Kahn, doctor Armand Bernard, the brother of Bernard Lazare, historian Jules Isaac, the faithful companion of Péguy.[49]

Historian Charles Seignobos, philosopher Gabriel Séailles, linguist Ferdinand Brunot, German scholar Charles Andler, all former Dreyfus supporters, associated with the Ligue des Droits de l'Homme, had already been approached by the Franco-Zionist League in 1915, but they do not seem to have been further involved after that time.[50] *Menorah*, which was published from 1922 to 1933, took over for Spire's little bulletin, *La Palestine nouvelle*, and then there was Albert Cohen's *La revue juive* in 1925 and the review *Palestine*, a mouthpiece for the France-Palestine Association, published by Rieder between 1927 and 1931, first subtitled *Revue mensuelle internationale*, and then *Nouvelle revue juive* beginning in 1929.[51] Spire was part of all these enterprises by the Zionist press, as was Cattaui who, as we will see, would publish the article "Proust et les Juifs" in *Palestine* in February 1928, his own in-depth contribution to the debate.

Thus Spire was one of the first critics, if not the first (the Proust obituary by his young friend Cattaui in *Menorah* preceded his) to raise the question overtly of Proust's Jewishness. Despite the summer vacation, and contrary to what he claimed to hope, according to his letter to Ludmila Savitzky, his article in the July 1923 issue of *Les nouvelles littéraires* hardly went unnoticed. Urbain Gohier (1862-1951), an expert in anti-Jewish sentiment—although he was nonetheless a Dreyfus supporter, his antimilitarism and anticlericalism being even more virulent than his anti-Semitism—must have been waiting for Spire's article for the proof of Proust's Jewishness it provided him, as he reported it in *La vieille France*, his anti-Semitic weekly, on 23 August 1923 under the title, "Marcel Proust était juif": "Recently deceased is a novelist whom I have never been able to read, not fifty consecutive lines; he gave his books extravagant titles; he wrote four hundred pages without starting a new paragraph; these two cheap tricks and his money won him a kind of reputation ... I always smelled a Jew. I was right!"[52] In conjunction with Proust, Gohier mentions Bernstein and Bauer as ostensibly Jewish literary hacks, that is, the playwright Henry Bernstein (1876-1953) and Henry Bauër (1851-1915), illegitimate son of Alexandre Dumas, or more likely Gérard Bauër (1888-1967), Henry Bauër's son, literary and drama critic for *L'écho de Paris* from 1906 to 1935 (he would later adopt the pseudonym "Guermantes" in *Le Figaro*).

Gohier apparently suspected Proust was Jewish but could not be certain of it until Spire's article appeared in *Les nouvelles littéraires*: "the Jew André Spire, one of the most fanatic and aggressive Hebrews of the Paris ghetto, revealed Marcel Proust's Jewish ancestry. . . . Of course the Jew Marcel Proust owed all his superiority to his race." No doubt Émile Cahen had not read *La vieille France* when he affirmed that anti-Semitism had disappeared since the war, but in insulting Spire, Gohier may have been thinking less of Spire's present Zionism than his 1895 duel and conflicts over the Dreyfus affair. In any case, he attributed a decisive role in divulging Proust's Jewishness to Spire's piece with its "flashy" title, improvised by Maurice Martin de Gard and expressly associating, the first time to our knowledge, Proust's name with the Jewish people.

Again, Gohier excerpts this sentence from Spire's article: "Proust's mother and grandparents were Jewish as well, despite appearances and although in his books, through literary prudence and not lack of courage, Proust made them into Christian characters."[53] For Gohier, this was a matter of hypocrisy and guile. Certain readers today may still share that opinion. But far from condemning those fictions, Spire justified the conversions to which Proust subjected his family in his novel, considering them opportune and reasonable in the contemporary literary landscape.

In 1928, hence when the publication of *À la recherche du temps perdu* was complete, Spire, who had reproduced his 1923 *Jewish Chronicle* and *Menorah* article almost verbatim in his chapter on Proust in *Quelques juifs et demi-juifs*, apparently remained untroubled by the treatment of Jewish characters in the novel. It was Proust's snobbishness, on the other hand, that he had reproved since their first encounter. In the hall of the École des Sciences Politiques, the young man that Léon Blum introduced to him in 1893, dark eyelids, dull white complexion, trim overcoat, white kid gloves, was immediately categorized by him as "one more poseur." But that same Marcel Proust interested him, "whose mother was Jewish, and whose best friends were Jewish or half-Jewish." Nor was Spire troubled that Proust had received the Prix Goncourt thanks to Léon Daudet, who did not hold dear "men of Jewish blood, or pure-blood or half-blood Christians who had fought, like Proust, in favor of Dreyfus." Actually, and for once, the jury was not mistaken and had recognized "the work of a truly great writer, the greatest French novelist, perhaps, since Stendhal and Balzac." Such testimonials show that Spire recognized the exceptional originality of Proust's work, although he seemed to disapprove of the habitual comparisons it drew, since Thibaudet's article, to Saint-Simon's *Mémoires*, Montaigne's *Essais*, and, in this case ironically, to the "veiled composition" of the "Jewish mother."[54]

The entourage of men and women of leisure described by Proust, "a deceptive and delightful world," certainly prompted moral reservations in Spire, but interested him from a historical perspective in showing the pitfalls of assimilation. It was a circle that "had succeeded in including a certain number of Jews," because the July Monarchy and the Second Empire "had not been hostile toward them, and even took a certain pride in welcoming them."[55] This remark foreshadows Hannah Arendt's thesis in *The Origins of Totalitarianism* (1951) on the curiosity demonstrated by salons for the charm of Jews (and homosexuals), without altering the basic antipathy that was felt toward both groups and that would readily surface during the Dreyfus affair.[56] Proust shows a "particular indulgence in . . . portraying the manner, the life" of that society, but he took it upon himself to leave the social world after having gained much from it. Rachel, "the little Jewish courtesan," Nissim Bernard, and Bloch, "intrepid Dreyfus supporters like Proust, but who, unlike him, do not always have the gallantry of their Jewish blood" (this comparison between character and author does not appear in the *Nouvelles littéraires* and *Menorah* versions, it was introduced in the 1928 book) are "characters with an intense reality."[57] Proust participates in the revival of French literature through his way of presenting Jews: "Because, since the work of Zangwill has penetrated France, French writers have ceased to present the Jew in their books as a conventional figure."[58] Cattaui had already stressed this innovation, which, as we will see, would become an argument adopted by all Jewish champions of Proust.

If the mother and grandmother in the novel are Christians, if Swann is a convert, that is a matter, as we have seen, of "literary prudence" on the part of the writer. Spire defends this fiction, which does not bother him in the least. But it is very much Proust's Jewish grandfather whom Proust depicts, who sings Fromental Halévy's *La Juive* on Bloch's arrival: "It seems that this grandfather . . . Marcel Proust had loved him. After the deaths of his mother and grandmother, he did not fail to visit his tomb until illness confined him to his home."[59] And this is where Spire inserted the anecdote of the visit to the Jewish section of Père-Lachaise.

Finally, "Swann has some Jewish ancestry," but through a "singular lapse of memory, or the phenomenon of 'Marranism,'" Proust "develops his psychology as though he were a pure-blood Jew."[60] Thus Spire also seems to be the first to analyze Proust's novel in terms of Marranism, a critical framework often adopted thereafter. And he sees in that assimilation of a half-Jew—indeed even less in the case of Swann—into a "pure-blood Jew," as he says, an indication that the writer himself thought his own qualities, "his best gifts . . . came from his Jewish blood."[61] And thus, despite his discretion, even dissimulation, here lies proof that Proust recognized his Jewishness and that he was proud of his Jewish origins.

Having arrived at this point, Spire of course must quote the lines from *Sodome et Gomorrhe II* that would become the obligatory passage and emblem of all Zionist readings of Proust (without the least pause over the "abject anti-Semitism" decoded there by our contemporaries): "Swann belonged to that strong Jewish race, in whose vital energy and resistance to death its individual members themselves seem to share."[62] But the quote was so long and lagged so far behind that first sentence that the *Jewish Chronicle* took the liberty of cutting it. *Les nouvelles littéraires*, however, retained the rest of the quote in its entirety:

> Struck down by their particular illness, as it itself has been by persecution, they each struggle indefinitely in a terrible death agony that may be prolonged beyond any probable term, when all that can now be seen is a prophet's beard crowned by an immense nose, dilated in order to draw the final breaths, before the time comes for the ritual prayers and the punctual file-past to begin, of distant relatives, moving mechanically forward, as on an Assyrian frieze.[63]

Swann rediscovers the way of Zion during the Dreyfus affair and as death approaches. Thus Swann, "whose character bears so much resemblance to Proust's own that one often wonders whether Proust is speaking of himself or of Swann,"[64] allows Spire to conclude by noting the compatibility between Proust's work and Zionism.

Including his 1923 article in his 1928 collection, *Quelques juifs et demi-juifs*, Spire preceded it with a long introductory note in which he reminded readers that the piece aimed at "indicating what the work and its characters owed to the Jewish origins of their author." Then, to acknowledge the various and even contradictory positions taken over those years, he continues: "Léon Pierre-Quint, the Jewish critic, considers this pursuit pointless. Another Jewish writer, Benjamin Crémieux, usually disinclined to attribute undue importance to ethnic origins, nevertheless recognizes an author's work to be a function 'of the individual temperament, in which atavism undoubtedly plays a role.'"[65] During those five years, the question had preoccupied numerous critics, Jewish and non-Jewish, and they each seemed to project onto Proust's novel their own personal relationship to the Jewish community, their own sense of Jewishness. Between Pierre-Quint's denial of the question's relevance and Crémieux's moderate support, Spire leaned more toward Crémieux's side, and he went further: the contribution of Proust's Jewish heredity to his work seemed striking to him, and, he noted, "more than one critic has delighted in discovering what Proust's work owes to the Jewish part of his blood." To confirm this, Spire offers an article by Abel Bonnard (which may seem ironic given Bonnard's future role in the Vichy hierarchy) that appeared in the *Journal des débats* on 14 January 1927 on Robert Dreyfus's *Souvenirs sur Marcel Proust* (1926): "When I recall him in reading this memoir, he always appears to me a bit Oriental. He had those traits, the nose, mouth, beautiful eyes. He also had that specious, superlative politeness."[66] This is a description that our contemporaries would be quick to censure, but that Spire saw in an entirely positive light.

CHAPTER 3

A Pointless Question?

I f André Spire had to justify himself in a long introductory note when reprinting his Proust obituary in *Quelques juifs et demi-juifs* in 1928, it was in fact because since 1923, when he had launched—and not without some uproar—the discussion of Proust's Jewishness with the excerpt from his Proust obituary appearing in *Les nouvelles littéraires*, the bibliography on the question had grown substantially, with positions both for and against represented there.

LÉON PIERRE-QUINT, 1925

Considering the question "pointless," as Spire said, Léon Pierre-Quint had expressed a very guarded position on the influence of Proust's "Jewish origins" in his *Marcel Proust: Son vie, son oeuvre* (figure 10), published in June 1925 and advertised as "the first complete study on Marcel Proust"[1] (whose work, incidentally, was not yet complete at the time, or completely published).

Léon Pierre-Quint begins with this warning, even before he starts recounting Proust's life:

Some have tried to find in his Jewish ancestry an explanation for certain of his turns of mind. These are theoretical deductions that clarify nothing. The Jewish mind has given rise to diametrically opposed systems, the most contradictory theories: Spinoza's intellectualism, for example, and Bergsonian intuition. A race does not represent only one form of ideas. Perhaps Proust's astonishing resistance to suffering and death is more specifically characteristic. Is this not the only truly Jewish trait that appears in Swann, whom Proust depicts as entirely assimilated?[2]

Figure 10. Léon Pierre-Quint, *Marcel Proust: Sa vie, son oeuvre*, 1925. Photo © Bibliothèque Kra / Le Sagittaire / IMEC

Pierre-Quint refuses from the outset to explain Proust's work through the Jewishness of its "entirely assimilated" author. Emphasizing the contrast between the philosophical systems of Spinoza and Bergson, both philosophers with Jewish origins, he challenges the identification of Jewishness with one specific literary or philosophical form, according to an argument that would often be repeated by those proponents of creative freedom in their struggle against those supporting genetic fatalism and against the temptation to identify Jewishness with certain cultural traits. If there was one specific Jewish trait in the life and work of Proust, shared by author and character alike, again, it was Swann's resistance, already praised by Georges Cattaui and André Spire, that quality that we now call "resilience," the moral strength that allows us to face hardships.

Léon Pierre-Quint was the pen name of Léon Steindecker (1895–1958), born into a family of Jewish bankers, a writer and critic connected to Proust and Gide, friends with Max Jacob, Philippe Soupault, and André Malraux. Having read *Du côté de chez Swann* in 1917, he got in touch with Proust and dedicated a short story to him, published in the *Mercure de France* in 1921.[3] He then wrote an obituary for him published in *Le monde nouveau*, 1 December 1922. In 1923 he became an editor at Éditions de Sagittaire, founded by Simon Kra in 1919, and then served as

Sagittaire's literary editor until the 1950s. It was there he published most of his vast critical writing on Proust, returning to it and expanding on it over the years in a dozen volumes between 1925 and 1955, focusing on the comic aspect of *À la recherche du temps perdu* and the genesis and reception of the work. In the 1970s, the 1936 update of his 1925 monograph was still the most accessible introduction to Proust available in bookstores.[4]

Léon Pierre-Quint was among the first and the most influential critics of Proust's work in the years between the wars in France when academics would still not touch it (they are conspicuous by their absence in our inquiry, from beginning to end). In the early 1920s, barely cognizant of his own Jewishness, he did not belong to the group of young Proustian Zionists, and he did not contribute to the militant Zionist reviews *Menorah* and *Palestine*. He was nevertheless connected to *La revue juive*, published under the direction of Albert Cohen at Gallimard in 1925, a Zionist review, but with eclectic tastes in literature and staffing. Henri Hertz's review of Pierre-Quint's 1924 collection of short stories, *Déchéances aimables*, appeared there, published with his portrait by Robert Delaunay (figure 11).[5] Pierre-Quint himself wrote an article for the last issue of the review in November 1925 and thus numbers among its impressive contributors.[6]

Figure 11. Robert Delaunay, *Léon Pierre-Quint*, 1924.
Photo © Librairie Le Feu Follet–Edition -Originale.com.

The single specifically Jewish trait that Léon Pierre-Quint recognized in Swann as well as in his creator was thus endurance, resistance to suffering and to death, a concession that would become a commonplace for Proustian apologists returning always to the same page of *Sodome et Gomorrhe II* on Swann's transformation in the grip of illness and the Dreyfus affair. There are no other references to Jewishness to be found in Pierre-Quint's first book on Proust in 1925. A homosexual himself, he proves very discreet, for example, when he broaches the comparison of homosexuals and Jews in *Sodome et Gomorrhe I*. Instead of questioning its appropriateness, he generalizes and immediately dilutes it by seeing a universal there, the description of a "'hunted man' rejected by society and in latent revolt against it, the individual versus society, nature versus morality." The "sodomists," Pierre-Quint continues, are "the eternally damned, similar to the Jews to whom Proust compares them, because they both are victims of social prejudice, accused of having betrayed God or of violating the sacred laws of nature." Pierre-Quint does not dwell on the specifics of this parallel or how disconcerting it might be for the reader discovering it for the first time, except to suggest that, for "sodomists," "happiness has something exceptional, rare, beautiful, and sacred about it."[7] He says nothing here about Jews.

MARIE-LOUISE CAHEN-HAYEM, 1925

Thanks to Léon Pierre-Quint and under the signature of Marie-Louise Cahen-Hayem, Proust's novel made a timid entry into the publication that represented an increasingly conservative Judaism, the *Archives israélites*, or what it had become. Marie-Louise Cahen-Hayem (1905–1944) was the daughter of René Cahen, who had taken over the editorship of the *Archives israélites* with his brother Georges after the death of their eldest brother Émile Cahen in May 1924.[8] In her, two great dynasties of French Jews were joined.

On her father's side, she was the great-granddaughter of Samuel Cahen, the founder of the *Archives israélites*, and the granddaughter of Isidore Cahen, student at the École Normale Supérieure in 1846, classmate of Edmond About, Francisque Sarcey, Hippolyte Taine, Paul Challemel-Lacour, and Anatole Prévost-Paradol.[9]

Isidore Cahen remains a cause célèbre in nineteenth-century French Judaism. Appointed to the La Roche-sur-Yon Lycée (Napoléon-Vendée following the decree of 18 March 1848, later Bourbon-Vendée) at the beginning of the 1849 school year, he renounced public teaching after the bishop of Luçon, Monseigneur Baillès, hostile to the presence of a Jewish teacher holding a philosophy chair, demanded his dismissal and the Education Ministry yielded.[10] Subsequently a journalist, he was one of the founders of the Alliance Israélite Universelle in 1860, before succeeding his father as editor of the *Archives israélites*. And the father of young Marie-Louise, René Cahen, born the same year as Proust (1871), was one of Proust's classmates at the Condorcet lycée.[11]

On the side of her mother, née Marguerite Hayem, she was the great-granddaughter of Simon Hayem (1811–1895), who made his fortune as a shirt-maker in the Sentier garment district, and the granddaughter of Georges Hayem (1841–1933), doctor and professor of medicine, eminent hematologist known for his treatment of cholera, and colleague of doctor Adrien Proust at the Académie de Médecine.[12]

Doctor Hayem's older brother was Charles Hayem (1839–1902), who took over the family business and married Amélia Franck, the daughter of philosopher Adolphe Franck who taught at the Collège de France, the first Jewish teacher to pass the qualifying exams (Isadore Cahen was his student at the Collège Charlemagne), but Charles Hayem was better known as a great collector and patron of the arts, a friend of Barbey d'Aurevilly, and donator of numerous works by Gustave Moreau to the Musée du Luxembourg in 1899. Proust had seen those works in the salon of Madame Hayem, a sculptor herself, on Boulevard Malesherbes (figure 12).[13]

Their younger brother was Armand Hayem (1845–1889), writer and politician, a follower of social philosophy and Proudhon, whose daughter, Harlette Hayem, was married in 1903 to Fernand Gregh, a friend of Proust from the Condorcet lycée.[14] Fernand Gregh mentions Marie-Louise in his memoir: "this Marie-Louise Cahen, whose studies for abstract paintings, precursors for all that singular art, we own, as well as two large unpublished volumes on art history, which must be published someday to honor her memory."[15]

Marie-Louise Cahen-Hayem herself was related to Proust, however distantly: the mother of Simon Hayem, her great-grandfather, was born Sara Zarate Charlotte Oulman (1777–1830); her grandfather, doctor Georges Hayem, was thus a second cousin of Madame Georges Weil, née Amélie Oulman (1853–1920), Proust's aunt and owner of the apartment building on Boulevard Haussmann where Proust roomed from 1907 to 1919, and where *À la recherche du temps perdu* was written.[16]

Figure 12. Edgar Degas, *Soirée* (Madame Charles Hayem, Barbey d'Aurevilly, and Adolphe Franck), c. 1877. Photo © The J. Paul Getty Museum, Los Angeles.

Who was it who called the hyphen "the democratic particle"? In 1897, Proust attributed the phrase to Anatole France, but there is no supporting evidence.[17] According to the press at the time, it might have been coined by "a senior Council of State member, speaking of one of those Worms-Clavelins whom M. Anatole France has just immortalized as a type."[18] The allusion is to the character of the prefect Worms-Clavelin in *L'orme du mail* (1897), the first volume of *L'histoire contemporaine*. The phrase was used in 1898 in *La revue blanche* in an article signed "A Lawyer" on the repression of anarchists by the Council president: "M. Charles Dupuy, who does not yet use the hyphen, that "democratic particle."[19] The "lawyer" hiding behind anonymity was none other than the young Council of State auditor and friend of Proust, Léon Blum. It comes as no surprise that Marie-Louise Cahen-Hayem took an interest in the life and work of Proust.

The young woman (she was not yet twenty years old) wrote a literary column for the *Archives israélites* beginning in July 1924. Her first review addressed *L'an prochain à Jérusalem!*, a book by the Tharaud brothers on Zionism (1924): "Our debut as a literary critic for the *Archives* is greatly facilitated by the quality of the work we are reviewing," she wrote at the beginning. And she ended her first article with this statement that summarized the position of the *Archives israélites* on Zionism and thus received the endorsement of Hippolyte Prague, its editor-in-chief: "This book with its pessimistic conclusions for Zionism will no doubt please French Jews. First, as Jews, they have proven by their abstention that a return to Zion could not satisfy them; next, as French, they have sensed Palestine becoming an English colony to the detriment of our country."[20] This balanced judgment allowed the Jewish community to add the French-British rivalry in the Middle East to their other reasons for distrusting Zionism, but her way of expressing herself could suggest that Marie-Louise Cahen-Hayem did not entirely share the French Jews' satisfaction with a negative prognosis for Zionism.

Once established, the novice critic would reveal her independence and a certain liberalism, as well as a more sympathetic view of Zionism than found in the rest of the weekly, more tightly controlled by the editor-in-chief. That was why, in 1925, she recommended Léon Pierre-Quint's book, by "one of our young fellow Jews," she felt compelled to note, despite the pseudonym. But she was more aligned with the André Spire camp and deemed it useful to consider Proust's Jewishness. She and Proust had crossed paths in Plaine-Monceau society, as Proust was an exact contemporary of her parents. She basically considered Proust to have demonstrated "qualities characteristic of his Jewish origins," in his life and work, and

she recalled that Spire, in the famous "flashy" *Nouvelles littéraires* article, emphasized that Proust had "sketched with much sympathy many Jewish figures," which
confirms that, two years later, Spire's article continued to have an impact.[21] The
brief review ends with a comparison that suggests the range of this young, very
intellectually awakened reader of Proust in 1925, as she mentions the recent French
translation of a work by Freud, *Le rêve et son interprétation*.[22] She concludes: "It
makes us proud to think that Israel continues to provide humanity with some of
its geniuses."

Léon Pierre-Quint—and our *Archives israélites* columnist disagrees with him on
this point—comes first in the line of critics who contest the relevance of Proust's
Jewish origins with regard to reading his work. Whereas, curiously, Quint's influence was decisive in the emergence of a Jewish, rabbinical, and even kabbalistic
interpretation of *À la recherche du temps perdu*. This is an ironic paradox, since he
himself granted hardly any importance to Proust's Jewishness, much less his own.
But some critics, as we will see, would exploit or even distort his analysis of Proust's
style in his 1925 book in order to compare *À la recherche du temps perdu* to the Talmud or the Zohar.[23] This comparison would meet with great success—even to this
day. At the time, it could be viewed either negatively or positively, with the young
Proustian Zionists of *La revue juive* proving to be ambivalent, reluctant to lay claim
to it, and making reference to it without expressing an opinion.[24] But we will
return to examine all this later in detail.

BENJAMIN CRÉMIEUX, 1925

The second critic whom Spire cites in his introductory note in 1928 is Benjamin
Crémieux (1888–1944) (figure 13), who would adopt a moderate position, not
granting "ethnic origins" excessive importance, but nevertheless recognizing "the
role of atavism," to use Spire's terms, in the work of Proust.

Crémieux, born in Narbonne, son of a tailor, scholarship student, was not
related to the famous Adolphe Crémieux, Jeanne Weil's great-uncle and witness
at her wedding, Minister of Justice on 4 September 1870, and author of the decree
that made Algerian Jews French citizens. He earned a teaching degree in Italian
in 1911, was called up for military duty in October 1913, and was demobilized as
an officer in August 1919. He gave up teaching in 1920 to begin his career with
the Ministry of Foreign Affairs in the information and press department where

Figure 13. Benjamin Crémieux.
Photo © Archives Gallimard.

he would remain until 1940. Serving as secretary general for the French PEN Club from its inception in 1921, Benjamin Crémieux was a regular contributor to *L'Europe nouvelle* under Louise Weiss and to *La nouvelle revue française*.[25] Friends with Jean Paulhan, he was later a member of the reading committee for Éditions Gallimard. The doctoral thesis on contemporary Italian literature by this translator and promoter of Luigi Pirandello was published in 1928 by Simon Kra, for whom Pierre-Quint worked as literary editor.[26] Crémieux's sweeping overview was meant for a cultivated readership, rather than scholars and academics: "M. Crémieux has undisguised disdain for precise research," noted the dissertation committee when he was a doctoral candidate at the Sorbonne in 1935. Crémieux continued to publish criticism in reviews and journals.[27]

Like Pierre-Quint, Crémieux was one of those young men who sought out Proust during the final years of his life. The relationship got off to a bad start with Proust wishing that Crémieux had not made so much of Proust's preface to Paul Morand's *Tendre stocks*, a book that Crémieux reviewed in *La nouvelle revue française* in April 1921.[28] Crémieux made up for it by citing Proust inopportunely but most favorably in a review of a Georges Duhamel novel.[29] After Crémieux published his first novel, *Le premier de la classe* (1921), he was a candidate for the

Blumenthal Prize, financed by a rich American. He feared an anti-Semitic reaction by the jury and confided to Morand, who reported to Proust: "Crémieux tells me that Mme Muhlfeld will influence the jury against him because he is Jewish."[30] The widow of the writer Lucien Muhlfeld, née Jeanne Meyer (1875–1953), long hosted an influential literary salon where such selections were made and unmade. Proust made an effort to support Crémieux, who won the prize (coming in second was Maurice Genevoix), but Proust had to apologize to Crémieux afterward because he had missed the jury meeting on 13 June 1922.[31] Neither their misunderstandings nor the capricious diva behavior that Proust adopted with young men diminished Crémieux's admiration for him and their last letters were friendly.

In 1924, in his *XXᵉ siècle: Première série*, Crémieux collected his studies on several contemporary writers, among them Proust, Jean Giraudoux, Valery Larbaud, Pierre Benoit, Jules Romains, Pierre Mac Orlan, Paul Morand, Pierre Drieu la Rochelle, Jean Paulhan, and so on (figure 14).[32] The first chapter, the longest one, taking up more than one third of the volume, concerns Proust and includes two articles that appeared in *Les nouvelles littéraires* and *La revue de Paris*.[33] This was a pioneering essay on the work of Proust, one of the most complete to date, but the author's Jewishness is hardly mentioned in it.

Figure 14. Benjamin Crémieux, *XXe siècle*, 1924.
Photo © Archives Gallimard.

In this detailed and penetrating hundred-page study covering all aspects of the novel (*Albertine disparue* and *Le temps retrouvé* were still unknown), the one and only reference to Jewishness is found in an inventory for *À la recherche du temps perdu* of characters whom Crémieux describes as all marked in one way or another by the duality of their personalities. That is the case, among many others, of "Jews in whom an oriental and oppressed atavism struggles with the more or less clumsy desire to *assimilate*, which can produce types as dissimilar as a Swann or a Bloch."[34] The italicized "*assimilate*" seems to indicate a citation from Proust, but the Proust never uses that verb for Jewish characters, and the noun is associated with them only once, in this sentence on the Blochs at the seashore: "Balbec, in this respect, was rather like certain countries—Russia or Romania, for example—where, as geography classes inform us, the Jewish population does not enjoy the same favor and has not attained the same degree of assimilation as in Paris, say."[35]

That is all that Crémieux finds to say about Jewish characters in the novel, whereas the Jewishness of its author is almost ignored, with the exception of that remark on the "split personality" of Swann as an expression of Proust's "need to externalize completely his personality, in which the Jewish heredity on his mother's side mixed with the Catholic and undoubtedly Touraine heredity on his father's side; the hero who says 'I' is his Catholic half."[36] Here we find Cattaui's and Thibaudet's thesis again, but not developed any further.

Thus Proust's Jewishness does not seem to have mattered any more to Crémieux in 1924 than it did to Pierre-Quint in 1925, and it is not to this Proust study in *XXᵉ siècle* that Spire refers in 1928 to offer Crémieux's opinion on "the role of atavism" in Proust's work, but to a much more ephemeral yet very remarkable piece that, moreover, had nothing to do with Proust. Appearing in *Les nouvelles littéraires* on 10 October 1925 under the title "Judaïsme et littérature," it was an overview that opened with this bold assertion: "Judaism is in fashion in France."

This portrait of contemporary Jewish literature made a deep impression on readers and became the subject of attentive reviews in the Zionist periodicals *Menorah* and *La Revue juive*.[37] Although Proust's name does not appear in it, he could well have figured into the paragraph in which Crémieux mentions those Jewish authors who "do not address Jewish subjects" and who do not seem "to possess distinct enough characteristics to be differentiated from other French writers."[38] In short, those who appear to be "entirely assimilated," to quote Pierre-Quint.

Crémieux thus attempts to catalogue a recent Jewish trend in literature, principally in France:

> One could already build a small library of all the books that have appeared in the last two or three years addressing Israel in one way or another.
>
> We have only just realized, with some surprise, that the Jewish soul may not have been entirely contained within the Bible and high finance and that, since Hebraic prophetism and especially since the diaspora, an infinite number of feelings, psychological attitudes, and religious and social forms, often contradictory, have sprung from Judaism or been grafted onto it.
>
> All the complexity of Judaism is now being delivered to us wholesale, so to speak, and it is about time for someone to establish a little order in this confusion where a jumble of orientalism appears side by side the highest aspirations of messianism.[39]

For books before the war in 1914, Crémieux mentions, on the heels of Israel Zangwill's *Chad Gadya!*, which appeared in a French translation in Péguy's *Cahiers de la quinzaine* in 1904, Spire's *Quelques juifs* (1913), *Écoute, Israël* by Edmond Fleg, also in the *Cahiers de la quinzaine* (26 October 1913), and the stories by Jean-Richard Bloch collected in *Lévy* (1912). By non-Jewish writers, he lists *L'ombre de la croix* by brothers Jérôme and Jean Tharaud, which was serialized in *L'Opinion* between April and June 1914 (1917).

After the war, according to Crémieux, *Menorah* and *La revue juive* took over, as well as the "Judaism" collection at Rieder, while the Tharaud brothers and Pierre Benoit exploited the possibilities of fiction.

Crémieux's detailed, informed list distinguishes the following categories: 1. "specifically Jewish works," especially written in Yiddish; 2. "Jewish novelists who escaped the ghetto," like Zangwill; 3. "works of French Jewish writers that address contemporary Jewish subjects," like Jean-Richard Bloch; 4. "French non-Jewish writers taking up the study of Jewish society," for example, the Tharaud brothers in *L'an prochain à Jérusalem!* (1924), Lacretelle in *Silbermann*, and Pierre Benoit in *Le puits de Jacob* (1925);[40] 5. "novelistic variations on modern Judaism" through Christianity, especially stories of false messiahs; 6. "documentary works and catalogues," like *Le livre du Zohar*, translated by Jean de Pauly, with a preface by Edmond Fleg (1925); 7. "books written directly in French by non-French Jews," like Albert Cohen and Georges Cattaui.

Then taking an overview, Crémieux discerns in the Jewish literature of earlier decades a tension between a specific Jewish identity, similar to a kind of regionalism, and a mystical universalism, having to do with a kind of internationalism. But at present that tension seems to him either overshadowed by Zionism, aiming toward internationalism following an identity phase, or by prophetism, sometimes approaching Christianity. According to him, Zionism and prophetism represented the two paths of contemporary neo-Judaism. His assessment was accurate, for the paths of Albert Cohen and of Georges Cattaui, then colleagues at *La revue juive*, would soon split following those two models.

All these categories are thus fleshed out without considering "French Jewish writers who do not address Jewish subjects." Confident in their full assimilation, Crémieux in fact doubted that such writers possessed "characteristics distinctive enough to differentiate them from other French writers." He disputes, for example, the existence of "a 'Jewish theater' that had supposedly taken over the French stage and, especially, light comedy" in the past fifteen years—as some claimed, often to condemn it—with the plays of Georges de Porto-Riche, Edmond Sée, and Tristan Bernard. If "some traits of the Jewish mind can be recognized" in their works, "it would not be impossible to trace them to the individual temperament of each of these authors (in which atavism undoubtedly plays a role) instead of seeing them as traits of the race." Here is the bit of that convoluted sentence that Spire must have remembered for his introductory note in 1928 on the "individual temperament, in which atavism undoubtedly plays a role," even though those words did not refer to Proust at all in Crémieux's piece, but rather to the said "Jewish theater" and to express doubt about the validity of that epithet. Crémieux proceeds tactfully, conceding, for example, that the exquisite French irony admired by *L'action française* in the early books of André Maurois ("*délicieux*" is the usual praise in *L'action française* for Maurois's novels *Les silences du colonel Bramble* and *Les discours du docteur O'Grady*)[41] could have been a matter of Alsatian Jewish humor. He makes "atavism" a sort of middle ground between "traits of the race" and "individual temperament," before concluding prudently: "In any case, it is difficult to generalize about this matter." Nevertheless, this is the passage that Spire cites to justify looking into what "Proust's work owes to the Jewish part of his blood."

Thus, Proust was not cited by Crémieux in his 1925 piece "Judaïsm et littérature." Neither was Henry Bernstein, moreover, certainly the most visible Jewish playwright, and the one most often attacked by Léon Daudet and *L'action française*, but Henri Duvernois was included, as an assimilated and not identifiably Jewish writer.

I do not know how Duvernois came to be another of those young or less young Jewish admirers of Proust. His real name was Henri-Simon Schwabacher (1875-1937); his father was a Hungarian diamond merchant. Duvernois was a journalist, storywriter, scriptwriter, playwright, secretary of the Bibliothèque Charpentier, founder and, most important, editor of the periodical series "Les Oeuvres Libres" at Fayard, in which Proust published "Jalousie," an excerpt from *Sodome et Gomorrhe*, in November 1921, despite the objections and displeasure of Gaston Gallimard.

In 1927 Crémieux would write a study that was published in 1929, this time focusing directly on the omission in his 1924 Proust chapter and titled "Proust et les juifs."[42] Just as balanced as his survey of Jewish literature in 1925, it follows the 1927 publication of *Le temps retrouvé* and marks the exact end point of the early reception of Proust's work among young Jews and Zionists in the 1920s. We will return to it later.

Crémieux was no more of an engaged Zionist than Léon Pierre-Quint was, but in its ecumenicalism, *La revue juive* gave him as warm a reception as it did Pierre-Quint. Armand Lunel wrote an enthusiastic review of his *XXe siècle* for the last issue of *La revue juive* in November 1925, devoting most of it to Crémieux's study of Proust.[43] And his article "Judaïsme et littérature" in *Les nouvelles littéraires*, distinguishing Zionism and prophetism as the two paths of neo-Judaism, was quoted at length in the final pages of that same last issue of *La revue juive*, with this introduction: "M. Benjamin Crémieux published in *Les nouvelles littéraires* 10 October 1925 an excellent article entitled 'Judaïsm et Littérature,' the conclusion of which appears here."[44]

The excerpt emphasizes how Crémieux understands Zionism as a new universalism, since "the Palestinian homeland is . . . destined to become a model of social life for the rest of humanity, a microcosm of what human intelligence and solidarity can succeed in achieving on this earth," whereas Jewish prophetism, another universalist ambition seeking to "reestablish the worship of the soul and of man," "is not afraid to approach Christianity here." The final words of Crémieux's article touch on the very contradictions of *La revue juive*, which could also explain why, with the end of that issue, the review ceased publication: "That is the dilemma whenever Judaism is debated: whether it should be confined to its specific identity, thus losing any universal raison d'être, or universalized, and thus dejudaized in the process."

LUDMILA SAVITZKY, 1925

The name of one and only one woman appears regularly in these pages. Not Jewish herself, she was a faithful companion of Zionists throughout the 1920s and remains a remarkable figure. Ludmila Savitzky (1881–1957) was born in Yekaterinburg, in the Urals, to an aristocratic Lithuanian Catholic father and a Ukrainian Orthodox mother, both of whom were politically active and who emigrated to Lausanne in 1897 (figure 15). After spending time in England and then returning to Russia, Savitzky settled in Paris in 1902, frequented the Sorbonne and Montparnasse, knew Apollinaire, Picasso, Marinetti, and Max Jacob, was friends with Mireille Havet, become a poet and actress, wrote children's stories and criticism for literary reviews. At a very young age she married an actor; her second

Figure 15.

Ludmilla Savitzky.

Photo © Archives Ludmila Savitzky / Institut Mémoire de l'édition contemporaine, Abbaye d'Ardenne.

marriage was to Jules Rais, né Jules Cahen, also called Nathan (1872–1943), a child-hood friend of André Spire in Nancy, doctor of law, parliamentary editor, and art critic, whom she left during the war. She and Spire got to know one another in 1908.[45]

In 1925 her husband was Marcel Bloch (1881–1951), Polytechnique graduate, engineer for the railways, an aviator during the war, squadron commander beginning in 1917, and, with five major victories, honored as one of the "175 French Flying Aces."[46] He was the older brother of the writer Jean-Richard Bloch (1884–1947) and of Pierre Bloch, known as Pierre Abraham (1892–1974), also a Polytechnique graduate and aviator during the war, and a Proust admirer, whom we will discuss later.[47] Savitzky was a translator of Russian, English, and German, and most notably the translator of James Joyce's *A Portrait of the Artist as a Young Man* into French, under the title *Dedalus: Portrait de l'artiste jeune par lui-même* (1924).[48] But she also translated Ezra Pound, Leonid Leonov, Virginia Woolf, Waldo Frank, and Christopher Isherwood well into the 1950s.

She remained close to André Spire after her separation from Jules Rais (whereas Rais, a declared anti-Zionist, had a falling out with Spire) and during her marriage with Marcel Bloch. They were actively engaged correspondents and she was a regular contributor to *Menorah*.

Cattaui is often mentioned in the letters between André Spire and Ludmila Savitzky in 1922, in the days surrounding Proust's death. They all had lunch together on Sunday, 12 November 1922.[49] Having received *La promesse accomplie*, Cattaui's newly published collection of poems, to which we will return, she wrote to Spire on 15 November 1922: "Dear André, I am happy; I like Cattaui's poems very much, with all their awkwardness and inexperience. You will see that I am right: there is more than intelligence and enthusiasm in this child, there is inspiration, vision, and music. . . . Henri Franck is not completely dead if he leaves us such comrades."[50] She even imagined writing "a study of Judeo-French poetry" for *Menorah*, bringing together Spire, Franck, Cohen, and Cattaui, and yet wondered in a note if: "It might be more worthwhile to inform Christians and not Jews about this poetry?" That clearly raises the question of *Menorah*'s readership, which Ludmila Savitzky did not think extended beyond the Jewish community. Spire responded the next day, 16 November: "Am glad that you like Cattaui's verse. Have you written to him? He will be very happy." Proust died on 18 November. On 20 November Ludmila wrote to Spire: "Received the very kindest of letters from Cattaui in response to my own. . . . Will you go see him on Friday? If so, we will, too."

On Sunday, 17 December, Ludmila noted once more in her daybook: "Met the Spires in Neuilly. Tea with Cattaui." Clearly, Spire and Cattaui saw each other often at this time, frequently with Ludmila Savitzky, which explains the similarities between their two articles written in early December for *Menorah* and the *Jewish Chronicle*, both claiming Proust as a Jew.

In January 1923 there was even talk of Ludmila Savitzky becoming literary editor of *Menorah*, but she preferred keeping her time free to write and she suggested Cattaui instead, or her brother-in-law, Jean-Richard Bloch. For his part, Spire proposed Henri Hertz, seconded by Cattaui, and his recommendation was accepted.[51] But Ludmila Savitzky remained very active with *Menorah*. She translated from Russian the poems of Constantin Balmont, "Médaillons juifs," for the January 1923 issue.[52] She published a personal account in December 1923.[53] In a September 1925 issue in which she reviewed Benda's *Lettres à Mélisande* (1925), she noted the influence of Zionism on literature: "The achievements and successes of Zionism have some very curious repercussions in the literary life of our time. 'Am I not more Jewish than European?' asks every Jewish writer today, a question that not long ago seemed to trouble only a certain isolated few."[54] That is exactly the question that his companions posed to Proust retrospectively. Some responded for him in a decidedly positive way, emphasizing his Jewish heredity, even his rabbinical style, while others proved more prudent, like Crémieux, and others even more reticent, like Pierre-Quint.

Ludmila Savitzky wrote a long review of Léon Pierre-Quint's *Marcel Proust: Sa vie, son oeuvre* for a November 1925 issue of *Menorah*. She was not completely aligned with her friends in their Proustian infatuation: "To celebrate Proust, to write about Proust, to have known Proust has become a kind of snobbery," she wrote, thus demonstrating a certain resistance to the trend.[55] But she praised Pierre-Quint's book, which she said would convince Proustians and "anti-Proustians" alike (without specifying to whom she was referring, perhaps herself), and she used the opportunity to state her own position on Proust's Jewishness, weighing both sides:

> The author puts little stress on Proust's half-Jewish origins. He is not wrong, in principle. Nothing is more annoying than overscrupulous efforts to render to Israel what is Israel's, to the point of extending Israel's claims to beings and things in which the spirit of the race has long been extinguished. And nevertheless, from the whole of this truthful book emerges a moral atmosphere

that urgently reminds us of certain distinctive traits of the Jewish soul, so distinctive, so particular, that even without knowing his biography, we would be inclined to wonder: did Marcel Proust not have a bit of Jewish blood?[56]

Ludmila Savitzky found herself in agreement with her friend André Spire—no surprise for us—and considered Pierre-Quint's reticence excessive. She lists a series of Proust's character traits that she would be tempted to attribute to what she, like Spire, calls the "Jewish soul":

Those excessive, somewhat morbid friendships, those immediate and tangible demonstrations of gratitude for the smallest favor, that art of offering the most pleasing thing at the moment when it would be received with the most pleasure, that anxiety over not giving enough—as we well recognize, as we "have spotted" such traits if we have spent any time with the Jewish bourgeoisie!

On the other hand, no one is more attuned than certain Jews to the prestige of the aristocracy, to the signs of confidence, and especially of gratitude, that they receive from them.[57]

And a bit further on: "The son of Professor Proust views his father's compatriots with an oriental gaze, which he got from his mother, Mlle Weil. He is of their blood, but he is not completely of their blood." The portrait is not very flattering, and Ludmila Savitzky concludes with a mixed verdict. She still characterizes Proust as "French, but gifted with the Hebraic genius for penetration and divination; Jewish, but disillusioned, 'demysticized' through French culture," and thus reasonably well assimilated. But unlike her friends, this translator of Joyce was clearly not a Proust enthusiast, which colors her appraisal when she declares her preference for works that also reach toward the sun and the open air, far from the inner depths. That is why, in her opinion, Proust's novel was not "the supreme expression of humanity."[58]

Contemporaries could get things wrong: the review of Pierre-Quint's *Marcel Proust* by Ludmila Savitzky, almost the only woman in the group, and not Jewish, belongs in the file of young Zionist readings of Proust, not only because it appeared in *Menorah*, an incarnation of *L'illustration juive*, but also because certain readers inferred from it that she was, in fact, Jewish. That was the case with Benjamin Crémieux, moreover, who would cite the *Menorah* review in his own contribution to the subject, "Proust et les juifs," at the end of the decade: assuming that Ludmila Savitzky was Jewish, he noted it expressly, as if that information was useful in appreciating her opinion of Proust.

But we will come back to this. For the moment, examining the ample space made for Proust in *Menorah* has let us consider not only André Spire and Georges Cattaui, the first to have broached Proust's Jewishness following his death, but also Léon Pierre-Quint and Benjamin Crémieux, authors of early and insightful critical essays on Proust, and Marie-Louise Cahen-Hayem and Ludmila Savitzky as well, who took positions in the two influential publications of the Jewish press and did not consider the question of Proust's Jewishness "pointless." We are not through with this handful of protagonists in the reception of *À la recherche du temps perdu* during the first half of the 1920s in the Jewish community, and they will all reappear in what follows.

CHAPTER 4

"The Same Degree of Heredity as Montaigne"

The bibliography on Proust's Jewishness grew significantly between the time of André Spire's 1923 article, first in English in the *Jewish Chronicle*, then in French in *Menorah*, and his 1928 collection *Quelques juifs et demi-juifs*. Spire cites Léon Pierre-Quint and Benjamin Crémieux in the introductory note he added in 1928 to the 1923 piece. He mentions their more (Pierre-Quint) or less (Crémieux) circumspect perspectives on the validity of a Jewish reading of Proust's novel. He could have also mentioned Albert Thibaudet's and Albert Cohen's contributions to the debate as early as 1923, and then those of Denis Saurat in 1925 and René Groos in 1926 (we will return to them), as well as the many references to Proust sprinkled throughout Albert Cohen's *La revue juive* in 1925.

A second commonplace found in a number of these studies, in addition to the ubiquitous quote from *Sodome et Gomorrhe II* on the atavistic tenacity of Swann, very ill during the Dreyfus affair and rediscovering Zion, is the comparison to Montaigne, partly Jewish like Proust. The reference to Montaigne serves, moreover, to introduce the philosophical kinship supposedly linking Proust to Bergson, with regard to their mobility of thought, which resembles that of Montaigne in his *Essais*. The critical tradition gives Albert Thibaudet credit for first tracing the lineage between these two or three writers in his article "Marcel Proust et la tradition française" for the "Hommage à Marcel Proust" issue of *La nouvelle revue française*, 1 January 1923.[1]

But Georges Cattaui, as we have noted, had already cited Montaigne in his Proust obituary for *Menorah* a month earlier, in December 1922: "I do not know if Montaigne's name has been uttered yet," he adds, thus claiming a kind of priority. Then he mentions in a note his meeting with Thibaudet, after the fact, as though by chance: "by one of those coincidences that I do not try to explain, I happened to meet M. Thibaudet, completely fortuitously, a few days after having jotted down the remarks I make here on Proust and Montaigne."[2]

In fact, the yoking of Proust and Montaigne, or of Proust's prose—both its style and thinking, or its style of thinking—and that of *Essais*, had occurred much earlier, but without any overt allusion to their common Jewishness. Montaigne's Jewish heredity, real or imagined, was familiar to cultivated readers at the turn of the century (even though the Marrano origins of his mother, Antoinette de Louppes, were still not established with certainty, much less the extent to which Montaigne could have been aware of them).

Théophile Malvezin was the first Montaigne biographer to stress his maternal heredity, in *Michel de Montaigne: Son origine, sa famille*.[3] It was published in 1874-1875, at the time of *Histoire des juifs à Bordeaux* by the same author.[4] Barrès, as we have seen, was not unaware of this conjecture and referred to Montaigne's Jewish origins in his *Greco ou le secret de Tolède*, but not without some discomfort and quickly exercising his right to retraction: "All these assertions are too rash. Herein lies an issue that I am not entitled to resolve regarding a great French writer."[5]

The connections between the two writers may seem self-evident (I find them both interesting because they wrote in a somewhat similar manner, endlessly expanding a single work until their dying day), but for a long time it may have served (this is the hypothesis I will formulate here, in any case) to let Proust's Jewishness be understood and not expressly stated, which might have seemed indelicate during his lifetime. It is indeed remarkable that, immediately following Proust's death, Montaigne was used to justify analyses—which quickly proliferated—of the influence of Proust's Jewish origins on his work. Until then Montaigne had been a convenient euphemism, a kind of coded message, that intimated without declaring that Proust was Jewish and that certain characteristics of his thinking and his style thus ensued.

In addition, the legendary friendship between Montaigne and La Boétie ("Because it was he; because it was I"), often misunderstood, could provide grounds for comparing Proust to Montaigne. As a philosophy student at the Condorcet lycée, Proust forced his attentions on his classmate Daniel Halévy through an apologia for pleasure in which he named Montaigne as his authority: "I will gladly tell you of two masters of expert wisdom who plucked only the flower in life, Socrates and Montaigne."[6] After the publication of *Sodome et Gomorrhe I*, in which Proust compares homosexuals and Jews, how to avoid letting the misinterpretation of Montaigne's feelings for La Boétie reinforce the temptation of finding similarities between Proust and the author of *Essais*?

HENRI GHÉON, 1914

One of the first reviews of *Du côté de chez Swann*, by Henri Ghéon in *La nouvelle revue française* in January 1914, already plays on these similarities:

> Here is a work of leisure in the full sense of the word. I draw no argument against it from this. Clearly, leisure is the essential condition for a work of art, is it not? But it can also make it superficial.—The whole question lies in knowing if excess leisure has led the author to go too far and if, whatever pleasure we take in following him, we can follow him forever. His book is "lost time:" we read it page by page, we waste time, as when we read Montaigne's *Essais*. With all its faults, it offers us a treasure trove of documents on modern hypersensitivity.[7]

Henri Ghéon (1875-1944), a doctor, close friend and companion of André Gide, was one of the founders of *La nouvelle revue française* in 1908 and 1909, as well as the Vieux-Colombier theater with Jacques Copeau in 1913. He returned to the Catholic faith on the front in 1915, became involved with *L'action française* after the war, and distanced himself from the literary circles in which he had formerly traveled. "Ghéon was a nationalist and traditionalist," said Maurras of him when he died.[8]

Likening Proust's novel to Montaigne's *Essais* under the pretext of leisure and idleness here seems at least ambiguous if not malicious. It was certainly not a matter of unadulterated praise, as Ghéon claimed in his ensuing correspondence with Proust, who took offense at the expression, "work of leisure."[9] In two heartfelt letters, Proust wrote to Ghéon that he had read his article, as "had everyone," as a "savage attack."[10]

JACQUES BOULENGER, 1920

In January 1920, after Proust received the Prix Goncourt for *À l'ombre des jeunes filles en fleur*, the critic Jacques Boulenger also used the Montaigne connection to defend Proust against Jean de Pierrefeu (1883–1940), better known in those same years for his attacks against the official history of the war, based on his experience with the Grand Quartier Général, the Chantilly GQG where he had been responsible for written communiqués beginning in November 1915.[11] This supporter of the "Pour un parti de l'intelligence" manifesto, launched in July 1919 by Henri Massis and inspired by Maurras, remained duly faithful to classicism, supposedly scorned by Proust, and thus lay into him in the *Journal des débats*: "M. Proust has made neither a novel, nor a play, nor anything resembling a work of literature. It is a sort of psychological inquiry, very thorough, very informed, aligned with the latest discoveries in modern psychiatry," Pierrefeu proclaimed, denouncing the danger of confusing literature and science, demanding respect for the literary genres, and declaring himself in favor of "common sense."[12]

Jacques Boulenger (1879–1944), who responded to Pierrefeu in *L'Opinion*, a weekly for which he served as editor-in-chief and literary columnist, was a paleographer and archivist, as well as a voluminous writer, light theater and sports enthusiast, and dandy who flew planes during the war. He was also a scholar, one of the founders of the *Revue du seizième siècle* in 1913, adapter of the four-volume *Romans de la table ronde* (1922–1923), disciple of Abel Lefranc and editor of Rabelais, for example, in Gallimard's "Bibliothèque de la Pléiade" (1934). Connected with *L'action française*, he declared himself a "fascist" in his *Entretien avec Frédéric Lefèvre* in 1926.[13] He even published an anti-Semitic pamphlet in 1943.[14]

Enthusiastic about *À l'ombre des jeunes filles en fleurs*, he was one of the first to mention Montaigne favorably in connection with Proust and to propose him as a model for reading Proust to counter to the complaint of idleness lodged against Proust by Pierrefeu during the controversy that followed the Prix Goncourt:

> And then, there is Montaigne, was he more a man of action than M. Marcel Proust? Yet in considering his usefulness, you may find it to be greater than that of most of his contemporaries. *À la recherche du temps perdu* is, if you like, a new, psychological *Essais*. And then, one of the reproaches you direct at the book is that it cannot be assigned to any genre. So assign it to the genre of essays. At least there is a great precedent for this.[15]

Thus Montaigne was formally called on to come to Proust's aid, with no mention of his "actions," serving as mayor of Bordeaux and negotiator between Henri III and Henri de Nevarre, or that his life had never been purely contemplative. But

Boulenger, a Renaissance scholar, knew what he was doing in summoning Montaigne to defend Proust, even though, during Proust's lifetime, no explicit reference was made to their shared maternal heritage.

ANDRÉ BEAUNIER, 1906

In fact, the parallel between Proust and Montaigne turns out to be even older and very deeply rooted, predating even the appearance of *Du côté de chez Swann*, and always undoubtedly as a circumlocution for Jewishness. André Beaunier (1869–1925), an editor at *Figaro* from the time that Gaston Calmette had become its director in 1902, made the connection as early as 1906, in his review of Proust's newly published Ruskin translation, *Sésame et les lys*.

He focused on Proust's long preface to the translation of Ruskin's lectures, "Sur la lecture," a text that prefigures *À la recherche du temps perdu,* both the account of childhood in "Combray" and the theory of literature in *Le temps retrouvé*:

> He reads Ruskin a bit like Montaigne read Plutarch: he "tries out" his thinking in contact with another's thought; he wonders about the greater or lesser credence he gives to the opinion of another whom he respects; he has doubts, he notices multiple differences between the other's claim and one he would have liked to formulate: and imperceptibly he becomes aware of himself. This is the game of a delicate moralist, unresolved because he has a sensitive mind and sees the various aspects of things.[16]

Graduate of the École Normale Supérieure with a degree in literature, André Beaunier, a friend of Paul Bourget and hostile to the modern humanities, returned to Catholicism and distrusted modernism.[17] He was among the first to sign the "Pour un parti de l'intelligence" Manifesto in 1919. His opinions were "strictly antidemocratic and even reactionary," wrote Léon Daudet at the time of his death.[18]

Proust was aware of his praise, which he brought up a year later in a letter to Robert de Montesquiou, recounting his visits among society to receive compliments (this is what the narrator of *Albertine disparue* will do after his article appears in *Le Figaro*): "Since he compared me to Montaigne and various other persons of quality, I was not upset at realizing what effect that had produced."[19] In fact, Beaunier had proposed only one model: Montaigne.

Beaunier had emulators and the comparison reappears in other reviews of *Sésame et les lys* that focus on the translator's preface. In *Le Mouvement*, a short-lived review published in 1906-1907: "Montaigne would have been delighted by the way Proust translates; abundant notes accompany his translation, which is perfect, and those notes, or rather those *commentaries*, informed and amiable, are an added pleasure to the translated work."[20] The article, which was unsigned, was written by a distant cousin of Proust, Marcel Cruppi (1883-1958), the son of Jean and Louise (née Crémieux) Cruppi, whom Proust thanked.[21]

Again, in *La revue idéaliste*: "M. Proust is very fond of Ruskin. He has already introduced to us the *Bible d'Amiens* that he enjoyed embellishing with notes and long commentaries. *Sésame et les lys* was only a happy pretext. This is the way Montaigne read 'in leaps and bounds' his dear Plutarch in Amyot's French, forgetting himself in endless reveries, meditations, or memories. M. Proust is a delightful poet. He knows how to muse over books."[22] The author, Jean Bonnerot (1882-1964), was a librarian at the Sorbonne, young poet, and future editor of Sainte-Beuve's *Correspondance générale*. He used the occasion to recount his own memories in the manner of Proust and he submitted his article to Proust before publishing it.[23]

Of course, it is impossible to be sure that the comparison of Proust with Montaigne always includes their Jewishness, but for Beaunier, author of an anthology of French moralists,[24] for Ghéon, a close friend of that fine connoisseur of Montaigne, Gide, and for the Chartist Boulenger, there seems to be no doubt about it, and even less after Proust's death, when his Jewishness was acknowledged.

ANDRÉ GIDE, 1921

Despite these few antecedents, the seminal text for establishing the parallels between the two writers, including their half-Jewishness, really was Thibaudet's tribute in *La nouvelle revue française* in January 1923, "Marcel Proust et la tradition française," much more influential even than Cattaui's Proust obituary in *Menorah* a month earlier. According to Thibaudet, Proust belonged to what he would call in his *Histoire de la littérature française* the "Montaigne party."[25] This label served to defend him against the charges of excessive intellectualism and endless psychological analysis: "Over the past six years it has become a commonplace in

France to evoke on the subject of Proust two names, Saint-Simon and Montaigne. And it actually deserves to become a commonplace, to be incorporated into our lineages of literary history. We must think of Saint-Simon and Montaigne to understand the French depths that underlie the work of Proust, the masses of lost time that this time regained restore to us."[26]

Like bedrock, humus, or leaf mold, Montaigne and Saint-Simon resurface in Proust, which was a way for Thibaudet to include Proust in the French tradition, according to the title of the article and despite those who refused him a place there and insisted upon the foreign nature of his work. Barrès, as we have seen, had ventured to call Montaigne a "foreigner," before correcting himself. For Thibaudet, who was closer to Barrès than to Proust, to associate Proust with Montaigne was to integrate him even while categorizing him, the reason no doubt that André Spire rejected this search for "precedents" to explain a "new 'species'" and refuted the comparison of Proust to Montaigne, as well as to Saint-Simon, in his Proust obituary for the *Jewish Chronicle*, claiming that: "Proust resembles no one.... Proust is a unique case."[27] In doing so, Spire introduced a rare distinction between his own reading of Proust and that of his young friend Cattaui who was partial to Montaigne.

But the comparison of Proust to Montaigne had supposedly become a "commonplace" over the past six years, Thibaudet announced in January 1923. The cliché thus seems to date back to 1916 or 1917. What event was he thinking of? Neither the publication of *De côté de chez Swann* in 1913, nor that of *À l'ombre des jeunes filles en fleur* in 1919 seems right, and Proust published nothing during the war. The date could correspond to when Proust broke with Bernard Grasset, in autumn 1916, to return to Éditions de la NRF in order to publish the rest of his novel with them. At the height of the war, a sacred union formed around classicism and the public expression of anti-Semitism abated. Established at Éditions de la NRF, Proust became a classic author, but a modern classic author, like Saint-Simon and Montaigne, not appreciated by *L'action française* but prized at *La nouvelle revue française*, in keeping with the audacious traditionalism of Gide. To Henri Clouard, a literary historian close to Maurras, who excluded Pascal and Saint-Simon from the French literary canon, Gide responded in 1909 that he had no doubt "they will be found, as Montaigne has just been found, to have some shameful origin, which will allow for them to be kicked out."[28] For Gide, who was thus aware that Antoinette de Louppes could have been a Marrano, Montaigne might well have been the greatest French writer, equal to Goethe for German literature.[29] If he defended him against Clouard, he did not do so without "afterthoughts," but in full consciousness of his "shameful origin."

Indeed in 1923, Thibaudet expanded on a brief but striking suggestion made by Gide in his "Billet à Angèle" piece for *La nouvelle revue française* issue devoted to Proust in May 1921. Gide was then immersed in reading *Le côté de Guermantes*, in this case *Le côté de Guermantes I*, which had appeared in late summer 1920 and which he had been slow to open, not *Le côté de Guermantes II* followed by *Sodome et Gomorrhe I*, for which the publication date was 30 April 1921. Immediately Gide came upon the discourse on the "*race maudite*," which shocked him. He paid a visit to Proust on 13 May, bringing him *Corydon* in exchange, and that evening they had their notorious conversation on homosexuality, over the course of which, according to Gide's journal, the comparison between homosexuals and Jews was not broached.[30] When speaking of "uranism," Gide seemed to prefer the Greek metaphor.

Thus it was his reading of *Côté de Guermantes I* that prompted this reaction from Gide:

> If I now try to find what I admire most in this work, I think it is its gratu-
> itousness. I know of nothing more useless, with less to prove. . . . It seems that
> turn by turn each page perfectly finds its end within itself. Hence this extreme
> slowness, this lack of desire to go more quickly, this continuous satisfaction.
> I experience similar nonchalance only with Montaigne, and that is no doubt
> why I can only compare the pleasure of reading a book by Proust to the plea-
> sure I derive from *Essais*. These are works of long leisure.[31]

Praising leisure and pleasure, uselessness and nonchalance, Gide seems to coun-ter, point by point, Ghéon's review of *Du côté de chez Swann* from *La nouvelle revue française* in January 1914. And by insisting on the independent closure of each page, its self-sufficiency, as it were, he also distances himself from the interpretation of Jacques Rivière, a rival at *La nouvelle revue française* who was also vying for Proust's good opinion in the early 1920s, and who delighted Proust in 1914 by find-ing his book to be "a dogmatic work and a construction."[32]

But if we need to verify that the reference to Montaigne really was a euphe-mism for evoking Proust's Jewishness, there could be no more opportune con-firmation than remarks Gide made in private, recounted by Maria van Rysselber-ghe, "la petite dame," at the time he was writing his "Billet à Angèle" on *Le côté de*

Guermantes I in spring 1921: "He read to us the column that he about to send to *La NRF* on Proust.... He said, 'I do not want to do it, but in discussing the suppleness of his style, I could say that it is Jewish; it is curious, he has exactly the same degree of heredity as Montaigne' (to whom he compares him)."[33] Gide lets the cat out of the bag: behind the noble parallel between these illustrious men hide Jewish suppleness, "shameful origin," and the ordinary anti-Semitism of the Paris literati, their mistrust of Jewish literature and its invasiveness (figures 16 and 17).

Figure 16. Félix Vallotton, portrait of Léon Blum, 1900.
Photo © BnF, Paris.

Figure 17. Félix Vallotton, portrait of André Gide, 1896.
Photo © BnF, Paris.

Following a luncheon in January 1914 with Léon Blum, three years his junior and his schoolmate at the Henri-IV lycée in 1888, Gide made this note in his journal, prompted by the feeling of Jewish superiority and its ostentation, which bothered him in Blum:

> It is absurd, it is even dangerous to deny the qualities of Jewish literature; but it is important to recognize that, in our day, there is a Jewish literature in France that is not French literature, that has its own qualities, meanings, particular directions. . . . Of course I do not deny in the least the great merit of a few Jewish works. . . . But how much more easily I could admire them if they only came to us in translation! . . . If the time comes when French no longer has sufficient power, it would be better to let it die than to let some boorish lout take over in its place, in its name.[34]

Deploring the triumphant arrival on the literary scene of Catulle Mendès, Henry Bataille, Henry Bernstein, Georges de Porto-Riche, Julien Benda over the past twenty to fifty years, Gide does not mention Proust. But in January 1914, and considering the blunder committed at *La nouvelle revue française* in refusing the manuscript of *Du côté de chez Swann*, Gide certainly had Proust in mind in these thoughts on Jewish pretension and arrogance. To correct the error in 1916, Montaigne's tutelage would be invaluable.

ALBERT THIBAUDET, 1923

Thus the parallel with Montaigne already had a long history, going back at least to 1906, when Thibaudet gave it definitive form in the January 1923 "Hommage à Marcel Proust" issue of *La nouvelle revue française*. This issue took the opportunity to advertise the most visible title published by Éditions de la NRF that fall, *Silbermann*, along with an excerpt from Jean de Pierrefeu's column from the *Journal des débats*.

Seeking to inscribe Proust in the "French tradition," and after having indicated what Proust owed to Saint-Simon, Thibaudet moves to Montaigne's *Essais*:

> At first glance, the name of Montaigne seems less relevant than that of Saint-Simon. . . . It is not over the world of men or the figures of his time that

Montaigne throws the net of his experience, but over himself and the human condition for which each individual is a figure. In his book there is no other living portrait than his own. On the contrary, in the portion of *À la recherche du temps perdu* published so far, the portrait of the author appears rarely and poorly, and should not be mistaken for those of Swann and Charlus.

However, let us not let Proust the portraitist, the memorialist, the novelist, make us forget the moralist! Someday, certainly, the psychological and moral reflections that he has scattered throughout the pages of his work will be collected in one volume, and we will see the extent to which he is bound to the pure line of great French moralists. For some sensible minds that cannot bear him, this will be a revelation and a source of confusion. From this perspective, he may be considered the present-day representative of the family of subtle analysts who, since Montaigne, have so rarely stood idle among us.[35]

Thus Proust was another of the moralists in the great tradition of French thought, whereas Montaigne was another of the novelists, or at least in Montaigne there was a potential novelist, and in his *Essais* the seed of the modern novel that would become the novel of the human condition, brought to fruition in French literature by Proust. In any case, that is what Thibaudet maintained in one of his last articles, "Le roman de Montaigne," in 1935, which completed the parallel he drew between the two writers.[36]

Moreover, Montaigne and Proust were both thinkers of movement, of mobility, and of relativity, which connected them to a third thinker, Henri Bergson, Thibaudet's former professor and the leading philosopher of that time:

His sickroom was his version of Montaigne's tower, and, if the spirits of solitude spoke to him and made him speak a different language, it is remarkable to see how that language is conveyed through images strikingly similar to those of Montaigne. Proust and Montaigne both belong to the family of creators of images, and Proust's images, like Montaigne's, are generally images of movement. The forms, the outer shells of things, represent for them only appearances to be traversed in order to find the inner movements that are fixed or expressed by them. Proust's and Montaigne's worlds both project dynamic schemas, and it is with these dynamic schemas that their styles, through the intermediary of images, strive to coincide. Their styles do not put movement into thought, according to the classic definition, rather they put thought into preexisting movement, which it happily follows or interrupts.

One will recognize Bergsonian expressions in these last lines, leading us to evocative views that I introduce here with some reservations.[37]

As a matter of form at least, it is this dual affinity linking Montaigne to Bergson and to Proust through the movement of their thought that leads Thibaudet, as though inadvertently, as though it had just occurred to him, to their Jewishness, where he proceeds with caution, with great delicacy, "with some reservations." His thesis is posed as a question, but it will soon become part of the standard line and will itself engender a considerable lineage:

> These similarities between Proust and Montaigne, the remarkable mobility of both authors, might they not have some connection to another type of kin-ship? It is certain that Montaigne's mother, a Lopez, was Jewish. Of our great writers, Montaigne is the only one in whom Jewish blood is present. We know the analogous heredity of Marcel Proust. And that is also the mixed heredity of the great philosopher whom I just mentioned and paraphrased, the founder of a philosophy of mobility that he has expressed in mobilist images, in visual-motor images, so analogous to those of Montaigne and of Proust.... An instructive story, here, of a drop of Jewish blood in our current literature![38]

The kinship of the three works is at least suggested: their mobility is an extended family affair. Thibaudet may not have known that Bergson had married Proust's cousin, Louise Neuburger, a great-grandchild, like Proust, of Baruch Weil (Proust was best man at their wedding in 1892). Although Jewish on both sides, the phi-losopher's "mixed heredity" points to his Polish origins on his father's side and English origins on his mother's side, thus toning down the suggestion even more.

Thibaudet then compares Proust with Henry Bernstein, a familiar pairing in the 1920s, as we have seen with Urbain Gohier. And then:

> A Montaigne, a Proust, a Bergson: they establish in our rich and complex lit-erary universe what could be called the Franco-Semitic doublet, as there are Franco-English, Franco-German, Franco-Italian literary doublets, as France itself is a doublet of North and South. But let us consider this only as an expe-dient and without indulging in belabored mobility ourselves. The French

tradition in which we must place Marcel Proust is a living, unpredictable, singular tradition, a tradition of irregular, serpentine movement, turning and returning, which, as in a sentence, as in a page of Proust, always transcends its precise subject through its inner elasticity and its overflowing profusion.[39]

Thibaudet trivializes his "Franco-Semitic doublet" (the phrase will enjoy wide success) by likening it to many other familiar doublets in comparative literature (Franco-English, Franco-German, Franco-Italian) and even provincial ones (North-South, as with *langue d'oc* and *langue d'oïl*), even more suitable and less suspect, since contained within the nation. As he insists, he "will not belabor it," because these are sensitive matters and require tact and indirection. But we have definitively abandoned the euphemism or implication, and discussing Montaigne with regard to Proust now comes down to underlining Proust's Jewishness without having to hide behind a paragon anymore. The Proust obituary in *Menorah* by Cattaui had been more measured: "Perhaps Proust's sympathy for Jewish characters benefitted from his maternal heredity." Nothing more, and in the form of a hypothesis ventured as though in passing. But once Thibaudet had cleared the way, with all the authority of a regular columnist for *La nouvelle revue française*, no one hesitated to "belabor it" anymore, from various angles, in a positive or negative light, and according to how one felt about Montaigne, Proust, and the Jews, to the point of Céline's giving us the "Prout-Prousts" in *Bagatelles pour un massacre* and "Mr Ben Montaigne prêchi-prêcha, madré rabbin" in *Les beaux draps*.

ALBERT COHEN, 1923

Following Thibaudet and thus authorized by him, the young Proustian Zionists of the 1920s quickly adopted the reference to Montaigne's heredity, with no uncertainties and even with pride, as a way of affirming Proust's Jewish side. That was immediately the case with Albert Cohen (1895–1981), born in Corfu, raised in Marseille, a student in Geneva of law and literature, and initiated into Zionism by André Spire as early as 1917, the author of poems collected in *Paroles juives* (1921). He became a Swiss citizen in 1919 and married Élisabeth Brocher, daughter of a Protestant pastor. The author of *Belle du seigneur* (Paris: Gallimard, 1968) is not an unknown figure, so this short note will suffice (figure 18).

Figure 18. Albert Cohen, c. 1930.

Photo © Archives Gallimard / Collection A. Cohen.

While he was attempting to establish himself as a lawyer in Egypt between autumn 1920 and autumn 1922 (his daughter Myriam was born in Geneva in his absence), Albert Cohen came across *À l'ombre des jeunes filles en fleurs* one day in a bookstore in Alexandria. Reading the novel made him a devoted Proustian. After returning to Europe in late 1921, his Egyptian ambitions thwarted, he met doctor Robert Proust in Paris "a few months after the death" of Marcel Proust.[40] He embraced the analogy between Proust and Montaigne, launched for better or for worse by Thibaudet in January 1923, adopting it as his own. In March 1923, Cohen published an article entitled "Le juif et les romanciers français" in *La revue de Genève*, where he had already introduced "the Jewish question and Zionism" two years earlier.[41]

Founded in 1920 by Robert de Traz, this periodical advocated for European reconciliation and spread the word of the League of Nations, as did Louise Weiss's *L'Europe nouvelle* to which Benjamin Crémieux contributed in Paris. The International Labor Organization, connected to the League of Nations, employed Cohen beginning in1926, after he rose to the head of *La revue juive* in 1925 (his *Belle du seigneur* would draw on this experience). The rubric under which his article appeared in *La revue de Genève* is a good illustration of that publication's sensitivity to Zionism, as it fell under the heading of "National Columns," followed by the subtitle, "Israel."

Cohen considers the usual suspects: the Tharaud brothers, Julien Benda, Jean-Richard Bloch, and Andrew Spire. But, as in the case with Spire's article, "Romans judéo-français," which appeared a few months earlier in *Menorah*, he essentially offers an analysis of Lacretelle's *Silbermann*. Proust, who is not discussed directly, nevertheless makes numerous appearances over the course of the article's twelve pages. For example, Lacretelle's hero is compared to Bloch: "Akin to Marcel Proust's Bloch, I believe, in speaking of Victor Hugo, he calls him *un coco*, 'that great bloke.'"[42] Now Silbermann considers "le père Hugo" a god, whereas it is not Hugo but Musset whom Bloch calls *un coco*, "an extremely pernicious individual and a rather sinister brute."[43] Nevertheless Cohen was one of the first to note the similarities between these two high school characters. Later in the article, we read that exile brought Jews "that 'immense and tranquil skepticism' of which Jacques Rivière speaks with regard to Marcel Proust."[44] Here Cohen cites and draws from the article by Jacques Rivière, "Marcel Proust et l'esprit positif," which had just appeared in the same "Hommage à Marcel Proust" issue of *La nouvelle revue française* as the article by Thibaudet.[45]

But Proust serves most importantly to characterize "the Jewish contribution, or at least the Jewish leaven," that "critical mind" that "has enriched the dry logic of the West," that has "given France that glowing, unsatisfied philosophy where the substance is inflamed and, as in Einsteinian or Proustian works, Duration sits enthroned, old wandering Jewess."[46] The image is appealing, even if Einstein seems to appear by mistake in place of Bergson, the undisputed master of duration. Although Bergson had just published *Durée et simultanéité: À propos de la théorie d'Einstein* in order to "compare our conception of duration with Einstein's views on time."[47]

Thus, with Proust, the Jewish mind had revived the French novel: "Is it not thanks a bit to that "destructive" Jewish mind that French genius has just burst forth in a new form of the novel that is positive and perceptive, a living being, uncorseted, richly dissociative and relativist?"[48] *À la recherche du temps perdu* was perceived by Cohen as the product of the "Jewish mind," characterized by skepticism and relativism, renewing and enriching the dry, rational French tradition with its critical sense.

Now this hypothesis called for an important footnote, "*capitalissime*" as Proust would say: "To be noted, in passing, that marvelous weakness, that inability to choose, for which the Jewish mind of the third period could justly be reproached and which makes Montaigne's *Essais* or *À la recherche du temps perdu* a river carrying along in its slow current so much alluvia, sending out so many branches to explore in so many foreign lands."[49] The river and alluvia recall here the Bergsonian connection revealed by Thibaudet, whereas the contradictions and complications of the characters in *Recherche*, simultaneously ashamed and proud of their origins, hiding them and then proclaiming them, split or divided (Swann in particular, whom Cohen does not name), are thus related to the writer's Jewishness, expressly associated with Montaigne.

A small clarification is necessary here, because Cohen's note linking Montaigne's and Proust's relativism and indecision to the "Jewish mind of the third period," that is, the period of exile, gave rise to an unfortunate confusion. The critic Alain Schaffner made the following comment: "Taking Montaigne and Proust as examples, Cohen develops the idea that Judaism can bring new life to the French novel both in terms of content (by creating new characters who are tormented, split between two cultures) and on the stylistic level (the Proustian sentence is compared here to Talmudic discussions)."[50] This reading was accepted as a given and henceforth generalized: "Albert Cohen was the first to notice, as early as 1923, the coincidences between the Proustian sentence and the Talmudic sentence," states Patrick Mimouni, for example, without looking back to Cohen's text.[51] Now this thesis is based on a mistaken reading. In Cohen's article, nowhere is there any mention of the slightest similarity between the "Proustian sentence" and "Talmudic discussions," or the "Talmudic sentence." That comparison would come much later, and it would not be made by Cohen. As it would enjoy great critical success and it is much debated, the question of its first attribution is not immaterial, and it is irresponsible to impute it to Albert Cohen.

The source of the misinterpretation is clear: in fact it comes from another note on the same page (note 3, whereas Montaigne and Proust are invoked in note 1) in which Cohen finds in Freud, and not Proust, the "Talmudic passion for contorting concepts, threading long black needles with very red thread and embroidering sometimes appalling and refined systems" that nevertheless inspire his admiration: "Is it not a beautiful Talmudic 'success' that makes Freud understand the resistance of his adversaries through psychoanalytic explanations?" But Proust's name is not uttered in this regard. Freud and Proust are sometimes compared (by Marie-Louise Cahen-Hayem, for example), but they are not interchangeable. We will return later to the circumstances under which the first mention of an affinity between Proust's style and rabbinical writing appeared in 1925. That thesis was immediately cited in Albert Cohen's *La revue juive*, but not under his signature, and nothing guarantees that he himself ever supported it.

During summer 1923, a few months after his article appeared in *La revue de Genève*, Albert Cohen, "of *La nouvelle revue française*" (he had published all of two articles there), gave four classes on Proust for the University of Geneva "Summer School."[52]

Two years later, *La revue juive* of 15 March 1925 announced that he would give a lecture on 2 April 1925 at Cercle Israélite, 18 Rue Lafayette, under the auspices of the Union des Femmes Juives Françaises, on "Quelques écrivains juifs de ce temps" (A few Jewish writers of our time).[53] In between those two engagements, his wife had died of cancer, in 1924.

On this occasion, he could not avoid discussing Proust as he had in his 1923 article. Gradually, however, he would prove more reticent, becoming more critical of a work about which he had mixed feelings of wonder, irritation, and rivalry. In *Belle du seigneur*, he reproaches the writer's snobbishness, the "perversity of dipping a madeleine into linden tea" and "his hysterical flatteries of the Noailles," as revealed in his letters.[54] As Proust's letters to Anna de Noailles were published in 1931, we can guess that Cohen's reaction against Proust took shape at that time.[55] And never, to my knowledge, did he return to the parallel between Proust and Montaigne, or, moreover, respond to the claims of anti-Semitism in Proust's work.

But the association between Montaigne and Proust (as well as Bergson) would be taken up again by many young Jews who lay claim to Proust in the 1920s and who did not at all condemn his portraits of Swann or Bloch. These contradictory, even pathetic, characters corresponded to the images that young Proustian Zionists themselves held of the Jews of the Diaspora, alienated through assimilation. In the same way, Cohen, no more than Spire, could perceive anti-Semitic reflexes in Lacretelle's writing—"We must not seek in *Silbermann*, in these exceptionally lucid, spiteful, and slightly mad visions of Jews, what we find in the works of Nietzsche."[56] The theory of an anti-Jewish Proust, widespread today among our own contemporaries who consider themselves above the fray, did not occur to Zionists of the 1920s, admirers of Proust as Jew, or half-Jew, for having given voice, through his characters, to the complexity and the contradiction of the being Jewish.

Cohen eloquently concludes his article by expressing the hope that David Silbermann, who, persecuted by his anti-Semitic high-school classmates, leaves Paris for New York at the end of the novel, will not settle there for good, but will himself set off for Israel: "Will he turn his gaze toward the land of refuge? He has never completely forgotten Jerusalem. Did he not hide Zionist newspapers behind his dear sixteenth-century writers?"[57] (this is possibly a misprint for the seventeenth century—although Silbermann appreciated Ronsard, he especially admired Racine). *Le retour de Silbermann*, which Lacretelle published in 1929 and in which the hero dies in Paris in abject poverty, intellectual impotence, and moral decay—"at the end of his lamentable fate . . . he was the most unfortunate of Jews"—could not help by disappoint Albert Cohen's expectations.[58]

In the meantime, everything would revolve around Proust in *La revue juive* in 1925.

CHAPTER 5

La Revue Juive

I n 1925, from January to November, six issues of *La revue juive* were published by Librairie Gallimard, Éditions de la Nouvelle Revue française
(the two imprints still coexisted) under the direction of Albert Cohen.[1]
The Zionist Organization financed the publication in order to promote Zionism among the French political and intellectual elite and enlightened francophone opinion in general. It employed Cohen, connected to Chaim Weizmann,
president of the Zionist Organization since 1921, while André Spire, éminence
grise and senior government official, remained in the background, as he had
previously done with the Ligue des Amis de Sionism and *Menorah*. The name of
the review summarized its agenda: *juive* and not *israélite* as with the *Archives*
and *L'univers*, that is, it was Zionist and not assimilationist. During the brief
but brilliant existence of *La revue juive*, its contributors were numerous, eminent, and very diverse: Pierre Benoit, Léon Blum, Georges Cattaui, Ilya Ehren-
bourg, Albert Einstein, Élie Faure, Sigmund Freud, Waldo Franc, Pierre
Hamp, Henri Hertz, Max Jacob, Jacques de Lacretelle, Armand Lunel, Louis
Massignon, Jean de Menasce, Léon Pierre-Quint, André Spire, Rabindranath
Tagore, and so on.[2]

Proust is ubiquitous throughout the pages of *La revue juive*, invoked in every
issue and at the slightest provocation: "The review set out to annex Proust," wrote
Gérard Valbert, Albert Cohen's biographer, although Cohen himself never signed
his name to anything on Proust in the review or elsewhere after those few remarks
in his early article in *La revue de Genève* in 1923 and prior to his criticisms in *Belle
du seigneur*.[3]

FIRST ISSUE

Jacques de Lacretelle entrusted to the inaugural issue of *La revue juive* a long commentary on his *Silbermann*, written at Cohen's request. The two were first in contact following Cohen's article in *La revue de Genève*. When Lacretelle mentions how difficult it is to represent Jewish characters in literature, the reference to Proust is inevitable:

> When representing in literature a type according to race, one must be careful never to fall into a conventional portrait that is easy to understand but often false. That is a particular danger for the type of the Jew, whose legend is as cliché as an Épinal print. Thus Bloch, as created by Proust, is certainly not one of the best characters in Proust's work. He is drawn with broad strokes, crudely colored in. One would like to perceive some regrets in this portrait. How much more original, finer, and more lifelike is the figure of Swann. In my opinion, he is, along with Gutlib [sic] of *Israël*,[4] the most interesting Jewish character we can find in our literature. And notice how both of them are very far from the conventional type.[5]

As early as 1922 or 1923, we may recall, Cattaui and Spire praised Proust for having created Jewish characters who could not be reduced to conventional types. Where Lacretelle mentions Swann, contrasting the subtlety of his portrayal to the caricature Proust draws in the case of Bloch, a note rightly refers to Spire's "flashy" 1923 article in *Les nouvelles littéraires*, "Marcel Proust et les juifs," that brought the question into the limelight by approaching it for the first time in the mainstream press.[6] But the comparison between Swann and Gutlieb may seem surprising. This character in *Israël*, a melodrama by Henry Bernstein written in October 1908 and full of clichés, is a banker provoked into a duel by a young aristocratic anti-Semite; when the young man discovers that Gutlieb is his own father, he commits suicide.

Also in this first issue of *La revue juive*, a certain Emmanuel Arié reviews the book of a certain Jaime de Beslou, *Idéologues*, or rather the first of the short stories, "Les systèmes du baron T'Phlex," collected in this volume published by Éditions du Sagittaire (where Léon Pierre-Quint, connected to the children of Simon Kra, served as literary editor).[7]

Emmanuel Arié (1887-1944) was born in Sofia, the capital of Bulgaria (which had only recently gained independence from the Ottoman Empire), to a family of Sephardic Jews who had left Spain for the Balkans after 1492. He was educated at the Alliance Israélite Universelle school in Smyrna, the Alliance professional school in Jerusalem, and then, after a brief time at the École des Arts et Métiers in Châlons-sur-Marne in 1901, at the École Pigier in Paris, where he learned accounting. After entering the pearl trading business he married Lucie Nestor Weill in Geneva in 1914, and they had two sons, Pierre and Georges. We know all this because his older brother Gabriel Arié (1863-1939), who was some twenty years his senior and raised him, was a key figure in the Alliance Israélite Universelle and left behind an autobiography and a journal.[8] A former student at the École Normale Israélite Orientale (ENIO) in Paris, where he was classmates with Abraham Benveniste, father of Émile Benveniste, a former teacher and director of Alliance schools in Constantinople, Sofia, Smyrna, and then a businessman, he was also the Alliance's historian and author of *Histoire juive depuis les origines jusqu'à nos jours* (1923), widely used in the Alliance school system.[9] It was "a good textbook," according to the *Revue des études juives*, with a "substantial summary of Graetz's *Histoire* and Narcisse Leven's *50 ans d'histoire 1860–1910*. Especially valuable, among others, are the last two chapters, a short, objective account of Zionism and the most recent events."[10] This review refers to the history of the Alliance that was issued to celebrate its first fifty years and published under the name of its director, Narcisse Leven, but actually written by Gabriel Arié. And by "objective account of Zionism," the *Revue des études juives* meant that Gabriel Arié evoked the Alliance's "declaration of neutrality" with regard to Zionism, a "partial solution to the Jewish question."[11] Nevertheless, there are advertisements for Gabriel Arié's *Histoire juive* in *La revue juive*.[12] Although Emmanuel Arié was interested in poetry, I have not found his name in any journal other than *La revue juive*. His Zionist activism seems not to have lasted either; as secretary general of the fine pearl brokers union in the 1930s, he gave lectures on "the treasures of the Law of Israel," and he was a member of the Consistorial Association of Paris, from which he was removed in 1936 for protesting the welcome given to fascist colonel François de La Rocque and a delegation of the Croix-de-Feu at the Rue de la Victoire temple.[13]

His review starts by repeating the new commonplace on Proust in the mid-1920s: "From Montaigne to Proust, what is more curious to observe than a half-Jew. That is the case with Baron T'Phlex, whose systems and surprising adventure are reported by Jaime de Beslou."[14] The filiation of Proust to Montaigne was henceforth so well accepted that it did not require an explanation and could simply be cited. Why did Arié concern himself with this book even though he notes at the very beginning, "some have criticized this short story's author for peddling an old collection of Jewish caricatures"?

To justify his interest despite that, Arié reveals the author hidden behind the pseudonym of Beslou: "Proust was not wrong to defend Blanche against this charge (anti-Semitism). Because for those who have read the *Cahiers d'un artiste*, it will not take long to recognize that Jaime de Beslou and Jacques-Émile Blanche are one and the same." Jacques-Émile Blanche: painter, son and grandson of the doctors Blanche, friend of Proust, maker of the famous portrait of the young Marcel as a dandy sporting a white orchid, but also the writer for whom Proust wrote a preface to his *Propos de peintre* (1919). His *Idéologues* brings together four short stories, comic portraits of limited interest. Arié comments on only one of them, that of the baron T'Phlex, because of the character's Jewish origins and especially because it allows him to cite Proust's unpublished letter to Blanche, to which Blanche gave his access. "Race does not explain everything," Arié points out. Nevertheless, "when we encounter certain shared traits in Blanche and in Proust, that may be because they are both (Proust only half) of Norman origin. And when, on the contrary, Proust and Blanche seem profoundly different, we are tempted to attribute those differences to the Jewish blood that Marcel Proust got from his mother." Arié expresses no criticism here and simply laments the title chosen for this book: "*Le Baron T'Phlex, histoire juive*, by J.-É. Blanche would certainly have prompted more interest among readers than *Idéologues* by J. de Beslou."[15]

The review must not have displeased Blanche since—and here is another indication of the complicity between *La revue juive* and the small circle of Proustian reviewers—the fourth issue of the review, in July 1925, offered generous excerpts from Proust's letters to Blanche, entrusted to Albert Cohen by their addressee and constituting some of the first publications of Proust's correspondence.[16]

Emmanuel Arié also wrote a review of the collection *Poésie, 1916–1923* by Jean Cocteau (1924) in the penultimate issue of *La revue juive*, in September 1925. He stresses the presence of angels in Cocteau and praises a poetry that has "let itself be permeated with the scents of the Judaic desert."[17] He even discerns here an interest in the Kabbalah and quotes the poet: "The Bible, which offers to the non-believer only a surface of crude images, naive and sometimes completely obscure anecdotes, is in reality made of many layers of meaning that cannot be understood without knowing the code."[18] But Arié again returns to Proust, because Cocteau is "too intense to be pretending, or even, as Proust liked to do, "to assume a posture, to mime naïveté and incommensurable modesty." This was a line he took from Anna de Noailles's contribution to "Hommage à Marcel Proust" in the January 1923 issue of *La nouvelle revue française*.[19] Thus Proust has the last word.

Again, in that first issue of *La revue juive*, the review that follows the one by Emmanuel Arié bears the signature of Georges Cattaui, who also finds a way to cite Proust, this time with regard to Péguy's *Note conjointe sur M. Descartes*, preceded by the *Note sur M. Bergson*, published posthumously in 1924 in the *Oeuvres complètes*.[20] Péguy presents a Jewish-Christian dialogue, in this case between Julien Benda and Péguy himself. To Péguy, who proposed that "Every Jew proceeds from a certain fatalism" (a traditional prejudice that, incidentally, is accompanied by its opposite, an anxiety over Jewish impatience and revolt), Cattaui responds that he "can no longer follow him." This offers Cattaui a good opportunity to contrast Péguy to Proust and repeat the usual quote on Swann's endurance: "Swann belonged to that strong Jewish race, in whose vital energy and resistance to death."[21] Then a Zionist activist, Cattaui uses Proust to refute the image promoted by Péguy of the Jewish people as victims; he chooses Proust over Péguy, despite his admiration for the latter.

ISSUES TWO TO FIVE

In the second issue of *La revue juive*, in March 1925, a long unsigned column under the heading of "Israël et les nations" addressed "La France et le sionisme." For Albert Cohen and his associates, it was a matter of anticipating the objections that French Jews, supporters of assimilation, would raise against Zionism. Proust is cited in it twice as a favored ally. The first time is with regard to the parallel that Proust's novel traces between Jews and aristocrats: both of them, the Guermantes and the Blochs alike, demonstrate inherited characteristics acquired through the marriages of individuals of the same blood.[22] That comparison was not problematic. In fact, during the Ancien Régime the notion of race was long used exclusively to speak of nobility, through blue blood or birth, and of Jews, the people or the chosen race.[23]

The second time is to emphasize that, no matter what happened, France and Israel would never be separate, estranged from one another, because of the ancient ties that bound them and "French genius continually bearing the mark of Jewish genius," as Proust's novel again illustrated.[24] The aim in invoking Proust was to reassure French Jews that Zionism would never isolate Jews from France or its culture, and that the "Jewish soul," and the "French mind," habitual categories in the thinking of Cohen as of Spire, would continue to enrich each other.

In the third issue of *La revue juive*, André Spire reviewed the latest book by Myriam Harry (1869–1958), the pseudonym of Maria Rosette Shapira or Mme Émile Perrault, half-Jewish like Proust, born in Jerusalem to a Protestant mother and a Jewish father who had converted to Christianity. Raised in Germany by her mother after her father's suicide, she became a successful French novelist with *La conquête de Jérusalem* (1904), a transposition of her father's misadventures. When the novel failed to win the Prix Goncourt due to the jury's misogyny (and no doubt its anti-Semitism), it was awarded the Prix Femina (first called Vie Heureuse), created as recompense.[25] It would be nice to pause here to consider the novelist's romances and travels, but this is not the time or place. Proust never mentions her, although he may have met her at Mme de Caillavet's salons, which she frequented, and although Philip Kolb finds in a letter from Proust to Reynaldo Hahn a possible allusion to a letter of condolence that Proust might have sent her in 1914 upon the death of Jules Lemaitre, who had promoted her literary career and with whom she had had an affair.[26]

Following her first return visit to Palestine, *Les amants de Sion* (1923) is the account of her voyage and the rediscovery of her Jewish roots. Spire compares Myriam Harry's discovery of Zionism and return to Israel not only to the realization of "Zangwill's dejudaized hero in *Chad Gadya*," his own model for his Zionist activism in 1904 (or negative model, since assimilation leads to suicide in Zangwill's story), but also to Proust's trajectory: "It is an aspiration analogous . . . to that invincible sympathy that drove Marcel Proust, half-Jew, baptized, raised outside of Judaism, to prefer his Jewish relatives and to choose his friends especially among Jews and half-Jews, to construct his story of late nineteenth-century French society around a good, proud, intelligent Jewish hero."[27] The trio of Marcel Proust, Israel Zangwill, and Myriam Harry? It is powerful and surprising connection, but Proust is dragooned in effect, or "annexed" as Valbert said, counted among the proselytes of Zionism by Arié, Cattaui, and Spire himself in *La revue juive*.

A letter from Georges Cattaui to Albert Cohen appeared in the fifth issue of *La revue juive* in September 1925, proposing that a monument to the memory of Proust be erected in the Jardin des Champs-Élysées for the third anniversary of his death: "Let all Marcel Proust's friends and admirers join us, regardless of political or literary party, from Léon Blum to Léon Daudet, from André Gide to Pierre Benoit, and from André Breton to Rosny aîné. . . . It is a matter of commemorating one of the purest and brightest literary lights of contemporary France."[28] The plan confirms the remarkable ecumenicalism of the Zionist review, coupling names in a way that seems bizarre to us today, but that did not seem so in the eyes of Cattaui, since all these figures venerated Proust. And Cohen supported his plan, since *La revue juive* would dismiss the arguments of a critic who protested the project, calling Cattaui, in his love for Proust, a victim of "exasperated—and exasperating—snobbishness," and "a Zionist to boot."[29]

LAST ISSUE

Albert Cohen met Robert Proust and obtained from Gallimard advance pages of *Albertine disparue* for the sixth and final issue of *La revue juive* in November 1925.[30] Entitled "Mademoiselle de Forcheville," this long excerpt of almost twenty pages presents Gilberte Swann, the narrator's childhood friend whom he no longer recognizes under her new name, that of her adoptive father, Odette's second husband. The passage published in *La revue juive* is particularly well chosen because it describes, according to Proust, "the time when the aftermath of the Dreyfus affair gave rise to an anti-Semitic movement, in conjunction with a movement toward a greater infiltration of society by the children of Israel."[31]

These are terrible pages: they recount the second death of Swann, renounced by his daughter and his friends, the duke and duchess of Guermantes, who, after having always refused to receive Gilberte while Swann was alive, henceforth open their salon to her. Proust targets the bad manners of high society, for example those of the duke of Guermantes who speaks of Swann as he would a servant: "So it is when an anti-Semite tells a Jew of the faults of Jews in general while smothering him with affable remarks, thus enjoying being hurtful without seeming to be rude."[32] Proust must have often experienced affronts like this in Paris salons. One of them was actually documented in a letter to Robert de Montesquiou from May 1896, the period of the Dreyfus affair, after the count had lashed out against Jews in front of Proust, who took it upon himself the following day to warn him: "if I am Catholic like my father and my brother, on the other hand, my mother is Jewish"; thus, "you could have hurt me unintentionally in a discussion."[33]

As for Gilberte, she hides her origins through snobbishness, but she reveals them all the more sharply following a blunder that has all the markings of a Freudian slip: "Thus it happened one day, when a young lady who, whether from malice or from tactlessness, had asked her the name of her true rather than of her adoptive father, that Gilberte, in her confusion and in an attempt to disguise what she was forced to say, had pronounced the name as 'Svann' instead of 'Souann,' a change which some time later she realized was pejorative, since it turned an originally English name into a German name."[34] This recalls the French-Jewish joke about a man named Katzmann who went by Shalom, because if you had a German-sounding name in France it meant you were Jewish.

The end of the excerpt puts the final nail in the coffin: "Gilberte's presence in a drawing-room, instead of being an occasion for people still to speak sometimes of her father, was an obstacle preventing them from seizing those increasingly rare occasions when they might still have been able to do so. Even on the subject of the words he had spoken and the gifts he had offered, people acquired a habit of no longer mentioning his name, and she who should have renewed, if not perpetuated, his memory turned out to be precisely the one who hastened and consummated the process of dying and forgetting."[35] Read in *La revue juive*, the advance pages of *Albertine disparue* take on a different meaning than in the novel, or a more evident and more irrefutable meaning: they denounce an integration, assimilation, or absorption that entails the erasure of one's name and denial of one's origins. Albert Cohen's choice of an excerpt worked well for making Proust into a critic of Franco-Judaism and a prophet of Zionism. It is doubtful that Robert Proust was aware of the maneuver he assisted by entrusting to Cohen this section of *À la recherche du temps perdu*.

The last issue of *La revue juive* also included Armand Lunel's review of Benjamin Crémieux's collection, *XXᵉ siècle*, an analysis that, as we have noted, essentially considers Crémieux's first study, "the longest and richest of them all," devoted to Proust.[36] The article is entirely in praise of the writer "who, through the horizons that he discovers for our literary future, may occupy the same position for the twentieth century as Chateaubriand did for the nineteenth century, as its innovator, and moreover, in an entirely different domain."[37]

And if *La revue juive* did not review *Marcel Proust: Sa vie, son oeuvre* by Léon Pierre-Quint, it was not for lack of trying but because plans unexpectedly fell through. The letters exchanged between Albert Cohen and Pierre-Quint during spring and summer 1925 discussed both the letters of Jacques-Émile Blanche to appear in the fourth issue in July 1925 and Pierre-Quint's book on Proust. Cohen was also trying to recruit him; on 12 June 1925 he entrusted to Pierre-Quint "the typed text of Marcel Proust's letters" to Blanche, writing, "Let me take this opportunity to tell you how happy I would be to see you give the support of your great talent to *La revue juive*. / If you would like, for example, to give us a note on a work by a Jewish author, we would do our best to publish it in our fourth issue." Pierre-Quint's book was published at the end of June and Cohen wrote to him as soon as 2 July: "Thank you for so kindly sending me your book on Marcel Proust, and for the gift of your generous inscription. I read with very great interest this precious contribution. The part devoted to the work seems to me particularly remarkable."[38] But Cohen says nothing about the very limited role given to Proust's Jewishness in this book. On 23 July Pierre-Quint proposed to Cohen a note by his friend Robert Desnos, who "would be very happy to talk about my book in a publication with a wider distribution than the *Révolution surréaliste*," while he himself would write a note on Carl Sternheim (1878–1942), a German expressionist writer.[39] Cohen answered him on 7 September, accepting the note on Sternheim, which appeared in the last issue of *La revue juive*.[40] But he rejected the text by Desnos: "I am returning to you the note by Mr. Desnos whose poetic talent I admire very much. But I believe as you do that it would be better not to publish this critical piece. / We will be very happy to talk about your Proust in our upcoming issues. Would you be so kind as to send a copy to me and have another one sent to Mr. Georges Cattaui, 35 Rue Madabegh Le Caire, who will probably review your work."[41] Thus, Robert Desnos did not contribute to *La revue juive*, Cattaui did not have time to submit his piece before the review ceased publication, and there was no further mention of Proust in *La révolution surréaliste*, except for a strange and beautiful portrait of his eye by Georges Bessière (figure 19).[42]

JEAN DE MENASCE, 1925

By focusing on Proust in 1925, *La revue juive* was fully part of a literary movement. Also in the last issue, and by an interesting coincidence, there was a long piece

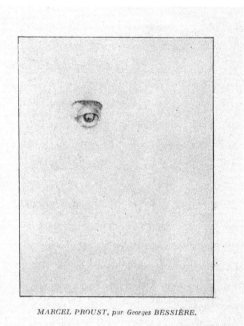

MARCEL PROUST, par Georges BESSIÈRE.

Figure 19. *La révolution surréaliste*, January 1925. Photo © BnF, Paris.

on James Joyce's *Ulysses*, published in English in Paris (Shakespeare and Company, 1922). It was signed by a very young Jean de Menasce (1902–1973), a brilliant student.[43] Born in Alexandria to a prominent family of bankers, he was the cousin of Georges Cattaui. His father, the baron of Menasce, came to Albert Cohen's aid during a disastrous trip Cohen took to Alexandria in 1920–1921.[44]

Educated at Oxford, introduced particularly successfully and at a very early age into modernist intellectual and literary circles, friend of Bertrand Russell, T. S. Eliot, E. M. Forster, Charles Du Bos, Constantine Cavafy, and so on, he appears in photographs of the Bloomsbury Group taken by Lady Ottoline Morrell, Russell's mistress and the model for D. H. Lawrence's Lady Chatterley. In 1925, Jean de Menasce was employed in the Geneva office of the Zionist Organization, where Albert Cohen would succeed him that summer, and he also worked as assistant editor for *La revue juive*. His zeal for Zionism was manifest. After having attended the inauguration of the Hebrew University of Jerusalem in April 1925, he wrote to his cousin Georges Cattaui: "I am dead to the Jewish people. I am Hebrew and Judean. I must live here; elsewhere is death and starvation."[45] A superb profession of Zionist faith! But also a good example of the bridge between the two paths of Zionism and prophetism that Benjamin Crémieux noted in neo-Judaism: Jean de Menasce converted to Catholicism in May 1926; resisted threats by his father, who made him return to Egypt; joined the Dominican order in 1930; and was ordained a priest in 1935. Introduced to the Pahlavi language by Émile Benveniste at the École Pratique des Hautes Études (EPHE) in 1937–1938, he brought the linguist to Fribourg during the war. Beginning in 1948, he served as chair of Iranian Religions at the Fifth Section of the EPHE.

An early reader of *Ulysses* (in the original English, because he says nothing about the French translation that appeared in 1924), he was very interested in the character of Bloom and speaks forcefully about him: "Bloom is a typical Jew, but not, as in most 'Jewish novels,' by virtue of his mannerisms or his preoccupations; he is Jewish in a unique and irreparable way, through the schema of his daydreams. He does not think about Jewish things, he thinks 'Jewish.' Or rather, he does not think it, but 'it thinks in him.'"[46] This insight demonstrates a surprising maturity for a young man of twenty-three. He discovered in Joyce the same novelty that his friends Spire and Cattaui appreciated in Proust, that is, the invention of a Jewish character who is unconventional but no less undeniably Jewish, "in a unique and irreparable way." "To think Jewish": the expression may seem suspect. Hitler wrote in *Mein Kampf*: "When he speaks French, he thinks Jewish, and while he turns out German verses, in his life he is expressing the character of his nationality."[47] This was also a phrase that French Jews used with regard to foreign Jews or recent immigrants from central or eastern Europe who still spoke Yiddish while they themselves "thought French." Jean-Jacques Bernard (1888–1972), son of Tristan Bernard, would say of the French Jewish elite arrested in December 1941 during the "roundup of the notables" and held with him at the Compiègne-Royallieu camp: "like me, they only knew how to think French. They did not know how to think Jewish."[48] Menasce turns the expression around, into a Freudian "it thinks in him," to praise Joyce, formally introducing the question that his friends did not yet dare to ask of Swann and Proust: "Do they think Jewish?" Or more precisely, "Does it think in them?"

Jean de Menasce contributed faithfully to *La revue juive*, where his signature appeared in every issue without exception. In the fourth issue, in July 1924, he offered an important column entitled "Antisémitisme," regarding the works of Hilaire Belloc, Franco-British historian and militant Catholic; Hans Blüher, German philosopher and militant homosexual; and René Groos, French journalist and writer, characterizing all three as "anti-Semites of good faith." "Jews," observed

Jean de Menasce, "have much to learn from anti-Semites," among them men like René Groos, an "Action Française Catholic," whose "Jewish origin only makes his testimony more interesting."[49]

RENÉ GROOS, 1926

This René Groos (1898–1972) should be introduced here for the record. Further on, we will consider his treatment of Proust's Jewishness, because he too examined the question and devoted a study to it that would attract, for example, the attention of Benjamin Crémieux at the end of the decade. As an *"Action française Jew,"* his perspective will complete the panorama.

Born in Paris, growing up not far from Rue des Rosiers, Groos was part of the "class" of 1918. Mobilized in 1917 and demobilized in 1920, his hero was Pierre David (1886–1918), a young *Action française* Jew who died at the front on 1 August 1918, and to whom Maurras paid tribute.[50] A private school teacher turned journalist, René Groos's many responsibilities in the press during the 1920s included writing literary columns for *L'intransigeant* and helping to edit *Les Marges*, a review directed by Eugène Montfort, one of the founders of the first, short-lived *Nouvelle revue française* in 1908.[51] Menasce called him a Catholic, but the date of his conversion is unknown. Following the model of *Enquête sur la monarchie* (1909) that launched Maurras's career, he published an *Enquête sur le problème juif* with the Nouvelle Librairie Nationale in 1923, with a preface by Eugène Marsan, literary critic for *L'action française*.

Thus it was this work that Menasce considered "interesting." In it, Groos exploits Maurras's notion of "intelligent Jews whom the war definitively incorporated into the French people."[52] That is how he distinguishes between the rest of the Jewish people and the "wellborn Jews," or "Jewish patriots of France," French "by the baptism of blood," on the model of Pierre David or Amédée Rothstein, killed at Verdun and celebrated by Barrès in *Les diverses familles spirituelles de la France*. According to Groos:

> There is a Jewish conspiracy against all the nations. And first of all against France, against the principle of order that it represents in the world. This conspiracy occupies, almost everywhere, the avenues of power. In France, it veritably reigns. . . . Also let us witness, parallel to and as a result of the spread of

this universal Jewish conspiracy, a rebirth of anti-Semitism. More precisely perhaps, its extension. . . . The universal Jewish conspiracy will be broken, brought down, quelled; or it is France that will perish, as Russia has. . . . What is the attitude in this tragic affair of that minority of wellborn Jews whom the War definitively incorporated into the French people? It is the duty, it seems, of these Jews, who repudiate all solidarity with international finance and revolution, these patriots above all others, to fight against the universal Jewish people who are trying to destroy, to assassinate France.[53]

Barrès's response to Groos's inquiry was evasive: "Do not waste too much time on polemics. We can argue on one side or the other and those speeches have very little effect." And few "wellborn Jews" would respond to it. Salomon Reinach was the exception: "Take 75 grams of stupidity; add 25 grams of malice, *misce secundum artem* and serve hot: that is the recipe for the anti-Jewish cake. It is unsavory and not nourishing."[54] Sarcasm would not stop Groos.

A figure with a complicated career in journalism and teaching between the two wars, and then, after 1945, in publishing, René Groos worked closely with Jacques Schiffrin on the first "Bibliothèque de la Pléiade," for which he would procure Racine's plays (1931), La Fontaine's *Fables* (1932), and Voltaire's *Romans et contes* (1932). The texts that he edited for Schiffrin were long kept in print by Gallimard and then by Raymond Picard in the new Pléiade edition of the works of Racine in 1951.

In *La revue juive* of July 1925, Jean de Menasce reconsiders the contradiction that Groos postulates in his *Enquête sur le problème juif* between Judaism and the nations that host Jews, a premise with which Menasce does not disagree. Nonetheless, if Groos holds "that the Jewish ideal is international, democratic, revolutionary, and plutocratic," he does not see Zionist separatism as a solution; as Menasce points out, he "rejects Zionism and advocates for the rehabilitation of Jews, *as individuals*, in the national . . . assimilationist sense."[55] For Groos, "the 'wellborn' Jew who wants to become French must prove himself, that is, resolutely denounce manifestations of the Jewish mind contrary to French doctrine," in short, convert, and even more, convert to full nationalism, the royal way, as opposed to democracy and the republic identified with the Jewish mind, since assimilation requires total repudiation of any allegiance to the Jewish people and since Groos sees "a real danger in considering conversion to Roman Catholicism as a solution to the Jewish problem," that is, as sufficient.[56] Groos's mistake, counters Menasce, a fervent Zionist at this point, is that he "does not consider the case of 'wellborn' Jews for whom the antithesis of the cosmopolitan internationalism that he denounces would not be French nationalism, but a separatist Jewish nationalism, straightforward and therefore legitimate. And Zionism would fulfill those conditions."[57] For Menasce, just back from Palestine and a year before his conversion, there was no doubt that Zionism was superior to assimilation.

Now René Groos, "Action Française Catholic," and of "Jewish origin" according to Jean de Menasce, or "*Action française* Jew," as a more blunt Benjamin Crémieux would call him, or again "anti-Jewish little Jew" according to the even more dismissive phrase of *L'univers israélite*,[58] was himself an admirer of Proust, and he was among the first to take a position on Proust's Jewishness. His article, "Marcel Proust et le judaïsme" appeared in 1926 in *Marcel Proust*, part of the "Les contemporains" series published by Éditions de la revue Le Capitole, with a preface by Colette and including texts by Léon Pierre-Quint on "Le sens du comique," and Benjamin Crémieux on *Les plaisirs et les jours*, and so on.[59]

The previous year the same series had published *Charles Maurras*, and the following year it would publish *Jacques Bainville*, titles that provide information on its ideological bent (Gustave Pigot, the head of the publishing house, was a regular contributor to *L'action française*).[60] Groos's contribution to the debate, to which we will return when discussing Benjamin Crémieux, unsurprisingly denies any influence of Proust's maternal heredity on his work, which Groos dissociates from romanticism, held in contempt by Maurras, and links instead to classicism.

But the encounter of Jean de Menasce, a Zionist soon to be baptized, and René Groos, an "*Action française* Jew," in the pages of *La revue juive*, the former a devotee of Joyce, the later of Proust, illustrates the intellectual ferment that animated that publication. Menasce could be interested in Groos because, in his eyes, "anti-Semitism has the extreme merit of underlining the reality—the depth—of the Jewish problem, whereas there are a great many people for whom this problem does not exist. For the most part, these are Jews, especially Western Jews. They consider the Jewish problem to be the offspring of anti-Semitism, both of which will disappear together."[61] For Menasce and his comrades at *La revue juive*, the "Jewish problem" could not be deduced from anti-Semitism and could not be reduced to it (this is the opposite of Jean-Paul Sartre's thesis in his 1946 *Réflexions sur la question juive*); it would not be resolved by ending anti-Semitism but by returning to Zion.

GEORGES CATTAUI, 1925

In 1925, Albert Cohen's other accomplice at *La revue juive*, in addition to Jean de Menasce and spiritual director André Spire, was Menasce's cousin Georges Cattaui. As we have seen, interpretations of Proust's Jewishness began with him, discreetly, through his Proust obituary in *Menorah* in December 1922. His presence extends through the whole first period of the reception of *À la recherche du temps perdu* in the 1920s, before continuing as part of Proust criticism for a very long time, until my own youth, since he translated into French and wrote a preface for George D. Painter's famous Proust biography in 1966.[62] Over the course of the year of 1925, his contributions to *La revue juive* were as numerous as those of Jean de Menasce, even though he spent at least part of the year in Cairo. For the third anniversary of Proust's death, as we have noted, he proposed erecting a monument in the Jardin des Champs-Élysées (it was not until 1966 that Jacques de Lacretelle, president of the Société des Amis de Proust, managed to get the garden's central lane, which runs along Avenue Gabriel, renamed Allée Marcel-Proust).[63]

Héli-Georges Cattaui (1896–1974), born in Paris, belonged to one of Cairo's most prominent Jewish families, both liberal and francophone, and his early years were divided between Cairo and Paris, where he attended the Carnot lycée. His father, Adolphe Cattaui Bey (1865–1925), lawyer, businessman, and Egyptologist, founder of the Geographic Society of Cairo, had been a student at the Condorcet lycée, where he was friends with the Reinach brothers, Victor Basch, and Henri Bergson. Following Adolphe Cattaui's death on 11 June 1925, the same year that witnessed *La revue juive*, *Menorah* ran a fine obituary for him.[64]

Georges Cattaui met Albert Cohen in Egypt in 1920–1921, the period in which they were both discovering Proust's work following the Prix Goncourt. Cohen wrote to him in 1925, when they were involved in the *La revue juive* venture: "What a pleasure to receive your letter. It felt like old, pre-Lutetian times. The time of greatest innocence when we conversed in Alexandria, in Cairo. And I do not know why, rereading your letter, that the beautiful, unforgettable, luminous gaze of your mother suddenly arose." The rest of the letter addressed Cattaui's collaboration with *La revue juive*: My dear Georges, work for our review. Make it even better. . . . Send me notes, columns, poems, even studies. Would you like books to review for our *Regards* and our *Notes* features? . . . I give you perfect freedom to send me other things. You see that I have complete confidence in you." And the closing evokes their shared faith: "To you, in Israel, my dear Prince and dear friend."[65]

After French law school in Cairo, an undergraduate degree in Paris, and the École Libre des Sciences Politiques, Georges Cattaui became King Fuad's secretary before launching a diplomatic career that took him to Prague, Bucharest, and London, which he then abandoned to become a poet and man of letters from the 1930s to the 1970s. A passionate Zionist at the time of *La revue juive*, he also converted to Catholicism, in April 1928 and not without first consulting Bergson before taking the leap. Their intermediary was Jacques Chevalier, disciple of Bergson, ardent Catholic (and future secretary of public education in the Vichy government for a few months in 1940-1941), who reported back to Cattaui: "With regard to your question, these are his exact words: If M. Cattaui feels called to Catholicism, I believe he must respond. And he should not be deterred by any external consideration such as my own attitude."[66] In his "Testament" from 1937, made public in 1941, Bergson would write, in keeping with his recommendation to Cattaui: "My thinking has brought me closer and closer to Catholicism in which I see the complete realization of Judaism. I might have converted, had I not seen rising for years ... the formidable wave of anti-Semitism that is about to sweep through the world. I wanted to remain among those would be the persecuted of tomorrow."[67] Thus Cattaui followed the path taken by Jean de Menasce, as well as many of his other relatives, for whom Zionism had not satisfied a mystical aspiration, but not without a crisis of conscience similar to that which Bergson experienced. And afterward, he had to admit, came a "tragedy that would rip apart my youth," because, "in discovering Christ, I had also discovered Israel," and "by embracing the Messiah, I did not want to abandon his unfortunate people, his despised people, his rejected people."[68]

In autumn 1922 Cattaui published in Paris a collection of poems, *La promesse accomplie: France-Égypte-Judée*, which was very well received, as we have seen, by Ludmila Savitzky.[69] The poems had been written in Cairo between 1917 and 1919, according to the introduction, and the title was inspired by the Book of Ezekiel (12:28). Pierre Benoit found the Zionist ideal to be as vivid there as on his trip to Palestine that had inspired his novel *Le puits de Jacob* (1925). Just as Albert Cohen had invited Lacretelle to revisit *Silbermann* in the first issue of *La revue juive*, he asked Pierre Benoit to comment on his "encounter with the Jewish soul": "The emotion that seized me, a Catholic, at the sight of the plain of Jizreel, over which the smoke from Zionist colonies rose at twilight, I rediscovered, explained and illuminated, in a precious little book of poems published in Paris in 1922. In this book, the twenty-five-year-old poet, Héli Georges Cattaui, celebrates the *Promesse accomplie*, that is, the coming of Zionism." The name of one of the collection's dedicatees made a strong impression on Pierre Benoit (the other is Sir Herbert Samuel, the British high commissioner in Mandatory Palestine): "Now, and this is, for me, the surprising and essential point, consider the dedication that the author believed it necessary to put at the beginning of his book: 'To Maurice Barrès, through whom I rediscovered Unity, in myself, and in my race, and in the human race.'"[70] Pierre Benoit might also have noted that one section of the book, "La double face de Janus," was dedicated "to the memory of Charles Péguy, dead at the Marne for France, and Amédée Rothstein, dead at Verdun for France and for Judea."[71]

Rothstein, born in Cairo in 1891, enlistee in the Foreign Legion, second lieutenant cited by the Ordre de l'Armée, knight of the Legion of Honor, was killed leading his men at Verdun in August 1916. The model of Maurras's and Groos's "wellborn Jew," he had been praised by Barrès in his chapter on "Les Israélites" in *Diverses familles spirituelles de la France*: "The most zealous was a Jew, twenty-two years old, engineering student at the École des Ponts et Chausées, small and frail, with fiery, almost feverish, eyes, and a strong, overpowering soul. An enthusiast, he dreamed of assembling a true Jewish legion. Rothstein was a Zionist. Through his allegiance to France, he never questioned that he was serving the cause of Israel."[72] As a young Zionist poet and Proustian (although Proust's name did not appear among the dedicatees in *La promesse accomplie*, which predated Cattaui's discovery of him), Cattaui could present himself equally as a Péguyist and a Barrèsian. All enthusiasms that could still be reconciled on the eve of the war. But by 1925, Proust would triumph over his rivals.[73]

PÉGUY, BARRÈS, OR PROUST

In May 1925, in its third issue, *La revue juive* ran a long excerpt of an article published in a special issue of *Les cahiers du mois* entitled "Les appels de l'Orient." *Les cahiers du mois* had been launched in 1924 by François and André Berge, the grandsons of Félix Faure and sons of Antoinette Faure, a childhood friend of Proust. André Berge had just discovered the famous questionnaire completed by the adolescent Proust in his mother's English book and he had published it two months earlier in *Les cahiers du mois*.[74] The issue "Les appels de l'Orient" contained a famous survey to which about a hundred important figures had responded, as diverse as Louis Massignon and René Guénon, Sylvain Lévi and Henri Massis, Antoine

Meillet and André Breton, Henri Maspero and Claude Farrère, Léon Brunschvicg and René Crevel, Émile Bréhier and Philippe Soupault, André Siegfried
and Henry de Montherlant, Henri Barbusse and Abel Bonnard, Paul Valéry,
André Gide, and even Reynaldo Hahn.

Now among "Les appels de l'Orient" compiled by *Les cahiers du mois* in 1925
appeared "Le sionisme, essai de renaissance juive," an article signed by André Desson and André Harlaire. After Zangwill, the poets André Spire, Henri Franck,
Albert Cohen, and Georges Cattaui are named as Zionism's representative writers
in the French language, while *La promesse accomplie* reveals in Cattaui "the avowed
influence of Barrès, but what subtle currents come to merge there: Maurras, Claudel, Péguy.... And more recent writings let us glimpse that secret rhythm of souls
over whom Marcel Proust has become master, through absolute conquest."[75] Cattaui was certainly not an "*Action française* Jew" in the style of René Groos, but the
young writers interested in Proust in the early 1920s also read, or had previously
read, Claudel and Péguy, and even Barrès and Maurras.

In addition to the many Proustian pieces already mentioned, the last issue of
La revue juive in November 1925 also contained a review of *La promesse accompli*.
Its author was none other than André Harlaire, signer of the article on Zionism
in *Les cahiers du mois* a few months earlier.[76] He emphasized the syncretism that
animated the mystical messianism of Cattaui, who rediscovered Judea in the
Gospels and letters of Saint Paul and celebrated "a curious (fertile) fusion:
Christian values in which Jewish prophetic passions come to be magnified."[77]
Professing the same kind of ecumenicalism, Albert Cohen also cited Saint Paul,
the Gospel of Matthew, and even *L'imitation de Jésus-Christ*, among the epigraphs
in his *Paroles juives* in 1921, a collection dedicated to his "Jewish brothers" as well
as to his "Christian brothers who will see the love in my words" (Cohen, let us
recall, had just married the daughter of a Protestant pastor). The young Zionists
of *La revue juive*, at least the two Egyptians, Cattaui and Menasce, were on a
curious path, well before the "realization"—to use Bergson's term—of their Judaism in baptism.

Again in that same last issue of *La revue juive*, following the "Mademoiselle de
Forcheville," the excerpt from *Albertine disparue*, a final article by Cattaui appeared,
entitled "Barrès et les Juifs."[78] This piece extends a line of thought begun the year
before, under the same title, in a Montparnasse review, *Critique art philosphie*, an
article that already had taken as its pretext René Groos's inquiry into "the Jewish problem," before Jean de Menasce's piece in *La revue juive*.[79]

But Cattaui, disciple of Barrès though he was, reproaches his master, under the influence of Taine, for "his too narrow, too exclusive conception of race." And he reconsiders Barrès's discrediting of Montaigne in *Greco ou le secret de Tolède* (I have already noted his fixation on that remark by Barrès): "Thus when, taking as his premise ethnic theories of nationhood, he wants to see Jews only as foreigners, logical consistency leads him to deny the quality of Frenchness in the son of the Marrano Antoinette Lopez, this Montaigne, father of French prose, whose 'doubt' gave rise to Descartes and Pascal, and who, through his humor and imagination, already prefigured Voltaire and Renan, France, and Barrès himself."[80] For Cattaui, Barrès had crossed a line beyond which he could no longer follow him, just as he had had to part ways with Péguy when Péguy repeated the cliché of Jewish fatalism. As in the first issue of *La revue juive*, Cattaui had contrasted Péguy to Proust, now in the last issue, he brought up Montaigne as an objection to Barrès. Thus the die was cast: for Cattaui, Montaigne and Proust were related. In 1925 Proust gave Cattaui permission to take leave of Péguy and Barrès, the two masters to whom he paid homage in his first collection of poetry, or at least to distance himself from their vision of Jewishness.

Nevertheless, Cattaui clears Barrès of the accusation of anti-Semitism, thanks to a circular argument that likens his irony to Jewish double entendre:

> As an anti-Dreyfusard, he once testified that the same chivalric spirit was evident in both camps, and he willingly wrote a preface for the political writings of Péguy, a Dreyfus supporter.[81] In his book on the diverse spiritual families of France, we must read the chapter he devotes to the Jews. How he praises the heroism of Amédée Rothstein, a militant Zionist who died at Verdun for France and for Judea. Some tell me that in Barrès, each time he speaks of Jews, and no matter how sympathetic he is toward them, a secret irony always comes through. I do not know. . . . But that irony, you must recognize it, my Jewish brothers, of whom they say that when your lips move, no one can tell if it is in jest or prayer.[82]

L'univers israélite was more dubious about Barrès: "maybe he was not openly anti-Semitic, but we prefer an honest adversary to a false friend. / Even the chapter that he devoted to Jews in his famous study on 'Les familles spirituelles de la France' during the war contains reservations, and last year he gave an equivocal response to the anti-Jewish little Jew who had opened a pretentious inquiry into 'the Jewish problem'" (that is, René Groos).[83]

Among the Proustian Zionists of *La revue juive*, Cattaui was hardly alone in redeeming Barrès. André Spire himself, who introduced Zionism to Albert Cohen and his friends, was a native of Nancy as was Barrès. Six years younger than Barrès, and after the death of this "prince of youth," Spire composed "Quelques souvenirs sur Maurice Barrès," dated February 1924, published in a special memorial issue of *Le pays lorrain* in March 1924,[84] and included in *Quelques juifs et demi-juifs* in 1928, which amounted to assimilating him, more or less.

For the rhetoricians at the Nancy lycée in 1885, Spire recalled, Barrès was already an important figure: "We were reading les *Taches d'encre* in class. . . . As for me, I often think back to a certain copy of *Sous l'oeil des barbares*, lying open on a big Directoire-style desk, between containers of gun powder, shot, and wadding." All the same, Spire adds by way of excuse: "we read him, and we went to his public gatherings because it annoyed our parents." In these few pages, Spire is strangely silent about the Dreyfus affair, jumps from the Boulangist campaign in 1889 to the year 1909, ignores a long interval in Barrès's political and literary career, and then mentions bumping into him again in Neuilly: "I suddenly saw, very close to me, in a small group of people, Maurice Barrès, whom I had not encountered in twenty years."[85]

At the end of these pages, written directly following Barrès's death in late 1923, Spire recalls that it was Cattaui who gave him the news: "On 5 December, at about eight o'clock, my young friend Georges Cattaui, who had just dedicated his first book of poems to him, called me by telephone, deeply distressed."[86] After having celebrated Proust together a year earlier in their parallel obituaries, Spire and Cattaui were united once again in mourning Barrès. Their literary, philosophical, even religious eclecticism, their indulgence with regard to Barrès in memory of *Le culte de moi*, will surely be judged as compromising or even culpable by some readers today, but Spire never denied that his search for what he called "the Jewish soul" was modeled after that of the bard of the "Lorraine soul."[87] He recognized Barrès's influence on his generation and on his own Jewish consciousness, but considered him an adversary, a tension perfectly summarized in the dedication of his 1908 *Versets: Et vous riez—Poèmes juifs*: "To Maurice Barrès, from his compatriot, admirer, enemy."[88] The ambivalence of his feelings toward Barrès inspired his reaction to Cattaui's article in *La revue juive* as well:

My dear friend,

> I just read the R.J. and your article on Barrès, fairer and kinder toward him
> than I might have been myself. But perhaps you knew him better than I did. I
> think that in Barrès, the forces of hatred were more powerful than the forces of
> receptivity. And his attitude in all things was always so sharply opposed to my
> own that I was not able to keep from feeling a bit of hostility. You did not know
> the wicked Barrès of my youth, an avid man . . . self-involved. You only see the
> work! Maybe that is how we must judge great writers.[89]

If the editors of *La revue juive* accommodated Barrès's anti-Semitism, how sensitive would they have been to excesses in Proust's portraits of Bloch or Rachel?
Jean de Menasce and friends very clearly identified the anti-Semitism of René
Groos, whose "Jewish origin only makes his testimony more interesting." Was it
because Barrès and Proust were great writers that such indulgence was necessary?
I do not think so. The period immediately following World War I, in particular
the year between the deaths of Proust and Barrès, was a time when anti-Semitism
decreased dramatically in its public expression, only a pause no doubt. But Émile
Cahen himself, editor of the *Archives isréalites*, noted it in his review of *Silbermann*:
"That does not mean, sadly, that those hideous sentiments, so unFrench, have
vanished completely with the invigorating and liberating winds of our stunning
victory, not at all; but we must admit—and reading the most notoriously nationalist Parisian papers easily proves it—that this hateful mindset has seriously
shifted in a favorable direction for us. Let us hope it will last."[90] Even in the eyes
of young Zionists, Barrès's *Les diverses familles spirituelles de la France* made up for
his anti-Dreyfus stance, as Proust offered them grounds for pride and a vehicle
for propaganda. No one at *La revue juive* in 1925 disavowed Barrès. That tolerance
was safeguard enough against any attempts to challenge Proust's treatment of
Jews in his novel.

Nevertheless, we are not completely finished with Proust's appearances in *La
revue juive* in 1925. A few remaining pieces will introduce us again to the commonplace of his "rabbinical style."

CHAPTER 6

"The Style of the Rabbi"

1925 was a good year, a crucial year, for reflecting on Proust's Jewishness, with the contributions of Léon Pierre-Quint, Benjamin Crémieux, Georges Cattaui, Marie-Louise Cahen-Hayem, Ludmila Savitsky, and others. The last issue of *La revue juive*, in November 1925 and closing out the year, was decidedly Proustian: we have already noted the advance pages of *Albertine disparue* and the review of Benjamin Crémieux's *XXᵉ siècle* by Armand Lunel. Now, last but not least, let us note the long excerpts from an article that had just appeared in *Les Marges* on 15 October 1925 (the review where René Groos, Proust lover and "*Action française* Jew," was, for the moment, the assistant editor). The article was entitled "Le judaïsme de Proust," and the author was Denis Saurat.[1]

DENIS SAURAT, 1925

La revue juive added no commentary to the long excerpts, but their length is proof that Saurat's article was deemed worthy of serious attention by editor-in-chief Albert Cohen and his close associates, André Spire, Jean de Menasce, and Georges Cattaui.

Denis Saurat (1890–1958) was born in Toulouse to parents from Ariège and raised in Nord, where his father worked for the post office. He earned a teaching degree in English in 1919 (he had married an English woman in London in 1911) and a doctorate in literature in 1920. In 1925, he had just been appointed director of the Institute Français of the United Kingdom in London and would soon become professor of French language and literature at King's College of the University of London, positions he would hold for more than two decades (1924–1945 for the first, 1926–1950 for the second), and he was a regular contributor to *Les Marges* beginning in 1924. His specialty was John Milton, the eighteenth-century English poet, on whom he wrote his thesis in 1920 at the Sorbonne, "La pensée de Milton."[2] He adored the Romantic poet William Blake, to whom he devoted his subsequent thesis, "Blake and Milton."[3] This learned academic was obsessed by occultism and passionate about the Kabbalah.

Tackling Proust this time, he pulled no punches: "The Proustian style is the style of the rabbi commenting on the Scriptures," he asserts at the outset to introduce his brief, sensational article.[4] This theory, thus openly defended for the first time, will mark a milestone, thereby attracting the interest of *La revue juive* editors, who seem to confirm Saurat's argument by reprinting it as is, unaccompanied and without the slightest reservation, as if giving their approval:

The style thus defined is not French in its formation. Long, complicated sentences, overloaded with parentheticals, ending in small, precious, disjointed discoveries, and offering glimpses of other subjects. *A kind of foreign language*, in truth. This is clearly the style that was invented in the Christian era by the Jews of Babylon and Jerusalem to comment on their sacred books. *Long* sentences of commentary, *complicated* because a commentator considers all possible meanings of the text, *overloaded with parentheticals* thus rendered necessary, *ending in small, precious discoveries*, because the goal of commentary is precisely to bring to light the suggested meanings, often more important than the direct meaning, *disjointed* in order to pursue all the ramifications of an idea at the same time, *offering glimpses* that are, consistently, deliberate references to other texts, other confirming facts. In defining Proust's style, Léon Pierre-Quint defined the style of the Talmud or the Zohar. *The short, light sentences* are also in those commentaries; because if we look at an entire passage, the short sentences are only fragments separated by a confusing period. It is the thinking itself that takes these forms, the inevitable forms of commentary, added to which are repetitions and the apparent lack of any immediate plan.[5]

The point of departure or pretext for Saurat's article is nothing other than the chapter, "Le style" in the book by Léon Pierre-Quint already mentioned, *Marcel Proust: Sa vie, son oeuvre*, published just three months earlier, at the end of June 1925.[6] All the expressions in italics above, italicized by Saurat, are literal quotations from

Pierre-Quint, who did not himself make the slightest allusion to Judaism in his analysis of the style of À la recherche du temps perdu and who, as we have seen, strongly resisted the theory of Proust's maternal heredity influencing his work. Nevertheless, Saurat deduced from Pierre-Quint's chapter this categorical proposition: "In defining Proust's style, Léon Pierre-Quint defined the style of the Talmud or the Zohar," that is to say, not only the style of rabbinical discussions of the Jewish Law collected in the Talmud, but also the style of kabbalistic exegesis, more esoteric and mystical, of the Torah in the Sepher ha-Zohar (the Book of Splendor), based on oral tradition, collected in the thirteenth century, and published for the first time in Mantua in 1558, but long presented as more ancient, predating Christianity.

Saurat continues, completely counter to Pierre-Quint, and La revue juive reprints this without batting an eyelid:

> Thus we can understand how the reader may be put off: the French reader feels he has left his country. Again I borrow a phrase from Pierre-Quint, drawn from Proust, and offered as characteristic (I prefer not to choose them myself): Swann caresses Odette and begins to touch her flowers, "either from dread of offending her, or from fear of appearing in retrospect to have lied, or from lack of audacity in formulating a greater demand than this one (which he could renew since it had not angered Odette the first time)."[7]

Commenting on this sentence from "Swann in Love" Pierre-Quint contrasts the famous strings of soit or soit que . . . (either, either, or . . .), so frequent in Proust, with the structure of the classic French language:

> It is curious to find the very frequent que of the seventeenth century replaced in Proust by the soit que or peut-être. The seventeenth-century que controls subordinate clauses, which follow each other as in a simple enumeration. On the contrary, Proust's strings of soit que nearly always explain the various and often contradictory motives of an act or attitude. A given gesture, a feeling that our language expresses with a single word, is, in reality, the effect of multiple desires and thoughts. Each soit of Proust represents one of those desires; from the converging ensemble of these soits comes a state of consciousness, a decision, as from many simple bodies, oxygen, hydrogen, comes a single compound body, water.[8]

Following after Pierre-Quint, Saurat gives this mannerism of Proust an entirely different interpretation, heavily informed by Judaism:

> We immediately recognize here the first law of the commentator: to give an event or a text all the possible explanations, and to do so without having to make them consistent. For the rabbis, one passage has many meanings that are not necessarily connected, and they must all be noted. Now that is the form that is most characteristic of Proust's mind, and he often applies the rabbinical method to texts, to the words of his characters, whose sentences have many completely probable meanings, all of which he gives, and without choosing between them. It would require citing whole pages of the Talmud and the Zohar to trace the similarities. I offer just one short passage. Do not consider the thoughts here but rather the thought process: the *parce que, pourquoi, puis, à plus forte raison* (repeated), *et encore, car.*[9]

Saurat gets straight to the point; he simply juxtaposes quotations, Proust on one side, the Talmud on the other, as one would make columns to catch a plagiarist, and as if the conclusion ought to be self-evident to the reader: Proust writes like a rabbi. But actually this examination of Proust's writing style mostly served as a roundabout way for Saurat to approach the question closest to his heart. This stylistic comparison allowed him to argue that Proust's Jewish heritage was a more profound and determining factor than critics had recognized until then. If Proust had the style of a rabbi, it was because of his intimate familiarity—whether of cultural or natural (or even supernatural) origin—with the Talmud and the Zohar.

MILTON, BLAKE, PROUST

This was not new territory for Saurat, which is why he had responded so quickly to Pierre-Quint's chapter on Proust's style. He had taken the same approach in his research on Milton and the Zohar, following his graduate thesis in which he had already introduced, albeit with "the greatest caution," the question of the poet's "Hebraic sources."[10] Nevertheless, as soon as his thesis was defended, all caution was thrown to the wind, notably in a 1922 article in English that resorted to the same tactics Saurat would use with Proust. It began will equal force: "I propose to prove that Milton knew the Zohar and other kabbalistic documents."[11]

His theory, integrated into the 1925 English version of his Sorbonne thesis, *Milton, Man and Thinker*—"roughly speaking, the whole of Milton's philosophy is found in the Kabbalah"—prompted a long and heated debate across the Channel and across the Atlantic.[12] One of the unforeseen consequences of this dispute was to unmask the anti-Semitism of some of Milton's adversaries who, like T. S. Eliot, would discover here a new pretext for disparaging the poet in finding their prejudices confirmed by the revelation that non-Christian texts influenced his work.

The debate over whether Milton was familiar with the Hebraic tradition continues to this day, but it has shifted away from Saurat's hypothesis that proposed a direct link between rabbinical texts, in Hebrew, Aramaic, Chaldean, or even in translation, and the inventions of *Paradise Lost* and even more of *Paradise Regained*. Although Milton might have been able to decipher the Hebrew of the Bible, it is inconceivable that he could have accessed texts as esoteric and difficult as the Talmud and the Zohar, as Saurat postulated.[13] His 1925 book in English, initially hailed for its unorthodox originality as a "radical turning point" ("a watershed moment in the field"), is now considered "an aberrant curiosity."[14] But encouraged by his success, Saurat would soon reveal that William Blake, Milton's spiritual and poetic heir, was under the influence of the Zohar as well, and he proved just as peremptory in this case: "the Cabala [sic] explains much more of the detail of Blake's visions. Indeed the Cabalistic [sic] element is so closely woven into the very fabric of the *Prophetic Books*."[15]

ZOHAR AND INVERSION

In the case of Proust, Saurat does not offer an opinion on the origin of the similarities that he discovers between *À la recherche du temps perdu* and the Zohar. He proceeds once again by comparing quotes without adding much commentary, according to the method he had already followed with Milton and as if such a demonstration would be argument enough. He does not maintain that Proust had access to Hebraic sources and knew the rabbinical books, as he proposes in the cases of Milton and Blake, but he lets it be understood that "this or that specific trait may very well reappear here and there throughout the lineage of a race," or more precisely, "of the race," with the definite article, the variant chosen for the essay as included in his book. Later he writes, "this is a bit of the rabbinical mentality that he inherited," though we are not told how.[16] Nevertheless, for Saurat, the basic traits of a lineage can resurface from the depths at long intervals through transmigration or metempsychosis. In other words, and as Jean de Menasce expressed it with regard to the character of Bloom in Joyce, Proust "thinks Jewish," or rather, "it thinks Jewish in him" (Saurat himself was not a fan of Joyce and had compared him unfavorably to Proust in an earlier issue of *Les Marges*, because, after Proust, it was impossible "to go on longer, or more subtly, or more deeply," it was only possible "to be filthier").[17] For Saurat, Proust's rabbinical style is only a superficial effect, a visible symptom, whereas the critic's real concern is to reveal Hebraic influences that act at great depths and animate all the writer's thinking, as with Milton and Blake:

> Now it is not only the thought process, but also the fabric of thought, the subject of thought (I am not speaking of ideas and systems) that are identical. Half of the Zohar is devoted to stories of souls that take refuge in other souls, in particular the souls of their mothers; and souls that are simultaneously male and female, or seem to be male when they are female and vice versa, are analyzed there for hundreds of pages. If Proust dared to throw inversion into the literary bargain it is because the speculation of his race over the course of two millennia had prepared the way. Rabbinical literature is the only kind that has approached directly this subject of the changing sexes of souls.[18]

On the basis of Pierre-Quint's literal and technical observations on Proust's style, Saurat permits himself to go into esoteric reflections to establish that Proust's theory of sexual inversion as presented in *Sodome et Gomorrhe I* had its antecedents in the Zohar and in the androgyny of the original soul (he is greatly exaggerating when he claims that "half of the Zohar" discusses migration of souls and changes of sex): "Thus, regarding his favorite subject, Proust is only a product of the debasement of rabbinism. But in fact, this is a bit of the rabbinical mentality that he inherited. As is the marvelously undulating, comprehensive, and complicated style of the Jewish commentators, which he transposed into this good, clear French language that undoubtedly offered no resistance."[19]

The article was included by Saurat in his 1928 volume entitled *Tendances*, along with other studies on Proust and other writers.[20] Saurat was a provocateur and in the very next issue of *Les Marges*, in November 1925, he would publish a second article on Proust that was just as equivocal, titled "Le génie malade." He was merely situating the writer, he claimed, and did not mean to belittle him, but he went on at length about his abnormality. He asserted that "the genius is, morally, a true hermaphrodite," but that "should he lose his balance, he falls into inversion," and does not know "the ordinary experience of humanity."[21] In fact, he had already dealt out praise and blame in his first article where, after calling Proust "a product of the debasement of rabbinism," he ends by reiterating his admiration for the writer and the work, permitting himself to conclude thus: "to avoid any misunderstanding . . . to my mind, this is in no way *against* Proust, any more than it is *for* him. Proust has given us a masterpiece. I am only calling attention to one of the most curious aspects of this masterpiece," that is, its rabbinical and kabbalistic filiation.[22]

From January to August 1926 Saurat published new studies on Proust as a series in Sully-André Peyre's Provençal review *Marsyas*, to which he contributed regularly, beginning with the third issue in 1921, under the pseudonym of Lucilius.[23] These studies were first given as lectures at the University of London, where he got his start.[24] Completed following the publication of *Le temps retrouvé*,[25] they were also collected in *Tendances* in 1928. Saurat returns here to the similarities that he had discovered between *À la recherche du temps perdu* and the Zohar, but without pointing to Proust's rabbinical style this time, which was, in truth, only a pretext, an entry point. What interests him is a theme that is "at the very essence of his thought . . . of his Jewish heritage," the theme "of the division, and then the reconstitution of the One," "which seems to come from Plotinus, but which, in Proust, is actually kabbalistic." With his theory of the original man-woman, "Proust is in full harmony with the sentiments of the kabbalists," he "rediscovers within himself both the feelings of the great Zohar rabbis on this point and their myth of the primitive hermaphrodite," far more profound and poetic than Plato's "amusing parody" in *The Symposium*. "These ideas inhabit the depths of his Jewish and pagan soul," Saurat continues.[26] Still he does not claim that Proust had actual book knowledge of the Jewish Kabbalah, but cites instead, a bit further on, Charlus's famous "little laugh" "that had probably come down to him from some Bavarian or Lorraine grandmother, who had herself got the identical laugh from one of her forebears, so that it had been ringing out like this, unchanged, for a good few centuries in the lesser courts of old Europe, and its precious quality had been enjoyed, like that of certain old musical instruments now grown very uncommon."[27] Proust can thus serve willy-nilly as support for the hereditary argument, applied here to Jews as well as aristocrats and homosexuals.

None of this keeps Saurat from insisting equally on the "the very French character of Proust's intelligence," on the way the writer privileges reason over the unconscious life, or from reporting this remark that he attributes to literary scholar Fernand Baldensperger: "Proust is the French response to Freud." Thus Saurat, who mistrusted both Joyce and Freud for their explorations into the subconscious, surely preferred Proust, who "expressed the deepest needs of two races, the Jews and the French," who, "through his Jewish roots, plunged back into the great intuitions of the Kabbalah," and who, through his "French side," brought to bear "his clear intelligence, capable of mastering the original chaos."[28]

Abandoning *Les Marges* and *Marsyas*, Saurat, a friend of Jean Paulhan and ever prolific and categorical, would contribute a great number of reading notes to *La nouvelle revue française* in the early 1930s. He often mentions Proust in them, in his opinion, the greatest modern writer. For example, he reviews Benjamin Crémieux's last book, *Inquiétude et reconstruction: Essai sur la littérature d'après-guerre*, in 1931. Crémieux notes in it that henceforth Proust no longer shocks readers, and Saurat regrets this development because it marks the exhaustion of the "modern style," which no one embodied better than Proust and which Saurat now defines through "the cult of sensation," no longer linked to rabbinism. "The field is wide open," he concludes, "who will take on Proust?"[29] For Saurat, Proust would remain the modern ideal, through the combination of incredulity and mysticism.[30]

HUGO, MALLARMÉ, BAUDELAIRE, AND RIMBAUD

But Saurat was not finished with the mysterious history of literary ideas. He repeated his kabbalist operation, following Milton, Blake, and Proust, first on Victor Hugo, who was supposedly introduced to the mysteries of the Zohar by Alexandre Weill (1811–1899), a prolific writer, originally a romantic and a socialist, then a republican, then a legitimist, before rediscovering Judaism and practicing prophetism. This legendary figure was supposedly introduced to the Kabbalah himself during his childhood in Alsace by his Talmud teacher, the rabbi Lazarus Ben Aaron.[31]

Then Saurat set his sights on Mallarmé, Baudelaire, and Rimbaud. He finds in Mallarmé's "child of an Idumean night," from his "Gift of the Poem," intimations of the primitive hermaphrodite of the Zohar.[32] In the "dark unity" of Mallarmé's "Correspondences," and then in Rimbaud's sonnet, "Vowels," he finds "the kabbalists' dark Aleph." From this he deduces that "Hugo, Baudelaire, Rimbaud, and Mallarmé knew more or less precisely the old theories," and that "many things we call 'modern' are continuously present in history."

Thus it was not only Proust but all Romantic poetry, all modern literature that conveyed beneath the surface ideas coming from the Kabbalah and from "before the kabbalists, probably from Egypt on one side, Mesopotamia and India on the other," in order that an original pantheism and cosmic metaphysics could be revived.[33]

If Saurat's conjectures about the influence of Jewish mysticism on the thinking of Milton, Blake, Hugo, Baudelaire, Mallarmé, and Rimbaud are now considered "aberrant curiosities," that does not necessarily mean that Saurat was wrong in Proust's case, but he would have had to provide solid arguments to prove himself. As with Milton, Blake, or Hugo, he failed to produce kabbalistic sources, but since he believed in the transmigration of souls and the deep affinity between poetry and creation myths, and since parallel passages resembled each other, he could not conceive of objections to his thesis. Moreover, it does not seem that he ever perceived the racial implications that follow from his tenet of a rabbinical Proust based on style and thought process. Saurat admired Proust and he was even relatively tolerant of sexual inversion; although he thought homosexuality limited the writer's human experience and thus the universality of his work, he nevertheless considered Proust to be "the great modern master."[34] In his dogmatic and visionary innocence, Saurat put Proust in harm's way.

PROUST THE KABBALIST

In fact, criticism has rarely embraced Saurat's explanation that Proust's theory of men-women in *Sodome et Gomorrhe I* is based on the Zohar's transmigration of souls. References to the Jewish Kabbalah are found neither in Proust's published works nor in his known correspondence. One mention of the Zohar does appear, however, in a draft of *À la recherche du temps perdu*. It is in Cahier 5, part of the series of notebooks for *Contre Sainte-Beuve* in 1909, in an additional note to his musings on Padua's Campanile:

ZOHAR
This name remained caught among my hopes at that time, it recreated around itself the atmosphere I inhabited then, the sun-warmed wind it stirred, the idea I created for myself of Ruskin and Italy. Italy contained less of my dream at the time than this name that lived there. There are

names, things that are not names, things that, as soon as we think them, become thoughts, they line up in the series of thoughts and mix with them, and that is why Zohar became something analogous to the thought I had before reading it, gazing at the restless sky, thinking that I would go to see Venice.[35]

One notation in Carnet 1, which can be dated to the second half of 1909, refers to this addition in Cahier 5: "See in the big notebook the arrival at the Campanile. —and also Zohar."[36]

The whole thing remains a mystery. The theme is familiar, however. It is that of the seductive power of names and the disappointment felt in encountering things. *Zohar* was a name with promise "before reading it," like the "sun-warmed wind," and the "restless sky," and the word *campanile* prefigured the trip to Italy, to Venice and Padua. Ruskin prompted a desire for Italy, as the word *Zohar* prompted dreams. The analogy centers on the word *Zohar*, which it links to words that prompt a desire for Italy, prior to reading the book or going to the country. These few lines do not imply that Proust had actually read the Zohar or that he owned a copy of it, but they recount his musing on names. *Zohar* is a poetic, suggestive, mysterious, secret word, but reading the book would inevitably be disappointing, as disappointment is inscribed in the transition from the age of names to the age of things. It is hard to say more than this.

Of course Saurat did not know about this draft, archived at the BNF in the 1960s with the Proust Collection. Since researchers discovered it, some have considered it positive proof of Saurat's kabbalistic theory. Based on these few lines, Juliette Hassine, in a book entitled *Ésotérisme et écriture dans l'oeuvre de Proust*, once again connects "Zoharic metempsychosis" as she calls it, with the Proustian theories of inversion and of men-women. This book appeared in 1990, after an interval of more than six decades, and it pays homage to Saurat. She insists on the "convergences on the phenomenal level of the inversion of souls between the Zohar and the work of Proust," discovered by Saurat, whose "intuition" she admires, as it predates the availability of manuscripts that made plausible "the influence of the Zohar on Proust's writings." Wavering between plausibility and certitude, she then adds: "What is very certain is that Proust had knowledge of this book and it is very probable that he had read it." Hassine does not offer a categorical opinion on the language or edition in which Proust would have encountered the Zohar, although it seems to her "very obvious" that he could only have had access to it "in the translation by Pauly."[37] She is referring to the first translation from the Chaldean into French of the *Sepher ha-Zohar* by Jean de Pauly, published between 1906 and 1911.[38] Recalling the similarities in thinking between Neoplatonism and the Kabbalah, Hassine further proposes that "Proust could only have studied the texts of Plotinus in French through the critical edition of Plotinus's works by M. Bouillet." Published by Hachette in 1857-1861, this edition includes numerous commentaries referring to the Kabbalah and the Zohar (Bouillet still thought that the Kabbalah was very ancient and influenced Neoplatonism, not the other way around).[39] But was Proust any more familiar with Plotinus's *Enneads* in the Bouillet translation than with the Zohar in the Pauly translation? Is this "very certain," "very probable," or "very obvious?" Here is a mystery as impenetrable as those of the Kabbalah. Like Saurat, Hassine proceeds by juxtaposing excerpts from the Zohar and quotes from Proust, letting the obviousness of the affinities convince the receptive reader.

More recently, Patrick Mimouni has taken up and even expanded Saurat's theory, revived by Hassine. He announces that Proust "owned," and then, some thirty pages later and even more peremptorily—unless it is a matter of expressing reservations through irony—that Proust "surely owned" a copy of the *Kabbala denudata* (1677-1684), the Latin translation of the Zohar by Christian Knorr von Rosenroth.[40] The reasons behind his certainty remain unknown to us (figure 20).

In the interval between these two works, Julia Kristeva asserted in her 1994 *Le temps sensible: Proust et l'experience littéraire* that "[at] the time when Proust was composing his Renan pastiche, he [had] read the translation of the Zohar by Pauly."[41] And she refers in a footnote to the collection of Proust's pastiches edited by Jean Milly.[42] As Jean Milly cites neither the Zohar nor Jean de Pauly in his edition of the pastiches, we can only guess about the source of Kristeva's certainty (she may have read Juliette Hassine, who, on the first page of her *Ésotérisme et écriture dans l'oeuvre de Proust*, cites both the Zohar translation by Pauly and the Renan pastiche by Proust in the Milly edition, but in two separate paragraphs and without establishing a link between the two references).[43] Similarly, a bit further on, Kristeva states: "We know that the Jewish tradition, and especially the talmudic tradition, of which Proust was keenly aware, multiplied interpretations." This time she cites in a note the work by Albert Mingelgrün, *Thèmes et structures bibliques dans l'oeuvre de Marcel Proust* (1978), which allows her to conclude by affirming the theory of Proust's rabbinical style: "Considered thus, the Proust experience can be called talmudic." Whereas there is no more mention of the

Figure 20. *Kabbala
denudata*, 1677–1684.
Photo @ wellcomecollec
tion.org/works
/pbtznu76.

Talmud in Mingelgrün's book than there is of the Zohar in Milly's. Mingelgrün
and Milly limit themselves to the Bible, but for Kristeva, who defines Sodom
and Gomorrah as "Hebraic cities," as if there were only Hebrews in the Bible, it
is also as if the Bible contains the Talmud and the Zohar (which, all things considered, is figuratively but not textually true).[44]

Saurat did not make his claims with as much temerity as his successors,
Hassine, Kristeva, and Mimouni. He cited the translation of the Zohar by Jean
de Pauly, which he had consulted and in which he had happened upon his idea
of the transmigration of souls from one sex to another, but he did not assert
that Proust was familiar with it. The coincidence was enough for him since he
himself believed in the transmigration of souls. He was unaware or rather had
forgotten that Pauly's translation of the Zohar into French was the work of a
falsifier who omitted some texts, added others, invented notes, and whose

intention was to show that the teachings of the Zohar "although predating Christianity, corroborated Christian truths."[45] Nor would Hassine, Kristeva, or Mimouni point out Pauly's literary hoax, chronological error, or apologist intentions. Following Saurat, none of them would think to question whether the Zohar itself might be a hoax, a thirteenth-century manuscript presented by kabbalists as the oldest book in the world, which cannot help but bring to mind the reviews of the Pauly translation in publications that Proust read and he would have found hard to ignore if he was interested in the Zohar.[46] But it is impossible to assert that he ever had the Zohar in hand, either Christian Knorr von Rosenroth's Latin *Kabbala denudata* or Jean de Pauly's French *Le livre de la splendeur.*[47]

A selection from Pauly's translation, "carefully reviewed" by a "learned rabbi" according to the foreword by Edmond Fleg, was published in 1925, under the title *Le livre du Zohar*, in Rieder's "Judaïsme" series, and it would subsequently appear in many library collections, but that was after Proust's death.[48]

Prior to Pauly's translation, the text itself of the Zohar was not available, but the doctrine of metempsychosis included in the Zohar had been discussed by Adolphe Franck (1810–1893), Victor Cousin's disciple who taught at the College de France, after having been the first Jew to pass the qualifying exams in philosophy. He was also, we will recall, the father-in-law of the art collector Charles Hayem, great-uncle of Marie-Louise Cahen-Hayem. In his *La Kabbale ou la philosophie religieuse des Hébreux* (1843), the first work in French on the subject, reissued in 1892 at the end of Adolphe Franck's life (it was both his first and last book, demonstrating this spiritualist's attachment to his Jewish origins), Franck showed more curiosity and indulgence toward the Kabbalah than did rabbinical institutions and Jewish academia (Franck's *La Kabbale* was also Bouillet's essential source for *Les Ennéades*, his edition of Plotinus's work). Franck, who was wrong about the date of the Zohar and imagined it to be very ancient, briefly mentions the "Pythagorean dogma of metempsychosis" adopted by the kabbalists, but says little about the transmigration of souls from one sex to another. All in all, he states that if a weaker soul unites with a stronger soul, "the latter then becomes a kind of mother to the former; it carries it within and nourishes it on its substance as a woman does the fruit of her womb." Franck describes such ideas as "details in which the most poetic imagination is sometimes revealed," and concludes, "but let us leave these musings, or, if you will, these unimportant allegories, and let us confine ourselves to the text of the Zohar."[49]

It does not seem that Alexandre Weill ever mentioned the transmigration of souls from one sex to another. In 1925 the work of Paul Vulliaud, former disciple of "Sâr" Péladan, had just been published. More a matter of esotericism than erudition, it briefly mentions metempsychosis and primitive androgyny, and Saurat could have found it interesting reading, but not Proust.[50] If we try to imagine what books Proust read or owned, it seems that Franck's *La Kabbale* remains more "plausible" than Christian Knorr von Rosenroth's *Kabbala denudata*, Jean de Pauly's *Le livre de la splendeur*, or even Bouillet's *Les Ennéades*, and Franck's book was Michelet's only source on the Zohar in his *Histoire de France*.[51] But there is still no proof that Proust ever opened it (of course I am only asking to be refuted).[52]

CHARLATANS AND DREAMERS

By categorically linking Proust's style with rabbinical writing, Saurat inaugurated a long—and dubious—tradition favoring hasty comparisons to methodical philology and reducing argument to self-fulfilling prophecy. Before Céline's eructations over "the teeny tiniest analysis of Pou-Proust, of ass-reamings, of 'nuance humping' half the stinger of a quarter of a fly's ass" in *Bagatelles pour un massacre* in 1937, and then in his wartime letters with coarse remarks of this kind: "The Talmud is more or less constructed and conceived like Proust's novels, a tortuous, ornamented, disorganized mosaic," the connection had already been made; Saurat's thesis simply stated it in a more neutral way.[53] Saurat discovered the Kabbalah in most French writers from Hugo to Proust, but he did so under the influence of a poetic pantheism that made him pro-Semitic. He himself did not see his thesis as negative, but he expressed it ambiguously enough for readers to interpret it as they chose. Proust's book was a masterpiece, he declared, but "the French reader feels that he has left his country." From the perspective of an excellent English scholar, future Occitan specialist, and passionate occultist, the foreign nature of Proust's novel, of Proust's style and thinking, in relation to the French tradition was surely not displeasing, but Saurat was playing with fire.

In Albert Cohen's *La revue juive*, however, readers could encounter directly Saurat's theory on the influence of the Talmud and the Zohar on Proust's thinking, or the spontaneous resurgence, the instinctive emergence of rabbinical commentary in his writing, just as in the *Revue des études juives* where Saurat's reflections on Milton and the Kabbalah were published in 1922 without any editorial interference. Moreover, Saurat was not unknown to the young editors of *La revue juive*; he was a well-established critic. He was especially important to Jean-Richard Bloch, who considered him a friend.[54] Following Bloch's trip to Palestine in spring 1925 for the inauguration of the Hebrew University of Jerusalem, thus just before Saurat's article on "Le judaïsme de Proust" appeared, the two of them had a serious conversation on the "God of the Jews," according to Bloch's notes.[55] Even though the Kabbalah was discredited by rabbinical authorities and Judaic scholars, its rehabilitation as a source for the best modern literature, from Hugo to Proust, had somehow captivated the Zionists, in conflict with institutional Judaism. This affinity is borne out elsewhere. Gershom Scholem, also connected to Zionism, turned toward Jewish mysticism in Berlin, also in the 1920s, despite warnings by rabbis and academics and in reaction to the disdain of rationalist historians, and he became its undisputed scholar. There is no doubt that the Kabbalah attracted young Zionists and young Jews who were dissatisfied with the consistorial tradition. In the tribute that Saurat wrote in 1957 for the tenth anniversary of Jean-Richard Bloch's death, he recalls how Bloch, the nephew of Sylvain Lévi (professor of Sanskrit language and literature at the College de France, president of the Alliance Israélite Universelle, faithful to Franco-Judaism and the Haskalah, hostile to political Zionism as well as mysticism), had been "delighted" in 1929, as a reader at Éditions Rieder, to receive Saurat's manuscript entitled *La littérature et l'occultisme* and had insisted on its publication.[56]

Saurat was more than a little proud of the role he took credit for playing in the rehabilitation of the Kabbalah:

> The Kabbalah was regarded in the Jewish tradition as highly infamous. It was the Jewish soul indulging all its extravagances, and yet a university professor (me), Director of the Institut Français (in London), that is, someone in a perfectly official position and with credentials from the French University, saw in the Kabbalah the glory of the Jewish people and found in the work of all the great poets of our civilization indisputable similarities to these musings of the Jews from the Middle Ages or earliest antiquity.[57]

Let us note how Saurat wavers in the final phrase, "musings of the Jews from the Middle Ages or earliest antiquity," which allows him to avoid the debate over the Zohar's date and its authenticity.

Suspicious of the "indisputable similarities" spotted by lovers of esotericism between products of the human mind very far removed in time and place, critical of their generalized comparativism and their cosmic metaphysics, Scholem set out to base his study of the Kabbalah on textual, historical, and philological analysis. As he declared in 1941 at the beginning of *Major Trends in Jewish Mysticism*, a landmark book, he intended to refute the legends cherished by those he called "charlatans and dreamers," who had appropriated the Kabbalah by decontextualizing it, as rabbis and scholars would have nothing to do with it.[58] He might have counted Saurat among the best of the dreamers, the worst of the imposters being the mysterious Jean de Pauly, whose French Zohar, "packed with shameless falsifications" according to Scholem, was the "useless and infamous hoax of a half-educated charlatan from eastern Galicia."[59] The haste with which Albert Cohen and his friends published Saurat's peremptory speculations on the affinities between the style and thinking of Proust and the rabbinical and kabbalistic tradition, including the migration of souls across sexes, suggests that they were not insensitive to the better side of his imaginings, which allowed them to claim Proust for Judaism, albeit a Judaism at odds with the official authorities.

Again in 1929, André Spire took up Saurat's comparison between Proust and the rabbis in an article on Israel Zangwill published by *L'univers israélite* (despite this weekly's hostility—it was connected to the Paris consistory—toward Zionism as promoted by Spire, who was accused, as we will see, of secularizing Judaism). Spire's article begins like this: "A young French academic, M. Denis Saurat, attributes certain characteristics of Marcel Proust's style, the lengthy and tangled sentences, with the parentheses, incidentals, and repetitions that overload and clarify them, to his Jewish origins. For him, the richness of this complicated style is "that of a rabbi commenting on the Scriptures."[60]

Spire immediately extends this diagnosis, without the slightest nuance, to Bergson, to the "mechanism of his metaphysical thinking, which could easily be shown to be related, without his knowing it, to that of Jewish mysticism as it has been preserved for us, for example, in the Zohar, the Book of Splendor."[61] For Spire, to discover in Proust or Bergson traces of the Talmud and the Zohar poses no problem whatsoever and is clearly grounds for praise. It is a way of identifying their roots in Judaism, or rather in a Judaism independent from religion, a free Jewishness. In 1932, Spire still maintained his enthusiasm for Saurat, whose "critical powers and penetration" he "admired," he wrote to Cattaui, following "a surprising article on J.-R. Bloch" in *La nouvelle revue française*. Nevertheless,

Saurat begins that article by denying the existence of a "Jewish literature" and affirming that Bloch was "French first of all." But he concludes with a high compliment: "There is no one in French letters from whom we can expect more."[62] Spire confides to Cattaui that he was just discussing Bloch in a lecture on "a few Jewish writers of the French language," but that he would have "spoken better of him" had he read this article by Saurat.[63]

Saurat, still director of the Institut Français in London, sided with Free France in June 1940. De Gaulle sent him on an AEF (French Foreign Affairs) assignment in 1941, which led to his book on Free France in Africa.[64] But since he resisted the French takeover of his Institut, his relations with the General deteriorated, so much so that he became an anti-Gaullist, was ousted from the Institut Français directorship in 1945, and following a very harsh letter from René Cassin, failed to obtain the position of rector that he sought in 1949.[65]

But he remained friends with Jean-Richard Bloch, who, on returning from the USSR in 1945 and reconnecting, coldly and tragically mocked Saurat's mania for the Kabbalah, which Saurat never abandoned: "I do not know how the Kabbalah explains or justifies the gas chamber where my mother died, the execution post where one of my daughters died, the cell where one of my sons-in-law was massacred, the concentration camp that killed my mother-in-law, the wall at the foot of which my oldest nephew was shot, and that immense No Man's Land of blood and pus where some of those closest to me disappeared."[66]

If Saurat abandoned Proust after the 1930s, he was ever more occupied with mysticism and occultism, and published books on metempsychosis and the origins of Atlantis, some of which were long available in a paperback series for enthusiasts of "the mysterious adventure of the cosmos and lost civilizations."[67]

Gradually the Occitan language of Saurat's Cathar ancestors, lost for generations, resurfaced in him from the depths of time, like Charlus's little laugh or Proust's rabbinical style, and "at over the age of sixty-five, aided by sleep and dream, [he] suddenly found himself endowed with a perfectly accurate subdialectical language that he did not remember having ever spoken." He called this phenomenon the "resurrection of a language" in an autobiographical account he sent to Paulhan, who chose not to publish it.[68] Having retired in the 1950s, he began composing a vast poetic work in the Argos dialect, *Encaminament catar* (1955, 1960). Paulhan wrote a sympathetic tribute at the time of his death, even while making light of his obsession with occultism: "Not one of his sentences lacks an idea. I am not saying necessarily a sound idea, but a thought that give us something to consider—and, of course, to debate and dispute."[69] Even if Saurat's theory on Proust's rabbinical style was not "necessarily a sound idea," his few pages on Proust and the Zohar in 1925 are still being discussed, and he still has followers among twenty-first century occultists who are republishing his work.[70]

Following Denis Saurat, all those participating in the debate over Proust's Jewishness would take a position for or against the thesis of his rabbinical style (the inversion of sexes in the Zohar would get less attention), like André Spire, as we have just seen, but also Georges Cattaui, René Groos, Benjamin Crémieux, and so on.

CHAPTER 7

"Making a Niche for Themselves in the French Bourgeoisie"

The premature end of *La revue juive* in November 1925 remains unexplained, after six high quality issues in which Proust was omnipresent. Chaim Weizmann might have gotten tired of financing it, considering the return on his investment insufficient and thinking that a more political, less literary periodical, like the soon-to-be *Palestine*, might have more influence on French public opinion. The review's abrupt demise was followed by a mysterious quarrel between André Spire and Albert Cohen that lasted for years, until 1933.[1] And we do not know how Spire reacted to the conversions of Jean de Menasce and Georges Cattaui, the two Egyptian cousins whom he had introduced to Zionism. The friendship and correspondence between Spire and Cattaui remained ongoing.[2] In the 1960s, Cattaui sent his book *Proust perdu et retrouvé* (1963) to Spire with this dedication: "For André Spire, remembering those years long ago when we read Proust together, to poet, prophet, friend, in faithful friendship and gratitude, Georges Cattaui." As for Menasce, he wrote a letter of condolence to André Spire's widow when Spire died in 1966.[3] But the little group of young Proustian Zionists had disbanded. None of them renounced the author of *À la recherche du temps perdu*, although Cohen would mock Proust later in *Belle du seigneur*. But he took it badly that Cattaui never acknowledged receipt of his novel in 1968 (did Cattaui refrain because Proust had not been well treated in it?) and sent him a letter to break off their friendship: "Despite our rare encounters and the distance between us, I did love you, I will hold dear my memory of our talks (affectionate, I believed) in Alexandria, Cairo, Lutetia at the time of *La revue juive*, and I believed in our friendship, naive though I was. . . . Nothing, not a line, not a word. . . . Even in bidding you farewell, I no less declare my affection, which is my business and not yours."[4]

The enthusiasm for Proust among the contributors to *Menorah* and *La revue juive* in the 1920s deserves notice especially because the more accredited Jewish press said almost nothing about Proust in France, whereas in Chicago, Philadelphia, Pittsburgh, Detroit, Minneapolis, and Montreal, the Jewish community periodicals, provided information by the Jewish Telegraphic Agency, a news service with its headquarters in New York, were eager to pay tribute to the writer. If the *Archives israélite*, as we have seen, made a little space for him beginning in 1925, that was at the initiative of the young Marie-Louise Cahen-Hayem, while *L'univers israélite*, closer to the Paris consistory and the more conservative tradition (at the *Archives* the year began on 1 January, but *L'univers* followed the Hebrew calendar), associated Proust with André Spire, who had publicized Proust's Jewishness in 1923 in *Les nouvelles littéraires*, and mistrusted them both with regard to Zionism as affirmation of a non-religious Jewish identity.

ANDRÉ SPIRE AND MAURICE LIBER, 1926–1927

In December 1926, Proust's name was mentioned for once in *L'univers israélite*. It was precisely on the occasion of a lecture given by André Spire at the École des Hautes Études Sociales, an annex of the Sorbonne founded following the Dreyfus affair by the writer Dick May (1859-1925), pseudonym of Jeanne Weill (no relation, but identical, almost to the letter, to the name of the young Madame Proust), sister of the historian of socialism Georges Weill and sister-in-law of Bernard Lazare.[5] *L'univers israélite* claimed to provide a "faithful analysis," though unsigned, of Spires's remarks, but if his talk on "La renaissance juive en France" was summarized, it was to affirm the conflict *L'universe israélite* had with it—"even though we consider it paradoxical"—and to announce a refutation for the following week.

Spire maintained that day that a Jewish renaissance had taken place following *Chad Gadya!* by Zangwill, which appeared in French translation in 1904: "A Jewish literature of the French language was born, cultivated even by Christians (the Tharaud brothers, Jacques de Lacretelle), by the half-Jewish Marcel Proust and the half-Jewish Myriam Harry, by Jews Albert Cohen, Jean-Richard Bloch, Armand Lunel, by the converted Jew Max Jacob, by Henri Franck who had lost his faith, and by Edmond Fleg who had rediscovered his faith." Nothing out of the ordinary here. Benjamin Crémieux, we may recall, proposed the same thing in his panorama, "Judaïsme et littérature," in *Les nouvelles littéraires* a year earlier, and we find the usual names surrounding Proust's. What followed was more offensive to *L'univers israélite*, which reported that Spire attacked French Jews hostile to this new literature: "But this revival is not to the liking of the Jewish bourgeoisie, who consider themselves an elite because they have succeeded in making a niche for themselves in the French bourgeoisie."[6]

The periodical's annoyance was understandable: while Spire paid tribute to half-Jews and converts, and even to non-Jews, considered actors in a "Jewish renaissance," he freely expressed his disdain for the assimilated Jewish bourgeoisie, concerned most of all with discretion, anxious that no one mention them, no one take notice, no one imagine them "making a niche for themselves in the French bourgeoisie," a very condescending remark, if it really was Spire's and not the reporter's. Unlike the Zionists who lay claim to Proust and made use of him, these were Jews supposedly in favor of erasing Jewishness in French society who might have had reasons for resenting a novelist who created indestructible and unforgettable Jewish characters. The very next week, Strasbourg's *La tribune juive*, a mouthpiece for "Judaïsme de l'Est de la France," reprinted this ill-intentioned account of Spire's talk at the École des Hautes Études Sociales.[7]

A piece in the following issue of *L'univers israélite*, under the signature of Judaeus, returned to Spire's lecture to dispute his argument and illustrations of a supposed "Jewish renaissance."

Judaeus was the pseudonym of Maurice Liber (1884–1956).[8] Liber was rabbi at the Grande Synagogue de la Victoire, professor of Jewish history and literature at the Séminaire Israélite de France, director of studies in Talmudic and Rabbinical Judaism at the École Pratique des Hautes Études Section V, and author of the definitive monograph on Rashi, published in London and Philadelphia in 1906.[9] He entered the debate and repudiated Spire with all the authority conferred by the Paris consistory and the university, and he did not pull any punches:

> This is precisely an intellectual and literary movement, in large part a sham, which is far from being "specifically Jewish." Let us put to one side Edmond Fleg, whose work is completely imbued with Judaism and who is fully immersed in the Jewish tradition; the appearance of *Écoute Israël* in the *Cahiers de la quinzaine* truly marks a milestone in the history of French Judaism. May he gain a following! But the others? It is ridiculous to applaud the Tharaud brothers who exploit Judaism as a kind of exoticism; you could just as well say that

Galand's [*sic*] translation of *Mille et une nuits* marked an Islamic "renaissance" in France. It is a mockery to claim for Judaism the apostate Max Jacob with his incongruities, or Marcel Proust whose mother was of Jewish origin, or Myriam Harry whose father had converted to Protestantism. And the same is true for other non-Jews curious about Judaism or those Jews anxious about having lost it.[10]

The battle went beyond Myriam Harry, Proust, and Max Jacob. Two conceptions of Judaism came into conflict here: Spire wrote in 1921 that Judaism "was simultaneously a religion, a race, and a nationality."[11] He advocated for a secular and cultural definition—racial in that sense, or a matter of identity, and thus fully including Proust—but this was unacceptable to the Paris consistory, Judaeus, and *L'univers israélite*, according to whom Judaism and religion were inseparable. That was why Judaeus concluded with this cutting remark: "Modesty has kept M. André Spire from including himself in this gallery and that is truly a shame, because this pagan poet, this coryphaeus of Judaism is the best illustration of M. Spire's paradoxes."[12] The paradox in the eyes of rabbi Liber was that a freethinker lay claim to Judaism, that a Zionist recommended half-Jews and converts as exemplary representatives of a kind of Jewishness having nothing to do with religion. A nonreligious Jewish renaissance made no sense to Maurice Liber, who expressed the viewpoint of the consistory.

The debate did not end there. Spire was a hardheaded militant and, far from backing down, responded at length to Judaeus-Liber a week later. He condemned the illusion that the path of assimilation represented for Jews and insisted instead on Proust's clear-sightedness, his awareness of the debasement, humiliation, and loss not only of faith but also of pride implied by the emancipation of French Jews: "And it is not just one particular case like the one described by Marcel Proust in *Le côté de Guermantes*, when he presents the writer Bloch in an aristocratic salon responding to a duke who alludes to Bloch's Jewish origins: 'But *how* did you know? Who told you?' And Bloch pronounces these words 'as though he had been the son of convict.'"[13]

Thus the debate between Spire and Maurice Liber, spokesperson for the rabbinical institution and Judaic scholarship, confirms the way Zionists could make use of Proust's novel: it simply provided them with arguments against assimilation. Zionists found among their adversaries a good portion of their fellow Jews, silent and consenting victims of anti-Semitism, that is the "Jewish bourgeoisie" who "succeeded in making a niche for themselves in the French bourgeoisie" or who just dreamed of doing so. In a letter to Jean-Richard Bloch from March 1919, Spire already harshly attacked "the Jewish plutocracy and clericalism" for whom, in his eyes, Sylvain Lévi was a puppet. Spire had just come from the Paris Peace Conference where he had argued with this eminent representative of official Judaism, professor at the Collège de France and soon-to-be president of the Alliance Israélite Universelle, for whom Zionism was "an anti-French undertaking."[14] Thus the Zionists' resentment toward shameful Jews, as well as the institutional Judaism of the Paris consistory and the Alliance, led them to express themselves like anti-Semites ("Jewish plutocracy" was a refrain from *La libre parole*) and explains how differently they read Proust from the way we are tempted to read him today when we accuse him of anti-Jewish sentiments. For them, he was clearly one of their own.

ROBERT DREYFUS, 1926

Robert Dreyfus (1873–1939), connected to Proust from their days at the Condorcet lycée and the Jardin des Champs-Élysées (or even from the "cours Pape-Carpantier" with Jacques Bizet) was the first, I believe, to publish an account of his memories, entitled *Souvenirs sur Marcel Proust accompagnés de lettres inédites*, and appearing in Grasset's "Les cahiers verts" collection, edited by their friend Daniel Halévy (1926).[15] Dreyfus (figure 21) was certainly no Zionist, but he earns a place here because of the reception given his book.

During their adolescence Proust did not feel the same passion for him as he did for the cousins Jacques Bizet and Daniel Halévy, his two other friends a year or two behind him at the lycée. Their relationship was subsequently more serene. They read each other's work and did each other favors. As Proust said to Halévy in 1907: "Robert Dreyfus? I adore him and admire him, but we do not have a single literary taste in common."[16] Among Proust's friends, he was one of the most faithful and obliging: "you, one of my oldest and dearest friends," Proust wrote to him in the last letter that Robert Dreyfus received.[17] But he numbers among those about whom we know the least (I think that was in keeping with his wishes, which I am going to disregard).

His father, Adolph Dreyfus (1826–1878), left few traces after the liquidation of his banking firm, Dreyfus, Scheyer et Cie, involved in the Honduras

Figure 21. Robert Dreyfus, at the Condorcet lycée, c. 1890.
Photo © Wikimedia Commons.

transoceanic railroad affair, prefiguring the Panama scandal, that exploded in 1875.[18] (Robert Dreyfus was not the son of Auguste Dreyfus [1827–1897], the tycoon of Peruvian guano importation, as Patrick Mimouni wantonly claims).[19] In the final years of the Second Empire and the beginning of the Third Republic the firm developed into a government bank.[20] Adolphe Dreyfus was a prominent figure at the time, invited to the Élysée on 27 April 1873 to dine with the president of the Republic, Adolphe Thiers, who would resign a month later. Among the dinner guests were a few "notables of finance, banking, and industry" including Baron Alphonse de Rothschild, and Monsieurs Stern and Halphen, listed with him in the *Archives israélites*.[21] But the first alarm was sounded by *Le Figaro* on 31 October 1875:

Dreyfus-Scheyer et Cie, —National Credit Bank, Limited Company—closed its offices last Friday. Here is the word on the street on this topic: M. Scheyer left Paris without warning—not even telling his wife, who, in an uproar, went to the Chausée-d'Antin offices asking for her husband "who had stayed out all night." M. Dreyfus bravely remained to face the situation. The debacle is primarily due to industrial speculation. The establishment's capital was in the ten millions. M. Scheyer is a knight of the Legion of Honor; he was responsible for the firm's internal business, leaving external affairs to M. Dreyfus. The roles seem to have changed for the moment.[22]

Le Figaro was a bit more reassuring two days later: "We know how easily rumors spread and grow in Paris. Thus it was reported that M. Scheyer, one of the administrators of the National Credit Bank, had fled. Whereas M. Scheyer did not leave Paris, and the entire board of directors met yesterday to deliberate on the adoption of appropriate measures to safeguard all interests and to weather a difficult, but temporary, crisis."[23] But nothing was settled, and the bank soon collapsed. In a second affair of the same kind, one involving Swiss property tax, Martin Scheyer, Adolphe Dreyfus's partner, was sentenced in 1876 to three years in prison for breach of trust and accessory to fraud and then struck from the Legion of Honor, but the court acknowledged that "with regard to Dreyfus, the charge does not seem sufficiently established."[24]

The affair involving the Honduras debt, in which Dreyfus, Scheyer et Cie had served as intermediary in 1869 to sell bonds on the French market, dragged on before the courts until 1881, when the bankers were finally sentenced.[25] In his introduction to *La France juive* in 1886, Édouard Drumont recalls this scandal, as emblematic as the embezzlements attributed to the Rothschilds: "the Bischoffsheims, the Scheyers, the Dreyfuses were able to collect from savings banks, in England and in France, a sum of 157 million, *one hundred fifty-seven million*, of which Honduras has always claimed to have received absolutely nothing."[26] The Bischoffsheim and Goldschmidt bank had sold bonds in London, and Raphaël Bischoffsheim (1823-1906), because he was not only a banker and a member of the supervisory committee that oversaw the Honduras loan in France but also a republican representative for Nice beginning in 1881, particularly excited Drumont's rage.[27] In his *La fin d'un monde* in 1889, Drumont came back to the eighty million "swiped" from the French savings bank by "the Bischoffsheims, the Dreyfuses, and the Scheyers."[28] And he denounced them again in 1890 in *La dernière bataille*.[29] Those three names composed a litany often repeated by *La libre parole*, as late as 1919, following the Dreyfus affair, following the war![30] Thus the father of Robert Dreyfus was one of the regular targets of anti-Semitic outbursts by Drumont and *La libre parole* for more than three decades.

But Adolphe Dreyfus, "senior banker, fifty-two years old," born in Belfort, 15 May 1826, son of Moïse Dreyfus, draper, and Pesselé Bloch, died on 2 November 1878, the same day that the newspapers announced the suspension of payments of Dreyfus, Scheyer et Cie, when his son Robert was five years old.[31] The death certificate states that he died on Rue Taitbout and was transported to his home on Rue Richer, but the circumstances of the event remain shrouded in mystery.[32]

His partner Martin Wolfgang Scheyer, born in Frankfurt in 1835, left France for America, where he went into the business of refining silver ore through lixiviation in Denver, Colorado. He took over a refinery there and impressed his interlocutors with the breadth of his experience: "Mr. Scheyer is from Paris, France, where, as in Stockholm, he was connected with the mints. He therefore understands his business thoroughly."[33] Avoiding prison in France, he supposedly found the time to learn the art of lixiviation in Sweden. But on 10 March 1879, a few months after Adolphe Dreyfus's death, he met his death as well, the circumstances of which are unknown.[34] In any case, neither of them lived to learn the judicial decisions on the Honduras affair.[35]

Nowhere does Proust mention Robert Dreyfus's father in their extensive correspondence, although he rarely fails to ask about Madame Dreyfus or convey his regards to her through his friend. In fact, Robert Dreyfus never left his mother, née Isabelle Bernheim (1833–1925), who died in her nineties.[36] He lived with her and his older brother Henri, also unmarried, at the end of Boulevard Malesherbes, not far from Proust, at the same address as Gabriel Fauré. A bank employee who suffered from neurasthenia and like Proust was a patient of doctor Paul Sollier, Henri Dreyfus, returning from a stay at the Boulogne-sur-Seine sanatorium, threw himself out the window of the family apartment.[37] It was 7 November 1910, and he was fifty-four years old (*La petite république* and *La petit parisien* do not agree either on the apartment floor in question or the time of death).[38] Born in 1857, Henri was sixteen years old than his younger brother. Proust spoke of him as "one of the familiar figures of [my] childhood."[39] But he missed the funeral in the Montmartre cemetery on 9 November 1910, where many of his friends and acquaintances gathered, like Daniel Halévy, Jacques Bizet, Bertrand de Fénelon, Léon Yeatman, Geneviève and Émile Straus, Marie Schiekévitch, Joseph Reinach, Gaston Calmette, André Baunier, René Blum, Dick May, Julien Benda, Paul Hervieu, Tristan Bernard. . . .[40] In his affectionate letters, Proust never uses the word "suicide," but he assures his friend that his grief is too much for one letter of condolence and that he will write again, as well as to his mother, a month after Henri Dreyfus's death, as he observed the rite of Sheloshim and scrupulously respected the first thirty days of mourning: "Do not believe that I have stopped thinking of you, I think of you always, my sympathy is without end, it has not been offered once and for all with my letter, it continues, as your grief does!"[41]

After attending Collège Rollin (renamed Lycée Jacques-Decour in 1944), Robert Dreyfus went to the Condorcet lycée, where he won the Prix d'honneur for a French dissertation in the 1890 general exams for philosophy.[42] (Robert Proust had to make do with the third certificate of honor).[43] He then went on to studies in law and letters. As the *Journal des débats* would phrase it at the time of this death: "Circumstances led him to technical studies and occupations in which his methodical nature, his concern for clarity and exactitude, were very soon appreciated. But he always retained a taste for literary and historical studies, and he devoted a great deal of his time to them, with a passion that lasted all his life."[44] That all seems full of innuendo. Robert Dreyfus has always been presented to us as a writer and journalist, a publicist, as they were called, but the realities of his career seem to have unfolded in a "little office on Rue Lafitte," in the shadow of the Rothschilds.[45] Most notably he worked as secretary general for the French boards of railroad companies for which James de Rothschild had financed construction in Italy and Spain, the Lombard Railways and the Railway Company of Madrid to Saragossa and Alicante.[46] Alone with his mother and brother, and then with just his mother, Robert Dreyfus's life seems to have provided him few joys. He died on the afternoon of 18 June 1939 on the Avenue de Marigny, at number 23—that is, the townhouse of Gustave de Rothschild, and then of Robert de Rothschild. (Muammar Gaddafi would stay there during an official visit very much later.)[47] Nevertheless, his last book, *De Monsieur Thiers à Marcel Proust* (1939)—that very M. Thiers who had invited his father to dinner at l'Élysée when Robert was only a month old—which included memories of Péguy, Madame Straus, and Élie Halévy, had just been published and was being well received (figure 22).[48]

Of his misfortunes, his "moral sadness" as Proust said, nothing shows through in his "Notes d'un parisien" signed simply D. in *Le Figaro*, "exquisite" and "delightful," according to Proust's usual comments, or even "splendid," but we can better understand Dreyfus's attachment to Halévy and his frequent visits to the more entertaining homes of the Strausses in Trouville, or Proust's kindnesses toward him, once we know his secrets, what the *Journal des débats* discreetly called his

Figure 22. Robert Dreyfus,
De Monsieur Thiers à Marcel Proust, 1939.
Photo © Librairie Plon.

"circumstances." By publishing his account of Proust very early, and by omitting in it, for example, most of the letters related to the illness and death of his brother, notably Proust's letter of condolence ("In November 1910, I suffered the grief of losing my brother. / The reader will understand that I am refraining from publishing many letters that my mother and I received from Marcel Proust"),[49] he succeeded in damping the curiosity of biographers regarding his own tragic story.

If I have engaged in this little inquiry, it is because I had nothing to say by way of introducing Robert Dreyfus in a few lines. We knew nothing of his father, his family, his occupations, although he was one of Proust's most affable and stead-fast confidants and although we believe we know his two sidekicks, Daniel Halévy and Jacques Bizet, the sons of Ludovic Halévy and of Georges Bizet and Geneviève Straus, née Halévy. The fact is that we do not know much more about them than we do Dreyfus. When Proust, over the course of his analogy in *Sodome et Gomorrhe* between homosexuals and Jews, compares the fate of those who hide their Jewish or homosexual identity to "something as simply atrocious as suicide (to which, whatever precautions we may take, madmen revert, and having been rescued from the river into which they had thrown themselves, take poison, procure a revolver, and so on,"[50] he refrains from mentioning those who threw themselves out a window, like Robert Dreyfus's brother and possibly his father.

During the "Marie Scandal" in *Jean Santeuil*, Charles Marie, representative and former minister of finance (whose wife, although Jewish, was Madame Santeuil's best friend and had entrusted her husband and son to the Santeuils on her deathbed), "enjoy[ed] dabbling in a number of decidedly shady concerns" and "frequent[ed] the company of two or three rather doubtful bankers." What became of them when their embezzling was exposed? No mystery in this case: "one committed suicide, another is now living in America, and a third managed to keep on the right side of the law, but found that not many hats were raised, nor many hands stretched out to him in welcome."[51] Novelistic solutions appear: America, suicide, shame, "social distancing" before its time. Proust did not need to know all the details to imagine the life of a disgraced financier.

In *À l'ombre des jeunes filles en fleurs* appears this exchange between Odette and Madame Cottard we all know by heart: "'Aren't you beautiful today! Is it one of Redfern's creations?' 'No, no, as you know that I'm a disciple of Raudnitz. In any case, it's just something I've had remodeled.' 'Well, I never! It's so smart!'"[52] This passage is famously prefigured by Proust in his November 1915 letter to Marie Schiekévitch regarding the next part of his novel.[53] But who knew that Ernest Raudnitz (1850-1906), the couturier on Rue Louis-le-Grand (said to be frequented by Madame Proust), and later on Rue Royale (1901), was related by marriage to Robert Dreyfus? Raudnitz had married Alice Brunschwig (1859-1957), the daughter of Robert Dreyfus's aunt, Palmyre Bernheim (1836-1906), and of Léopold Brunschwig (1829-1897), the Sentier merchant who signed Adolphe Dreyfus's death certificate in 1878.[54] Dreyfus's aunt and uncle were buried at Père-Lachaise, in the former Jewish section that became the seventh division, facing Rue du Repos. These small details may seem insignificant, but they add to the tangled web of destinies of this new Jewish bourgeoisie of Paris, and Robert Dreyfus, always obliging, does mention this allusion to his relative when he announces the publication of the second volume of *À la recherche du temps perdu* in *Le Figaro* in July 1919.[55]

Like Halévy, with whom he translated Nietzsche very early on, Dreyfus aligned himself with Péguy, the Universités Populaires, and the École des Hautes Études Sociales after the Dreyfus affair, and he contributed to the *Cahiers de la quinzaine*, where he published his introduction to the ideas of Joseph Arthur de Gobineau in 1905.[56] Then followed his introduction to the ideas of Alexandre Weill in 1908.[57] Yet ideological affinities between Robert Dreyfus, a devotee of Thiers, and Péguy were by no means certain. A historian of the Third Republic like Daniel Halévy, conservative in his literary tastes, contributor to *Le Figaro* beginning in 1908 (he made his debut in the *Supplement littéraire* of 22 February 1908, which, incidentally, ran the first "Pastiches" of the "L'affaire Lemoine"), Dreyfus facilitated Proust's appearances in Gaston Calmette's daily newspaper, where, along with Robert de Flers, he was Proust's ever devoted and admiring contact.

His own Jewishness seems to have left him completely indifferent. In his book on Alexandre Weill he relates a conversation with Barrès. Because Barrès was surprised that no young Jewish writer sought to "portray the 'Jewish soul' in a work of fiction, as he himself had tried to portray the 'Lorraine soul,'" Robert Dreyfus explained to him that "the Jews of France are at present too identified with French society, too similar to other French of all groups and all origins, to be tempted or capable of expressing a sensibility, ideas, and inclinations that are *different* and uniquely Jewish, and that we no longer find in ourselves."[58] Great-grandson and grandson of Belfort merchants, son of an apparently unscrupulous Paris financier, brother of a suicide victim, Robert Dreyfus found no refuge in Judaism. He seems to have been an excellent example of the dejudaized Jew, absorbed by the French mind.

That was not the case for his entire family, especially for his maternal uncle Alfred Neymarck (1848–1921).[59] Neymarck had served as Dreyfus's father's witness, signing Robert Dreyfus's birth certificate.[60] He was a prominent member of the Jewish community, continually reelected to the Paris consistory from 1897 until his death and serving as its longtime treasurer. A liberal economist, disciple of Léon Say, editor and owner of *Le Rentier*, a newspaper he had founded in 1868, he publicized the loan for the Honduras railways there.[61] Meanwhile his competitor, Paul Leroy-Beaulieu, warned investors away in *L'économiste française*.[62] Named commander in the Legion of Honor in 1907,[63] he was the author of numerous works, including a reference manual for investing money, *Que doit-on faire de son argent? Notions et conseils practical sur les valeurs mobilières, placements et operations* (1913), which Robert Dreyfus could have recommended to Proust.

But what do we know of the last thoughts of this friend of Proust? At the time of his death, *L'univers israélite*, less hostile, as we will see, than Strasbourg's *La tribune juive*, tried its best to recuperate him: "A few weeks ago, he had promised us some *Souvenirs* to publish in *L'Univers.*"[64] What *Souvenirs* could Robert Dreyfus have intended for *L'univers israélite* in 1939? Unlike his friend Daniel Halévy at the time, would he have reclaimed his heritage as son of Israel, or declared his solidarity with the Jews driven from Germany?[65] In his *Souvenirs sur Marcel Proust* in 1926, Jewishness is only mentioned on one occasion, and that is through Proust, in a letter that Proust wrote to Dreyfus in May 1905, but that passage seems important and could not have escaped the attention of vigilant readers.

MARIE-LOUISE CAHEN-HAYEM, 1926

Marie-Louise Cahen-Hayem was one of those readers and she duly noted the passage in her March 1927 piece for the *Archives israélites*. Of another generation that Judaeus-Liber, she took a huge step toward André Spire and proved responsive to the work of Proust and the possibility of secular Judaism. In commenting on the letter from Proust that Dreyfus mentioned, she praises Proust's faithfulness to his Jewish identity: "We already knew that Proust had never dreamed of renouncing his Jewish ancestry, but he did better than that. He recounts to his friend that, in an article on Barrès, several Jewish writers were attacked, and he was among them. 'I did not protest one bit, he says, 'because it would have been necessary to say I was not Jewish and I did not want to do that.' Such loyalty is rare."[66] Proust did, in fact, refrain from responding to the article in *La libre parole* of February 1898 that, in the midst of the Dreyfus affair, linked him with the Jewish contributors to *La revue blanche*, Gustave Kahn, Romain Coolus, Lucien Muhlfeld, Fernand Gregh, Tristan Bernard, and Léon Blum, characterized as "Dreyfus intellectuals," after *La revue blanche* had published a condemnation of Barrès's anti-Dreyfusism signed by Lucien Herr.[67]

Proust's letter to Robert Dreyfus reconsidering that affair dates from May 1905. In his book on Gobineau, a copy of which he sent Barrès, complete with a reverent dedication ("A token of my absolutely indestructible admiration!"), Dreyfus had nevertheless committed a blunder that hurt Barrès.[68] According to gossip reported to Dreyfus by Proust, Barrès "thinks that you accused him of plagiarizing Gobineau."[69] Dreyfus did in fact view the author of the *Essai sur l'inegalité des races humaines* (1853 and 1855) as the precursor of "contemporary nationalist doctrines," notorious for " 'integral nationalism' and its basic corollaries: anti-Semitism, anti-Protestantism, traditionalism, regionalism, neo-monarchism, and so on." Surprised that these doctrines were said to draw inspiration from Joseph de Maistre, Louis de Bonald, even August Comte, but that no one spoke of Gobineau, Dreyfus added as a precaution, "it goes without saying that I absolutely dismiss and repudiate any explanation of that silence that would tend toward incriminating as philosophical and literary *plagiarists* those whom I have called just now the 'well-read theoreticians of French nationalism.' " Then with regard to Barrès, who mentions Gobineau's name once in relation to Stendhal in *Leurs figures*, he writes: "From this passage, it is evident that M. Maurice Barrès knows the name of Gobineau, some facts about his masterpiece, but it is not at all clear that he has read that work, or especially thought about it."[70] Dreyfus's precautionary note was insufficient.

Responding to Proust, Dreyfus acknowledged his error: "It is my fault in the Barrès business (thank you for telling me, I promise my complete discretion)."[71] Then followed an imbroglio typical of Proust, who proposed intervening through his source—who was not, he specified, Anna de Noailles—to mollify Barrès but in the end did nothing.[72] "This mysterious source would permit me, I am sure, to give you her name. But I cannot ask for authorization since you have forbidden me to say that I told you."[73] Dreyfus seemed to mistrust Proust's skills at diplomacy and preferred that he involve himself no further in the affair. Moreover, is it possible that the gossiper was Proust himself, whose first reaction when he received Dreyfus's book was to wonder "if basically, despite your protests, you are making an accusation of plagiarism. But against whom? Barrès? Léon de Montesquiou? Marras?"[74]

It is under precisely these circumstances that Proust reminds Robert Dreyfus of the misunderstanding that cooled his own relationship with Barrès in 1898, following the article in *La libre parole*. He recommends that his friend refute the rumor publicly, which he himself was not able to do at that time: "To set it right, it would have been necessary to say I was not Jewish and I did not want to do that. Thus I let it stand that I had come out against Barrès, which was not true."[75] His silence, he seemed to suggest, was a way of expressing his Jewish solidarity. At least that was how Marie-Louise Cahen-Hayem chose to interpret it. But what could he have denied? When he writes, "I was not Jewish," he means that he was Catholic, like his father and brother, as he had responded to Montesquiou in 1896, but he then added, we will recall, "on the other hand, my mother is Jewish."[76] What good would such a correction have done among readers of *La libre parole*? Or with Barrès? Might not the cure have been worse than the disease? "To set it right, it would have been necessary to say I was not Jewish and I could not do that:" such was the situation in which Proust found himself, and there was no way out. That is why Marie-Louise Cahen-Hayem's interpretation (and those of all who followed her) could well have erred on the side of generosity.

LA TRIBUNE JUIVE, 1927, 1937, 1939

Be that as it may, thanks to Marie-Louise Cahen-Hayem, the *Archives israélites* recognized the importance of Proust's work and paid tribute to him for claiming his Jewishness, but the assessment by the Jewish press as a whole seems better summarized by this article in *La tribune juive* of Strasbourg on the fifth anniversary of Proust's death in 1927:

> Paris. An anniversary mass in remembrance of Marcel Proust, who died 18 November 1922, was celebrated on Friday 18 of this month, in the Église Saint-Pierre de Chaillot, in Paris. All his friends were invited by way of the press.
>
> Marcel Proust has his place in the pages of literary reviews, but nowhere else.[77]

The judgment was final and the rejection total. Nevertheless, if *La tribune juive* thought it essential to bring to its readers' attention such a minor news item and to accompany it with a condemnation, to blacklist Proust, as it were, it was undoubtedly because, whether *La tribune juive* liked it or not, Marcel Proust really did have a place other than "in the pages of literary reviews," for example in *Menorah*, *La revue juive*, and soon, *Palestine*, and no doubt also among its very own subscribers, who had to be warned against bad books.

Ten years later, in 1937, Proust as well as Bergson had "no place in a history of Judaism," according the *La tribune juive*, which resorted to the same image of a "place" wrongly held by those authors and expressed the same desire to expel them. This time it was with regard to a *Histoire des juifs de France*, edited by no less than the head rabbi of Lille, Léon Berman (1892–1943), who, horror of horrors, cited Bergson and Proust under the heading of "our contribution to the sciences and intellectual life of our era."[78]

Proust, "son of a Jewish mother," was a model of the apostate and illustrated "what Théodore Lessing called *jüdischer Selbsthass* (self-hating Jew)," again according to *La tribune juive* in 1937, in a positive review of the study by Siegfried van

Praag, "Marcel Proust, témoin du judaïsme déjudaïsé," then in the process of being serialized in *La revue juive de Genève*.

Van Praag, to whom we will return, was, in fact, one of the first critics to denounce the treatment of Jewish characters in *À la recherche du temps perdu*, and his study is evidence of a noticeable change in perspective on Proust in the second half of the 1930s. He would inspire the influential analysis of anti-Semitism presented by Hannah Arendt, beginning with the case of Proust, in *The Origins of Totalitarianism*.[79]

La tribune juive was also Zionist, but Zionism in Strasbourg was different from Zionism in Paris. Lacking patience for literature, it would never have the least sympathy for Proust, "the famous half-Jewish novelist," as it called him in 1939, at the time of Robert Dreyfus's death. Considering that Dreyfus had invented the prophet of modern racism in the figure of Gobineau, his obituary in *La tribune juive* was particularly mean-spirited, with the sarcastic title, "The Charming Chronicler Robert Dreyfus, or: In Place of a Kaddish."[80]

Like Proust, Robert Dreyfus would have no "place" in the memory of *La tribune juive*, harsher toward him than *L'univers israélite* was, which, as we have seen, recuperated him at the time of his death. But *La tribune juive* failed to report that Henri Schilli, the future head rabbi of France for the period from 1952–1955, led the prayers for Robert Dreyfus's funeral at the Montmartre cemetery, in the presence of a large contingent of the Rothschild family, as well as Madame Robert Proust and her daughter, Madame Gérard Mante, Daniel Halévy, Fernand Gregh, Robert de Billy, Gérard Bauër.... Madame Alfred Neymarck, the aunt of Robert Dreyfus, was also there, so that the funeral procession did not take place "in the absence of any family," as the *Journal des débats* reported.

Thus, the enthusiasm for Proust among the young Paris Zionists of *Menorah* and *La revue juive*, and later, *Palestine*, clearly distinguished and isolated them from institutional Judaism. One swallow—by the name of Marie-Louis Cahen-Hayem—does not make the summer, as the saying goes, because Proust's contribution to the "Jewish renaissance," as André Spire called it, was not recognized by the Jewish press. The cruelty of *La tribune juive* toward Robert Dreyfus illustrates the divide: no stone to lay on his tomb any more than on Proust's.[81]

The debate between Spire and Judaeus-Maurice Liber in *L'univers israélite* in December 1926 and January 1927, like the reception to Dreyfus's *Souvenirs* in the *Archives israélites* in March 1927, signaled that the late 1920s would be a time of taking stock.

CHAPTER 8

The Zohar or L'Astrée?

By the end of 1927, the publication of *À la recherche du temps perdu* was complete; the question of Proust's Jewishness and the influence of his maternal heritage on his work had been thoroughly discussed from multiple and contradictory perspectives, ranging from being dismissed as irrelevant, in the manner of Léon Pierre-Quint, to being considered essential and seminal, in the manner of Denis Saurat. Two major studies came out at that time, in 1928 and 1929, written by Georges Cattaui, for whom the subject was nothing new, and Benjamin Crémieux, who had not yet addressed it.

GEORGES CATTAUI, 1928

Georges Cattaui (figure 23) had been the first to underscore Proust's Jewishness in his *Menorah* obituary in December 1922. In 1925, his contributions to *La revue juive* distanced him from Péguy and Barrès, the idols of his first poetry collection published in 1921, *La promesse accomplie*, and led him continually back to Proust. Having abandoned his diplomatic career, he would go on to publish essays on Léon Bloy, Péguy, Paul Claudel, T. S. Eliot, Constantin Cavafy, and others.[1] He would also publish the first biography of Charles De Gaulle at the end of 1944.[2]

But most important, he was the author of numerous books on Proust, following his *Amitié de Proust* in 1935. Between 1953 and 1972, Georges Cattaui published five volumes on Proust with various publishing houses, among them an invaluable collection of photographs, *Marcel Proust: Documents iconographiques* (1956). For over fifty years, from the 1920s to the 1970s, Cattaui maintained the Proust cult, facilitating communication between firsthand witnesses, historic Proustians, and university

Figure 23. Georges Cattaui by Thérèse Le Prat.

Photo © Thérèse Le Prat / Bibliothèque de Genève– RMN–Grand-Palais–gestion des droits d'auteur.

professors and researchers who gradually took an interest in Proust, first in Great Britain, the United States, Germany, and Italy and only later in France. Serving as the bridge between generations, Cattaui codirected with Philip Kolb, the dogged and learned editor of Proust's letters for sixty years (from the 1930s to the 1990s), the colloquium held in Cerisy-la-Salle in July 1962, the proceedings of which they published under the title of *Entretiens sur Marcel Proust*.[3] As we have seen, Cattaui translated and wrote a preface for the Proust biography by George D. Painter, which was published in French at a pivotal moment in the reception of Proust's work, in the mid-1960s, at the time when *À la recherche du temps perdu* was made available in a paperback edition, thus democratizing its readership.

Following his Proust obituary in *Menorah*, Cattaui's most important contribution on the subject of the author's Jewishness appeared under the title "Proust et les juifs" in the fifth issue of the *Palestine* review in February 1928, at which time he was experiencing the painful turmoil brought on by his desire to be baptized.[4]

Palestine was published by the Association France-Palestine, "the French committee of the friends of Zionism," founded in December 1925, with seven very eminent honorary presidents: Raymond Poincaré, Aristide Briand, Édouard Herriot, Paul Painlevé, Louis Barthou, Gaston Doumergue, then president of France, and Jules Cambon. It was presided over by Justin Godart, radical, former minister and senator from the Rhône, future "Righteous Among the Nations" for his role during the Occupation.[5]

The committee included many political radicals and socialists, mostly Protestants and Freemasons: Anatole de Monzie, Marius Moutet, Albert Thomas, Joseph Paul-Boncour, Léon Blum.[6] It also included Jewish and non-Jewish scholars, many of whom taught at the Collège de France: Jacques Hadamard, mathematician; Charles Gide, social economist and uncle of André Gide; Paul Langevin, physicist; Louis Massignon, Arabist; Jean Perrin, physicist at the Sorbonne; Paul Lapie and Paul Appell, director and former director of the Académie de Paris; the composer Maurice Ravel; André-Ferdinand Herold, symbolist poet and vice president of the Ligue des Droits de l'Homme; and writers familiar to us: André Spire, Jean-Richard Bloch, Edmond Fleg, Henri Hertz, Gustave Kahn.

The first issue of *Palestine* appeared in October 1927.[7] And in the first four issues, articles by André Spire, Edmond Fleg, Henri Hertz, Armand Lunel, Albert Cohen, and Jean-Richard Bloch, the whole team of the defunct *Revue juive*, preceded the one written by Cattaui for the fifth issue in February 1928. From *Menorah* to *La revue juive* to *Palestine*, no solution of continuity but increasing political ambition. Cattaui would expand his *Palestine* article in *L'amitié de Proust*, his 1935 book with the ambiguous title, since he had never met Proust.[8] On the last page of this book, as we have seen, Cattaui dates its composition to 1930, when the first cycle of public reception to Proust's work had come to an end, after the appearance of *Le temps retrouvé*.[9]

In the course of his article Cattaui evokes "the one who taught me to understand and to love Marcel Proust, and who, if I am to believe Jacques-Émile Blanche, resembles him in her facial features, as well as her sensitivity, heart, and intuition."[10] That allusion cost me much time by piquing my curiosity about the woman who had introduced Cattaui to Proust's work. Nothing in Blanche's writings revealed her identity to me.[11] Could this be Anna de Noailles or Marthe Bibesco? Or why not Natalie Clifford Barney, whom André Spire knew and whose salon Blanche frequented? But Cattaui, who calls Barney "the vestal of friendship" in a 1962 tribute, recalls meeting her only much later, not until 1936.[12] No leads paid off until one day when I realized the answer was quite simple and that Cattaui was thinking of his own mother, Rachel Cattaui, née Francis (1873–1924).

According to Edmée de la Rochefoucauld's memoir, it was Georges Cattaui's mother who gave him *À l'ombre des jeunes filles en fleurs* when it was first published in 1919, before it won the Prix Goncourt, while he was recovering from "a stubborn case of typhoid fever." "It was love at first sight," she adds, for "the young Egyptian invalid," who tore up "the letters he prepared for the writer he so admired," and never met him.[13] By mentioning Jacques-Émile Blanche, Cattaui had thrown me off track, and into Blanche's *Cahiers*, by too subtly suggesting that Rachel Cattaui might have resembled Blanche's famous portrait of Proust as a dandy sporting an orchid, just as she shared with that portrait's model the winning qualities of his novel: sensitivity, heart, intuition. Cattaui wanted to say (and not to proclaim it from the rooftops) that his attachment to Proust was, for him, inseparable from the memory of his mother, that Proust connected him to his mother's side.

Just as Spire did in his 1928 introductory note to his 1923 Proust obituary, reprinted in *Quelques juifs et demi-juifs*, Cattaui starts his article by parting ways with Léon Pierre-Quint who, in his 1925 book, had minimized or even denied any Jewish influence in the work of Proust. To counter Pierre-Quint, Cattaui evokes Proust himself, whom, he insists, "attaches such great importance to the laws of heredity." For examples, he notes Proust's descriptions of Bloch, of "Oriental type," and with his "body bent forward like a hyena," expressions that seem not to bother Cattaui, as they do some twenty-first-century commentators who find them offensive. "From Montaigne to Proust, what is more captivating than a half-Jew?" asks Cattaui moreover, recalling that Bernard Faÿ insisted on Proust's "Jewish race" as Blanche did on his Oriental eyes and young Assyrian face.[14] Proust "gets from Israel his nervousness, his memory, his acute sensitivity, that anxiety from which arises in him the torment of jealousy, his psychological imagination, his sense of mobility, his intuitive faculties and analytic mind," that is to say, many of the essential qualities of *À la recherche du temps perdu*.[15] A note here refers to Denis Saurat on Proust's rabbinical style, but Cattaui remains cautious, consigning this interpretation to a footnote while in the body of the text he continues by attributing Proust's professional awareness and his concern for structure to the influence of his Normand, paternal side (in his 1935 book, Cattaui would no longer show such reticence, since there he cites Saurat's position in the body of the text itself, although without expressing his personal opinion either in favor or against it).[16]

Cattaui again insists on Proust's kindness, tenderness, and leniency, even toward Bloch, and he refers to Benjamin Crémieux to explain Proust's interest in the "condemned race" among "all the humiliated, all the solitary, all the condemned:" servants, inverts, snobs, and Jews.[17] Following Spires's example, he reads the grandfather of Combray to be a version of Nathé Weil, humming an air from *La Juive*, and this is where he finds a place for the Père-Lachaise anecdote.

Then Rachel, Nissim Bernard, and Bloch are examined one by one, and, "if they all have the flaws of certain Jews, they are at least more true, more alive, more recognizable than those Jewish entities that unflaggingly, for over fifty years, have been trotted out for us in plays and novels." As for Swann, who rediscovers his Jewish heritage during the Dreyfus affair, he "only remembers that he is Jewish on the day when the Jew is persecuted."[18]

As we can see, Cattaui covers the entire ground of what could be said on the subject since Proust's death. Thus, Swann "is Jewish as well through the feeling he gives us of a continual flow, a constant mobility; and in that, as in many other things, it is of Montaigne more than any other French writer that we must think." Thibaudet's article, published in "Hommage à Marcel Proust" in *La nouvelle revue française* in January 1923, is cited at length in a note, linking Proust with Montaigne and Bergson through their "Jewish blood." All this is recalled without the slightest hesitation on the part of Cattaui, who repeats the words of his 1923 Proust obituary in *Menorah*: "Like Montaigne, Proust was born of a French father and Jewish mother. Such marriages are often rich and fertile. It seems that crossing the strong, clear logic of the French with the nervous sensitivity of the Jews produces the most precious fruits." Nevertheless, Montaigne lacks warmth of the soul: "Proust is Montaigne, but Montaigne corrected by Pascal, his skepticism tempered by such passionate love for humans." Thus Proust rejoins—a curious turn that gestures toward Cattaui's imminent conversion—"the old ardent prophets, the mystics of Israel . . . and the last of them, the one who, on Golgotha, wanted to suffer and shed blood for men."[19] After having been co-opted by *La revue juive*, Proust is again claimed by young Zionists on their way toward baptism. As we have said, one invests one's own singular Jewishness in *À la recherche du temps perdu*.

Nothing very new in these pages, but all the participants in the debate over Proust's Jewishness since 1922 are cited in this summary: André Spire, Albert Thibaudet, Léon Pierre-Quint, Denis Saurat, Benjamin Crémieux, with the exception of René Groos, the "*Action française* Jew." Ideas introduced in the 1922 *Menorah* obituary are developed, with Cattaui claiming responsibility for the parallel between Montaigne and Proust, repeating again in 1935 that he was the first to mention their shared "maternal heredity:" "And first of all, let me offer a personal testimony: I was struck immediately by the strange parallelism between Proust's and Montaigne's thinking. . . . even more than intellectual affinities, there was a kind of consanguinity."[20] Thus Cattaui did not need Thibaudet's January 1923 article to note, in December 1922, that Proust, like Montaigne, was born of a Jewish mother. Cattaui was all the more eager to claim credit for being first to consider Proust's maternal side because he first read Proust with and thanks to his own mother, as she was the one who taught him "to understand and love Marcel Proust."

L'amitié de Proust, in which Cattaui expands his 1928 *Palestine* article, was published in 1935 in Gallimard's "Cahiers Marcel Proust" collection. Following the reissue of "Hommage à Marcel Proust" by *La nouvelle Revue française* (1927), the *Répertoire des personnages* (1928) and the *Morceaux choisis* (1928), both by Ramon Fernandez, the memoir by the Princess Marthe Bibesco, *Au bal avec Marcel Proust* (1928), the memoir by Lucien Daudet, *Autour de soixante lettres de Marcel Proust* (1929), the *Lettres à la NRF* (1932), and a *Répertoire des thèmes* (1935), this was the eighth volume in the series and (a sign of the small purgatory Proust entered, even at Gallimard, in the second half of the 1930s) the last of them until the resurrection of the "Cahiers Marcel Proust" in 1970. With the preface by Paul Morand, it remains an authoritative introduction to the work of Proust.

BENJAMIN CRÉMIEUX, 1929, RENÉ GROOS, 1926, AND GUSTAVE KAHN, 1925

Benjamin Crémieux wrote the date "February 1927" at the end of his article "Proust et les Juifs," which remained unpublished until he included it in his book *Du côté de Marcel Proust* in 1929, along with other studies complementing the one that had appeared in his *XXᵉ siècle* in 1924, and followed by the letters he had received from Proust.[21] These pages close the first cycle of the posthumous reception of Proust's work, now including the publication and reception of *La prisonnière, Albertine disparue,* and *Le temps retrouvé.*[22]

In his widely read article "Judaïsme et littérature," in *Les nouvelles littéraires* on 10 October 1925, Crémieux, we will recall, does not mention Proust's name. His presence remains vague among the "French Jewish writers" not possessing "characteristics distinctive enough to be differentiated from other French writers."[23] Crémieux's perspective had evolved, and this time, he begins by recalling that

André Spire, Denis Saurat, and René Groos had all posed the question of Jew-ishness in the life and work of Proust. His own contribution would take the form of a measured assessment. Further on, he cites Léon Pierre-Quint and links him to Groos—"(both Jews)," he notes in parentheses—for whom "Proust's work dis-plays no specifically Jewish character." As Crémieux summarizes it: "M. René Groos, *Action française* Jew, distinguishes in Proust only lucidity, which is a French quality, and states that 'in terms of moral atmosphere, he stands head and shoul-ders above talmudic moralism.'"[24] The whole spectrum of opinions will be surveyed by Crémieux, from Groos to Saurat, by way of Pierre-Quint, Spire, Ludmila Savitzky, and Albert Thibaudet. Crémieux seeks a middle course between the extreme positions supported by Saurat and Groos: Proust is a rabbi; Proust is a classical writer.

Just before Crémieux addressed this subject in February 1927, Groos was the last to express himself, in his article "Marcel Proust et le judaïsme" (the publica-tion date of Groos's *Marcel Proust* was 30 December 1926) (figure 24).

Proust posed a dramatic problem for Groos: How could he resolve the contra-diction between his faithfulness to Maurras, anti-Semitic defender of classicism, and his admiration for Proust, half-Jew suspected of romanticism? To do that he had to begin by refuting Saurat's sensationalist theory on Proust's rabbinism, first put forward in *Les Marges* in October 1925, and then immediately picked up by *La revue juive*. *Les Marges* was not hostile to Action Française (its editor, Eugène Montfort, had refused to belong to the "Parti de l'intelligence" in 1919, but also to Henri Barbusse's "Clarté" movement),[25] and Groos had ties there, as assistant editor and literary columnist in 1924 and 1925. But no review was free of dissen-sion, and Groos hardly saw eye to eye with Saurat.

Before watching Crémieux find a path between Groos and Saurat, we need to take a brief look at Groos's argument. In order to deny that Proust's style has any-thing to do with rabbinism, Groos begins by quoting the poet Gustave Kahn: "if someone tells us that the proof of Proust's Semitic origins is to be found in the lengths of his sentences, we would argue that some of the most beautiful work issuing from the Jewish mind" is characterized by concision and brevity, the work of Spinoza, for example, and the poetry of Heine. Through this argument, which Groos calls "simplistic," Kahn contests all ethnic determinism of Proust's long sen-tences (Pierre-Quint, we will recall, had already evoked Spinoza, with the same intention). For Groos, such objections against Saurat were "infantile," because the

Figure 24. René Groos, "Marcel Proust et le judaïsme," engravings by Louis Caillaud, *Marcel Proust*, 1926.

Photos © BnF, Paris.

complexity of Proust's sentences is not characterized by their length alone.[26] On this point, Groos concedes, Saurat was not wrong.

But Groos gives no source for his Gustave Kahn quote, and Kahn had never been included, so far, among the protagonists in the debate over Proust's Jewishness. The words that Groos attributes to him come from an unsigned editorial titled "Le judaïsme et le style," from an issue of *Menorah*. Kahn was then editor-in-chief of that review, and the issue in question is dated 1 November 1925.[27] Thus it appeared immediately after Saurat's article, "Le judaïsme de Proust," in *Les Marges* on 15 October 1925. That issue of *Menorah* is very Proustian (that is how I happened upon the passage quoted by Groos and attributed to Kahn): in addition to the editorial, this is the issue that includes the review by Ludmila Savitzky of Pierre-Quint's book.[28] Also featured there, in the "Revue de presse" section, are excerpts from Crémieux's article, "Judaïsme et littérature," from *Les nouvelles littéraires* of 10 October 1925.[29] As we have already noted, the theme of literary Jewishness, and Proust's Jewishness in particular, were in the air in autumn 1925.

Thus in November 1925, while *La revue juive* reproduced Saurat's article without commentary, that is to say, tacitly approving it, *Menorah* took a stand against his theory. Gustave Kahn, Proust's contemporary who shared with him the honor of appearing on the list of "Dreyfus intellectuals" drawn up by *La libre parole* in 1898, had no love for Proust. Nor did he approve of *La revue juive*'s infatuation with the author of *À la recherche de temps perdu* or the credit it gave to Saurat's theory. Groos parts ways with him even more when he belittles Proust: "'Proust lacks something,' writes M. Kahn, 'that would rank him among the great Jewish thinkers and writers.'" Groos then turns toward Léon Daudet, satirist for *L'action française* and Proust's champion for the Prix Goncourt, to refute both Saurat and Kahn: "Proust's analysis, which 'goes farther than that of Balzac,' as M. Léon Daudet has said, achieves a different grandeur than talmudic hair-splitting. Proust is the genius of pure reflection."[30] Hostile to what he calls the "charlatan eloquence" of the Talmud, Groos manages, through this three-part maneuver, to acquit Proust of any ties to romanticism, Maurras's bête noir.[31] Quite familiar with the literature, he again cites the articles by Spire and Thibaudet from 1923, and Pierre-Quint's book and Ludmila Savitzky's article from 1925, before concluding confidently, "Marcel Proust's art is lucidity," another name for classical clarity.[32]

What would Crémieux say about all this in his own "Proust et les juifs?" He notes first that by defining Proust's grandeur in terms of lucidity, "a French quality," Groos was in fact reacting to Ludmila Savitzky's review of Pierre-Quint's book, in the same issue of *Menorah* as Kahn's editorial against Saurat: "In writing this, M. Groos is responding to Mme Ludmila Savitsky (Jewish as well) who, while in basic agreement with M. L. Pierre-Quint, thought she recognized in Proust 'a moral atmosphere that urgently reminds us of certain distinctive traits of the Jewish soul.'"[33] To reveal Savitzky's contradictions, Groos finds inconsistencies between the reviewer and the author Pierre-Quint, and points out that "Mme Ludmila Savitzky in a study in *Menorah* (1 November 1925) notes that M. Pierre-Quint 'hardly insists on Proust's partly Jewish origins'; she acknowledges that 'he is not wrong' but wants to find in Proust 'a moral atmosphere that urgently reminds us of certain distinctive traits of the Jewish soul.' Certain ones, but which ones?"[34] Groos, as we can see, was anxious to invalidate any participation by Proust in "the Jewish soul," however modest, as Savitzky envisaged it, adapting the opinion of Pierre-Quint.

The fact remains that it is Crémieux, not Groos, who finds it useful to add that Ludmila Savitzky, a contributor to *Menorah*, is Jewish. Crémieux thus considers this information relevant for understanding how she finds "distinctive traits of the Jewish soul" in Proust. He is careful to note whether each participant in the debate is Jewish or not, before presenting that participant's position. That gesture seems noteworthy, as it is the first time we have observed it. In Cattaui's synopsis in *Palestine*, he did not note that Pierre-Quint was Jewish or that Thibaudet was not. Crémieux, on the other hand, must have wanted this information included because he must have considered it relevant to each participant's perspective on Proust's work.

Now, in seeking a middle path, he carefully weighs the pros and the cons on both sides. Thus he mentions Andre Spire's initial hesitations in 1923 (in *The Jewish Chronicle* and in *Menorah*, because the passage he quotes does not appear in the excerpt in *Nouvelles littéraires*), Spire, for whom, rather than Proust's maternal heredity, it was "a long heredity of spiritual exercises and habitual suffering" that contributed to his gift of an extremely refined sensibility." (Crémieux, whose text dates from February 1927, could not yet know of Spire's introductory note to his 1923 article, revised for his 1928 collection *Quelques juifs et demi-juifs*, which takes more seriously the theory of Jewish influence on Proust's novel.) From Spire's circumspection in1923 and Pierre-Quint's in 1925, Crémieux then distinguishes the convictions of Thibaudet in 1923 and of Saurat in 1925: "two non-Jewish critics . . . who have tried to analyze most precisely Proustian Judaism." But Crémieux seems skeptical about the comparison Thibaudet makes between Proust's mobility and that of Montaigne and Bergson: "It remains to be seen whether this 'mobility' is specifically Jewish," since, he remarks with good humor, it may undoubtedly be found in Ecclesiastes, but also in the Greek philosopher Heraclitus, or the in the Sicilian Catholic Pirandello (whom Crémieux translated).[35]

As for Saurat, who recognized "in Proust's reasoning processes and style the same type of reasoning and style as in the Talmud and the Zohar," Crémieux treats him with even more skepticism. He argues that French literature has habitually featured complications in style and that this was already evident in others long before Proust, for example, "our court poets of the Middle Ages, the author of the *Le roman de la rose*, and the author of *L'Astrée* were quite the hair splitters." Crémieux thus refuses to make Saurat's amphigory, any more than Thibaudet's mobility, a specifically Jewish feature. For Crémieux, who doubts all such comparisons, "the Talmud quibbles about words, plays with an often empty formalism."

Whereas Proust repudiates "fixed ideas" and works with the concrete, the impression. Saurat's thoughts on the transmigration of souls and their changing sexes in the Zohar, as model for the theory of inversion and the description of men-women in *Sodome et Gomorrhe I*, make little impression on Crémieux, who, not without scornful irony, dismisses them with a stroke of the pen, noting that there is nothing "specifically rabbinical in believing that a man can resemble his mother."[36] This quip steals the last word from Groos, and strips the sentimentality from Cattaui's discovery of his mother's traits in Jacques-Émile Blanche's portrait of Proust.

Thus, methodical academic that he is (even if the Sorbonne considered his thesis too cavalier, as we have seen), Crémieux refuses to be caught on one side or the other, or rather in one corner or another in this game of four square between Jews who make Proust a non-Jew, non-Jews who make Proust a Jew, and so on. Although he concedes that mobility and "the taste for and art of dissecting feelings" are "characteristic of many Jews," he immediately adds to their characteristic traits, the "passionate worship of intelligence and knowledge," "respect for culture," "unhealthy emotionalism," "nervous hypersensitivity," "love of music," "faculty for . . . *alienation*," "plasticity," "power of adaptation and imitation," "relentless determination to dissociate everything, dismantle everything." And that is not all, since "the vision of the world that Proust proposes to us reunites oriental fatalism and the highest Jewish wisdom: 'God gave them to me, God took them from me, God's will be done!' says the rabbi who returns one evening to find his two children dead." For Proust, as for Montaigne: "Our life is a succession of uninterrupted deaths. Here again, how not to think of Ecclesiastes?" So much so that it all blends together, impossible to make sense of it, and "such a general view of Proustian Judaism is undoubtedly . . . subject to caution . . . and it is better not to insist on it too much."[37]

Finally, by dismissing two non-Jews (Thibaudet and Saurat) who insist too much on "Proustian Judaism" and two Jews (Pierre-Quint and Groos) who deny any influence of Proust's "Hebraic origin" on his work, Crémieux achieves a balance approaching the position defended by Spire and Cattaui in *Menorah*, *La revue juive*, and *Palestine* throughout the 1920s. By noting whether or not each participant in the debate is Jewish—although he is wrong in the case of Ludmila Savitzky—Crémieux clearly hypothesizes that the diversity of perspectives on Proust and his work could reflect the ideas held by the individual participants on Judaism and, in the case of Jewish critics, on their own Jewish identity. People always act in their own interest. That is why Robert Le Masle (1901–1970) would perceive nothing Talmudic in Proust's complicated language in 1935, but only his paternal heritage: "Like the doctor, Marcel Proust dissects, analyzes, and diagnoses passions, feelings, and vices."[38] It is from doctor Adrien Proust that his son Marcel Proust must have gotten his rabbinical style. Duly noted.

Thus Crémieux completes the first cycle of Proust's critical reception with a judicious appeal to moderation. He himself evolved between 1925 and 1927. Certainly, as for Spire and Cattaui, Proust's maternal heredity mattered for him, but it did not explain the style or the thought processes in Proust's work: "What is clear is that Proust always had a keen awareness of the Jewish portion of himself and he never sought to repress it."[39] That was how Marie-Louise Cahen-Hayem interpreted, perhaps generously, the words Proust wrote to Robert Dreyfus: "To set it right, it would have been necessary to say I was not Jewish and I did not want to do that." Thus Proust could not be made into "the greatest 'witness of dejudaized Judaism,'" as Hannah Arendt would maintain in *The Origins of Totalitarianism*, and especially not the "model representative" of a certain French Jewish circle at the turn of the century, assimilated to the point of becoming blind to the rise of modern anti-Semitism once the Dreyfus affair was settled.[40] Arendt, like Spire in his Proust obituary, recognized moreover that Proust had been "ready, when the circumstances required it, to affirm his Jewish identity." Thus let us be content to read Proust, Crémieux recommends, without denying the "marks of his Hebraic origin," but without exaggerating them, without making them the alpha and omega, or the aleph and the tav, of *À la recherche du temps perdu.*[41]

L'UNIVERS ISRAÉLITE, 1927, 1930

Crémieux's moderation, and his irony with regard to extreme theories, was nevertheless not sufficient to defuse the hostility of *L'univers israélite*, which reported, 4 March 1927, on a lecture on Proust and Judaism that Crémieux had come to Mulhouse to give for the Société d'Histoire et de Littérature Juives. This talk clearly provided him the opportunity to write the text we have just analyzed, dated February 1927 by Crémieux and included in his *Du côté de Marcel Proust* in 1929.

According to the account in *L'univers israélite* of Crémieux's lecture at Mulhouse, he supposedly said of *À la recherche de temps perdu*: "In studying this book from the Jewish perspective, we see only characters disagreeable by nature. Because Proust presents to us the Jew, especially the Parisian Jew, as a type distinguished by ostentation, avarice, and great physical awkwardness. Fortunately, French Judaism still possesses a fine elite of a different stock than the one depicted by Proust."[42]

Unless Crémieux was making immense concessions to his Alsatian audience, how to recognize his cautious and balanced approach in such a scathing summary of Proust's representation of Jews? The last sentence seems to reflect the reporter's opinion rather than that of the lecturer, who was applauded by his civilized Mulhouse listeners all the same: "With much witty verve, Crémieux was able to show the value of Proust's works for Judaism." That conclusion does not seem to have convinced the Paris editors of *L'univers israélite*; it must have annoyed them, since, in their fit of ire, they thought it judicious to add to the local dispatch this dubious and telegraphic, but no less expeditious and executory, commentary: "(*Editor's note?*)" Clearly, it was less the lecturer's "witty verve" that needed to be called into question than the usefulness of his demonstration of the "value of Proust's works for Judaism."

The opinion of Strasbourg's *La tribune juive* (we will recall how it treated poor Robert Dreyfus at the time of his death) was no more sympathetic toward Proust's novel following Crémieux's Mulhouse talk: "In this book, Proust did not use his great writing talent or the resources of his intelligence to serve Judaism. It is not in studying the works of this half-Jew that one will find an explanation for the miraculous existence and the eternal continuance of Judaism."[43] Once again, if *La Tribune* deemed such aggressions necessary in 1927, it was because its readers were not all insensible to Proust's novel.

In December 1930, following the publication of his book *Du côté de Marcel Proust*, Benjamin Crémieux gave a talk on "Les juifs dans la littérature française d'aujourd'hui," this time in Paris, for the Cercle d'Études Juives gathered at the home of its president, the baron James-Henri de Rothschild (1896–1984), son of the baron Henri de Rothschild (1872–1947). The elder Rothschild, an imposing figure, doctor, playwright, race car pioneer, philanthropist, collector and patron of the arts, was also friends with Proust.[44] He might also have been a student at the legendary "cours Pape-Carpantier," with the Proust brothers, Jacques Bizet, Robert Dreyfus, and Daniel Halévy.[45] He financed their review *Le Banquet*, and Proust dedicated an article to him in 1892.[46]

When Crémieux gave his talk in 1930, the Cercle d'Études Juives had just been created and wanted to think of themselves as openminded, offering invitations to both the side of the consistory and the rabbinate as well as the side of the Zionists.[47] During their first meeting in May 1930, at a lecture given by André Siegfried, André Spire and the rabbi Maurice Liber may have crossed paths, as the presence of both men was noted by *L'univers israélite*, as well as that of the Zionist Fernand Corcos, and writers Lily Jean-Javal and Jean-Jacques Bernard, son of Tristan Bernard.[48] Henri de Rothschild spoke first, happy that his son presided over the new circle. Then the lecturer defended French assimilation, contrasting it to the situation of Jews in the United States, where, according to him, a "Jewish question" was on the rise, "whereas in France, one perceived only sympathetic motives, elements of fruitful collaboration." The author of the report, Pierre Paraf (1893–1989), one of the pillars of the Ligue Internationale Contre l'Antisémitisme (LICA), founded in 1928, editor-in-chief of *La revue littéraire juive*, which took over from Albert Cohen's *La revue juive* in 1927, was very pleased that André Siegfried had spoken of Judaism "with such perceptiveness, refinement, and loftiness as I might often wish from our fellow Jews." And he had no objections to the father of French political science defending the determinism of ethnic heredity.[49]

André Spire's poetry was even the subject of a talk by René Lalou for the Cercle d'Études Juives in 1932. It is true that at the end of the lecture, Baron James-Henri de Rothschild offered a firm reminder of the position of French Jewish institutions and their hostility toward Zionism, carefully distinguishing Spire the poet from Spire the politician, but nevertheless accepting, unlike Rabbi Liber, the idea of a "Jewish renaissance:"

> Many of us do not share in the least M. André Spire's opinions on the various problems facing Jews today. Some of us are even hostile to them. But we are in agreement about recognizing him as a writer who does credit to Judaism, a forerunner and driving force who has contributed greatly to this Jewish renaissance that we have been witnessing for several years in France. André Spire is a merit to French Judaism, and it is with deference that I offer him this expression of our gratitude and our admiration.[50]

L'univers israélite's review of Crémieux's lecture on "Les juifs dans la littérature française d'aujourd'hui" for the Cercle d'Études Juives in December 1930, under the signature of Lily Jean-Javal (1882–1958), was just as dismissive as ever. This woman of letters was especially known for her children's books, but her adult novels expressed nostalgia for traditional Judaism. *Noémi: Roman d'une jeune fille juive en pays basque* (1925) describes the customs of a small Portuguese Jewish community in the Basque country that the heroine leaves to become a nurse in Paris, and *L'inquiète* (1927) tells of Noémi Valdès's return to her people and her marriage to another Jew, after having been disappointed by the secular world.[51] *La revue juive* gave *Noémi* a fairly positive review in 1925.[52] Marie-Louise Cahen-Hayem wrote about *Noémi* and, less favorably, about *L'Inquiète*, which she found more stereotyped, in the *Archives israélites*.[53] The work illustrates the tension between the Jewish tradition and European modernity, still in the manner of *Chad Gadya!* dualism, which Crémieux, in his lecture for the Cercle d'Études Juives, made precisely the characteristic feature of the contemporary Jewish condition, as represented by literature.

A regular contributor to *L'univers israélite* where she also published poems, Lily Jean-Javal does not seem accurately informed about Proust in her account of Crémieux's talk: "Proust, Jewish by way of his grandmother, devoted numerous pages to the Semite friends of Swann, sympathetic and not sympathetic, experiencing, one after the other, 'the age of the boor and the age of the prophet.' He described Jewish avarice, vanity, and snobbery at the same time as familial solidarity. As for Swann, heir to heavy blood, he suffers from 'the eczema and constipation of the prophets.'"[54] Crémieux must have quoted the page from *Sodome et Gomorrhe II* on Swann's return to his community:

> Perhaps, in any case, in recent days the race had caused the physical type characteristic of it to reappear more pronouncedly in him, at the same time as a sense of moral solidarity with other Jews, a solidarity that Swann seemed to have neglected throughout his life, but which the grafting one on to the other, of a mortal illness, the Dreyfus affair, and anti-Semitic propaganda had reawakened. There are certain Israelites, very shrewd and refined men of the world though they be, in whom a boor and a prophet remain in reserve, or in the wings, so as to make their entrance at a given moment in their lives, as in a play. Swann had arrived at the age of the prophet.[55]

But she criticizes the lecturer, despite his talk being "full of substance, humor, and sometimes a very Jewish (not displeasing) causticity"—a dig at his parsimonious Judaism—for not recognizing "kinship" among the writers whom he discusses, not "acknowledging a special link between their inspirations, their sensibilities," refusing to define Judaism except by the formula, "to be Jewish is to be Jewish," and she concludes disdainfully, taking on the tone of Rabbi Liber against André Spire: "To feel what is Judaism, one must love it. Does M. Benjamin Crémieux love it?"[56]

This is a rhetorical question, beyond a shadow of a doubt, since *L'univers israélite* refused to dissociate Jewish identity from Jewish religion and reproached Benjamin Crémieux, as it did André Spire and the Zionists, for secularizing Judaism. However, unless one speculates on the rabbinical nature of Proust's writing and thinking, as Saurat did, to separate Jewishness from religion, to understand it as a mind, a soul, or a culture, was the necessary condition for judiciously incorporating into it the author of *À la recherche du temps perdu*, as Georges Cattaui did in 1928 and Benjamin Crémieux did in 1929.

And here we have arrived with them, at the end of the 1920s, "the end of the postwar," as Robert Brasillach would say as early as 1931. In what follows we will witness the reversal of general opinion in the 1930s, not only from the perspective of the Catholic reaction against Proust, as in the 1937 book by Henri Massis, *Le drame de Marcel Proust*, gathering together ideas expressed in reviews from the beginning of that decade, but also from the perspective of the Jewish community.

CHAPTER 9

The End of the Postwar Era

The first critic of Jewish origin to express serious reservations, with arguments, on the representation of Jewish characters in *À la recherche du temps perdu* was Siegfried Emanuel van Praag. His long article "Marcel Proust, témoin du judaïsme déjudaïsé," published in three successive issues of *La revue juive de Genève* in May, June, and July 1937, had unexpected and long-lasting repercussions, however indirect. Hannah Arendt's reading of Proust's novel, to which she would soon devote herself, owed very much to it in fact, as did her subsequent depiction of assimilation and her analysis of anti-Semitism in *The Origins of Totalitarianism*, a fundamental work first published in 1951 and still widely read.[1] By what combination of circumstances was Hannah Arendt led to Siegfried van Praag? Who or what served as that link? We will venture a hypothesis further on.

In 1941, a few years after van Praag's study, a work by Chanan Lehrmann, *L'élément juif dans la littérature française*, also published in Switzerland but this time in Zurich, contained a chapter on Proust entitled "À la recherche du Judaïsme perdu." Although this book was republished in Paris in the early 1960s, it had less influence than van Praag's articles did on Proust's fate following World War II, but it tended toward the same conclusions.[2]

"Dejudaized Judaism," for van Praag, "lost Judaism" according to Lehrmann: these titles say it all. They reveal a very different assessment from the somewhat earlier, much more conciliatory views of André Spire, Georges Cattaui, Benjamin Crémieux. We have moved beyond the 1920s, which had witnessed an abatement in the public expression of anti-Semitism, noted by the editor of the *Archives israélites* himself, Émile Cahen, at the time when Lacretelle's novel *Silbermann* was published. The historical moment no longer had anything in common with the mid-1920s, when the question of literary Jewishness prompted the curiosity and the sympathies of the press: "It is the end of the postwar," proclaimed Robert Brasillach in 1931 in *L'action française*, with regard to the novel by Pierre Drieu la Rochelle, *Le feu follet*.[3]

By 1931 political Zionism seems to have lost the fight in France, where institutional Judaism prevailed. On the literary front, counterattacks by *L'univers israélite* multiplied during the 1930s, under the signatures of Judaeus-Maurice Liber or Lily Jean-Javal, who made it their business to refute the thesis of a "Jewish renaissance" defended by Spire and Crémieux, for whom Proust was one of its major figures. The review *Palestine*, inaugurated in 1927, ceased publication in 1931; *Menorah* appeared sporadically in 1931 and stopped appearing for good in 1933; *La revue littéraire juive*, edited by Iehouda Gheler and Pierre Paraf, which had taken over from Albert Cohen's *La Revue juive* in 1927, was discontinued in 1931.

La revue juive de Genève succeeded it beginning in 1932, under the direction of Josué Jéhouda, a Zionist writer of Russian origin . Its first issue opened with an article by André Spire, who returned once more to the Zionism of Israel Zangwill.[4] Another clear sign of continuity: this issue included an article by Ludmila Savitzky, friend of Spire, who reviewed Hans Kohn's book *L'humanisme juif: Quinze essais sur le juif, le monde et Dieu* (Rieder, 1931).[5] Hans Kohn (1891–1971), to whom we will return, was a captivating figure. Born in Prague, raised speaking German, trained in philosophy, mobilized in 1914, taken prisoner in Russia in 1915, not returned to the West until 1920, militant Zionist, he lived in Paris in the early 1920s before emigrating to Palestine in 1925, and then leaving for the United States in 1934, where he would become a university professor and public intellectual, specializing in nationalism.[6] He served briefly as intermediary between the Paris Zionists and the Berlin Zionists, clearly less tolerant of French-style assimilation.

Spire's and Savitzky's participation in the first issue in 1932 must not mislead us, however. *La revue juive de Genève* would be less Parisian than *Menorah*, *La revue juive*, or *Palestine*, and that gap also explains the shift in the perspective on Proust expressed in it. Siegfried van Praag's essay would find its appropriate place there in 1937, at a time when renewed racial anti-Semitism was spreading in Europe, and the reaction against it affected, collaterally, the exegesis of *À la recherche du temps perdu*.

Van Praag and Lehrmann, a Dutch Jew and a central European Jew, would read Proust with a different sensibility, more critical of the French model of emancipation than, for example, André Spire, who, although harsh with Franco-Judaism, was raised under its regime, served as senior French official, and wrote in the French language. Casting aside assimilation even while retaining his attachment to it and remaining its product, Spire is mentioned by Crémieux in an article, also in *La revue juive de Genève* in early 1937: "if I search, beyond the interest displayed by Spire for all the manifestations of Judaism, beyond his need to assert his Jewishness, what is there about him that is specifically Jewish? I admit I remain uncertain." Benjamin Crémieux's article, entitled "La littérature juive française" and repeating certain phrases from his December 1930 talk at the Cercle d'Études Juives, which Lily Jean-Javal had written about in *L'univers israélite*, attests to the evolution of critical expectations, even in a critic as detached from Judaism as Crémieux was, since 1925 and his article "Judaïsme et littérature" in *Les nouvelles littéraires*.[7]

SIEGFRIED VAN PRAAG, 1937

Siegfried Emanuel van Praag (1899–2002), born in Amsterdam, son of a diamond merchant, studied French and Russian at the University of Amsterdam, before becoming a French teacher, novelist, essayist, and journalist. He went into exile in London in 1940, where he worked for the BBC during the war, before returning to the Netherlands, settling in Brussels, publishing a vast opus, living to be over one hundred years old, and always sporting an impressive beard resembling the one that Courbet attributed to the "Assyrian side of (his) head" (figure 25).[8]

Before taking an interest in Proust in the 1930s, van Praag had already conducted research on the presence of Jewish characters in French novels, in Balzac, the Goncourts, Maurice Donnay, and Eugène-Melchior de Vogüé. An article on this subject appeared in 1922 in *Der Jude*, a fine Zionist review founded by Martin Buber and Salman Schocken, published in Berlin and Vienna between 1916 and 1928 and financed by the Zionist Organization, like *Menorah* and *La revue juive*, more politically oriented but equally ambitious in terms of literature.[9] Readers of *Der Jude* had been introduced to Henri Franck and André Spire specifically a few months earlier by Hans Kohn, one of the review's main contributors at the time. He lived in Paris in the early 1920s, as we have said, and he also discussed Albert Cohen in *Der Jude*, citing his *Paroles juives* and his 1923 article in *La revue de Genève* on "Le juif et les romanciers français." He commented on Julien

Figure 25. Siegfried van Praag,
in *Persoonlijkheden in het Koninkrijk
der Nederlanden.*

Photo @ Smoelenboek; N. Japikse, *Persoonlijkheden
in het Koninkrijk der Nederlanden in woord en beeld*,
Huygens Instituut voor Nederlandse Geschiedenis,
http://resources.huygens.knaw.nl/retroboeken
/persoonlijkheden, 1938.

Benda's novel *L'ordination*.[10] And he reviewed *La nuit kurde* by Jean-Richard Bloch
as well.[11]

In 1923, Van Praag had also given *Der Jude* an article on Alexandre Weill.[12] This
prolific friend of Nerval and Heine was trained as a rabbi in Frankfurt, before
turning from romantic socialism to republicanism, then to legitimism, and finally
to prophetism (Robert Dreyfus, we will recall, devoted a monograph to this
"obscure man" in the *Cahiers de la quinzaine* in 1908, and Denis Saurat credited
him with introducing Hugo to the Kabbalah).

In 1926, Van Praag published a book on the Jews in French, German, English,
and Dutch literature since 1860, but without citing Proust a single time, although
the usual Zionist poets, Edmond Fleg, André Spire, Henri Franck, Albert Cohen,
and Georges Cattaui, are well represented.[13] His long study on Proust of 1937 in
La revue juive de Genève is thus without precedent.

CHANAN LEHRMANN, 1941

The author of *L'élément juif dans la littérature française* in 1941, Chanan (also Cuno, Kuno, and Charles) Lehrmann (1905–1977), was born in Strzyżów, in Galicia, a province that was part of Austria-Hungary and then Poland after 1918.[14] He grew up in Stuttgart, where his father was established as a *sofer* (copyist of the Torah) and where his parents raised nine children. He must have been one of the two oldest sons in the family photo from 1922, but which one? The adolescent with the round cheeks or the one looking out from under the oversized hat (figure 26)?

He studied Roman philology at the University of Würzburg and was also trained as a rabbi at the Berlin Rabbinical Seminary. Converging remarkably with van Praag's research, his 1932 doctoral thesis addressed romantic socialism and the Jewish question (the curiosity of young Zionists regarding Romanticism and Alexandre Weill deserves a more in-depth study, including especially a reappraisal of the case of Robert Dreyfus, more invested in Judaism than his apparent indifference would suggest).[15]

By 1933, Lehrmann had left Germany for Switzerland, where he taught French and Jewish literature as a *Privatdozent* at the University of Lausanne (his 1941 book on *L'élément juif dans la littérature française* clearly grew out of his courses) and where he also served as rabbi for the Jewish community of Fribourg.[16]

"MARCEL PROUST, WITNESS OF DEJUDAIZED JUDAISM"

In the second half of the 1930s, van Praag and Lehrmann, from very far removed places and circles but demonstrating similar interests, both reacted in the same

Figure 26. Chanan Lehrmann with his parents, brothers, and sisters, c. 1922.

Photo © Collection particulière / private collection.

way—and differently from Spire, Cattaui, and Crémieux—to the descriptions of Bloch and Rachel in Proust's novel.

Van Praag's three articles in *La revue juive de Genève* in 1937, a total of twenty-five dense pages, form a single veritable essay that considers from all angles the Jewish question in the work and life of Proust. Van Praag is also the first to address the subject using a scholarly approach, because Thibaudet and Crémieux, although trained as academics, contributed to newspapers and reviews as literary critics, offering clear-cut opinions without worrying too much about supporting them. Again, *La Revue juive de Genève* had just published a quick study by Crémieux on "La littérature juive française," as cursory as his sweeping panoramas of the preceding decade: "The pages that Proust devotes to Swann and the Bloch family," Crémieux proposes, "are the most complete ever written on French Jews." But he gives no details and immediately follows with a generalization: "I am struck by the fact that the traits amassed by him are physical traits and character traits tied to ancient, enduring customs, on the way to transformation or extinction."[17] For Crémieux in 1937, Proust was describing a Jewish world in the process of disappearing. He would not have asserted that categorically in 1924 or 1929, but neither does he seem to regret that evolution or condemn it, as van Praag and Lehrmann will do.

Van Praag knew how things stood on the question. He had carefully perused all Proust's work and the secondary bibliography. This confirms—an often repeated observation—that Proust had long been better and more carefully read outside of France, that is to say, in Great Britain, Germany, Italy, or the United States, and thus the Netherlands as well, where the presence of firsthand witnesses and biographical illusions, the Sainte-Beuvian temptation to read a work biographically, weighed less heavily. As early as 1926, Benjamin Crémieux would suggest that "to size up Proust accurately, it is perhaps a great privilege not to have known him," a privilege extended to all those who, not sharing Proust's mother tongue or Parisian culture, are freer from the prejudices that inevitably accompany them.[18]

Van Praag's study rests on two premises, or rather, a single premise and its corollary. First, van Praag's hostility toward assimilation explains his interest in Proust, who as "half-Jewish, was the model of the perfectly assimilated western Jew." Second, "He was the greatest portrayer of assimilation, of that Jewish movement directed against the very existence of the Jewish race." Proust was not only a profoundly French writer, he was also a totally Jewish writer. Van Praag walks a thin line between harsh repudiation of Proust as shameful Jew and intense fascination for the eternal return of Judaism in a traitor, who becomes the best witness of assimilation as downfall. That is why van Praag begins by subjecting Léon Pierre-Quint to public discredit for claiming that Jewishness was not a relevant entry point for reading Proust: "Léon Pierre-Quint is wrong when he declares to us that the only truly Jewish element in the Proustian life and personality was a tenacious will to struggle against the treasons of a diseased body. Perhaps Proust's authorized biographer, Jewish himself, feels some repugnance at confronting the author with Judaism and offers us a preconceived idea that he has borrowed from the Aryans rather that pushing his analysis any further."[19]

In other words, to consider Proust's novel as having nothing to do with Judaism was supposedly an idea held by goyim or apostate Jews. Van Praag refused to reduce Proust's Jewishness to Swann's proverbial resilience, a commonplace or sentimental tendency shared by all Proust critics until then.

Inventorying the Jewish characters in the novel, van Praag proposes anti-Semitism as the explanation for certain character traits that Proust gives his creations, for example, the father of Albert Bloch: "One could even speak here of an anti-Semitic caricature, because the author especially brings out his avarice." The phrasing remains cautious nevertheless, and avoids placing responsibility on the author for this appearance: "One could even speak," if one absolutely insisted on attributing an intention to the writer. Van Praag does not say that the portrait of Bloch's father is anti-Semitic on account of its author, but that some could characterize it as such, since the reader can interpret it that way. His care is even more obvious in the case of Rachel, whose success on stage is a matter of fashion, not of talent: "I do not believe that Proust reflected on the danger of too hasty conclusions. Nevertheless, to characterize the career of a Jewish actress in terms of her undeserved fame constitutes a danger that modern anti-Semitism shamelessly hastens to exploit."[20] Thus Proust might not have been well advised, he might not have assessed the use to which his descriptions of Jewish characters could be put, and he might have inadvertently armed the anti-Semites.

But van Praag identifies especially in Proust, whether intended or not, his own distrust of assimilation: "when Proust imagines assimilation as a social phenomenon, this author who plumbs the Jewish soul, believes that such a tendency must inevitably lead to the decline of the race." The comparison between homosexuals and Jews made in *Sodome et Gomorrhe I* deeply shocks van Praag, who calls it "infinitely painful and startling": "That comparison, the darkest one ever drawn with regard to western Judaism, proves that Proust observed the morbid symptoms of the Franco-Jewish circles of his time. That ineluctable fatality of assimilation Proust saw as a situation with no way out."[21] There could be no stronger terms for designating assimilation as the mortal disease of Judaism, "ineluctable fatality," and Hannah Arendt would break no new ground on this front.

Van Praag, who had read Cattaui, Spire, Thibaudet, and Saurat, did not completely reject either the parallel with Montaigne or the reference to the Talmud, but he remained circumspect about the stylistic significance of such comparisons:

> The nearly casuistic discussions of all imaginable psychological possibilities that could have produced an event are his *sine qua non*. That is why Proust's "talmudism" is evoked to explain his curious sentences overloaded with considerations: the commentary by which he comments on his commentary. The Jewish liturgy is also distinguished by its desire to try to say everything, by the obsessive fear of not being absolutely complete. That same *frénésie d'intégrité* is a characteristic of Proust's work.[22]

But van Praag does not attribute this "frenzy for integrity" to Proust's Jewish culture, because he is well aware that Proust was never interested in "postbiblical Judaism," as he says, and he offers for proof the letter in which Proust thanked Robert Dreyfus for his 1908 book on Alexandre Weill. Prior to van Praag himself and Lehrmann, this childhood friend of Proust was, in fact, the first to deem this "obscure man" worthy of a monograph, less than ten years after his death.[23] Now Proust's indifference to Dreyfus's book surprised and disappointed van Praag: "Proust as much as says this: 'How can one write on a subject so disagreeable and so insignificant,' whereas this Weill, from the historical and psychological perspective, was so interesting a man!"[24]

Proust could not understand how Robert Dreyfus could devote a whole book (a long article, actually) to such a mediocre figure. Worried about upsetting his friend, he compared Dreyfus's assiduousness to his own devotion to John Ruskin, hardly less minor a writer, he conceded, before concluding, "But just the same, this Alexandre Weill!" Proust does not seem to have been amused by the warning that Alexandre Weill includes in his books (and that was noted by Dreyfus): "From the author at 11 Faubourg Saint-Honoré," adding fussily, "Do not confuse my name with the one of my wealthy homonym, 45 Rue de Courcelles."[25] By chance, this was Proust's very address from 1900 to 1907, the address where Adrien and Jeanne Proust had died, but also, a few years earlier, it had been the address of Alexandre Weill, a partner with the Lazard bank, whose son, David Weill (1871–1952), would also become a banker and who, again, was a student with Proust at the Condorcet lycée and Science Politiques (he married Flora Raphaël in 1897, daughter of the banker Edward Raphaël and Laetitia Dreyfus, who was herself the daughter of Mardochée Sourdis, the banker with whom Adolphe Dreyfus, Robert's father, did business at the end of the Second Empire and who also did business with his future son-in-law: at the banks Lazard, Raphaël-Berend, Sourdis, Bischoffheim-Goldschmidt, and Dreyfus-Scheyer, there was much speculating around 1870; some banks were successful, others failed).[26] All the same, Proust was not as close to the young David Weill, even if they appear together in a photo of their philosophy class, as he was to his cousin Jean Lazard (1871–1950), who visited him in Fontainebleau in 1896 and who comes up often in Proust's correspondence with his mother.[27]

But Proust may not have read the footnote in which Robert Dreyfus mentioned 45 Rue de Courcelles. In any case, he stops denigrating his friend's book and returns to his usual kindness: "I will reread it, I hope that I will understand the man and why you are so inclined toward him. Until then I remain unmoved."[28]

For van Praag, Proust's indifference to Alexandre Weill, and thus to the Jewish tradition, to "post-biblical Judaism," which included the Talmud and the Zohar, was far from insignificant. It meant that Proust did not owe his "frenzy for integrity," "his desire to try to say everything" to his reading and his Jewish culture: "Proust must have found this style in the depths of his soul, because it is not the product of his refined, literary education."[29] In the final analysis, although formulated as a hypothetical, this proposition reintroduces into van Praag's study the idea of an ethnic determinism shaping Proust's style.

Thus, like his predecessors from the 1920s, and even though he questions them, van Praag invests Proust's life and work with his own conceptions of Jewish identity and assimilation as the eradication of that identity. No one had described better than Proust the demise of Judaism through assimilation. That is why van Praag could conclude his study by acknowledging Proust's genius, equal to that of a prophet of Israel: "Proust was a Jew, a melancholic, disillusioned Jew, perhaps like Qoheleth, long ago king of Jerusalem."[30] So, *À la recherche du temps perdu* is the modern Ecclesiastes.

"À LA RECHERCHE DU JUDAÏSME PERDU"

In a work covering the whole history of French literature, Lehrmann inevitably passes more quickly over Proust, but he owes much to van Praag and uses the same words to express himself in a chapter with the emblematic title "À la recherche du judaïsme perdu." Thus he declares that "even while recognizing that assimilation involves humiliation, Proust considers the complete disappearance of Jews into their surroundings to be an ineluctable fatality."[31] The recurrence of the words "ineluctable fatality," already used by van Praag to characterize assimilation, attests to their shared thinking (and to the fact that Lehrmann had, of course, read van Praag).

That would not keep Lehrmann from also quoting the favorite line of Parisian Zionists in the 1920s on Swann's endurance and on his embrace of Israel at the end of his life, with the help of his illness and the Dreyfus affair, a declaration that Lehrmann is sure provides cover for Proust himself to take pride in his own membership in "that strong Jewish race." Lehrmann reproduces Proust's expression and comments on it without the least qualm in 1941: "He proclaims the purity of the Jewish race, which he compares to that of the native French," but that last sentence would be deleted from the second edition of the book in 1961, with the word "race" only appearing in the quote, between quotation marks and attributed to Proust, and not in the rephrasing by Lehrmann. And then this son of a *sofer*, a rabbi himself who, unlike most French Proust proponents in the 1920s, knew what he was talking about regarding talmudic matters, repeated the familiar comparison between the talmudic and Proustian style: "Like a biblical verse in the Talmud, the basic idea is accompanied by commentaries and super-commentaries" before a "luminous truth" appears to the reader wandering in that "inextricable labyrinth." This style, according to Lehrmann, was not something Proust had found in books, but in his soul, "steeped in the tribe of his mother."[32] Van Praag had said the same thing.

If Lehrmann displays no fondness for the society, Jewish or non-Jewish, whose decadence Proust describes like a biblical prophet, a "modern Jeremiah," he nevertheless concludes by evoking Bergson, Freud, and Einstein, and by noting that these "four men of Jewish blood," had transformed our conception of the world.[33] On this point he also follows van Praag very closely, who had already proposed: "It is curious to note nonetheless that four men of Jewish blood have contributed to the conception of a dynamic world: Einstein, Bergson, Freud, and Proust, a world whose relativity is one of its great characteristics."[34]

When Lehrmann updated his book for the second edition in 1961, that tribute to Proust in the company of Bergson, Freud, and Einstein disappeared, along with the words "Jewish blood," which van Praag had used previously to designate what connected them, and the conclusion of the chapter on Proust became less generous. Lehrmann now noted the comparison in *Sodome et Gomorrhe I* between the "inconsiderateness" of the Zionists "who declare they want to live as Jews" and that of homosexuals "who acknowledge their abnormality and cynically put it on display" as if Jewish origin was a "social defect more unpardonable than any other sin."[35] Twenty years later, the "philosophy of mimetism" adopted by Proust, forcing him to "go unnoticed," to conceal his "homosexual tendencies," like his "Jewish conscience," was now interpreted as self "shame."

The author, the chief rabbi of Luxembourg from 1950 to 1958, was then teaching in Israel at Bar-Ilan University, an institution recently created by religious Jews, where the foreword for the 1961 edition of his book was written.[36] A few chapters extend the presence of "the Jewish element in French literature" to Max Jacob, dead at Drancy, and Albert Cohen, although Lehrmann regrets that Cohen did not follow up on *Solal* and *Mangeclous*, published in 1930 and 1938 (*Belle du seigneur* would not be published until 1968). But three writers of the French language had "created monuments to the memory of their Jewish mothers": Proust, Romain Gary with *La promesse de l'aube* (1960), which had just appeared, and Cohen in *Le livre de ma mère* (1954). Lehrmann gives a long and beautiful quotation, without commentary, from Cohen's homage to his mother, and then, despite the academic nature of the work, he allows himself a personal digression in which he evokes the image of his own mother, "deported and dead somewhere in Poland," far from her children, "but united until the final martyrdom, to her husband, "pious and venerable scholar."[37] That was why the conclusion of the chapter on Proust had to be modified after the war, and Lehrmann's admiration toned down, even though the monument that Proust erected to his mother redeemed him in Lehrmann's eyes.

Rabbi for the West Berlin Jewish community from 1960 to 1971, honorary professor beginning in 1967 at the University of Würzburg, where he had studied Romance languages, Lehrmann eventually retired to Stuttgart, where he had spent his childhood.

Figure 27. *Stolpersteine*, in memory of Blume and Chaim Lehrman, Christophstrasse 41, Stuttgart.
Photo © Wikimedia Commons / DR.

Two *Stolpersteine*, those memorial "stumbling stones" or paving stones, created by the artist Gunter Demnig to honor the victims of Nazism, are embedded in front of the family home of the Lerhmanns on Christophstrasse in Stuttgart (figure 27). They memorialize the deportation of Chanan Lehrmann's father and mother in 1938 and their extermination in 1942.[38]

ROBERT DREYFUS, 1937

When Siegfried van Praag published his challenge to the circles of shameful Jews that Proust had frequented in his life and described in his work, it did not go unnoticed in Paris, where some of Proust's friends reacted. Following the publication of van Praag's first article in May 1937, Robert Dreyfus sent a letter to *La revue juive de Genève* that was published in the next issue, in June 1937, when the second part of van Praag's study also appeared. Dreyfus protested the way in which the Amsterdam critic depicted Proust's world, in particular the salons of Madame Straus and Madame de Caillavet, both of Jewish origin, where Proust, van Praag claimed, "must have encountered a number of Jews who still belonged, just barely or begrudgingly, to the Jewish race, the last deserters of French Judaism whom Proust could distinguish perfectly."[39]

The characterization of "the last deserters of French Judaism" clearly wounded Robert Dreyfus, who did not recognize the 1890s he had known in this caricature dating from the end of the 1930s: "How bizarre and distorting this reflection of a world I knew so well seems to me today!" Robert Dreyfus had just recounted his own memories of Madame Straus's salon in *La revue de Paris* in an introduction for Proust's letters to Madame Straus.[40] Thus he set about to defend the memory of his friends and those they welcomed to their salons:

> it is my duty to add nuance here as best I can to the portrait of those bygone times, and to assert that their salons never served as training grounds for a few Jews anxious to have their origins forgotten. The many "assimilated" Jews of that era (I could draw up a long list of them) proudly accepted a weighty heritage of opprobrium and resistance; they were not in the least shameful "deserters" of their birth, eager to conceal themselves. When could that have been better confirmed than at the time of the Dreyfus Affair, that touchstone of the diversity of human temperaments?[41]

Here lies the eternal conflict between historian and witness, which does not resurface in the chronicle created by subsequent generations based on documents and logical reasoning, not on feelings and memories. But this call to order provides an opportunity to retouch the portrait of Robert Dreyfus sketched earlier, in particular his apparent indifference to his own Jewishness, at least until then. By putting quotation marks around "assimilated," he seems to suggest in 1937 that assimilation, beginning with his own, must never be taken literally, that it is never a fait accompli but rather an idea. Nothing made this more obvious than the Dreyfus affair (although he himself only ever called it the affair, as though to distance it ever so slightly from his own patronymic).

Moreover, was Robert Dreyfus not among the first to point out, well before van Praag, the risks that Proust took by playing with his readers' anti-Semitism? In an 1892 article in *Le Banquet*, a review published by a group of young former Condorcet lycée graduates, including Daniel Halévy, Jacques Bizet, Fernand Gregh, and Proust, Proust mentioned, citing Théodore Reinach, the excessive luxury of Jewish women's clothing in Lyon in the thirteenth century and the repression that followed. That prompted a clarification by Dreyfus in this *Souvenirs sur*

Marcel Proust in 1926: "even though he himself was not the least anti-Semitic, as his conduct at the time of the Affair proved, Marcel Proust offers, through this pointed—if still witty and light—remark, evidence of the anti-Semitism of the salons, which would resurface later with much less sweetness and charm in certain passages of his books."[42]

That reflection comes retrospectively: Dreyfus made it after the fact, in his *Souvenirs*, not at the time, in 1892, but it proves that in 1926 he was already aware of the misunderstandings that "certain passages" of *À la recherche du temps perdu* could create, passages in which he does not seem, or no longer seems, to find "charm."

In 1936, in his memories of Madame Straus for *La revue de Paris*, he proves to be clear-sighted about the mounting anti-Semitism since the time of his friend's death ten years earlier: "sometimes I think that it is a good thing for her and her husband, as for many others, to be dead, because they had already suffered too much from a France ravaged by discord."[43] Robert Dreyfus died in June 1939, between the Munich agreement and the "phony war," leaving this world at a good moment. With the Dreyfus affair proof in hand, he intended, in any case, to contradict van Praag and affirm that the so-called assimilated Jews were never "deserters." That indicates to us how he perceived himself. Did his debate with van Praag lead him to mend his ways, that is, to "deassimilate" in the way of Swann under the effects of illness and the Dreyfus affair? I discovered a single variant in his memories on Madame Straus. Where, in *La revue de Paris* in 1936, he mentions without specifying Madame Straus's "origins" with regard to her attitude toward the Dreyfus affair, he speaks openly of her "Jewish origins" in his book in 1939. But to what feeling should we attribute his initial precaution? To his refined discretion? Or else to a premonition about the narrow-mindedness of readers of *La revue de Paris*? In any case, the variant does not seem insignificant and such discretion was no longer suitable in 1939. Dreyfus knew very well that it was no time to remain silent about "Jewish origins."

DANIEL HALÉVY, 1937, RACHEL BESPALOFF, 1938

It is a striking coincidence that the next issue of *La Revue juive de Genève*, in July 1937, contained not only the third and last installment of van Praag's study, but also, as though to verify its thesis, a letter from another Condorcet lycée friend with whom Proust had never lost contact, Daniel Halévy. Halévy wrote to Josué Jéhouda, the review's editor, to explain to him why he refused to contribute to his publication:

> unlike many of my fellow Jews in this way, first of all, I bear my name, and secondly, I am not Jewish. For to be Jewish requires first of all that from the person of my father I remove the person of his mother, a long-standing Catholic, to whom he owed practically everything, and to whom I owe much. Then it requires that I remove from my person the person of my mother, a long-standing Christian. I do not need to tell you that these operations are unthinkable. I know what I owe to my name and what I owe to my family.[44]

With a Protestant mother and a Catholic grandmother, Daniel Halévy claimed that there was nothing Jewish about him and that his grandfather Léon Halévy transmitted to him only his name, a bit like the prince of Guermantes, an anti-Semite friend of Swann, who tells himself stories to justify his friendship in his own eyes: "knowing that Swann's grandmother, a Protestant married to a Jew, had been the mistress of the Duc de Berry, he tried, from time to time, to believe in the legend that had it that Swann's father was an illegitimate son of the Prince. On this hypothesis, which was, however, false, Swann, the son of a Catholic, who had himself been the son of a Bourbon and a Catholic woman, was Christian through and through."[45] Even if Proust mixes up the religions, the genealogy resembles Halévy's.

Halévy continues his letter to Jéhouda by relating a scene that he had witnessed at about the age of ten, around 1882, at the time of the first republican—that is to say, anticlerical—laws. From this scene that pits his father, Ludovic Halévy, against the editor Calmann Lévy, he had drawn, he announced, a lesson to which he had remained faithful for his entire life. That day, voices rose between Ludovic Halévy, who became uncharacteristically "vehement," given his usual good manners, and his editor and friend. "The Jews," Halévy's father said, "have been generously welcomed in France, France has made them French. They should not do anything about France's anticlerical policy. If they do, they will be wrong and they will come to regret it."[46] Recommending that Jews be discreet, Ludovic Halévy marked "the limits that Jewish activity must observe" in French society, especially in its relations with the dominant religion. That was the very attitude that André Spire condemned, we will recall, among that "Jewish bourgeoisie, who consider themselves an elite because they have succeeded in making a niche for themselves in the French bourgeoisie." The friendship between Spire and Daniel Halévy was no less intense for this, just as Spire remained friends with Robert Dreyfus.[47] The ties they had established with the Dreyfus Affair, the *Cahiers de la quinzaine*, and the Universités Populaires allowed them to overcome their differences facing the rise of Nazi racism. But the letters from Dreyfus and Halévy in *La Revue juive de Genève* in June and July 1937 underscored their conflict regarding the solidarity that should be demonstrated, at that crucial time, with the Jewish community.

One year later, in June 1938 and following Hitler's "annexation of Austria" in March, *La revue juive de Genève* published a long, indignant response to Halévy's advice to Jews to practice restraint, summarized in this way: "Do not interfere in our quarrels, you tell us in substance. France has generously welcomed you: do not abuse that, or you could regret it. Respect the limits that your condition of ethnic minority imposes on your activity. In the guise of discretion, the threat is clear."[48] Halévy replied briefly that his contribution was in no way a threat and only "a bit of advice, inspired by moral considerations."[49]

The author of that letter knew Halévy very well: it was Rachel Bespaloff (1895–1949) (figure 28), a remarkable figure, like the handful of women encountered over the course of this inquiry, Ludmila Savitzky, Marie-Louise Cahen-Hayem, and of course Hannah Arendt, although this is not the time for a lengthy account of her accomplishments.[50]

Born into a family of Zionist intellectuals originally from Ukraine, raised in Geneva, a musician, Rachel Bespaloff had introduced herself to Halévy in 1933 precisely through a letter: her "Lettre sur Heidegger à M. Daniel Halévy," published in the *Revue philosophique*, was one of the first introductions in France to Heidegger's philosophy.[51] With ties to Lev Shestov, and friends with Jean Wahl, she was the author of articles on Søren Kierkegaard (to whom she briefly compares Proust with regard to romantic love as dupery),[52] Gabriel Marcel, Julien Green, André Malraux, and finally Albert Camus's *La Peste*, published posthumously.[53] Exiled to the United States in 1942, teaching at Mount Holyoke College in Massachusetts, she committed suicide in 1949. Her work is primarily scattered throughout letters.[54] But her major book remains her reading of Homer during the war, *De l'Iliade*, published in New York in French in 1943, and in English in 1947, this time with an introduction by Hermann Broch.[55] This text is often compared to the reflective piece by contemporary Simone Weil, who also had ties to Jean Wahl, "L'Iliade ou le poème de la force," published in the *Cahiers du Sud*

Figure 28. Rachel Bespaloff.
Photo © Éditions Allia.

under the pseudonym of Émile Novis.[56] Broch's introduction to *On the Iliad*, entitled "The Style of the Mythical Age," is a major text on the "style of old age" (the
old age of a creator and the old age of an epoch), which Broch defines as "violent
stylistic rupture" with the literary convention giving access to myth. For Broch,
in the aftermath of World War II, this "style of old age," exemplified in Kafka,
makes it possible to transcend literature and to save it, following and despite the
Shoah.[57]

At the time of her death, Rachel Bespaloff was working on a book that might
have included a chapter on Proust.[58] Everything we know about her is cause for
regret. Hannah Arendt, who met her during a stay in Paris between 1933 and 1940
and who saw her again in the United States after 1942, shared her interest in
Kierkegaard and, of course, in Heidegger, and she admired her work. Mary McCarthy would recall a dinner in New York held by Jacques Schiffrin in 1947, with
Hannah Arendt, Hermann Broch, and Rachel Bespaloff.[59]

When Arendt started her research on anti-Semitism, it stands to reason that
it was Rachel Bespaloff who directed her toward Siegfried van Praag's articles on

Proust in *La revue juive de Genève*, articles on which Arendt would so heavily rely. Thus Arendt could not have been unaware of the perspectives of Proust's friends on their Jewishness, expressed in the same issue of the journal: Daniel Halévy, whom Bespaloff put in his place in 1938, and Robert Dreyfus, who defended Geneviève Straus against van Praag in a kind of "Apology for our Past," or "Our Youth." But the fight was already lost and van Praag's thesis prevailed. Adopting his position, Hannah Arendt would pay no attention to Robert Dreyfus's response.

We no longer have Siegfried van Praag's restraint, which at least grants Proust the benefit of the doubt. Ours is a retrospective illusion, a very understandable form of prediction of the past, consisting for us in the twenty-first century of denouncing an anti-Semitic Proust or a Judeophobic narrator, applying criteria unfamiliar to readers in the 1920s, first and foremost the Zionist activists. Quite the contrary, André Spire used Proust's work expressly to illustrate the lure and even the trap of assimilation, and van Praag, basically, did likewise, if more bluntly. In the early 1950s, following the Shoah that cut history in two, the meaning of words was transformed, after which Jean-Paul Sartre defined Jewishness through anti-Semitism (his thoughts on the "authentic" Jew who chooses freely, like the Zionist or the Resistance fighter, made less of an impression). Jean Cocteau, through his envious and spiteful rereading of *À la recherche du temps perdu*, was undoubtedly one of the first to express himself in these terms: "Proust, who had a thousand reasons not to be anti-Semitic, manages to give the impression of being one in his book," he noted in his *Journal* at the time.[60] But this was still only an "impression"; soon it would be the thing itself.

Bloch would become an anti-Semitic caricature, worthy of Edouard Drumont, first for American critics, and then for French critics.[61] His presentation in the novel would be interpreted as the result of a maneuver by Proust to deny his own Jewishness, at best as "a precautionary, self-protective anti-Semitism," on the model of Bloch on holiday at Balbec and complaining about the overrepresentation of Jews:[62]

One day, as I sat with him on the sands, we heard a voice from a nearby tent bemoaning the dense infestation of Jews that one had to put up with in Balbec: "You can't walk ten yards without stepping on one! Not that I'm a dyed-in-the-wool enemy of the chosen people, but hereabouts there's a glut of them. One's surrounded by people saying, 'I say, Apraham, I've chust seen Chacob.' One might as well be on the rue d'Aboukir." Eventually, the man who found Jews so distasteful stepped out of the tent, and we glanced up to look at the anti-Semite: it was my old school friend Bloch.[63]

Hence, the thesis of preventative anti-Semitism in the manner of Bloch, conforming to Proust's flattery in his correspondence with recognized anti-Semites or his obsequiousness in salons, would prevail over the one of Swann's final turn against assimilation and his admirable resilience, in keeping with Proust's Jewish "loyalism." Defended by André Spire and Georges Cattaui at the time of Proust's death, and then by most of their successors in the 1920s, including Marie-Louise Cahen-Hayem and Robert Dreyfus, that earlier thesis found fewer defenders beginning in the 1930s, and it is still struggling to win them back.

CHAPTER 10

The Baruch Tomb

The question of Proust's Jewishness intrigued and even captivated his young Zionist readers in the 1920s, contributors to *Menorah*, *La revue juive*, and *Palestine*, as well as some Jewish and non-Jewish allies, and at least one "*Action française* Jew." All of them, within or without the Jewish community, invested *À la recherche du temps perdu* with their own conceptions of Judaism or Jewishness. They read the novel and perceived its Jewish characters, Swann, the Bloch family, Rachel, through the lens of their own positions on the emancipation and assimilation of Jews in France. Despite the writer's *ultima verba*, giving the impression that the meaning of ancestral customs could have been lost in the Weil family as early as the generation of Proust's grandfather, Nathé Weil (figure 29), the most committed of them put all the emphasis on the return of Swann—apparently as perfectly assimilated as his creator—to the Jewish people when under threat during the Dreyfus affair, and they insisted on his admirable endurance in the face of illness: "Swann belonged to that strong Jewish race, in whose vital energy and resistance to death its individuals themselves seem to share," according to the phrase that everyone liked to quote as a definitive truth, from Georges Cattaui and André Spire to Siegfried van Praag and Chanan Lehrmann.[1]

122.037

What could Proust really have meant in recalling his visits to the Jewish section of Rue du Repos with his grandfather? When he was a child (figure 30) it was enclosed by walls; he would return there as an adult, after the walls had come

Figure 29. Nathé Weil, Braun & Cie, c. 1865.
Photo © Sotheby's, Paris, 31 May 2016, lot 116.

Figure 30. Robert and Marcel Proust,
Hermann & Cie, c. 1882.
Photo © Photo12 / Heritage Images /
Fine Art Images.

down, since his grandparents were buried in the Baruch Weil family vault, his grandmother Adèle in January 1890 and his grandfather Nathé Weil in June 1896, his great-uncle Louis Weil also in 1896, then his aunt Frédérique, widow of his great-uncle Godchaux Weil, in 1897. On the death of Louis Weil in May 1896, Proust informed Laure Hayman, who had been his great-uncle's mistress: "In his religion, there is no service. People gather this afternoon at 3:30 at his home, 102 Boulevard Haussmann, and go from there to Père La Chaise [*sic*]."[2] This "people" included her, apparently. Proust's ill health kept him from attending the burial of his uncle Georges Weil in August 1906, however, in another plot in the seventh division.[3]

It took me a long time to locate this Baruch Weil family vault in the old Jewish section of Père-Lachaise (figure 31). I made a first unsuccessful visit many years ago, and then, as soon as confinement ended and we were free once again to move about Paris and visit cemeteries, I made a second expedition with my brother in June 2020. Discovering the Weil burial place among so many abandoned, moss-covered, broken tombs, where the names were no longer legible—that seemed a

Figure 31. Family tomb of Baruch Weil, Père-Lachaise Cemetery; behind it, David Sintzheim's tomb.

Photo © Collection particulière / private collection.

worthy challenge. It would have been humiliating to come up with nothing and to have to make do with an image of another tomb in the seventh division. We were almost ready to give up, however, when, wandering about the corner of the Worms de Romilly, among the tombs of a few great Jewish families of the early nineteenth century, we spotted the Weil sepulture, solid, even monumental, with an imposing obelisk on top, rather well preserved, and very moving. In *Les plaisirs et les jours*, Proust wrote that in cemeteries "the tombs disappear under inscriptions and ornaments in bad taste."[4] That was not the case here. Attesting to the social success of Baruch Weil and his kin, the Baruch Weil tomb has its place there no less than the tomb of Théodore Cerf Berr, son of Cerf Berr (or Beer) de Medelsheim, the family vaults of Salomon Dalsace, David Singer, Beer Léon Fould, and the most visited tomb in the division (with that of Rachel), always strewn with stones: that of the president of the Grand Sanhédrin in 1807 and first chief rabbi of France, David Sintzheim (1745–1812), buried in the Jewish section when it had just opened adjacent to the Paris cemetery.

According to the inscriptions engraved in the stone, beside Baruch Weil and his second wife, Marguerite Nathan, lie many of his children and their wives: Godchaux Weil (oldest son of Baruch Weil's first wife, Hélène Shoubach) and his wife, née Frédérique Zunz; Nathé Weil and his wife, née Adèle Berncastell; Louis Weil and his wife, née Émilie Oppenheim; Adèle Weil, widow of Joseph Lazarus, and her son Paul Lazarus; Alphonse Weil; Maurice Cohen, oldest son of Merline Weil and Benoist Cohen.[5] The names are worn, but most are still legible, and nothing seems to have been written there in Hebrew.

The cemetery archives provided some specific details. When Marguerite Nathan was buried on 1 May 1854, the Baruch Weil vault, initially designated as plot 323 in 1828, received its permanent number, 122.037 in the cemetery's general numbering system.[6] In the margin of the Père-Lachaise daily registry, on the page for 1 May 1854 and on the line 122.037, ten subsequent burials in the tomb of Baruch and his second wife were registered as they took place (figure 32).

3   No. 340935: that is no. 1964 of 3 February 1871, Émilie Oppenheim wife Weil;

4   No. 340936: that is no. 1965 of 3 February 1871, Paul Laruras (for Lazarus).[7]

Émilie Oppenheim, wife of Louis Weil, died on 22 November 1870 at the age of forty-nine in their home at 29 Rue Bleue, and the death was registered by Nathé

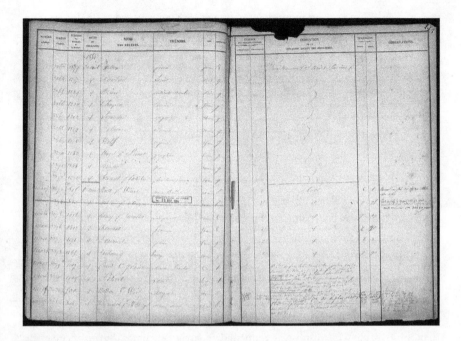

Figure 32. Daily registry of burials, Père-Lachaise Cemetery, 1 May 1854.
Photo © Archives de Paris, Service central des cimetières de Paris.

Weil, her brother-in-law, at the Ninth Arrondissement town hall. Paul Lazarus, son of Adèle Weil, died three weeks later, on 16 December 1870, at just twenty-three years old, at 8 Rue d'Enghien, and that death was also registered by Nathé Weil, his uncle, this time at the Tenth Arrondissement town hall. The Weils lived as neighbors: between Rue d'Enghien, Rue Bleue, and 40a Rue du Faubourg-Poissonnière, there were only about five hundred meters (Flora, the youngest sister of Nathé, died at Rue de l'Échiquier in 1867, five minutes away from 40a). The burials of Émilie Oppenheim and Paul Lazarus at Père-Lachaise could not take place until the end of the Siege of Paris by the Prussian army in the last days of January 1871.

We do not know the cause of these deaths, but there was an unusually high mortality rate in Paris during this "period of investing," as Maxime Du Camp called the months beginning with the first Prussian siege, through the Commune, and until the second siege of Versailles: "Paris went through a period of suffering and destitution that raised the level of mortality to extraordinarily grievous numbers."[8] Almost 13,000 deaths in December 1870 and more than 19,000 in January 1871, as opposed to about 4,000 over the course of a normal month; almost

75,000 deaths in 1870 and more than 85,000 in 1871, as opposed to 45,000 in 1869 and again in 1872.

Nor do we know what was done with the bodies between mid-December and early February. In the first days of September 1870, in anticipation of the siege, it was decided that bodies from the Ninth Arrondissement would go to the Montmartre cemetery, while those from the Tenth Arrondissement would go to the small, walled Belleville cemetery, hastily reopened.[9] But in late December 1870 and January 1871 the bombarding of the capital completely disrupted mortuaries, and "burials were haphazard," recalled Du Camp.[10] In the "Observations" column of the Père-Lachaise burial registry, on the line for Émilie Oppenheim, these words appear: "Israelite from the Cimetière du Nord," that is, Montmartre, a note repeated in the following line for Paul Lazarus. To the funerary worries of Nathé Weil during those terrible months were added the pregnancy of his daughter Jeanne, at the height of the "period of investing" in Paris, and the fate of his brother Alphonse, a prisoner of war following the siege of Strasbourg from August to September 1870. It was in the midst of major historical events, during a brief lull, that the Baruch Weil tomb was reopened in early February 1871 to receive the remains of the sister-in-law and the nephew of Nathé Weil.

The burials subsequently recorded in the margins of no. 122.037 were less remarkable:

5   No. 3731, June 1878: that is Godchaux Weil (Wiel in the register);[11]

6   No. 1313, December 1883: that is Maurice Cohen;[12]

7   No. 1628, December 1886: that is Abraham Alphonse Weil;[13]

8   No. 4768, January 1890: that is Adèle Berncastell wife Weil;[14]

9   No. 5324, June 1892: that is Adélaïde Weil widow Lazarus;[15]

10   No. 2282, May 1896: that is Lazard Weil;[16]

11   No. 2940, July 1896: that is Nathé Weil;[17]

12   No. 825, January 1897: that is Frédérique Zunz widow Weil.[18]

There is one curiosity of note: the same Alexandre Nerson registered the deaths of Lazard (Louis) and of Nathé Weil in 1896 in the Eighth and Tenth Arrondissements; this was many decades after his signature had appeared at the bottom of the death certificates for their sisters, Flora Weil Alcan in 1867 and Merline Weil Cohen in 1873, in the Tenth and Ninth Arrondissements, as well as the death certificate of Zélie Cerfberr, widow of Cerf Weil, the brother of Baruch

Weil, in 1874.[19] Listed as employee, he lived on Rue Notre-Dame-de-Nazareth in 1867, 1873, and 1874, then on Rue Notre-Dame-de-Lorette in 1896. As another indication of the close family ties among the Weils, for funerals they used the same Jewish funeral home, which was in charge of all the arrangements: "immediate dispatch of mourners of both sexes to keep vigil," purifications, funeral garb, tallith, funeral and burial, funeral processions, and carriages, including the registration of the death at the consistory and the town hall. Many funeral-home owners, like A. Cahen, 32 Rue Saint-Georges, across from the consistory, or Samuel Schnee-berg, and then his son Éduoard, Rue de la Victoire, across from the synagogue, advertised in the Jewish community newspapers (see figure 4). For many decades Alexandre Nerson worked as "adjuster," the "funeral consultant" of that time, for one of those enterprises, very likely Schneeberg, to whom the Weil family subse-quently remained faithful.[20] When Georges Weil died on 23 August 1906, Édouard Schneeberg, merchant, came in person to sign the death certificate (as director of the agency, he was also a lawyer), accompanied by a certain Maurice Weill, employee, who had already registered the death of Frédérique Zunz in 1897.[21] Thus the rites of Jewish law were still observed for Louis and for Nathé following their deaths.

Four Weil brothers (Godchaux, Alphonse, Louis, and Nathé), one sister (Adé-laïde), and three sisters-in-law (Émilie, Adèle, and Frédérique) were buried in the Baruch tomb. In addition to those of his grandparents and his uncle Louis, Proust could have attended some of those burials.

The following generation is represented by two nephews of Nathé, cousins of Georges and Jeanne Weil: these are Paul Lazarus and Maurice Cohen. The first was an employee when he died at a very young age during the Siege of Paris. The second was the oldest son of Merline Weil, the oldest of the Weil siblings. Mer-line Weil is also buried in the Jewish section of Père-Lachaise, not far away, with her husband Benoist Cohen. Maurice Cohen (1826–1883), an 1843 graduate of the École Polytechnique, chief engineer for the Ponts et Chaussées, knight in the Legion of Honor, bachelor, died on 3 November 1883 in Cahors, where he was director of the navigation service of Lot.[22] According to *La Dépêche*, he was a "solid and sincere republican" but a "difficult character," "frank and blunt," "very free-spoken," and above all, a scholar, "a true erudite," and a bibliophile.[23] He pub-lished pamphlets on literary history under the anagrammatic pseudonym of E. Marnicouche, as well as articles in scholarly reviews like *Le moniteur du biblio-phile* or *Le Moliériste*, for which Gustave Larroumet, Marivaux specialist and future

Sorbonne professor, wrote his obituary.[24] His precious library, with three thousand volumes, was sold to the Hôtel Drouot auction house in April 1884.[25]

Maurice Cohen's presence in the Baruch Weil tomb, rather than with his parents, intrigued me and led to an extension of my inquiry. A thirteenth body was actually buried in the Baruch tomb, although it was not noted in the margin of line 122.037, 1 May 1854. Maurice Cohen had a younger brother, also a bachelor and equally original. Léonce Cohen (1829–1901), the second son of Benoist Cohen and Merline Weil, just as precocious as his older brother, entered the Conservatoire de Paris at the age of thirteen. Violinist and violist at the Théatre-Italien, he won the Prix de Rome in composition in 1852, outmatching Saint-Saëns. Following in the footsteps of Fromental Halévy, he composed a solemn Mass sent to Rome in 1853, some operettas (*Mam'zelle Jeanne* in 1858, *Bettina* in 1866), as well as numerous melodies. He was a violist for the Société des Concerts de Conservatoire and second conductor for the Concerts Colonne. As a music teacher he published various musical theory and notation manuals, including *École du musicien, ou solfège théorique et pratique avec accompagnement de piano.*[26]

But his career advanced no further and even ended abruptly in November 1881 when, "struck with persecution mania," he was confined at Sainte-Anne.[27] "The unfortunate artist is the son of the late Benoît Cohen, president of the consistorial charity committee, and the nephew of the late Godchaux Weil (Ben-Lévi)," recalled the *Archives israélites.*[28] Edmond About, who had known him in Rome, reported that he had lived on "dry bread and fresh eggs" at the time, and that other boarders had tormented him.[29] For the last twenty years of his life, all trace of his existence disappears, so much so that the *Jewish Encyclopedia* lists the year of his death as 1884. But the Société des Auteurs et Compositeurs Dramatique allocated a pension to him in 1897.[30] In fact, he died in a hotel on Place de l'Odéon on 25 February 1901 and was buried in tomb 122.037 in Père-Lachaise on 28 February, near his grandfather, his uncles and aunts, and his brother.[31] The name of this thirteenth occupant, a promising musician in his youth, was not even engraved on the tombstone, but the registries offer proof. Now in 1901, the descendants of Baruch Weil most likely to take charge of Léonce Cohen's funeral and burial in the family vault were the children of Nathé, Georges Weil and his sister Jeanne, Madame Proust. Marcel Proust could not have been unaware of the fate of his mother's two Cohen cousins, a learned engineer and an accursed musician, worthy of being dramatis personae in *À la recherche du temps perdu.*

Baruch Weil, his second wife Marguerite Nathan, five of his children (Godch-aux; Nathé; Lazard Louis; Adélaïde, who was called Adèle; and Abraham Alphonse), three daughters-in-law (Frédérique Zunz, Adèle Berncastell, and Émi-lie Oppenheim), and then three grandchildren (Paul Lazarus, Maurice Cohen, and Léonce Cohen) are buried in the tomb in the little Jewish cemetery on Rue du Repos that Proust regretted he could not visit anymore as he had in his grand-father's time, due to his ill health. When we finally came upon the tomb of Baruch Weil and his descendants, we saw that no stones had been laid there; we left one.

"JEWISH CLANNISHNESS"

This tomb is imposing. Nevertheless, Nathé Weil consented to the marriage of his daughter to a Catholic, unless it was against his wishes, unless he did not want the complete assimilation of his branch of Weils in its fourth generation. In the family of his son Georges, unlike that of his daughter, the precepts of Judaism continued to be observed. But his grandson Marcel was baptized at birth, even though Adrien Proust was a freethinker and Jeanne Weil had not converted. Nev-ertheless, the grandfather, acting with discretion, managed to impress the child, then the adolescent, with his ancestral gesture, which Proust never forgot. And this custom from time immemorial was forever inscribed in his memory, as his *ultima verba* demonstrate in a lost letter.

Without knowing the addressee of that letter, most likely a mutual friend of Proust and André Spire, since Spire was the first to quote it—someone like Daniel Halévy or Lacretelle?—how to decide if Proust meant to put more emphasis on the forgetting or on the remembering, on a rite's loss of meaning or on a venerable gesture's continuity despite the sense of it fading away?[32] When his mother died in 1905, remaining faithful to the religion of her family (figure 33), Proust wanted a rabbi sent from the Paris consistory to recite the Kaddish, the prayer for the dead. There is no reason not to think that he left a stone on the tomb that day after the burial in Père-Lachaise, as he had done with his grandfather at the Baruch Weil tomb. Similarly, he went to the cemetery in March 1903 for the burial of Daniel Mayer, the cousin of his mother, to whom he wrote the day before: "There will not be prayers at the house and only a few words at the cemetery."[33] In any case, there is no doubt that young Proustian Zionists were aware of the transmission, through Proust, of a custom they took as a proof of identity and a duty to memory.

Figure 33. Jeanne Weil, Otto,
c. 1870.
Photo © Rue des Archives / Tallandier /
Bridgeman Images.

    Not a single one of them ever believed that there was the least trace of an anti-
Semite or anti-Jew in Proust, or found in him self-hatred or shame regarding his
Jewishness, or even raised an eyebrow over the comparison between homosexuals
and Jews in *Sodome et Gomorrhe I*, or reacted to the preference expressed for the
choice of the "sodomists," not to "rebuild" Sodom, which would have been a "fatal
error," but to spread out among the nations and prosper there as a diaspora, even
while the Zionists were demanding the rebirth of Israel.[34] Very much to the contrary, *Menorah* and *Palestine*, mouthpieces for the Zionist movement, reserved their
warmest welcome for Proust and recruited him to serve their cause, seeing in him,
in the manner of Swann, a model of Jewish tenacity and the recognition of Israel
from the moment that he was persecuted. Proust was ubiquitous in *La revue juive*,
a periodical intended for the cultivated French elite and financed by the Zionist
Organization, a kind of Jewish version of *La nouvelle revue*, because reading *À la
recherche du temps perdu* encouraged Albert Cohen's contributors in the feeling of
their Jewishness and in its affirmation in the form of Zionism. Proust hardly spoke
of Zionism, never quoted Israel Zangwill, and of course was not an actual Zionist.
In *Sodome et Gomorrhe I* he treats the Zionism of "apostolic zeal" like "conscientious

objection, Saint-Simonism, vegetarianism, or anarchy."[35] Categorizing it in that way seems to trivialize it, reduce it to one more cause among others, a passing craze, a fad like the prophetism of Alexandre Weill embraced by Charles Fourier in his bohemian youth. In *À l'ombre des jeunes filles en fleur*, Proust nevertheless considers what he calls "Jewish clannishness" to be "inescapable...in people who believe they have risen above their race."[36] Although van Praag discovered and condemned in *À la recherche du temps perdu* the "ineluctable fatalism" of assimilation, an expression then adopted by Lehrmann, it was in fact "Jewish clannishness" that Proust deemed "inescapable," during the Dreyfus affair, for example. Now, in 1919, the date of the novel's publication and of the Paris Peace Conference, where André Spire and Sylvain Lévi had quarreled, the words "Jewish clannishness" were synonymous with the Zionism that opposed Franco-Judaism. On Proust's part, this was thus a recognition of the necessity of the return to Israel, of loyalty and solidarity under certain circumstances, during the Dreyfus affair as in the face of any rabid anti-Semitism. That was why Robert Dreyfus objected to the comparison between "the assimilated" and "deserters" in his 1937 response to van Praag.

The passage in which Proust presents his most anti-Semitic caricature is found in *Les plaisirs et les jours*:

As for the Jews, Bouvard and Pécuchet, without entirely proscribing them (you have to be liberal, after all), admitted that they hated finding themselves in their company; they all sold pince-nez in Germany in their youth, and even in Paris they insisted on preserving—and with a piety which, as impartial spectators, our heroes handsomely acknowledged—special practices, an unintelligible vocabulary, and butchers of their own race. They all have hooked noses, an exceptional intelligence, and base souls intent only on seeking their own advantage; their women, on the other hand, are beautiful, a little on the flabby side, but capable of the deepest feelings. How many Catholics ought to imitate them! But why are their fortunes always incalculable and hidden? In addition, they formed a sort of vast secret society, like the Jesuits and the Freemasons. They had inexhaustible treasures stowed away, nobody knew where, at the service of unspecified enemies, always available for some terrible and mysterious purpose.[37]

This was first published in 1893 in *La revue blanche*, edited by the Natanson brothers, whose contributors *La libre parole* would describe as "Dreyfus intellectuals," and it is a pastiche of Flaubert's *Bouvard et Pécuchet*. At twenty-two years old, Proust knew how to imitate perfectly, in a single paragraph, Drumont's *La France juive*. This was written twenty years before the publication of *Du côté de chez Swann*, but with the protection of this introductory note: "The opinions ascribed here to these two celebrated characters from Flaubert are, of course, in no way those of the author," a disclaimer repeated more emphatically in *La revue blanche* itself: "It must be understood that, despite the use of the present tense, the opinions expressed here are those of Bouvard and Pécuchet, not the signatory of these lines."[38] As Laurent Dispot summarizes it so well: "If anti-Semitism is present in *La Recherche*, and not in the novels by Céline or the operas of Wagner (except in some remote way), that is because Proust is combating it."[39]

Proust was no more anti-Semitic or anti-Jewish than the contributors to *La revue juive*, or else those young Zionists and sympathizers—André Spire, Albert Cohen, Georges Cattaui, Léon Pierre-Quint, Benjamin Crémieux, and a few others like Jean de Menasce and Emmanuel Arié—were as anti-Semitic and anti-Jewish as he was, since they saw no wrong in the treatment of Jewishness in his novel. To the contrary, they were very pleased that Proust had introduced into literature a whole cast of very diverse Jewish characters, far removed from the stereotypes and representing all degrees of assimilation, and they used a vocabulary to talk about this that present-day critics of Proust would consider even more offensive than Proust's own: not only "Jewish race," but "Jewish blood," and even "Jewish pure-blood," in Spire's case, "Parisian Jewry," for Crémieux, a vocabulary that resembles the one used by Charlus in his tirades against Albert Bloch and his family in *Sodome et Gomorrhe II*.[40] In fact, they "annexed" Proust, and the Zionist publications in the 1920s, *Menorah*, *La revue juive*, and *Palestine*, used him as a vector for propaganda. In 1928 the Jewish Telegraphic Agency once again distributed to the diaspora press an article in praise of Proust, "The Jew in Contemporary French Literature: An Appreciation of Marcel Proust," by David Ewen, a young musicologist.[41]

David Ewen uses the pretext of Clive Bell's book, *Proust* (1928), the first monograph on the writer in the English language, to assimilate Proust entirely on the side of Zion, not as a half-Jew but as fully Jewish. That is how, moderately informed about the life and work of the author of *À la recherche du temps perdu*, David Ewen makes both Proust's parents, not just his mother Jeanne Weil but also his father Adrien Proust, into Jews, and Proust himself into a disciple of Freud and of Bergson, thus a complete Jew, in his life and in his ideas. In Ewen's eyes, Proust is "a Jew who is likewise one of the literary giants of all times."[42]

ET ALIA

There are many other names still left to be mentioned among the young and less young Proustian Jews or Zionists who were oblivious to the anti-Semitism conveniently uncovered a century later in the life and work of Proust. First there are those of Proust's schoolmates at the Condorcet lycée and the editors of *Banquet*, the literary review they published in 1892 and 1893: not only David Halévy and his cousin Jacques Bizet—whose childhood photograph given to Proust bears this dedication: "To my dear friend Marcel (with Daniel Halévy) 18 February 1889, J. Bizet"—but also Robert Dreyfus (who became interested in Alexandre Weill before Siegfried van Praag and Chanan Lehrmann did), as well as Fernand Gregh, Léon Blum, and Horace Finaly.

They never parted ways with their young schoolmate: "one evening, after having let his beard grow for some time, it was suddenly the ancestral rabbi who reappeared behind the charming Marcel whom we knew," wrote Fernand Gregh many years later, after the war and the Shoah.[43]

That description is read today (as a way of feeling superior to one's predecessors or to ease one's conscience) as proof of anti-Semitism on the part of Gregh, or as Jewish self-hatred, even though in the last pages of his memoir, Gregh reviews with emotion and affection Proust's metamorphosis at the end of his life, on the model of the changes perceived in Swann (figure 34).[44]

Then comes Reynaldo Hahn, faithful to the very end, and then the second circle of René Blum, Jean-Richard Bloch, and Gabriel Astruc (1864–1938), organizer of the first season of the Ballets Russes in Paris in 1909, founder of the Théatre des Champs-Élysées, one of the first, and, without an occupation at the time, one of the most careful readers of *Du côté de chez Swann*—he sent his copy to Proust after having correcting the printing errors in it.[45]

And then there is the philosopher Léon Brunschvicg (1869–1944), another of Proust's classmates at the Condorcet lycée, a disciple of Alphonse Darlu, and contributor to *La revue juive*, which published an important article he wrote on Montaigne. He does not mention the mother of the author of *Essais* in that article, but where he notes that, in "Apologie de Raimond Sebond," Montaigne demonstrates "the moral inefficacy, and consequently the religious emptiness of Christianity," the editor of *La revue juive*—Albert Cohen? Jean de Menasce?—thought it wise to add a footnote: "It hardly seems useful to recall here the half-Jewish origin of Michel de Montaigne. (Editor's note)."[46]

Figure 34. Proust's friends André Rivoire, Daniel Halévy, Robert Dreyfus, and Fernand Gregh, 1897.

Photo © Beaussant Lefèvre et Studio Sebert.

And, further removed from the inner circles, there is Julien Benda, a contributor to *La revue Blanche* and Dreyfus supporter like Proust, but opposed to Proust's complicated way of writing and thinking, not yet in *Belphégor*, already finished in late 1913, at the time of the publication of *Du côté de chez Swann*, but in an article in *Le Figaro* in March 1920, where he makes Proust into an enthusiast of "hyper-romanticism," "full-scale romanticism," and "literary Asianism."[47]

Proust was not greatly affected by this, but he did not forget it, recalling again to Jacques Boulenger in November 1921: "Personally, I was neither very pleased nor very annoyed with him: he spoke of me in *Le Figaro* as an ultra-romantic, and as far as I can recall, he meant it as a reproach. But he included me in very 'noble company.'"[48] Benda would commit a second offense in *La France byzantine*, but without ever taking up the thesis of Proust's rabbinism.[49] In the meantime, he redeemed Proust in *La trahison des clercs*, pleased that he had risen up against the "Manifeste du parti de l'intelligence," the proclamation inspired by Maurras and launched by Henri Massis in 1919; thus, a few years after Proust's death, Benda called him "one of our greatest writers" who deplored "a kind of '*Frankreich über alles*,' gendarme of the literature of all peoples," and Benda declared himself "glad for this opportunity to pay homage to that true '*clerc*' and to say that we know there are still writers in France other than those who believe only in the virtue of the sword."[50]

There is also Pierre Abraham, younger brother of Marcel Bloch and of Jean-Richard Bloch, author of yet another *Proust*, published by Rieder in 1930, in which he cites Pierre-Quint, Saurat, and Crémieux but says nothing about Proust's Jewishness to explain his character, and objects to the comparison with Montaigne: "Some have tried to find an explanation for the sometimes profound similarities between Montaigne and Proust in the presence, in both of them, of Jewish blood," he recalls, before raising this nullifying objection: "If we accept heredity as the explanation, we would then have to find in the two paternal lines the reason for the equally profound differences between the works."[51] Moreover, indifferent to Judaism and drawn to Communism, Pierre Abraham considered Proust closer to Rousseau through their "analytical mania," which was his way of reconciling his literary tastes and political leanings.

And there is Emmanuel Berl (1892–1976), related to the Bergsons and the Prousts, a friend of Proust who welcomed him in 1917 and educated him until the day he drove him off, launching insults at him, "like slippers by the bathroom door," to settle their debate over the possibility, or not, of being happily in love.[52] Berl wrote an article on "Freud and Proust" for *Les nouvelles littéraires* in 1923, in which, to counter the idea of Proust's mobility and emphasize the subservience of individuals to the "laws of heredity," he recalled how Swann, "the friend of the prince of Galles, the darling of the Jockey Club . . . died a Dreyfusian and prophesying Jew."[53]

And finally there is André Maurois, né Émile Herzog (1885–1967), the husband of Simone de Caillavet (daughter of Gaston Arman de Caillavet and of Jeanne Pouquet, granddaughter of Léotine Lippmann, Madame Arman de Caillavet, a model for Gilberte), whose biography *À la recherche de Marcel Proust* (1949) fixed forever the image of the little Jewish cemetery on Rue du Repos with which we began.

IN MEMORIAM

The list of these young Jewish and Zionist readers of Proust brings to mind again a few far more serious fates. Proust would have been approaching his seventieth year in autumn 1940, when the Vichy government enacted the Law on the status of Jews. Many of the men and women that we have mentioned, or those close to them, did not survive the persecutions that followed.

Proust's first cousin, Adèle Weil (1892–1944), daughter of his uncle Georges, the brother of his mother, and of Amélie Oulman, was arrested on 4 July 1944, along with her husband Jules Maxime Weil (1877–1944) and their daughter Annette (1921–2020), in Toulouse, where they had taken refuge in 1940 (figure 35). All three were deported by convoy no. 81, one of the last to leave France, which departed from Toulouse on 30 July 1944 for Buchenwald, where Maxime Weil died on 30 November 1944, and then to Ravensbrück, where Adèle died on 5 December 1944.[54] Only Annette returned. Her married name was Madame Claude Heumann. We learned of her death in April 2020 at the age of ninety-nine. What might Proust's fate have been had he not died prematurely?

René Blum (1878–1942), Léon Blum's younger brother, whom Proust had seen in August 1902 at Larue and who, twenty-four years old at the time, was one of the models for the waiters at Balbec's Grand-Hôtel, "svelte, rosy, shy, smiling, and curly-haired, like a Hippolytus from the best times of Greek sculpture your friend M. R. Blum." Returning from the restaurant, Proust wrote this to Antoine Bibesco, but what follows is less pretty: "Rosy especially because of constipation of which he complains and which is symbolic of his difficulty to produce."[55] Proust makes him a prototype of Swann, "suffering from ethnic eczema and the Prophets' constipation."[56] (Contemporary detractors of the anti-Jewish Proust will perk up their ears.)

René Blum played a major role in the publication history of *À la recherche du temps perdu*. A journalist and secretary-general of *Gil Blas* at the time, he was the one who served as intermediary between Proust and Bernard Grasset in early 1913. Later, as director of the Théâtre de Monte-Carlo and founder of the Ballets Russes de Monte-Carlo, having refused to leave the country with his troupe, he was arrested on 12 December 1941 during the "roundup of the notables," held at the Compiègne-Royallieu camp, transferred to Drancy in March 1942 and then deported on 23 September 1942 in convoy no. 36 to Auschwitz, where he was executed on arrival.[57]

Figure 35. Maxime and Adèle Weil, front left, Annette, back center.
Photo © Mémorial de la Shoah / Coll. Ariel Conte.

Benjamin Crémieux, the most subtle analyst of Proust's Jewishness at the end of the 1920s, dismissed by the Vichy government in 1940, joined the Resistance in Marseille in 1941, was arrested in April 1943, transferred to Fresnes and then to Compiègne-Royallieu, and deported in January 1944 to Buchenwald, where he died of exhaustion on 14 April 1944, according to *L'univers concentrationnaire* by David Rousset, who arrived in the same transport.[58]

Emmanuel Arié was born in Sofia and educated at the Alliance Israélite Universelle school in Smyrna, then directed by his brother Gabriel Arié; a contributor to *La revue juive* in 1925, he used his articles on Jacques-Émile Blanche and Jean Cocteau as opportunities to discuss Proust. Naturalized as French citizen in 1925, a jewelry merchant, he was arrested in Lyon, 7 July 1944, transferred to the Montluc prison, then held at Drancy and deported by convoy no. 77 on 31 July 1944 to Auschwitz, where he died on 4 August 1944.

Jules Rais (Cahen known as Nathan known as Rais), André's Spire's childhood friend in Nancy, and Ludmila Savitzky's second husband, who became a passionate anti-Zionist and fell out with Spire, former head librarian at the Chamber of Deputies, was deported by convoy no. 62, leaving Drancy on 20 November 1943, and he died at Auschwitz on arrival.[59]

Louise Bloch (1858–1944), mother-in-law of Ludmila Savitzky and mother of her third husband, Marcel Bloch, as well as Jean-Richard Bloch and Pierre Abraham, was arrested in Néris-les-Bains, in Allier, on 12 May 1944, and deported by convoy no. 75 on 30 May 1944 from Drancy to Auschwitz, where she was gassed on arrival, at the age of eighty-six.

Chief rabbi Léon Berman, victim of the wrath of *La tribune juive* in 1937 for having included Proust in his *Histoire des juifs de France*, was arrested in Cannes on 15 October 1943 and deported with his wife and son, departing from Drancy on 28 October 1943 in convoy no. 61 for Auschwitz.

First cousin of Robert Dreyfus, one of Proust's oldest and most faithful friends, Henriette Neymarck (1873–1944), and her brother Pierre Neymarck (1875–1944), a former student at the Condorcet lycée who succeeded his father, Alfred Neymarck, in directing the journal *Le Rentier*, were interned at Drancy on 21 March 1944 and deported by convoy no. 70 on 27 March 1944 to Auschwitz, from which they never returned.

Dina Brach (1865–1943), née Sourdis, youngest daughter of Mardochée Sourdis, partner of Adolphe Dreyfus, father of Robert Dreyfus, was deported in convoy no. 61, which left Drancy, 28 October 1943, and she died in Auschwitz, at the age of seventy-eight.[60]

Édouard Schneeberg (1876–1943) was the funeral director, taking over from his father Samuel, of the "only essentially Jewish funeral home," according to advertisements in the *Archives israélites* and *L'univers israélite*, the largest specialized mortuary, close to the consistory, in charge of the free burials of indigent Jews, and where the Weils were loyal patrons. A longtime president of the employers' federation of funeral directors, knight of the Legion of Honor, administrator of Le Mont Sinaï society, former Parisian Jewish charity worker, Entente Républicaine candidate in the Paris municipal elections in 1932, he perished at Auschwitz, deported there in convoy no. 58 on 31 July 1943 after two detentions at Drancy, the first in September 1941.[61]

André Lévy, known as Arnyvelde (1881–1942), published an interview with Proust in *Le Miroir* on 21 December 1913, just after the release of *Du côté de chez Swann*, announcing the "sensational arrival" of a book that "has made quite a stir."[62] He was also arrested on 12 December 1941 during the "roundup of the notables" and then transferred to Compiègne-Royallieu, where he contracted pneumonia, from which he died on 2 February 1942 in the Compiègne hospital.[63] "He was one of a batch of five hundred intellectuals taken hostage, because of who knows what attack on the person of a Kraut officer," wrote Frédéric Joliot-Curie in his obituary of André Levy, who had become a journalist, writing popular science articles. Joliot-Curie was his friend and saw him last in the hospital morgue.[64] Fernand Gregh would mention him with Benjamin Crémieux and René Blum, among his exterminated friends, schoolmates, and relatives.[65]

The parents of Chanan Lehrmann, author of the 1941 book *L'élément juif dans la littérature française*, Chaim Frieder-Lehrmann (1882–1942), the *sofer* in Stuttgart, and Blume, née Kranzler (1880–1942), were expelled from Germany and deported to Poland during the *Polenaktion* of October 1938. They died in a concentration camp in 1942.

Marie-Louise Cahen-Hayem (1905–1944), who wrote positive reviews for the *Archives israélites* on the books on Proust by Léon Pierre-Quint, Robert Dreyfus, and Pierre Abraham, was arrested with her parents and deported from Toulouse to Germany by convoy no. 81 on 30 July 1944, one of the last and the same one that carried Proust's cousin Adèle Weil, her husband, and her daughter to Buchenwald and Ravensbrück. Cahen-Hayem died at Ravensbrück on 29 November 1944, as did her mother, Marguerite Cahen, née Hayem (1874–1944) on 20 November—Adèle Weil and Marguerite Cahen, we will recall, were third cousins—while her father, René Isaac Cahen (1871–1944), who edited the *Archives israélites* with his brother Georges, died on 8 November at Buchenwald.[66] He was the grandson of Samuel Cahen—the founder of the *Archives* in 1840, for which Godchaux Weil, Proust's great-uncle and the family writer before him, was the most assiduous contributor for about a decade—son of Isidore Cahen, and brother of Émile Cahen, who directed the review before he did. He was also an old schoolmate of Proust's at the Condorcet lycée, and he referred to him informally as "our friend Marcel Proust" in the *Archives israélites*.[67]

Compared to Proust's supposed anti-Semitism that good souls today find shocking, the anti-Semitism that exterminated so many of his relatives, friends, acquaintances, and admirers certainly deserves more attention.

CHAPTER 11

Manuscripts Regained

T here is a hidden god of research, one of a researcher's Graces. My investigations were finished; I had taken my inquiry as far as I thought possible; it seemed that there was nothing more to find or that I could add. Of course, I had hit one impasse and it still bothered me: "There is no longer anybody, not even myself, since I cannot leave my bed, who will go along Rue du Repos to visit the little Jewish cemetery where my grandfather, following a custom that he never understood, went for so many years to lay a stone on his parents' grave." I had not discovered to whom it was that Proust addressed these melancholic words on his Jewishness. Nonetheless I had established that the young Jewish and Zionist admirers of *À la recherche du temps perdu* in the 1920s saw nothing anti-Semitic in Proust's novel, no Jewish self-hatred or shame, but on the contrary, they claimed Proust as one of their own and made use of his work to demonstrate their pride in being Jewish. But the initial mystery remained unsolved. Soon I had a few drafts to share. I consulted a few trusted readers on future possibilities for these pages. Then I put them aside for some months and moved on to something else.

Then one morning I found in my email a note from Nathalie Mauriac Dyer, who was familiar with my research. It was accompanied by a file that I opened immediately. In it were photographs of a few pages written in Proust's hand.[1] Knowing my interest in the questions raised by this document that she had just discovered, she had sent it on to me (figure 36). Here is the transcript of it:

a bit reactionary for the tastes of Maman, who was the best and most tender-hearted and who said of such people, "they are not in favor of what lowers interest rates and railroad stocks," but since my grandfather's death, Maman has, with a kind of fetishism, accepted, imitated, and transformed into objects of worship what she might have found a bit exaggerated about him while he was alive; and my grandfather, as tender and good as she was, whom I watched pass sleepless weeks because he had seen a man on the street strike a child, who, even when he was very sick and almost unable to walk, made his cab stop two blocks from his house so that the sight of such luxury, which she could not share, would not upset his concierge, my grandfather believed [that] the good of the people could only be obtained through an authoritarian regime (and moreover, relatively anticlerical, not in today's sense but in the sense of Louis-Philippe sending his sons to the lycée). My grandfather, my dear Daniel, went to all the performances of La belle Hélène. My grandmother always said, when speaking of her husband, that La belle Hélène was the great event of his life, "much more than our wedding," she would add. My grandfather's memories of operas and operettas were my constant terror, because they were to him a kind of figurative language and less difficult to penetrate than he thought, which he used to say things to us about people, in front of them, and which they were not supposed to understand. He would claim that someone about whom we had spoken to him, despite a changed name, was Jewish, barely had this person entered, either his face or a few cleverly asked questions would leave him no doubt, and he would hum nonstop, "Israël romps ta chaîne, ô peuple lève-toi, viens assouvir ta haine, le Seigneur est en moi, etc." (*Samson et Dalila*) or "Ô Dieu de nos pères, parmi nous descends cacher nos mystères à l'oeil des méchants" (*La Juive*) or many others that I have forgotten. One particular bore was always greeted with the cavatine from *Barbier*, etc. But these are things that I could not keep myself from telling and alas, they have charm only for me. There is no longer anybody, not even me, who cannot leave my bed, who will go along Rue du Repos to visit the little Jewish cemetery where my grandfather, following a custom that he already no longer understood, went every year to put a stone on his parents' grave.[2]

The extract, beginning in the middle of a sentence (so who was "a bit reactionary for the tastes of Maman?"), then extends over four dense pages. As was his habit when Proust began a letter, he wrote it on a large sheet of paper folded in half, first on folio 1 recto and folio 2 recto, then, having turned the sheet forty-five degrees counterclockwise, on folio 1 verso, and finally on folio 2 verso. It seemed to be part of a long letter, but its beginning was missing, at least one double sheet

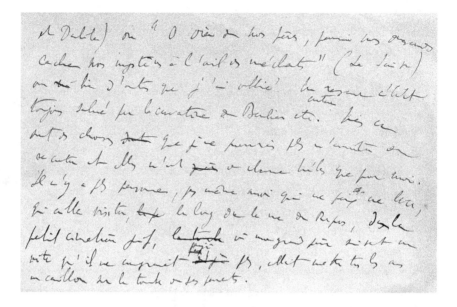

Figure 36. Proust, letter to Daniel Halévy, May 1908.

similar to this one, as well, probably, as its end, on a third sheet (the first double page preceding our manuscript was discovered after the publication of this book in French, as well as the inscription for which these two double pages were the draft). A good many corrections give the impression of a rough draft, or that the hypothetical letter, with more and more cross-outs, became a rough draft as it was being written, and that Proust then had to make a fair copy before sending it to its addressee.

At first I read distractedly, and then with growing curiosity, but when I came to the last lines of the fourth page the shock was so great that it took my breath away for a good while. I was holding the solution that I despaired of finding for years now. Like a gift from heaven, the fragment ends, at the bottom of the fourth page, with the famous sentence about the little Jewish cemetery on Rue du Repos. With minor variations—"not even me, who cannot leave my bed" becoming "since I cannot leave my bed," perhaps a variation in the fair copy—these are the exact words that André Spire quoted in 1923, Georges Cattaui in 1935, André Maurois in 1949, and so on. Spire and Cattaui come closer to the newly found manuscript than do Maurois and his successors, who prefer *puis* over *peux*, the first-person present form of *pouvoir* used by Spire, Cattaui and in this draft of the letter (honestly, the repetition of *puisque* [since] and *puis* had always bothered me).

Another slight variation did not seem insignificant to me: Nathé Weil, writes Proust, lay a stone on his parents' grave, "following a custom that he already no longer understood," a turn of phrase that, beginning with Spire and Cattaui, tradition transformed into "following a custom" or "the custom that he never understood." The nuance matters. If Proust's grandfather "already no longer understood" the meaning of the stone placed on the grave, that does not necessarily mean that he had "never understood" it, but it allows for possibility that he had forgotten it, that over the course of his lifetime the tradition was lost, and that his grandson no longer had reason for knowing it. In that "already no longer" there is a touch of regret, missing from the "never," not reproach but nostalgia, a "nevermore."

CREMATION

Restored to the context of a letter draft, the sentence on the "little Jewish cemetery" concluded a moving portrait of Nathé Weil, compared to his daughter by his grandson: more conservative than his daughter, but "tender and good" like her. Moreover, he was passionate about opera, quick to detect the Jewish origins of visitors, and faithful—apparently—to the traditions of Judaism. His grandson could have recounted much more, but he refrained for the moment, saving that for "Combray."

Now the annual index of burials at Père-Lachaise cemetery, already successfully consulted to understand the importance of the family tomb with regard to the Jewish world of Baruch Weil, held one last surprise for us, related to the meaning of Nathé Weil's gesture at his father's tomb. There appears a most important detail about Nathé Weil's death, a single but monumental detail that his grandson must have known. That piece of information, missed until now, leaves hardly any doubt about Proust's grandfather's attitude toward Judaism. On the same page of the registry are entered three successive burials, very close together in time: Weil Lazard (Uncle Louis), 12 May 1986; Weil Nathé, 2 July 1986; Weil née Zunz Frédérique, widow of Godchaux Weil, 17 January 1897, all three in the 122.037 plot of Baruch Weil. In the right-hand column, meant for "Observations," an extraordinary note appears at the end of the line for Nathé Weil: "Incineration" (figure 37).[3]

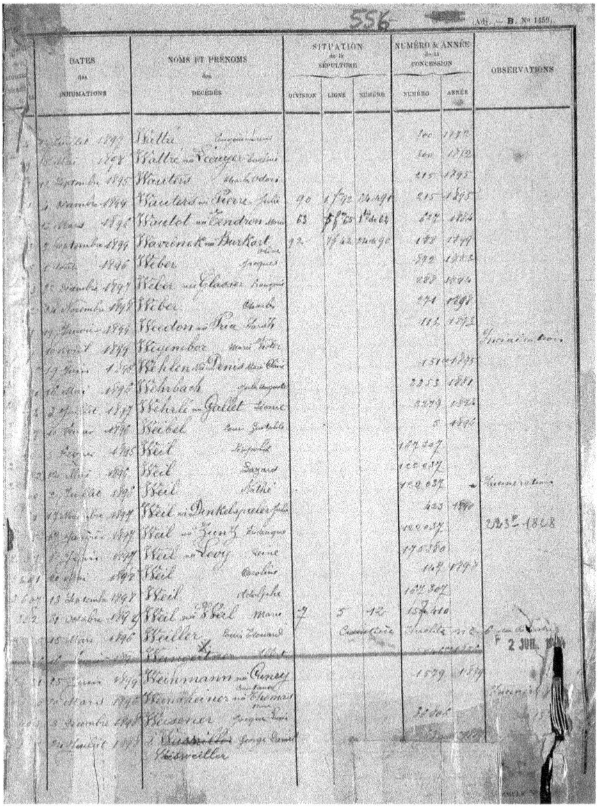

Figure 37. Annual index of burials, Père-Lachaise Cemetery (incineration note).

Photo © Archives de Paris, Service central des cimetières de Paris.

This disconcerting bit of information, repeated in the annual index, already appeared in the margin of the daily registry on the line for Nathé Weil.

At that time, in 1896, cremation was almost never a part of burials in France, especially for a Jew. To choose it was to profess one's atheism, to proclaim oneself a freethinker. The cremation of the body had been legal for less than a decade, following the 15 November 1887 law on the freedom of funerals (appearing in the *Journal officiel*, 18 November 1887, the implementation decree was made public 27 April 1889), a republican law, both hygienic and anticlerical. A decree from the Holy Office denounced cremation as early as May 1886, as the restoration of a pagan custom and instrument of masonic propaganda, while its authorization was debated in the National Assembly and the Senate, and Pope Leo XIII condemned it in December 1886 (canon 1203). The first cremation took place on 30 January 1889 at the Père-Lachaise crematorium, a large secular basilica that had just been completed, but demand remained low. According to the statement given in 1897 by the *Revue d'hygiène et de police sanitaire*:

> In Paris, the crematorium built at Père-Lachaise performed 28,000 cremations, from 1889 to the end of 1896, 4423 of them in 1896; but in reality only 1255 of them were requested by families over this whole period (203 of them in 1896); the rest include 17,006 for the remains of cadavers coming from hospitals (2587 of them in 1896) and 10,097 for embryos (1636 in 1896). The 203 bodies cremated in 1896 came from: 172 from Paris, 16 for the département de la Seine, 15 from twelve other départements often very far from Paris.[4]

Nathé Weil was thus one of 172 Parisians who asked to be cremated in 1896 (out of 50,509 deaths registered in the twenty arrondissements of Paris).[5] These statistics on cremation appear in the final pages of the June issue of the *Revue d'hygiène*. The following issue opens with the report by Adrien Proust himself on the International Sanitary Conference held in Venice in February–March 1897.[6] The rare individuals who then chose cremation did so because of their anticlerical convictions and they were, for the most part, freethinkers and Freemasons (Paul Casimir-Perier in 1897, Athénaïs Michelet in 1899), plus a few anarchists, former communards (Prosper-Olivier Lissagaray in 1901), and socialists (Paul Lafargue in 1911).[7]

Judaism categorically condemns cremation. In 1885, when there was first talk of authorizing it in France, *L'univers israélite* recalled the traditional doctrine:

> Cremation—which, moreover, presents certain drawbacks in addition to indisputable advantages—does not seem close to entering into our customs, by which we mean French customs. As for the Jewish sentiment, it is absolutely repugnant to it. The cremation of bodies, as a routine practice, goes against both the economy of our religious law and, no matter what has been said, against all the basic elements of the Bible and the Talmud. If it is ever adopted, we must believe that it will always remain optional and that few Jews will be in a hurry to take advantage of that option.[8]

Immediately following the vote on the law authorizing cremation, *L'univers israélite* published a long study by chief rabbi Michel Aaron Weill (1814–1889), the former chief rabbi of Algiers, the father of Dick May and historian Georges Weill.[9] This was his conclusion:

we are addressing, not the scholars, but the mass of faithful, all the sons of Israel, each having his own share in salvation and the future world, except for those who deny resurrection. We implore them not to expose themselves to this reprobation by associating themselves with measures running counter to our beliefs, traditions, all the teachings that encompass the past and the future of the people of God. . . . Cremation is incompatible with the spirit as well as the letter of the Law, both written and oral, forbidden to the Jew faithful to Jewish beliefs and traditions, and therefore, it cannot claim the support of our religion and its ministers.[10]

In 1888, in the *Archives israélite*, Hippolyte Prague violently denounced the actions of a rabbi from London who came "to recite prayers over the hot ashes" of the deceased following a cremation:

That Jews have themselves cremated, we have seen this and sadly, will see it again. When it is a matter of eccentricities, even posthumous ones, we can be sure that they will find favor with a few individuals among us. There are Jews who have themselves baptized, others who give in to that needless fuss called mixed marriage, still others who shout their atheism from the rooftops and wage war on the name of God in children's readers!

These peculiarities can and must offend the great mass of believers, rouse their indignation, but they should not surprise them. We find all kinds in the Jewish community. It is a herd in which the sheep cannot all be irreproachable.[11]

Thus Nathé Weil did not have a Jewish burial in the presence of a rabbi in 1896, but a civil burial, that of a freethinker and a Freemason. By the choice of this cremation he demonstrated his infidelity to the beliefs and traditions of Judaism.

In *Jean Santeuil*, Madame Santeuil, Jean's mother, imagines with terror and tenderness the death of her father, M. Sandré, old and resigned. Around him, her behavior is timid, "as, when we stand by the grave of someone we loved, we keep our voices low and tread lightly, while with trembling hand, we drop the ritual earth upon the unresponsive coffin which hides from us the unhearing dead, because there is present all about us something so tender that the least sound might bruise it."[12] Proust wrote that passage on Madame Santeuil's admiration and pity for her father in the very months leading up to Nathé Weil's death on

30 June 1896. He was thinking quite obviously of Jeanne Weil's devotion to her own father. Failing for some time, Nathé Weil, "seeing that he had digested nothing for two days, let himself die in eight days while continuing to be lifted into his bathtub three times a day while terrified Papa took his pulse the whole time," Proust related to Paul Morand a few months before his own death, when he could see it approaching.[13] But there was no "ritual earth" dropping on an "unresponsive coffin" for Proust's grandfather.

A cremation takes many hours, and generally the family is not present. Family members return to the cemetery to witness the urn being lowered into the tomb. A cremation accelerates absence at the same time as it delays it, and it alters the mourning process. Proust wrote to his mother in the early days of July 1896: "When one sees, as we saw the other day, how everything ends, what is the use of grieving over sorrows or devoting yourself to causes of which nothing will remain. One can no longer understand anything but the fatalism of Muslims."[14] There should be nothing disconcerting about the association, in Proust's letter, between Nathé's death and the cliché of Islamic fatalism. Moreover, Islam disapproves of cremation as much as Jewish law and the Catholic Church do. Without faith or hope, whether Jewish, Christian, or Islamic, there it is: "how everything ends" and "nothing will remain." Returning to what took place "the other day," Proust seemed to think of Nathé Weil's cremation as a sudden and definitive annihilation.

During the death of Bergotte before the little patch of yellow wall, the narrator would say the same thing, that "there is nothing in the conditions of our life on this earth to make us feel any obligation to do good, to be scrupulous, even to be polite, nor to make the unbelieving artist feel compelled to paint a single passage twenty times over, when the admiration it will excite will be of little importance to his body when it is eaten by worms."[15] But this time the fatalism would be overcome and the skepticism denied. "All these obligations which do not derive their force from the here-and-now," Proust continues, only make sense according to the hypothesis of an "earlier life" and a "world quite different" from this one, where "unknown laws" were traced in us, so "that the idea that Bergotte was not dead for ever is not at all implausible." We struggle along in this life as if there must have been another life in which we were accountable for our actions, whereas Proust calls "the fatalism of Muslims" a behavior that would not be dictated by the obligations of another life. It is the convention of immortality, that is to say, a suspension of incredulity, that the last wishes of Nathé, in skipping the "eaten by worms" stage, seem to have shaken.

The choice of cremation would surprise us less for Adrian Proust, professor of hygiene and noteworthy republican. He approaches the question in his *Traité d'hygiène* in 1877, when cremation was not yet legal:

> Another system borrowed from the Ancients has been revived in our time: we are speaking of *cremation*, for which various methods have been proposed, in France, in Italy, in the United States, and so on. It seems to us entirely useless to go into the details of this subject. Let us say only that the goal to be achieved is to incinerate the bodies completely and to consume totally the gases that result from this operation. . . .
>
>   Let us say in passing: we do not understand at all the sentimental and religious objections that have been raised against the combustion of bodies. . . . A single word suffices to overcome the arguments of those who claim to find an offense to spiritualism in the use of this process; it is that during the first century of the Christian era, in the Greco-Roman world, Christians universally practiced the cremation of bodies with the approval and under the eyes of the Church, whose orthodoxy could not be suspect in a period so close to the time of its origin. We can thus see that sentiment and religion have nothing to do with this, and that everything is reduced to a question of custom. While the pagans of Egypt were embalming their dead according to the custom of their ancestors, Christians were reducing the bodies of their kin to ashes. How can we justify, in the nineteenth century, any protests against such practices in the name of spiritualist doctrines?[16]

Doctor Proust returned to this subject in an addendum to the third edition of his manual in 1903, when cremation was henceforth legal but remained rare: "In France, cremation was only authorized in 1887; it is still not legal in Austria-Hungary or in Holland. On the other hand, in Japan it is extremely widespread, since the city of Tokyo alone has seven crematoriums that incinerated 42 percent of cadavers. In Europe, cremation has not made noticeable progress for several years." He notes that France has only four crematoriums, in Paris, Rouen, Reims, and Lyon. Then he details the process: "The combustion apparatus destroys a cadaver in one or two hours at little cost. The crematorium ovens at Père-Lachaise in Paris are constructed according to this principle; the fuel used is coke."[17]

But Adrien Proust was not cremated when he died, unlike his father-in-law, seven years earlier, at the age of eighty-three. Was that because his sudden death in 1903, at the age of sixty-nine, did not leave him time to express his final wishes, or because his wife survived him, whereas the death of Adèle Weil had preceded that of Nathé Weil, leaving Proust's grandfather more at liberty to decide the conditions of his funeral for himself before his death, as article 3 of the 1887 law permitted, and to compel his children to respect his convictions? The difficulties encountered by funeral homes during the 1870 and 1871 sieges of Paris contributed to the campaign in favor of cremation in the years that followed. "The idea is in the air," wrote Du Camp in 1874, and, despite opposition from the Church, "it will end up taking the form of a practical means," because it would be "a superior way of disposing of the dead than what is imposed upon us."[18] Nathé Weil, who experienced the funeral home backlogs during the terrible month of December 1870, after the death of his sister-in-law and his nephew, was clearly more receptive than others to the hygienic arguments favoring the cremation of cadavers. In 1896, nevertheless, the choice to be cremated represented, indisputably, a militant act; this was a provocative final wish on the part of Proust's grandfather, respected by his son Georges Weil, more religious than he was, and by his daughter Jeanne (the new law gave them no choice, moreover, if Nathé Weil, as is likely, had predetermined his method of burial).

The cremation of Proust's maternal grandfather establishes definitively that he was a freethinker and very likely a Freemason, like Adolphe Crémieux, great-uncle of Jeanne Weil (Amélie Crémieux née Silny, the wife of Adolphe Crémieux, was the sister of Rose Berncastell, née Silny, the maternal grandmother of Jeanne Weil).[19] On 3 September 1870, Adolphe Crémieux, a Freemason since the age of twenty as a young attorney in Nîmes in 1817, commander of the Supreme Council of France Ancient and Accepted Scottish Rite beginning in 1869, president of the Alliance Israélite Universelle beginning in 1863, who would be named Minister of Justice in the Government of National Defense the following day (4 September 1870), served as witness for Jeanne Weil at her marriage to Adrien Proust (that "needless fuss called mixed marriage" according to Hippolyte Prague). The hypothesis that Nathé Weil and Doctor Adrien Proust encountered each other in Masonic circles seems credible.

MONT SINAÏ

The "Bossu file" of the French Freemasons, compiled by Jean Bossu, acquired by the Bibliothèque Nationale in 1987, and containing 130,000 entries, mentions a certain Baruch Weil, Worshipful Master of the Mont Sinai Lodge, of the

Scottish Rite, in 1845.[20] The file's source is a news item from *L'Orient, revue de la franc-maçonnerie*: "An initiation of the greatest interest took place, 11 April, at the Mont Sinaï lodge, in conformity with the Scottish Supreme Council, under the direction of brother Baruch Weil, Worshipful Master of that atelier. The proposed candidate, M. Pélissier, teaches at the School for the Deaf and Mute, and is a deaf-mute himself." Since it was not possible to blindfold the candidate in order to interrogate him, he was asked to answer in writing. The Baruch Weil who directed this unusual initiation could not have been Proust's great-grandfather, who died in 1828. In the preceding issue of *L'Orient*, a brother Weil was also mentioned, raised to the rank of 30th degree by the Supreme Council of the Scottish Rite, in very good company: "Raised by the Supreme Council of the Scottish Rite to the rank of 33rd degree, brother James de Rothschild; to the rank of 32nd degree, brother Chasseloup-Laubat, Minister of France to the Germanic Diet; to the rank of 31st degree, brother Ch. Mayer, baron de Rothschild; to the rank of 30th degree, brothers Kloos and Weil."[21]

The brochure of the Supreme Council of France that published the minutes for the Fête de l'Ordre of winter solstice 1845 also lists the ateliers: Mont Sinaï lodge, symbolic lodge no. 6, had for Worshipful Master brother Desfammes and for deputy brother Weil, "30ᵉ, *ut supra*." One year later, during the winter solstice of 1846, the Worshipful Master of the Mont Sinaï lodge was brother Bancelin, while brother Weil remained the deputy.[22] This pamphlet further noted that brother Weil had been raised in rank to the 31st degree. Finally, these two publications list among active members of the Grand Council, under no. 3948, for the rank of 30th degree in 1846, the name "Weil (Godefroy). Huissier. / Boulevard Saint-Martin, 49, à Paris," and for the rank of 31st degree in 1847, "Weil. Huissier. / Boulevard Saint-Martin, 49, à Paris."

This brother Weil, deputy for the Mont Sinaï lodge, was called by the first name of Baruch in *L'Orient* in 1845 and by the first name of Godefroy in the Supreme Council's pamphlet in 1846. In fact, there was only one bailiff (*huissier*) in Paris with the name of Weil at that time. His name appears for the first time on the list of bailiffs for the département de la Seine in the *Almanach royal* de 1842.[23] His address is 59 Boulevard Saint-Martin, in the *Almanach royal* of 1842, 1843, and 1844, but it becomes 49 Boulevard Saint-Martin in 1845, 1846, and 1847.[24] And the 1842 *Almanach-Bottin* specifies that the first letter of his first name was, in fact, G.[25] Thus, this G. Weil could only have been Proust's own great-uncle, the only one of the 150 bailiffs in Paris with the name of Weil, and the first name not of Baruch or of Godefroy but of Godchaux (or Godecheaux or Godechaux). "By edict of the King, on the date of 8 September, M. G. B. Weil was named bailiff for the county court of the Seine. M. Weil, who has long been one of the Jewish community's most distinguished administrators, is the first Jew to assume the responsibilities of bailiff in Paris," announced the *Archives israélites* with pride in September 1841, just before noting that Rachel had "made a great impression" by attending the Rosh Hashanah service, Rue Notre-Dame de Nazareth.[26] *L'Orient* must have given him the first name of his father, a more striking Parisian figure (although Godchaux Weil was also known by the name of Godchaux Baruch Weil, Godchaux Baruch-Weil, or G. B. Weil), whereas the typographer of the Supreme Council must have transformed Godchaux into Godefroy, a lovely mistake in 1846, deleted in 1847. Having sold the porcelain factory he inherited from his father, he had bought a bailiff practice, but he continued to practice his new trade in the neighborhood of the family shops, between the Porte Saint-Martin and the Place de la République. He was still working in 1876, according to the *Annuaire-almanach du commerce, de l'industrie, de la magistrature et de l'administration*, but no longer in 1877, and he died in 1878.[27]

Godchaux Weil, the older half-brother of Nathé Weil, the great-uncle of Marcel Proust, the most assiduous contributor to the *Archives israélites* between 1840 and 1850 under the pseudonym of Ben Lévi, a moderately reformist Jew, was thus an active member of the Freemasons of the Scottish Rite during those same years. There was nothing irreconcilable about these two activities, Jewish and Masonic. Adolphe Crémieux, a longtime mason, presided over the Central Jewish Consistory of France from 1843 to 1845.

An article appeared in the *Archives israélites* in June 1844 entitled "Du rôle des israélites dans la franc-maçonnerie." Signed W. . . ., Worshipful Master of the Mont Sinaï Lodge, Orient of Paris," it was thus written by Godchaux Weil himself. According to him, "it was long believed that a Jew could not become a Freemason without renouncing the religion of his fathers, or at least without his faith suffering grievously," but that prejudice disappeared at "the beginning of our century," first among Christians, and then among Jews, and "Freemasonry . . . soon contained within it all those Jews considered eminent gentlemen and distinguished citizens."[28] Godchaux Weil prided himself on belonging to that elite group, his membership as a Freemason having helped him to arrive there.

In the 1840s, the *Archives israélites* and the masonic review *L'Orient* often returned to the "question of Jewish masons" and condemned in identical terms the Prussian

Freemasonry that refused access to Jews, unlike the French and British orders.[29] On 2 November 1844, in a letter to the Lieutenant Grand Commandeur du Rite Écossais, Général de Fernig, the Mont Sinaï lodge expressed their support for his interventions (which would prove fruitless) with the prince of Prussia, brother of the king and protector of lodges, asking that those masons "belonging to the religion of Moses no longer be turned away" from Prussian lodges. The name of the Mont Sinaï lodge, as well as "its composition," the letter explained, "made it obligatory" to write to him. The letter was adopted unanimously by the atelier and signed by "Le Vén. Weil, 30ᵉ Ch* K* S* [Chevalier Kadosh]" and other dignitary officers.[30] Godchaux Weil had surely initiated this process, which he summarized himself in the *Archives israélites*.[31]

When Adolphe Crémieux stepped down from the presidency of the central Consistory in July 1945, following the baptism of his wife and two children, Godchaux Weil supported his candidacy before the assembly of notables in preparation for the new elections, and then joined the delegation urging Crémieux to reverse his decision, an effort that temporarily succeeded.[32] This complicity may have worked against Weil when he was defeated in the next Paris consistory elections in August 1850, this time in the general vote, a loss that would lead to his withdrawal from official Jewish Community responsibilities.[33]

Godchaux and Nathé Weil, who was eight years younger, would remain close throughout their lives. Moreover, they were neighbors: at the time of his death in 1878, Godchaux lived at 36 Rue d'Enghein, three minutes from 40a Rue de Faubourg-Poissonière, home of Proust's grandparents. Accompanied by Edmond Revel (1847-1914), broker, stepson of Godchaux, born of the first marriage of Frédérique Zunz, it was Nathé Weil who registered his half-brother Godchaux's death at the tenth arrondissement town hall, 9 June 1878, just as he had registered the deaths of his sister-in-law Émilie Oppenheim and his nephew Paul Lazarus in December 1870, during the Siege of Paris.[34]

Three years later, in 1881, for the marriage of Clémence Weil (1854-1929), the only daughter of Godchaux and Frédérique Zunz, to Émile Jacob (1856-1928), a trader of semiprecious stones, at the 10th arrondissement town hall, the bride's witnesses were her uncle Nathé Weil and her cousin Georges Denis Weil.[35] The following year, Nathé was again the witness for Edmond Revel, who married Aline Aron (1860-1910).[36] Similarly in 1871, he served, along with his brother Louis, as witness to the marriage of Laure Lazarus (1849-1898), the daughter of his sister Adèle, to Gustave Neuburger (1836-1912).[37] He also served as witness for the marriages of the two daughters of his sister Flora, Emma Marguerite Alcan (1856–1926), to Élie Ernest Léon (1848–1909), merchant, in 1877, and Louise Alcan (1860–1950), to Adolphe Mayer (1844–1884), merchant, in 1882.[38]

About ten years earlier, the three daughters of Moïse Weil were married in Bauvais, their hometown, where their father was the state architect. For the marriage of Jenny Weil (1846–1922) to Xavier Boeuf (1830–1898) in January 1870, her uncles Godchaux and Louis Weil were witnesses. But for the marriage of Hélène Weil (1847–1925) to Casimir Bessière (1829–1892) in August 1872, no less than three uncles signed the registry, Godchaux, Nathé, and Alphonse Weil, a recently retired infantry captain. A few months later, for the marriage of Claire Weil (1848–1929) to Léon Neuburger (1840–1932) in December 1872, her uncles Godchaux and Nathé again made the journey to Bauvais.[39]

Half a century after the death of Baruch Weil, his sons remained close to one another and supportive of their nephews and nieces. Nathé Weil paid many visits to the Paris townhalls, especially in the tenth arrondissement, Rue du Faubourg-Saint-Martin, not far from Porte Saint-Martin and Rue de Bondy, where he grew up, but also in the ninth arrondissement, as well as the sixteenth, where, accompanied by his brother Louis Weil and doctor Adrien Proust, he registered the birth, 10 July 1871, of the oldest of his grandsons, Valentin Louis Georges Eugène Marcel Proust.[40] As the oldest child of Baruch Weil's second marriage, Nathé Weil was chosen to register the family's births, marriages, and deaths. His daughter, Jeanne Weil, could not have been unaware of her first cousins' fortunes and misfortunes, for example, the sons of Merline, Nathé's oldest half-sister, Maurice and Léonce Cohen, buried in the Baruch Weil tomb in 1883 and 1901, or the daughters of Flora, Nathé's youngest sister, Marguerite and Louise Alcan, who, as the young widow of Adolphe Meyer, married Gaspard Ernest Lévy (1861–1910) in 1887, with cousins Charles Nathan and Georges Weil serving this time as witnesses.[41]

Ernest Lévy, with his brother Abraham Lucien Lévy (1865–1917), owned Léon & Lévy, later called Lévy & Fils, the second largest postcard maker in France during the Belle Époque, known by the trademark L. L. Their father, Isaac Lévy, had started the business with his father-in-law, Moÿse Léon. Initially, as makers of stereoscopic images, they enjoyed great success during the International Exposition of 1867. "In those days I loved the theater, with a platonic passion since my parents had not yet allowed me to enter a theater, and I pictured to myself so inaccurately the pleasures one might experience there that I almost believed that each spectator looked as though into a stereoscope at a scene that was for him alone, though similar to the thousand others being looked at, each one for himself, by the rest of the audience," observed the narrator in "Combray," before adding: "Every morning I would run to the Morris column to see what shows were being announced," because the stereoscope and the Morris column were two inventions contemporary with Proust's childhood.[42]

The Léon & Lévy firm went into postcard making when tastes changed. Its two specialties were French cities and orientalist images, in particular women from the colonies displaying one or two breasts. Another sign of strong family bonds, Lucien Lévy would marry Noémie Neuburger in 1894, the daughter of Léon Neuburger and Claire Weil.[43] Thus the Lévy brothers married two Weil cousins, Louise Alcan, daughter of Flora Weil and granddaughter of Baruch Weil, and Noémie Neuburger, daughter of Claire Weil, granddaughter of Moïse Weil, and great-granddaughter of Baruch Weil.

We still lack proof that Proust's grandfather was himself a Freemason like his older brother (which brings to mind the obelisk on the family tomb in Père-Lachaise, a monument whose style and state of repair dates it to long after the death of Baruch Weil in 1828 and much closer to that of Godchaux in 1878). But Godchaux's Masonic activities and Nathé's cremation leave little doubt. Certainly, one would expect Adrien Proust, an important figure in the Third Republic, to belong to the Grand Orient de France, matrix of republicanism, opportunism, and radicalism, rather than the Suprême Conseil de France, more monarchist in its leanings. The Ancient and Accepted Scottish Rite, into which Godchaux Weil had been initiated in the 1840s, was more invested in hierarchy than the Grand Orient. At the time of the engagement of Jeanne Weil and Adrien Proust, toward the end of the Second Empire, called the Liberal Empire, these political nuances had nonetheless blurred. Adolphe Crémieux, who had evolved from liberal monarchism to republicanism in the 1840s, was the Minister of Justice from 25 February 1848 to 4 September 1870, and then commander of the Suprême Conseil of the Ancient and Accepted Scottish Rite from 1869 until his death in 1880. During the Third Republic, among the Worshipful Masters of the Mont Sinaï lodge, that is, Godchaux Weil's lodge, was Paul Strauss (1852-1942), Jew, journalist, radical senator and minister.[44] Édouard Schneeberg, director of the Jewish funeral home that the Weil family long patronized, also belonged to the Mont Sinaï lodge and was a dignitary of the Grande Loge de France, running advertisements for his business in the Jewish newspapers and in the *Bulletin de la LICA*, but also in *Le Radical* and the *Bulletin hebdomadaire des loges de la région parisienne*.[45] In his rediscovered letter, Proust insists nevertheless on his grandfather's enduring monarchist affinities, his liberal temperament, even "a bit reactionary," in Jeanne Proust's eyes, an attitude typical of the Jewish bourgeoisie of his generation, more sympathetic to the Grande Loge de France (which the Suprême Conseil created in 1894) than the Grand Orient. "Orléanism = Juiverie," claimed Urbain Gohier after having read Spire's article in *Les nouvelles littéraires* that had revealed to him Proust's Jewishness.[46] There was no contradiction in any case between belonging to the lodge of Mont Sinaï du Rite Écossais and the Société du Mont Sinaï, one of the oldest charity organization of Parisian Jews.

Proust rarely mentions Freemasonry in his novel, but this background information, which he must have known, increases the significance of the comparison he makes between homosexuals, Jews, and Freemasons in *Sodom et Gomorrhe I*:

> excluded even, save at times of high misfortune, when the majority rally around the victim, like the Jews around Dreyfus, from the sympathy—sometimes from the company—of their own kind, who are disgusted to be made to see themselves as they are, depicted in a mirror that no longer flatters them . . . forming a freemasonry far more extensive, more effective, and less suspected than that of the lodges, for it rests on an identity of tastes, of needs, of habits, of dangers, of apprenticeship, of knowledge, of commerce, and of vocabulary, in which even the members who do not wish to know one another at once recognize one another by natural or conventional signs, whether involuntary or deliberate, which indicate to the beggar one of his own kind in the great nobleman whose carriage door he is closing, to the father in his daughter's fiancé, to the man who had wanted to be cured, or to confess, or to be defended, in the doctor or the priest or the lawyer of whom he has gone in search.[47]

Nathé Weil, more of a rationalist than Godchaux, as his cremation demonstrates, or than their father Baruch, *mohel* for the Jewish community, nonetheless respected the traditions of Judaism and, "following a custom that he already no longer understood, went every year to put a stone on his parents' grave." His gesture, faithful to the ancestral observance, was symbolic and no longer comprised any religious intention on his part.

"WHAT A TRIAL, THE DEATH OF A FATHER!"

The mysterious addressee of Proust's final word on Jewishness was finally revealed, appealed to by name in the rediscovered draft: "My grandfather, my dear Daniel, went to all the performances of *La belle Hélène*." Proust was addressing his old friend Daniel Halévy (figure 38), fellow student at the Condorcet lycée and perhaps even at the "cours Pape-Carpantier" with his cousin Jacques Bizet. Daniel Halévy, one year younger than Proust, and, like Bizet, the object of Proust's passion for a brief time in their adolescence, founded a series of short-lived reviews—*La revue de seconde, La revue verte, La revue lilas,* and *Le Banquet*—with Proust, Robert Dreyfus, and Jacques Bizet. Their relationship was always strained and bumpy, often hurtful on one side or the other. "You deal me small blows according to the rules but your switches are so flowered that I cannot hold it against you," Proust wrote to him in

Figure 38. Edgar Degas, *Daniel Halévy,* 14 October 1895.

Photo © RMN–Grand Palais (Musée d'Orsay) / Hervé Lewandowski.

autumn 1888, after Daniel Halévy had rejected his advances.[48] Much later, in 1904, on receiving Proust's translation of Ruskin's *The Bible of Amiens*, Halévy thanked him, in a manner of speaking, in these candid terms: "I must tell you that I have not read it. I hate reading books just because they have been sent to me."[49]

Daniel Halévy totally disregarded his Jewish origins: grandson of Léon Halévy (1802–1883) and son of Ludovic Halévy (1834–1908), his paternal grandmother was Alexandrine Le Bas (1813–1893), the daughter of Hippolyte Le Bas (1782–1867), architect for Notre-Dame-de-Lorette during the Restoration and then for the Institut de France, and his mother was Louise Breguet (1847–1930), one of the great family of Swiss Protestant clockmakers. For the Halévy family, it was not that one "already no longer understood" Jewish customs as for the descendants of Nathé Weil (in Jeanne Weil's home at least, because her brother Georges's family was more observant), but that one deliberately ignored them and denied all Jewishness. Recalling the indifference of Geneviève Straus (her witticism is notorious: "I have too little religion to change it"), Robert Dreyfus described "the Halévy family, where all religions were mixed and fraternized going far back."[50] Léon Halévy, who had married a Catholic, and Ludovic Halévy, baptized in 1836, transmitted almost nothing of their Jewish heritage to Daniel and his older brother Élie, except their family name (and actually, their first names). "You are not Jews," Ludovic Halévy said to his sons, advising them only "not to forget the great Jewish qualities to which [they owed] much: work, persistence."[51] Here again: the legendary endurance of Swann during the Dreyfus affair and in the face of his illness.

The Halévy family (figure 39) acted as if they were not at all Jewish, and Léon Halévy was not the type to take his grandsons to leave a stone at the tomb of their great-grandfather Élie Halévy (1760–1862), son of a rabbi from Fürth in Bavaria, cantor in Paris synagogues, distinguished Hebrew scholar and learned Talmudist, member of and translator for the first central consistory appointed by Napoleon in 1808. According to his son Léon: "All of the Jews in Paris followed our father's funeral procession" to the Jewish section of the Montmartre cemetery.[52] Proust's great-uncle, Godchaux Weil, was present: according to his obituary in the *Archives israélites*, "at just twenty years old, [he delivered] a speech on behalf of the Consistory at the tomb of Élie Halévy, father of the famous composer, that was reprinted in *L'Opinion*, 6 November 1826, a literary newspaper edited by MM. de Jouy and Népomucéne Lemercier, of the Académie Française."[53] Godchaux Weil was introduced in *L'Opinion* as M. Baruch Weil the younger, and his speech, "remarkable for its lively sensibility and an ingenious comparison

Figure 39. Élie Halévy, Ludovic Halévy, M. Bodley, Émile Straus, Geneviève Straus, Mme Bodly, Mme de Gournay, Albert Boulanger-Cavé, and Ferdinand Brunetière. Photo © Beaussant Lefèvre et Studio Sebert.

drawn from the Scriptures" was quoted at length.[54] Élie Halévy and Baruch Weil were part of the handful of the first prominent Jews who established a Jewish community in Paris during the First Empire. Their great-grandsons had this genealogy in common, which had somehow made them like "two alley cats, in two opposite gutters, on the defensive, their fur bristling, and only drawing in their claws with infinite caution," as Sainte-Beuve described Stendhal and Hugo.[55]

In December 1913, we will recall, Proust asked Daniel Halévy to get copies of *Du côté de chez Swann* to a few contributors to the *Cahiers de la quinzaine*, among them André Spire, listed first. That is why I hypothesized earlier that Daniel Halévy could have been Spire's intermediary and the addressee of Proust's remark on the Jewish section of Père-Lachaise. Spire seems to have been familiar with the entire purported letter, or at least with the whole rediscovered extract, since just before quoting the sentence about the annual visit to the cemetery, he confidently identifies Proust's grandfather with the hero's grandfather in *À la recherche du temps perdu*. He cites as evidence the arias from Fromental Halévy's *La Juive* and Saint-Saëns's *Samson et Dalila*, which appear both in the rediscovered letter and in *Du côté de chez Swann*, but he cites neither those works mentioned only in the letter (*La belle Hélène*, the cavatina from *Barbier de Séville*) nor those that appear only in "Combray" (*Archers, faites bonne garde! . . . , De ce timide Israélite . . . , Oui je suis de la race élue*) and that are still not identified.

I also considered Lacretelle earlier (but with less conviction because the addressee had to share with the author a modicum of Jewish culture), but that was because Proust complained of his health ("since I cannot leave my bed") and because the hypothetical letter is traditionally dated to "the end of his life" as Maurois said, which picks up on Spire's 1923 note: "'There is no longer anybody,' he wrote not long ago to a friend. . . ." Whereas it turns out that the sentence is older than and predates the publication of *Du côté de chez Swann*, since it prefigures the portrait of the grandfather in "Combray," which Proust would not have reproduced after the fact in a letter to a friend.

The rediscovered manuscript could have been part of the letter of condolence, or more accurately, the draft of the letter of condolence, that Daniel Halévy received from Proust after the death of his father (this was my assumption in the French version of this book, before the first part of the draft as well as the fair copy resurfaced). Ludovic Halévy, novelist, playwright, librettist with Henri Meilhac for the masterpieces of Offenbach, *La belle Hélène* (1864) among them, as well as the author of the libretto for *Carmen* by Bizet (1875), and a true gentleman, died on 7 May 1908. "The letter from Proust to Daniel Halévy, written the day of the death of Ludovic Halévy, has not been found," note the editors of their correspondence.[56] The other letters from Proust to Halévy dating from the years 1907 and 1908 to which we do have access all come from the collection of Jean-Pierre Halévy (1927–2005), son of Léon Halévy (1902–1980) and grandson of Daniel, to which they belonged before going to the Bibliothèque Nationale de France in the early 2000s.[57]

Beginning in early 1907, Proust, gradually recovering from the loss of his mother, who died in September 1905, had started writing again and was publishing columns sporadically in Gaston Calmette's *Le Figaro*, and then his pastiches of the "Lemoine Affair" in the February and March 1908 *Supplément littéraire* of the daily newspaper. His first returning article was "Sentiments filiaux d'un parricide," published as the "lead column" in *Le Figaro*, 1 February 1907, on the murder of Henri Van Blarenberghe, whom he knew slightly and who had just killed his mother before killing himself. *Figaro* readers were used to shorter, wittier, and less scandalous "Premier-Paris" articles. These four plus columns made such a strong impression on Daniel Halévy that he cut them out and glued them on sheets of paper he had bound into a small booklet that he asked Proust to inscribe for him (the Halévys were collectors).[58] He was undoubtedly influenced by his father in this process, who had "marveled" at "Sentiments filiaux d'un parricide" and had let Robert Dreyfus know: "Your friend young Proust just wrote an astonishing article, full of talent and originality."[59] Proust was not unaware of Ludovic Halévy's reaction, which he reported immediately to Reynaldo Hahn: "And old Halévy did not write to me because this and that, but had me told this and that, and cut out the article, glued it, kept it, etc."[60] The idea of cutting and pasting might thus have come first from Daniel Halévy's father.

Learning of the death of Ludovic Halévy, "whom I knew very little, but whom I admired and loved deeply," as he confided to Geneviève Straus (figure 39), first cousin of the deceased, Proust immediately had the intention of "writing something on M. Halévy" for *Le Figaro*, as he had published there in July 1907 a short piece on the death of the grandmother of his friend Robert de Flers, another old Condorcet schoolmate and contributor to *Le Banquet*, now an editor at *Le Figaro*.[61] The mourning of his friends made Proust's own all the more intense.

A few months earlier, he had addressed Daniel Halévy as "the son of perhaps the only man since the days of Greece whose joking is as witty, as delightful, as poetic as Plato's, the best comic author of all time."[62] It is astonishing, in some perverse way, that the son of such a father could appreciate the heaviness of Péguy. In their youth Proust was not as close to the Halévy clan as he would have liked (Daniel Halévy no doubt had something to do with that), as Ludovic Halévy, in his eyes, embodied the quintessence of the French mind and the art of conversation, which the duchess of Guermantes would inherit in the novel: "the type of mind that is characteristic of Mérimée and Meilhac and Halévy, and was hers also, led her, in contrast to the verbal sentimentality of an earlier generation, to adopt a style of conversation that rejects everything to do with grandiloquence and the expression of lofty feeling."[63] Ludovic Halévy was the best friend of Degas, who had been his classmate at the Louis-le-Grand lycée and who often done his portrait, famously in the wings of the Opera which the two of them attended regularly. The photographs of the Halévy family taken by Degas, of young Daniel in particular, illustrate their daily intimacy, until the Dreyfus affair, which divided them.[64] Proust was more dazzled by the father, who fascinated him, than by the son, whose literary and aesthetic tastes, as well as his social and political ideas, did not attest to the same tact, style, and easygoing manner. Thus, after the "Victory," when Daniel Halévy, moving toward the right, signed with Henri Massis and Charles Maurras the "Pour un parti de l'intelligence" Manifesto in July 1919, Proust took up his pen immediately to rebuff him: "I must tell you this evening about how much I disapprove of your manifesto in *Le Figaro*." That proclamation, he continued, "unwittingly brings to mind 'Deutschland über alles' and therefore is somewhat unpleasant. It has been the nature of 'our race' (would a good Frenchman speak of a French 'race'?) to know how to combine much pride with even more modesty."[65] Ludovic Halévy, for whom Proust had imagined writing a tribute in 1908, might have shown better judgment and more discretion.

But on Sunday, 10 May 1908, the very day of Ludovic Halévy's funeral, Proust confided to Geneviève Straus that André Beaunier had "gotten there ahead of him."[66] In fact, an obituary written by Beaunier had appeared the day before, 9 May 1908, on the front page of *Le Figaro*. Proust's dream of "writing something on M. Halévy" could not have lasted more than a day. Nonetheless he offered Madame Straus some indication of what he could have said, had he had the opportunity, about Ludovic Halévy and her as well, those two beings "for whom conversation is a work of art," as would be true of Oriane. He mentions in passing the obituary that Sainte-Beuve wrote for Fromental Halévy (1799–1862), composer of *La Juive* (1835), Madame Straus's father and Ludovic Halévy's uncle.[67] Sainte-Beuve's "Monday" on Fromental Halévy reappears many times in the correspondence between Proust and Madame Straus, a bit like a password, and Proust would finally send her the article four years later.[68] In spring 1908, when he was not yet engaged in an in-depth reading of Sainte-Beuve in preparation for an essay on the critic that would consume him beginning in November of that year, Proust was already thinking about him, while in the newly discovered draft of a text intended for Daniel Halévy (in fact, the inscription in Daniel Halévy's booklet containing "Sentiments filiaux d'un parricide"), he was drawing the first sketches for the grandfather of "Combray."

In a letter written the same day, Sunday 10 May 1908, to Robert Dreyfus, a mutual friend who was closer to Daniel Halévy than Proust was, Proust confesses the "qualms" he felt with regard to Dreyfus after having sent his letter of condolence to Halévy: "I said to myself: Robert Dreyfus has the right to speak to him in that way, I do not, at all," as Dreyfus and Halévy were "best friends."[69]

Ludovic Halévy was most certainly a very amiable man, the father that all Daniel Halévy's friends might have dreamed of having. Daniel Halévy kept Proust at a distance from his family, but that was not the case with Robert Dreyfus who was welcome at the Halévy home, and who concludes his memorial tribute in *Pages libres* with this cry: "what a trial, the death of a father—and of such a father!"[70] That exclamation cannot help but recall that he himself had lost his father when he was a small child, and that Ludovic Halévy was the paternal ideal, the "complete Parisian," who put aside his own ambitions to be attentive to others and encourage them in their endeavors.

What might Robert Dreyfus have had the right to say to Daniel Halévy, a right that Proust may have exercised without possessing it? Was it not simply a matter of Proust evoking his Jewish heritage, that heritage that Daniel Halévy and his older brother Élie were even further removed from than the son of Jeanne Weil. Relations between Proust and Halévy were always complicated, brusquer than between Proust and Dreyfus, a devoted and admiring friend. They never saw each other again, it seems, after the 1890s, since Proust would say of him in 1920: "it has been twenty-five years since I last saw him."[71] That was in Proust's preface to *Tendres stocks* by Paul Morand, regarding their differing perspectives on the criticism of Sainte-Beuve, whom Halévy was defending at the time.[72] Beyond their complicity during the Dreyfus affair, Proust did not approve of Halévy's lingering admiration for Péguy, or for Péguy's vague style, humanitarian vocation, or return to Catholicism (Halévy broke with Péguy in 1910 following his *Apologie pour notre passé* and Péguy's reply in *Notre jeunesse*, but only to move further to the right).[73] Between Halévy and Proust, a blunder, an affront was always lurking. Their correspondence is made up of misunderstandings and hurt feelings, the letters sometimes being received "like slaps in the face."[74] Recalling to Daniel Halévy the inquisitorial behavior of Nathé Weil toward young Marcel's friends who denied their Jewishness: could this have been what Proust had no right to do (if not in his condolence letter, then in his inscription of "Sentiments filiaux d'un parricide")? But given that Robert Dreyfus was also discreet about his Jewish origins, would it have been any more legitimate for him to remind Daniel Halévy of his Jewish heritage? Not according to the opinion of Strasbourg's *La tribune juive*, we will recall, when they treated Robert Dreyfus as a renegade at the time of his death in 1939.

The letter to Robert Dreyfus from 10 May 1908 poses an additional question. Proust speculates, with regard to his project for *Le Figaro* that Beaunier's article forced him to abandon: "that what I said was perhaps more precise and specific, but lacked form."[75] What did he mean by "more precise and specific"? Here again Proust cultivates mystery. He did not know Ludovic Halévy well. The precious photo albums that Ludovic Halévy compiled include images of Robert Dreyfus, Fernand Gregh, and André Rivoire at Sucy-en-Brie (figure 34), where the Halévys vacationed, but of the core contributors to *Banquet*, only Proust is absent. What specific details could he have provided? His article could well have contained personal elements, autobiographical digressions, like his other columns for *Le Figaro* in 1907 and 1908. Nonetheless it is unlikely that he would have included the portrait of Nathé Weil and the account of their visits together to the Jewish section of Père-Lachaise cemetery.

A few weeks later, in a letter to Daniel Halévy that, this time, was not lost, Proust returns to the pain he feels knowing that his friend is unhappy, as well as his own "grief over never being able to see" Ludovic Halévy again, and he assures his friend that this grief is not "a one-time thing, like a letter," that is to say, like one of those condolence letters that one writes to relieve one's conscience. Proust would resort to the same stylistic device, as we have seen, in the letter he would write in November 1910 to Robert Dreyfus, a month after his brother Henri's suicide. So here was a custom that Proust honored: he sent a second letter of condolence to his friends after a month, as though he strictly observed the rite of *Sheloshim* and did not fail to mark the end of the first thirty days of mourning. Thus, he wrote to Daniel Halévy: "Know at least that my sorrow lasts, will last, and speaks to me often of you, of your father."[76] Indeed there was nothing conventional about Proust's first letter of condolence to Daniel Halévy, long lost, partially recovered. In it, Proust offered memories of his grandfather, the relationship between his mother and his grandfather, and other details we do not know.

COLLAGE

Nevertheless, two questions remain hanging, like loose threads or loose ends, that we would still love to tie up. First, this putative letter of condolence to Daniel Halévy: why would it include four pages on Proust's grandfather, Nathé Weil, on his political ideas, perfectly illustrating the monarchism of the liberal Parisian Jewish bourgeoisie, on his sense of injustice over the fate of the working classes, a feeling tinged with Hebraic *tsedakah* more than Christian charity, republican equality, or radical solidarity, on his anticlericalism, which Proust presents as worthy and respectable although Nathé Weil requested cremation, and which he compares to Louis-Philippe's assertion of neutrality, sending his five sons to the Henri-IV school, following the eldest Ferdinand-Philippe, in 1819, despite the annoyance of Louis XVIII?[77]

Was Proust's grandfather's love of opera, and especially comic opera, reason enough to justify this digression? His enthusiasm for Fromental Halévy's *La Juive* and for *La belle Hélène*, with its libretto by Meilhac and Ludovic Halévy, seems a bit ridiculous, a bit nouveau riche, in the way Proust describes it. Moreover, each time *La belle Hélène* comes up in Proust's writing, in his correspondence as well as his novel, it is always with a schoolboy's cheeky humor, for example, when he compares it to the plays of Paul Claudel, or when, in a letter to Daniel Halévy himself, he remembers how *La belle Hélène* saved him "forever and ever from tolerating the *Ubu-rois*."[78] And did Nathe Weil really go to "all the performances of *La belle Hélène*"?

Spire would note in his Proust obituary that "his Jewish grandfather [Proust's], that amiable old man...like many French Jews who had made their fortunes under Louis-Philippe and Napoleon III, had a passion for theater, knowing by heart a great number of pieces from operas and operettas and had the odd habit of singing them on any occasion" (a commentary that confirms that Spire had read the entire letter).[79] The portrait of Nathé Weil sent to Daniel Halévy prefigures "Combray" as early as spring 1908. In *Du côté de chez Swann*, the grandfather would sing the same arias from *La Juive* and *Samson et Dalila* when Bloch arrived, because he "claimed that each time I formed a closer attachment to one of my friends than others and brought him home, he was always a Jew,"[80] as Proust formed attachments to Jacques Bizet, Robert Dreyfus, and Daniel Halévy. No doubt "these little idiosyncrasies of my grandfather's did not imply any feeling of ill will toward my friends," and the hero's grandfather is not Jewish, but he inherits many traits from Nathé Weil. Just as Nathé Weil recognized "that someone about whom we had spoken to him, despite a changed name, was Jewish," the hero's grandfather would guess "the Jewish background of those of my friends who were in fact Jewish," even if the name "had nothing particularly Jewish about it," and he would "adroitly" ask questions, engage in a "subtle interrogation" to lead the visitor to "confess his origins," just as Nathé Weil confirmed his intuition through "a few cleverly asked questions" before that humming that caused young Proust "constant terror."

But was it really appropriate to recall to Daniel Halévy that no one who denied his Jewishness could fool Proust's grandfather? Was it polite, kind, generous to offer him this lesson on his Jewishness? No, one might think, as Nathalie Mauriac Dyer pointed out to me over the course of our conversations regarding the rediscovered letter, and Proust pretends to recoup his ill-advised indelicacy, or his deliberate tactlessness, or his calculated and disguised insolence, with his little sentence on the cemetery on Rue du Repos, since that grandfather, so quick to unmask assimilated and integrated Jews, might no longer have been so Jewish himself. Thus, the famous sentence, more than or as much as an avowal of his own Jewishness on Proust's part, might have been a ruse meant to soften a dig aimed at an old schoolmate with whom relations were always strained, even following the death of his father. Unless Proust was simply indulging in his taste for anecdotes and his comic sense, that "great freedom of speech" that gave the conversation of his distant cousin, the well-read engineer Maurice Cohen, "a particular, original, and pleasing turn."[81]

A second loose thread, or a second mystery, stems from the date on which Daniel Halévy showed Proust's autograph to André Spire. It was written in the spring of 1908; Spire quotes it fifteen years later, in May 1923 in the *Jewish Chronicle*. It seems certain that he had knowledge of the entire text, not just the sentence about the Jewish cemetery on Rue du Repos. Had Halévy shown it to him after Proust's death, when Spire was writing his Proust obituary? Or much earlier? And, a bonus question, did Spire make a copy of the manuscript? Or perhaps keep the letter, since it is not part of the Jean-Pierre Halévy collection now held at the Bibliothèque Nationale de France? Or did the sentence in question strike him so deeply that he remembered it at the requisite moment?

Spire wrote in 1923 that Proust had written that sentence "not long ago to a friend." Now, thanks to a final stroke of luck, Marie-Brunette Spire, alerted to it through my inquiry, has just rediscovered the manuscript of André Spire's Proust obituary in her father's archives. That twenty-nine-page manuscript, begun on 5 December and completed on 9 December 1922, just three weeks after Proust's death, is accompanied by a sheaf of preparatory notes and notes on *À la recherche du temps perdu*. In the middle of page 18 of the manuscript appears a little piece of paper cut from another piece, blue, serrated along the top edge, and glued onto the page. It is written in pencil, seven lines of handwriting that is neither Spire's nor Daniel Halevy's (figure 40). This piece is glued after the words "he wrote in a letter to a friend," and the famous sentence on the "little Jewish cemetery" does indeed appear there: "There is no longer anybody, not even myself, since I cannot leave my bed, who will go. . . ." This is the only note glued to the manuscript, which confirms the importance of the sentence for Spire, who first began to recopy it before sticking the scrap of blue paper to the very page that he was in the process of writing.

Two immediate observations are worth making: first, the blue sheet does read, *"puisque je ne* peux *me lever,"* not *"puisque je ne* puis *me lever,"* the change introduced by André Maurois in 1949 and wrongly repeated since then; second, and more significant, the phrase "not long ago" does not appear in Spire's manuscript. But two new questions immediately arise: in whose handwriting are the seven lines from Proust's letter to Halévy on the scrap of blue paper that Spire affixed to his manuscript? And why did Spire add, after the fact, that "not long ago," between the December 1922 manuscript and the 1923 publication of the obituary, perhaps in the typescript draft?

The correspondence between Spire and Halévy goes quiet in November and December 1922 and teaches us nothing. In Paris at the time, they did not exchange

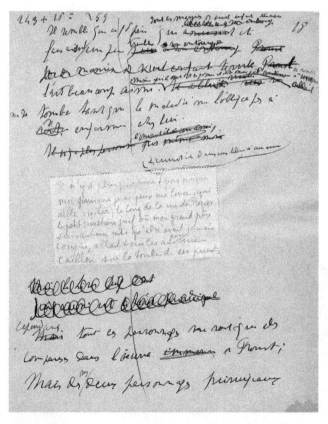

Figure 40. André Spire, manuscript. Photo © Collection Spire.

letters. But the affixed paper, easily recognizable thanks to the serration on two sides, is clearly one of those notecards or else one of those "*petits bleus*" that circulated in the underground pneumatic tube system in Paris. The model was still identical in the 1970s, a period in which we communicated by pneumatic tubes because one had to wait for several years in order to get a telephone line. Proust used that service, and "*petits bleus*" circulate abundantly in *À la recherche du temps perdu*, like those by which the hero communicates with Gilberte:

> Another time, still preoccupied by the desire to hear La Berma in a classical play, I had asked her if she happened to own a little book in which Bergotte talked about Racine, and which one could no longer find. She had asked me to remind her of its exact title and that evening I had addressed an express letter to her, writing on the envelope that name, Gilberte Swann, which I had so often copied out in my notebooks. The next day she brought me a packet tied up in mauve ribbons and sealed with white wax containing the little book, which she had asked someone to find for her. "You see? It really is the one you asked for," she said, taking from her muff the letter I had sent her. But on the address of this *pneumatique*—which, only yesterday, was nothing, was merely a *petit bleu* which I had written, and which, now that a telegraph boy had delivered it to Gilberte's concierge and a servant had carried it to her room, had become a priceless thing, one of the *petits bleus* she had received that day—it was hard for me to recognize the insignificant, solitary lines of my handwriting under the printed circle apposed to it by the post office, under the inscriptions added in pencil by one of the telegraph messengers, signs of actual realization, stamps from the outside world, violet bands symbolizing life, which for the first time came to espouse, sustain, uplift, delight my dream.[82]

Since the Proust quotation is not Halévy's handwriting, he may have had someone copy it onto a notecard for Spire's benefit. But these two questions remain unanswered: who copied the sentence, and when did Spire add the misleading phrase, "not long ago"? Not appearing in the first draft, those words did not flow spontaneously from Spire's pen. Thus, they need not be treated with the same respect given proven testimony. Was it perhaps "not long ago" that Halévy showed Spire Proust's letter? Spire did not have the letter in his possession at the time he was drafting the obituary, but he may have remembered the sentence and requested it from Halévy.

In late 1913, Proust had asked Daniel Halévy to see that a copy of *Du côté de chez Swann* reached Spire. Moreover he had used the occasion to remind Daniel Halévy of his respect for Ludovic Halévy: "How I would have loved for your father to have been able to read this book; I so sought his esteem."[83] Five years after Ludovic Halévy's death, he still held the same high place in Proust's estimation, and, as we have seen, Proust long imagined taking on the role for him that Sainte-Beuve had played for Fromental Halévy. Daniel Halévy and Spire had had a conversation about *Du côté de chez Swann* at that time, since Halévy reported certain parts of it to Proust, in particular, Spire's distrust of a novel lacking any philanthropic concerns.

What else had Halévy and Spire talked about in 1914 on the subject of Proust and his novel? Spire could have recalled to Halévy that Léon Blum had introduced him to Proust in the Sciences Po Hall twenty years earlier, and that Proust had impressed him as a "poseur." As a Zionist searching for the "Jewish soul," curious about vestiges of Judaism surviving in his most assimilated acquaintances, like Proust and Halévy, Spire, in reading "Combray," could not have helped noticing the grandfather's strange habit of sniffing out the assimilated Jews among the hero's friends. Was it in 1914 that Halévy showed him the letter he had received from Proust following Ludovic Halévy's death, with the sketches of the grandfather's tirades in "Combray"? Could Spire have remembered it in 1922 when he was writing his Proust obituary and have asked Halévy for the letter? That is a reasonable hypothesis.

If the account of the visit to the cemetery had not caught the attention of Daniel Halévy, whose Jewish origins meant little or nothing to him, it nevertheless struck André Spire, who read it in 1914 or in 1922, since it is to Spire that we owe these few winged words that have been circulating among Proustians, unattributed until now, for almost a century.[84] These are not literally Proust's final words on his Jewishness, since they date from 1908, but they were the definitive words.

The little Jewish section of Père-Lachaise lost its walls in 1881, when Proust was ten years old. It then merged into the large Paris cemetery, like a metaphor for the assimilation of French Jews. But Nathé Weil, who died in 1896 when Proust was twenty-five years old, so attentive to the Jewish origins of his grandson's friends, could "already no longer" understand the custom of leaving a stone at the family tomb when he performed that age-old gesture on the eve of Rosh Hashanah, or Yom Kippur, or the day of Shloshim, and guiding the hand of the future author of *À la recherche du temps perdu*. Proust knew perfectly what he was doing, as when he sent to his Jewish friends, those friends whose Jewishness his grandfather would

Figure 41. Eugène Atget, *Père-Lachaise, rue du Repos*, 1900–1901.
Photo © BnF, Paris.

unmask, a second letter of condolence after thirty days of mourning. It is said in *Le temps retrouvé* that "a book is a great cemetery where the names have been effaced from most of the tombs and are no longer legible."[85] No doubt, but a book, *À la recherche du temps perdu*, is also a little stone left at the tomb in remembrance, the little stone left at the walled Jewish cemetery on Rue du Repos (figure 41).

LATEST DEVELOPMENTS

In several digressions over the course of this chapter, I let it be understood that the story of Proust's sentence about his visits with his grandfather to the Jewish section of Père-Lachaise cemetery remained unfinished as my book went to print in France. I hypothesized, based on the incomplete manuscript of a rough draft provided by Nathalie Mauriac Dyer, that the mysterious sentence came from a letter of condolence that Proust sent to Daniel Halévy after the death of his father, Ludovic Halévy, on 7 May 1908. Now two invaluable manuscripts resurfaced in the year following the publication of my book in February 2022 and the exhibition at the Musée d'Art et d'Histoire du Judaïsm in spring and summer 2022, "Proust du côté de la mère," to which I contributed[86]—the book and exhibition both highlighting Proust's sentence.

The first treasure to appear was quite simply the small booklet in which Daniel Halévy had bound "Sentiments filiaux d'un parricide," Proust's article of 1 February 1907 that Halévy had cut out of *Le Figaro*, the true start of *À la recherche du temps perdu*. We knew about this booklet thanks to Proust's letters, but no one knew where to find it or even if it still existed. Then, in November 2022, it appeared in the catalog of the Jean-Baptiste de Proyart bookstore and was sold for a very high price.[87] We were able to examine it, and there we discovered, to our amazement, the long dedication inscribed by Proust at the beginning of the booklet, four large sheets, the second half of which is a fair copy, with just a few variants, of the text that we took for the draft of a condolence letter from Proust to Daniel Halévy. The error, happily, was not fatal.

Halévy had sent Proust his booklet "to sign" at the end of 1907.[88] Proust put off complying, and he still had not done so at the time of Ludovic Halévy's death in early May 1908, as he wrote to his friend toward the end of May or in June 1908 that he was thinking continually of his grief, thought "several times a week" of writing to him, and concluded: "Know at least that my sorrow lasts, will last, and speaks to me often of you, of your father."[89] He was writing to Halévy "today because you tell me that you need the little booklet that you made with my article." Then he wondered what his friend was waiting for from him: "You had asked me to "sign" it. What exactly does that mean? I must write what? Just my name? Where?" Thus, in all likelihood, it was in late May or in June 1908 that Proust finally wrote his dedication, a few weeks after Ludovic Halévy's death. And although that dedication is not, strictly speaking, a condolence letter from Proust to Daniel Halévy, it is not far removed from one, in time or in spirit, and it commemorates Daniel Halévy's grieving for his father.

Proust begins by mentioning "all that I know about the Van Blarenberghes." Mme Van Blarenberghe was "an old acquaintance of Maman," who often visited her, "an old reactionary lady," and it was M. Van Blarenberghe, and not Nathé

Weil, who was "a bit reactionary for the tastes of Maman," the transition through which Proust moves on from his memories of the Van Blarenberghes to recalling his grandfather, who was also rather conservative. Thus, Proust does much more than "sign" Daniel Halévy's booklet—and much more than their rocky friendship might require. He inscribed in it a dedication four pages long, which, in spring 1908, constitutes a very early draft of "Combray" and confirms that "Souvenirs filiaux d'un parricide" was a decisive step in the writing of *À la recherche du temps perdu*.

The second important discovery was of a double page identical to the one that had been sent to us and that in fact corresponds to the first part of the dedication.[90] Between the draft and the dedication, both now known, there are many but not significant variants. The last one must be mentioned to settle (for good?) the question that runs through the whole book: "There is no longer anybody, not even me, who cannot leave my bed, who will go along Rue du Repos to visit the little Jewish cemetery where my grandfather, following a custom that he already no longer understood, went every year to put a stone on his parents' grave," we read in the draft, a formulation that Proust corrected in the dedication—"following a custom that he never understood"—and that Spire quoted exactly in his Proust obituary, but that would become "following the custom that he never understood" in Cattaui and would remain so subsequently—at least until now. Can we assume that we are done with the stone that Nathé Weil left on the grave of Baruch Weil each year, when Proust accompanied his grandfather to the Jewish section of Père-Lachaise? As long as it is a matter of manuscripts—and collectors—we cannot swear to anything.

Postscript

During the confinement of spring 2020, the appeal of a new form of publishing and the weekly rhythm of a series allowed me to give shape to a research project I had begun years earlier on how Proust has been read in the Jewish community. The first stone was laid in a lecture I gave at the University of Tel Aviv in 2007, on "Israel before Israel," within the framework of a conference on "The French Intellectuals and Israel."[1] It was already a matter of French Intellectual Zionists, the few references to Zionism in *À la recherche du temps perdu*, and the Jewish journals: Albert Cohen's *La revue juive* and *Palestine*, published by the Association France-Palestine, that is, the French committee of the Friends of Zionism. Ten years earlier, in my article "Le 'profil assyrien' ou l'antisémitisme qui n'ose pas dire son nom: les libéraux dans l'affaire Dreyfus," I was interested in an image, that of the Assyrian beard, as a possible allusion to Judaism in late nineteenth-century culture and in Proust's novel.[2]

The bibliography on Proust and the Jewish question is extensive. The first book that I remember having read on the subject, when it was first published, is the one by Jean Recanati, *Profils juifs de Marcel Proust* (1979). I have just gone through it again to see what I owe to it. Recanati covers Proust's entire opus, pays particular attention to the representation of the Dreyfus affair in *Jean Santeuil*, but does not consider how the novel is read by the Jewish community.

Almost forty years later came the work of Patrick Mimouni, *Les mémoires maudites: Juifs et homosexuels dans l'oeuvre et la vie de Marcel Proust*, published in 2018 and cited on some occasions in the preceding pages. I became aware of it when my research was essentially complete, and our perspectives seemed to me incompatible. I do not think that Adrien Proust was the lover of Proust's uncle Louis Weil, who supposedly arranged the marriage with his niece to keep Adrien Proust close to him. Intrigues of this kind abound in *Sodome et Gomorrhe II, III*, and *IV*; they belong to the genre of the novel, but fabrications that blend fiction and factual history create confusion more than they advance our knowledge of the texts.

Between Recanati and Mimouni there have been countless contributions touching on the comparison between Jews and homosexuals, Sodom and Zion, beginning with the innovative article by Jeanne Bem in 1980, "Le juif et l'homosexuel dans *À la recherche du temps perdu*."[3] They appeared abundantly, first in the English language following *Epistemology of the Closet* (1990), the book by Eve Kosofsky Sedgwick, founder of so-called Queer Studies, and then in all languages.[4] But it was not this rich lode, this fertile line of interpretation, that it seemed opportune for me to continue to explore.

Many studies discuss the place of the Dreyfus affair in the life and work of Proust. It does not play an insignificant role: "I really believe I was the first Dreyfusard, since I was the one who went to ask Anatole France for his signature," Proust wrote to Paul Souday in 1919, after being awarded the Prix Goncourt.[5] But he keeps his distance from the affair in *À la recherche du temps perdu*, where it is seen through its social repercussions, usually laughable. In *Le temps retrouvé*, this reaches its height when it is treated as a distraction in relation to the vocation of the work, the discovery of the inner book: "Every major event, from the Dreyfus affair to the war, provided further excuses for writers not to decipher that book—they wanted to ensure the triumph of justice, to rebuild the moral unity of the nation, they were much too busy to think about literature. But these were simply excuses because they did not have, or no longer had, genius, or to put it another way, instinct."[6] Regarding the Dreyfus affair, we await the publication of the definitive book that Yuji Murakami will draw from his thesis, "L'affaire Dreyfus dans l'oeuvre de Proust," defended in 2012.

What matters to me is refuting the increasingly accepted idea that Proust's representation of Jews includes elements of anti-Semitism or Judeophobia. That is why it seemed to me crucial to concentrate on analyzing the earliest reception of *À la recherche du temps perdu* in the 1920s by the Jewish community, from the perspective of young Jews captivated by Zionism, as well as the perspective of consistorial and rabbinical institutions, as an antithesis. The still unsurpassed and irreplaceable research tool for conducting such an inquiry remains the bibliography established on the eve of World War II by Douglas W. Alden, "Marcel Proust and His French Critics," a meticulously detailed thesis defended at Brown

University in 1938. Inventoried there are nearly all the publications in which the signatures that interested me are to be found: Georges Cattaui, André Spire, Léon Pierre-Quint, Benjamin Crémieux, Ludmila Savitzky, Denis Saurat, René Groos. . . . Very few escaped the vigilance of Douglas Alden, only the young Marie-Louise Cahen-Hayem in the *Archives israélites*, for instance, or the anonymous Gustave Kahn in a *Menorah* editorial. Following that lead, the ground was prepared and the way marked in 2013 by Yuji Marakami in the introduction to his thesis, in which he refutes Alessandro Piperno's *Proust antijuif*, and by Joseph Brami in an article on the "Premières réceptions critiques 'juives' de *Swann*, 1923–1941."

For years this project was entitled "Jeunes juifs lecteurs de Proust" (Young Jewish Readers of Proust). That was still the title when I was invited by the Marcel Proust Gesellschaft to give a lecture in November 2019 at a conference on "Marcel Proust und das Judentum" in Berlin. Then, when it came time to post my first piece online, that working title seemed too descriptive, neutral, and flat to me. I improvised another one: "Proust sioniste" (Zionist Proust), since the young contributors to the Zionist reviews in the 1920s, *Menorah, La revue juive, Palestine*, publications financed by the Zionist Organization with Chaim Weizmann as its president, were Proust enthusiasts who saw him as a proud Jew whose novels could encourage other Jews to join their ranks. On the other hand, the reviews closer to consistorial authorities and institutional Judaism, *L'univers israélite* and the *Archives israélites* in Paris, *La tribune juive* in Strasbourg, had little use for Proust because they refused to separate Jewishness from religion.

The advantage of a series is that it prompts reactions while the work is in progress, and it allows for correction, reorientation, redress. "You could say instead 'Proust as viewed by a generation of Zionists,'" one friend wrote to me, "maybe 'Proust and Zionism,' but not 'Zionist Proust.'" Another reader suggested that the title "Proustian Zionists" would be more accurate. Yes, undoubtedly, since those young Zionists loved Proust (the work), whereas Proust (the man) never adhered to Zionism. Another objection to "Zionist Proust" was that the modifier was unfortunate and inopportune given the connotations that it could have today, evoking revisionist, nationalist, or religious neo-Zionism rather than secular post-Zionism. Those who raised this objection were surely recalling Resolution 3379 of the 1975 General Assembly of the United Nations, in which "Zionism is a form of racism and racial discrimination," a resolution revoked in 1991. But just as I protest the anachronism of now characterizing Proust as anti-Semitic or anti-Jewish, I do not want the connotations some might associate with Zionism in 1975 or 2020 tacked on to its meaning for Proust readers between 1922 and 1931. When I say "Zionist Proust," I do not mean, of course, that the man was a Zionist, but that for a few years those young Zionists readers lay claim to his work to advance their cause. Nevertheless, because of this ambiguity, I decided not to retain the title "Zionist Proust" for this book.

Certain leads could still be pursued. Until now we knew nothing about Robert Dreyfus, one of Proust's oldest and closest friends, or about his father's demise, or his brother's suicide, or even his professional life with the Rothschilds. What I learned led me gradually to revise my view on his relationship to Judaism, which I had considered to be as distant as the most assimilated Jews, like his friends Proust and Halévy. Contradictory reactions to his death in 1939 appearing in *La tribune juive* and *L'univers israélite*, one hostile, the other sympathetic, made me less certain, as did his response in *La revue juive de Genève* in 1937, following the first of Siegfried van Praag's articles that called the "assimilated" "deserters," and, as early as 1926 in his *Souvenirs sur Marcel Proust*, his warning against an anti-Semitic reading of *À la recherche du temps perdu*. Not to mention the fact that he was one of the first to take an interest in Alexandre Weill, before van Praag and Lehrmann, a shared curiosity that is worth considering, since some Zionists saw utopian socialism, espoused for a time by Weill, as anticipating Zionist messianism. To introduce his monograph on Weill, and without indicating what led him to this "obscure man," Dreyfus considers *Ma jeunesse*.[7] He finds Weill's memoir on his Alsatian childhood, his Talmudic initiation in Metz, and his rabbinical studies in Frankfort to be a "moving and delightful book," the one that, to date, had established the "Jewish soul," in the way that Barrès wanted to establish the "Lorraine soul."[8]

Later in his study Dreyfus offers proof, moreover, of his knowledge of "postbiblical Judaism" (as van Praag said, reproaching Proust for his lack of it), which shows that he received a Jewish education. And I noted earlier the presence of Rabbi Schilli at his funeral at the Montmartre cemetery in 1939. In short, my initial opinion—"His own Jewishness seems to have left him completely indifferent. . . . He seems to have been an excellent example of the dejudaized Jew, absorbed by the French mind"—now strikes me as excessive or even erroneous, to be revised, in any case.

My research into the Baruch Weil tomb at Père-Lachaise cemetery has given me the sense that we still have much to learn in this area. There were two architects among Proust's great-uncles, Benjamin and Moïse Weil, two scholars in the family, Moïse Weil again, who was interested in churches and archeology, and Maurice Cohen, passionate about literary history and bibliography, one unfortunate musician among Proust's mother's first cousins, Léonce Cohen, and a writer of some renown prior to Proust, Godchaux Weil, who mysteriously stopped writing, or at least publishing, at about the age of forty-five. It would be good to know more about them all, because their great-nephew or distant cousin would follow in their footsteps.

We should go more deeply into the relationship between Baruch Weil's sons and Freemasonry. Rumor has it that Moïse Weil, the Beauvais architect, and Louis Weil, the button maker, might have been Freemasons, but this is not established fact. I have, I believe, shown that Godchaux Weil was a dignitary for the Ancient and Accepted Scottish Rite, just as he was the most involved of the Weil brothers in the Jewish community. It remains to be definitely established that Nathé Weil was also a Freemason, as his choice of cremation and the mixed marriage of his daughter, with Adolphe Crémieux as witness, would lead us to conclude.

The series form won me over. For three months I lived according to the rhythm of Alexandre Dumas, impatient to begin the next episode, eager to keep my readers interested. In retrospect, it seems that allowed me to survive the trauma I experienced when my course at the Collège de France fell apart midsemester in the midst of the pandemic. Unfortunately called "The Ends of Literature," it was cancelled without being completed. In a series as in a course, you advance hypotheses, feel your way, weave a plot, "exchange" as we now say, an exchange all the more indirect for being completely virtual. No, actually the exchange was all the more positive as confinement made us all receptive to new forms of dialogue.

Of course, this book is very different from the series posted on the Collège de France website in spring 2020. Many essential new developments occurred afterward (even after the book was published in France). The two threads woven through these pages, the reading of Proust's novel within the Jewish community and the tomb of Baruch Weil at Père-Lachaise cemetery, were tied much more closely to Proust's so-called *ultima verba* on his Jewishness before the latest discoveries: the draft of Proust's inscription sketching out those *ultima verba* (later even the fair copy of that inscription)) and the manuscript of André Spire's article where they had appeared but without an identifiable source. Various leads, as yet unsuspected during the series, have been explored since, notably in the Archives de Paris.

Acknowledgments

My thanks to the internet and multimedia center at the Collège de France: week after week, under the conditions of strict confinement and then less strict deconfinement, they adapted my episodes for the unique digital format of the Collège, with its website that scrolls its contents laterally, like the Torah. I cannot name all those who sent messages to me over the course of the series. In subject they ranged from correcting misprints to providing essential documents that were then taken into account. I would like to thank Ruth Amossy, Pierre Assouline, Françoise Balibar, R. Howard Bloch, Évelyne Bloch-Dano, Dominique Bourel, Monique Canto-Sperber, Anne Carvallo, Bernard Compagnon, Jessica Desclaux, Max Engamarre, Anne Esmein, Valérie Fasseur, Pierre Force, Pierre Frantz, Andrée Hayum, François Heilbronn, Marian Hobson, Edward Hughes, Christian Jeanbrau, Alice Kaplan, Sandrine Kott, Lawrence D. Kritzman, Elisabeth Ladenson, Henry Laurens, Monique Lévi-Strauss, Françoise Leriche, Maureen McLane, Éric Marty, Pierre-François Mettan, Patrick Narzul, Dominique Panzani, Françoise Pitt-Rivers, Anne Pons, Christophe Pradeau, Emmanuel Rimbert, Philippe Roger, Thomas Römer, Serge Sur, Jean-Yves Tadié, Matthieu Vernet, and all those who enriched this research project with their reactions, encouragement, objections, and assistance. I am especially indebted to Nathalie Mauriac Dyer and Marie-Brunette Spire, who provided me with essential documents, as well as the collector who gave me permission to reproduce the important letter from Proust to Robert de Montesquiou. My deep gratitude for their generosity.

Notes

INTRODUCTION

1. André Spire, *Quelques juifs* (Paris: Mercure de France, 1913); *Quelques juifs et demi-juifs* (Paris: Grasset, 1928).

2. Alessandro Piperno, *Proust antiebreo* (Milan: FrancoAngeli, 2000); in French: *Proust anti-juif*, trans. Fanchita Gonzalez Batlle (Paris: Liana Levi, 2007). See the review by Stéphane Chaudier, "Proust, l'antisémitisme et le non-engagement," *La Revue internationale des livres et des idées* 4 (March–April 2008): 43–46.

3. "This passage seems a classic—if doubled—form of self-hatred." Jonathan Freedman, "Coming Out of the Jewish Closet with Marcel Proust," in *Queer Theory and the Jewish Question*, ed. Daniel Boyarin, Daniel Itzkovitz, and Ann Pellegrin (New York: Columbia University Press, 2003), 334–64, at 340.

4. Patrick Mimouni, *Les mémoires maudites: Juifs et homosexuels dans l'oeuvre et la vie de Marcel Proust* (Paris: Grasset, 2018), 314.

5. This study began with two papers on the "Amitiés sionistes de Proust," the first given at a Proust seminar for the CNRS Institut des textes et manuscrits modernes (Item), 13 May 2013, the second during an Item seminar organized by Yuji Murakami, "Autour de Proust: L'affaire Dreyfus, coda," 1 June 2013. See Joseph Brami, "Premières réceptions critiques 'juives' de *Swann*, 1923–1941," *Francofonia* 64 (Spring 2013): 141–59.

1. ULTIMA VERBA

1. Léon Kahn, *Histoire de la communauté israélite de Paris*, vol. 3, *Le Comité de Bienfaisance, l'hôpital, l'orphelinat, les cimetières* (Paris: Durlacher, 1886), 119–25. See Emmanuelle Polack, "À la fondation CASIP-COJASOR: Retrouvées, classées, enfin accessibles: Les Archives du Comité de Bienfaisance Israélite de Paris (CBIP)," *Archives juives* 36, no. 2 (2003): 131–38.

2. Maxime Du Camp, "Les cimetières de Paris," *Revue des deux mondes* (April 15, 1874): 812–51; *Paris, ses organes, ses fonctions et sa vie dans la seconde moitié du XIXe siècle* (Paris: Hachette, 1875), 6:107–74, at 148.

3. AP, Reconstructed registry, Deceased, 27 September 1836, former Third Arrondissement, V3E/D 1494, view 5/51; AP, Daily burial register, Père-Lachaise cemetery, 28 September 1836, no. 3135, general no. 54.180, 48 years old, CPL_RJ18361837_01, view 29/31; Régine de Plinval de Guillebon, *La porcelaine à Paris sous le Consulat et l'Empire: Fabrication, commerce, étude topographiques des immeubles ayant abrité des manufactures de porcelaine* (Geneva: Droz, 1985), vol. 18; R. de Plinval de Guillebon, *Faïence et porcelaine de Paris, XVIIIᵉ–XIXᵉ siècles* (Dijon: Faton, 1995); Rosine Alexandre, *Fontainbleau, naissance d'une communauté juive à l'époque de la Révolution, 1788–1808* (Privately published, 1991).

4. Léon Kahn, *Histoire de la communauté israélite de Paris,* vol. 1, *Histoire des écoles communales et consistoriales israélites de Paris (1809–1884)* (Paris: Durlacher, 1884), 9.

5. AP, D43 Z2, bill from day 27 in the month of Floréal in year 10 of the French Republican calendar (17 May 1802).

6. *Le moniteur universel* (Paris), 22 December 1826, 2.

7. *Le guide des acheteurs ou Almanach des passages de l'Opéra, Janvier 1826* (Paris: David, 1826), 23–28, at 27.

8. *Le moniteur universel* (Paris), 1 June 1825, 3; *Le drapeau blanc* (Paris), 2 June 1825, 2.

9. *Le moniteur universel* (Paris), 14 May 1825, 1.

10. Adolphe Blanqui, *Histoire de l'exposition des produits de l'industrie française en 1827* (Paris: Librairie du Commerce, 1827), 167. See R. de Plinval de Guillebon, *Bibliographie analytiques des expositions industrielles et commerciales en France depuis l'origine jusqu'à 1867* (Dijon: L'Échelle de Jacob, 2006), 88–89.

11. *Le Constitutionnel* (Paris), 23 October 1827, 4.

12. *Le Figaro* (Paris), 7 August 1827, 2.

13. Baruch Weil, *Lettre à M. Rey, membre du Conseil général des manufactures et du jury central de 1827, relative à son mémoire sur la nécessité de bâtir un édifice consacré aux expositions générales des produits de l'industrie* (Paris: Dondey-Dupré, 1827). See Joseph Rey, *Mémoire sur la nécessité de bâtir un édifice spécialement consacré aux expositions générales des produits de l'industrie* (Paris: Bachelier, 1827).

14. AP, Reconstructed registry, Deceased, 8 April 1828, former Fifth Arrondissement, V3E/D 1494, view 3/51; Tables of the deceased, former Fifth and Sixth arrondissements, DQ8 679, VEI no. 21, view 24/114: "Weil, Baruch, porcelain manufacturer, Bondy no. 16, 8 April 1828, 46 years, acceptance 3 June 1828, see the declaration entered Letter B folio 53 vol. 4 no. 3"; DQ8 632, BAR, no. 3, view 36/131: "Baruch Weil, Marguerite Pincas, Merchant, Bondy no. 16, 8 April 1828, Marguerite Nathan his widow / inventory 7 May 1828 [Antoine Simon] Hailig / marriage 2 September 1813 [for 1812] [Pierre Amable Ferinand] Viault / personal property 181 244.46 Children 8 October 1828 / various claims 69,000 Children, 28 fol. 13, 23 October 1829"; AP, D5U1 47, no. 414, 9 April 1828, seals after death of Baruch Weil, his wife has six minor children; no. 535, 7 May 1828, seals removed, 1 Marguerite Nathan, acting under her personal name (marriage contract before Mᶜ Viault 2 September 1812), in the name and as legal guardian of 1 Nathé Baruch Weil, 2 Lazard Baruch Weil, 3 Adélaïde Baruch Weil, 4 Salomon Baruch Weil, 5 Abraham Alphonse Baruch Weil, 6 Flora Baruch Weil; and 2 Godecheaux Barluch Weil, oldest major son, acting under his personal name as guardian of 1 Benjamin Baruch Weil, 2 Moyse Baruch Weil, 3 Joseph Pinckhas Baruch Weil; 3 Benoist Léon Cohen and Merline

Baruch Weil his wife, creditor of the estate; 4 Michel Goudchaux, banker [president of the Paris consistory, future finance minister of the provisional government 24 February 1848], surrogate guardian of the children of the second marriage; 5 Aaron Schmoll, proprietor [member of the central Consistory], surrogate guardian of the three minor children of the first marriage (he was named surrogate guardian of the children of Baruch Weil upon the death of Hélène Schoubach in 1811, because his wife, Hindel Benjamin, widow from first marriage with Mayer Schoubach, thus grandmother of the children, by deliberation of the family counsel before the justice of the peace for the Sixth Arrondissement 16 December 1811, D6U1 96, no. 1911; see deliberation of the family counsel before the justice of the peace for the Sixth Arrondissement 5 May 1828, D6U1 159).

15. *Le moniteur universel* (Paris), 12 April 1828, 2; *Le Constitutionnel* (Paris), 12 April 1828, 2; *Journal des débats* (Paris), 12 April 1828, 2; *Journal de commerce* (Paris), 12 April 1828, 2.

16. AP, Notifications of inheritance following death, Ninth Bureau, former Fifth and Sixth Arrondissements, DQ7 3623, no. 659, 8 October 1828, Godecheaux Baruch Weil under his personal name as heir for an eleventh of Baruch Weil his father and as guardian of Benjamin, Moÿse, Pinckhas, his brothers, heirs each for an eleventh, and as proxy of Nathé, Lazar, Adélaïde, Salomon, Abraham, and Flora. Marguerite Nathan is to receive a sum of 8,000 francs according to the contract of marriage before Me Viault, 2 September 1812; assets of 209,018 francs; children of the first marriage withdraw 27,773 francs, inventory of 23 December 1811; 181,244 francs remain; DQ7 3625, no. 693, 23 October 1829, Jean Godecheaux Baruch Weil, omission in the notification of 8 October 1828 of the payment of a debt of 69,000 francs accepted by the family counsel before the justice of the peace of the Sixth Arrondissement 23 June 1828, registered 30 June 1828.

17. Hélène Schoubach died in Paris on November 29, 1811 (composition of the family counsel 16 December 1811, AP D6U1 96, no. 1911; deliberation of the family counsel 5 May 1828, after the death of Baruch Weil, D6U1 159; act of marriage of his son Benjamin Weil in Algiers 16 November 1842, no. 192). A Schoubach plot already existed in the Jewish section: AP, Burial registry, Père-Lachaise cemetery, 29 March 1810, no. 366a, CPL _RJ18041818_01, view 21/31.

18. Léon Kahn, *Histoire de la communauté israélite de Paris*, vol. 4, *Les sociétés de secours mutuels, philanthropiques et de prévoyance* (Paris: Durlacher, 1887), 10–12; vol. 5, *Les juifs à Paris depuis le VIe siècle* (Paris: Durlacher, 1889), 225.

19. AP, D6UI 96, no. 1911, 16 December 1811, composition of the family counsel before the justice of the peace of the Sixth Arrondissement: Merline, born in 1804, seven years old, Mayer, 1805, six years old, Godechaux, 1806, five years old, Benjamin, 1807, four years old, Moyse, 1809, two years old, Jules, 1810, one year old, and Joseph Pinckhas, 1811, five months old.

20. AP, Died 4 March 1873, Ninth Arrondissement, no. 294, V4E 3504, view 10/31; domicile is 50 Rue de La Tour-d'Auvergne; witness is Alexandre Nerson; AP, Burial registry, Père-Lachaise cemetery, 6 March 1873, no. 1645, "Jewish, 2nd line to left entering no. 25, 132.890," CPL_RJ18731873_01, view 22/31; AP, Estates, DQ7 13021, view 35/50, Eighth Bureau, 13 June 1873, no. 611; assets of the estate 613 francs (DQ7 12347).

21. "Death of M. Benoist Cohen," *Archives israélites* 17 (August 1856): 436–41. AP, Recon-
     structed registry, V3E/D 312, view 19/51, Cohen, Benoist Lion, 15 July 1856, former
     Eighth Arrondissement, no. 2424; Burial registry, Père-Lachaise cemetery, 15 July 1856,
     order no. 271, general no. 132.890, CPL_RJ18561856_2, view 14/31.

22. AP, Estates, DQ7 13012, view 19/50, 9 June 1878, 36 Rue d'Enghien, Ninth Bureau, 4
     November 1878, no. 1347 (DQ7 12644). In 1836, he was still in the porcelain business,
     the victim of a creditor's bankruptcy. *Le Droit* (Paris), May 5, 1836, 2.

23. *Archives israélites de France* 2 (September 1841): 586.

24. His first contribution was an assimilation fable, "Première lettre d'un humoriste: les trois
     générations," *Archives israélites de France* 1 (October 1840): 527–30. Among his stories, see
     for example, "Mémoires d'un colporteur juif, écrits par lui-même," *Archives israélites de
     France* 2 (November 1841): 686–91, and 3 (August 1842): 459–66. The first part was repub-
     lished by Maurice Samuels in *Les cahiers du judaïsme* 29 (2010): 27–31. See his obituary in
     Archives israélites 39, no. 12 (15 June 1878): 381, and no. 13 (1 July 1878): 406–7 (signed "An
     old Parisian, former student of Jewish schools"). On Ben Lévi, see Maurice Samuels,
     Inventing the Israelite: Jewish Fiction in Nineteenth-Century France (Stanford, CA: Stanford
     University Press, 2010), 74–111.

25. Born in Paris 21 November 1807 (AP D6U1 159, deliberations of the family counsel
     before the justice of the peace of the former Sixth Arrondissement, 5 May 1828 and
     23 June 1828).

26. *Le journal des débats* (Paris), 23 June 1837, 4; *Le Constitutionnel* (Paris), 1 August 1837, 4.

27. *Moniteur algérien* (Algiers), 30 March 1851, 7.

28. Malik Chebahi and Claudine Piaton, "Les architectes d'Alger, 1830–1940," in *Alger, archi-
     tectures 1830–1940*, ed. B. Aïche, J. Hueber, T. Lochard, and C. Piaton (Arles: Honoré
     Clair, 2016), 30–49.

29. *Archives nationales d'outremer*, Algiers, 16 November 1842, no. 192.

30. Died 7 July 1866. *Archives des Bouches-du-Rhône*, Marseille, decennial table 1863–1872, let-
     ter V, AD13_201E_TD59_0245; register no. 3, act no. 830 of 8 July 1866, AD13_201E
     _4570_0140; the two witnesses are Édouard and Auguste Crémieux, his brothers-in-law.

31. Marcel Proust, *À l'ombre des jeunes filles en fleurs*, 526; *In the Shadow of Young Girls in Flower*,
     trans. James Grieve (New York: Penguin, 2004), 110. *À la recherche du temps perdu* is cited
     from the Bibliothèque de la Pléiade edition, 4 vols., ed. Jean-Yves Tadié (Paris: Gallimard,
     1987–1989). English translations are from *In Search of Lost Time*, 7 vols., ed. Christopher
     Prendergast (New York: Penguin, 2003–2023).

32. Proust, *À l'ombre des jeunes filles*, 531–32; *In the Shadow of Young Girls in Flower*, 120.

33. *La Presse* (Paris), 26 August 1906, 2.

34. Born in Paris 9 May 1807 (AP D6U1 159, deliberations of the family counsel before
     the justice of the peace of the former Sixth Arrondissement, 5 May 1828 and 23 June
     1828).

35. *Archives israélites de France* 6 (July 1845): 604, cited in the *Journal de l'Oise*, 3 May 1845. See
     also, with regard to a statue of Jeanne Hachette, *Archives israélites de France* 5 (August 1844):
     577–78.

36. Died 26 September 1874. *Archives de l'Oise*, Beauvais, act no. 732 of 27 September 1874,
     2MO/ECA 057 R9; the two witnesses are Casimir Bessière and Jean François Xavier
     Boeuf, his sons-in-law.

37. Moïse Weil, "Description des cryptes de département de l'Oise," *Mémoires de la Société académique, etc. de l'Oise* 1 (1847): 182–90; "Notice sur les souterrains-refuge, et en particulier sur le souterrain de Noyers-Saint-Martin," *Mémoires de la Société académique, etc. de l'Oise* 1 (1847): 191–200.

38. Proust, *Du côté de chez Swann*, in *À la recherche du temps perdu*, 1:61; Proust, *Swann's Way*, trans. Lydia Davis (New York: Penguin, 2003), 63.

39. AP D6U1 159, deliberations of the family counsel before the justice of the peace of the former Sixth Arrondissement, 5 May 1828 and 23 June 1828.

40. See Roger Duchêne, "Un inédit proustien, le testament de 'L'Oncle Adophe,'" *Revue d'histoire littéraire de la France* 104, no. 3 (2004): 673–85, see 680 and 683.

41. Only Godchaux (Godecheaux) and Benjamin appear, 16 April 1806 and 21 November 1807, in the registry files reconstructed after the Commune, V3E/N 2245, views 39/51 and 40/51.

42. Chevalier Drach, *De l'harmonie entre l'Église et la synagogue* (Paris: Mellier, 1844), 1:47–48.

43. *Temple israélite de Paris*, designed by Jeramec Raphaël, by Baruch Weil, print by Engelmann, *Bibliographie de la France*, 10 July 1830, no. 617 (Musée d'Art et d'Histoire du Judaïsme, Paris, Inv. 2000.14.001). See the subscription of the perspective view of the Jewish temple of Paris designed and lithographed by Moïse Baruch-Weil and Raphaël Jeramec, printer Dondey-Dupré, 1826, *Bibliographie de la France*, 21 April 1827, no. 2832. Raphaël Jeramac was the secretary of the consistory from 1844 to 1847. See Kahn, *Histoire des écoles communales*, 78.

44. Register of deliberations, Jewish Charity Committee of Paris, series 1B1, 22 November 1818, Fondation Casip-Cojasor.

45. Plot no. 323 of 1828, acquired 8 April 1828, day of the death of Baruch Weil, later CAP 122.037, 7th division, 3rd section, 2nd line of the wall. See Albert Fournier, "Du côté de chez Proust," *Europe* (August–September 1970): 246–63, at 247; Armand Lunel, "Marcel Proust, sa mère et les juifs," *Europe* (February–March 1971): 64–67, at 64; Madame Claude Heumann, "Correspondance," *Europe* (February–March 1971): 190–91; Frédéric Viey, "Historique du carré israélite du cimetière du Père-Lachaise"; Gilles Plaut, *Cimetière du Père-Lachaise: Division israélite* (Paris: Cercle de Généalogie Juive, 1999).

46. AP, Burial registry, Père-Lachaise cemetery, 1 May 1854, no. 3381, general no. 122.037, Third Arrondissement, no. 530, "Jewish no. 43 of map 5 m 90 right David Singer right Fould, 2nd line of Béral wall," CPL_RJ18541854_01, view 24/31.

47. AP, Estates, DQ7 13144, view 43/51, 30 June 1896, Ninth Bureau; 1 August 1896, no. 1186 (DQ7 12801), assets of 444,000 francs, principally in shares of the Compagnie Générale des Eaux and the Crédit Foncier de France; 16 December 1896, no. 1911 (DQ7 12804), remainder and rectification of the preceding declaration, 730,000 francs, 208,000 of which for the dowry of Madame Proust.

48. In March 1893 Nathé Weil's sentence by the commercial court was confirmed on appeal of a lawsuit pitting him against the stockbroker Alexandre-Auguste Blin, 5 Rue Taitbout, successor to Albert Ramel in 1882; Nathé Weil had been Blin's backer between 1882 and 1890, but losses were noted after the liquidation of the company in 1890; Nathé Weil was sentenced to paying Blin 80,000 francs plus interest, equivalent to more than 300,000 euros in 2020, plus costs. See *Gazette des tribunaux* (Paris), 25 August 1893, 1–2.

49. Formation of the Trelon, Weldon, Weil company, *Le Droit* (Paris), 19 September 1844, 4; company dissolved and new limited partnership formed, at the law office of Godchaux Weil, *Le moniteur universel* (Paris), 1 November 1863, 4.

50. *La république de 1848* (Paris), 26 October 1849, 3.

51. AN, Léonore database, L2751025. Adrien Proust was named knight on that same date, 8 August 1870, in the midst of the Franco-Prussian War, also on recommendation of the Minister of Agriculture and Commerce (L2233038).

52. AP, Estates, DQ7 13144, view 35/51, 10 May 1896, Seventh Bureau, 9 June 1896, no. 943, 16 June 1896, no. 991, 7 August 1896, no. 1263; Ninth Bureau, 7 August 1896, no. 1219 (DQ712280, 12281, 1282, DQ712801). The 1886 will of Louis Weil, which establishes Georges and Jeanne Weil, his favorite nephew and niece, as sole legatees, allows capital bequests to other nephews and nieces, the children of Benjamin in Marseille (bequest removed in an 1895 codicil), the daughters of Moïse, his Lazarus niece and his two Alcan nieces, or his half-brother Joseph in Algeria (bequest removed in an 1895 codicil, after the death of that brother), as well as life annuities for his sister Adèle, widow of Lazarus, and his sister-in-law Amélie, widow of Moïse. See Duchêne, "Un inédit proustien," note 42.

53. AP, Estates, DQ& 13144, view 9/51, 21 June 1892, 80 Rue de La Tour, Ninth Bureau, 15 November 1892, no. 1740 (DQ7 12763).

54. Their marriage was announced in *Le Constitutionnel* (Paris), 24 October 1845, 3. Reconstructed registry, Death of Joseph Lazarus, 28 January 1850, former Ninth Arrondissement, V3E/D 858, view 13/41.

55. In the reconstructed registry of Paris, only Nathé, Salomon, and Abraham Alphonse appear, 19 April 1814, 13 October 1820, and 29 June 1822, AP V3E/N 2245, views 45/51, 47/51, 2/3.

56. *Gazette des tribunaux* (Paris), 7 August and 18 September 1859; *Le Droit* (Paris), 6 May 1860 and 30 March 1861.

57. Witnesses for his birth certificate were Benoist Cohen, his brother-in-law, and Cerf Weil, his uncle, AN, L27l51009.

58. AP, Estates, DQl7 13144, view 7/51, 10 December 1886, 51 Rue Decamps, Ninth Bureau, 2 January 1888, no. 4 (DQ7 12719).

59. *Le Droit* (Paris), 2 October 1851, 4, and 18 January 1852, 7.

60. AP, Died 10 March 1867, Tenth Arrondissement, 11 March 1867, no. 850, V4E 1213, view 12/31; the first witness is Alexandre Nerson; AP Death registry, Montmartre cemetery, 12 March 1867, no. 226, MTM_RJ1867_01, view 12/31; AP, Estate, DQl7 12927, view 38/51, 15 Rue Mazagran, Ninth Bureau, 30 August 1869, no. 937; DQ7 13144, view 20/51, omission, 16 Rue de l'Échiquier, Ninth Bureau, 18 January 1889, no. 65, marriage contract of 11 December 1850 (DQ7 10798, 12728).

61. Godecheaux Baruch-Weil, *Réflexions d'un jeune israélite français, sur les deux brochures de M. Tsarphati* (Paris: Sétier, 1821), 23. If, with Godchaux, we add to the six living sons of the first marriage at the time of their mother's death in 1811 (Mayer, Godchaux, Benjamin, Moïse, Jules, and Joseph Pinckhas) the three sons of the second marriage born by this time (Nathé, Louis, and Salomon),we arrive at a total of nine, prior to the birth of Abraham Alphonse in 1822.

62. "Les succionnistes," *Archives israélites de France* 5 (December 1844): 825–27, at 827.

63. Marcel Proust, Letter to Madame de Brantes, 1 September 1897, *Correspondance*, ed. Philip Kolb (Paris: Plon, 1970–1993), 2:212.

64. Marcel Proust, *Jean Santeuil*, preceded by *Les plaisirs et les jours*, ed. Pierre Clarac and Yves Sandre (Paris: Gallimard, 1971); *Jean Santeuil*, trans. Gerard Hopkins (New York: Simon & Schuster, 1956).

65. *Archives israélites de France* 2 (May 1841): 323–33, at 324.

66. See Pierre Birnbaum, *La république et le cochon* (Paris: Seuil, 2013), 90.

67. Tsarsphati, *Première lettre d'un Israélite français à ses coreligionnaires, sur l'urgente nécessité de célébrer l'office en français le jour de dimanche, à l'usage des Israélites qui ne peuvent assister à l'office asiatique de la veille, comme unique moyen de rendre désormais l'éducation religieuse possible en France* (Paris: Bachelier, 1820), 12; *Projet de règlement concernant la circoncision, suivi d'observations sur une lettre pastorale du grand rabbin de Metz et sur un écrit de M. Lazare (aîné)* (Paris: A. Béraud, 1821).

68. Baruch-Weil, *Réflexions d'un jeune Israélite français*, 23.

69. Ben Lévi, "Les poissons et les miettes de pain," *Archives israélites* 7 (October 1846): 630–38.

70. Kahn, *Histoires des écoles communales*, 78 and 103; *Le Comité de Bienfaisance*, 156.

71. Ben Lévi, *Les matinées du samedi: Livre d'éducation morale et religieuse à l'usage de la jeunesse israélite*, 2 vols. (Paris: Bureau des Archives Israélites de France, 1842; 3rd ed., 1859; 4th ed., 1897); see *Archives israélites* 58, no. 18 (May 6, 1897): 143. On Samuel Cahen, see the obituary by G. Weil (Ben Lévi), *Archives israélites* 23, no. 2 (February 1, 1862): 81–87; see also Phyllis Cohen Albert, *The Modernization of French Jewry: Consistory and Community in the Nineteenth Century* (Waltham, MA: Brandeis University Press, 1977), 50; Jay R. Berkovitz, *The Shaping of Jewish Identity in Nineteenth-Century France* (Detroit: Wayne State University Press, 1989), 132.

72. Heidi Knörzer, "Isidore Cahen, directeur des *Archives israélite*," *Archives juives* 51, no. 1 (2018): 126–31.

73. *Archives israélites* 68, no. 33 (15 August 1907): 264.

74. André Maurois, *À la recherche de Marcel Proust* (Paris: Hachette, 1986), 14, 10; Jean-Yves Tadié, *Marcel Proust* (Paris: Gallimard, 1996), 34; Évelyne Bloch-Dano, *Madame Proust* (Paris: Grasset, 2004), 29.

75. E. Bloch-Dano, *Madame Proust: A Biography*, trans. Alice Kaplan (Chicago: University of Chicago Press, 2007), 264 (note 14 for page 15).

76. Georges Cattaui, *L'amitié de Proust* (Paris: Gallimard, 1935), 203n35.

77. Georges Cattaui, "Proust et les juifs," *Palestine* 5 (February 1928): 196–205, at 203.

78. Spire, *Quelques juifs et demi-juifs* (Paris: Grasset, 1928) 2:45–61, at 56.

79. Georges Cattaui, *Marcel Proust: Proust et son temps, Proust et le temps* (Paris: Julliard, 1952), 27; Georges Cattaui, *Proust perdu et retrouvé* (Paris: Plon, 1963), 22.

80. Pages 53–60, from "La Société, sous Louis-Philippe et le Second Empire n'avait pas été hostile aux Juifs . . ." to ". . . on se demande souvent si Proust parle de lui-même ou de Swann" ["Society, under Louis-Philippe and the Second Empire, had not been hostile to Jews . . ." ". . . one often wonders if Proust is talking about himself or Swann"].

81. *Les nouvelles littéraires* (Paris), 28 July 1923, 1; the article was reprinted in an Alexandrian daily newspaper, *La Réformes*, 14 August 1923, and in a Cairo weekly, *Israël*, August 21, 1923.

82.   *The Jewish Chronicle Supplement* 29 (25 May 1923): 6–7.

83.   *The Jewish Chronicle Supplement* 29 (25 May 1923), 7.

84.   It almost ceased publication in April 2020, a victim of the coronavirus pandemic: https://www.thejc.com/news/uk-news/an-announcement-from-the-jewish-chronicle-1.498949.

85.   See David Cesarani, *The Jewish Chronicle and Anglo-Jewry, 1841–1991* (Cambridge: Cambridge University Press, 1994), 103–33.

86.   Jean-Richard Bloch and André Spire, *Correspondance, 1912–1947: "Sommes-nous d'accord?"* ed. Marie Brunette Spire (Paris: Éditions Claire Paulhan, 2011), 20 (preface).

87.   *The Jewish Chronicle* (London), 2 February 1923, 15.

88.   *The Jewish Chronicle* (London), 19 October 1923, 25.

89.   "Marcel Proust," *The Reform Advocate* (Chicago), 23 June 1923, 755–60; "Marcel Proust—His Jewish Traits: Eminent French Writer's Works Have Jewish Interest," *The Jewish Exponent* (Philadelphia), 13 July 1923, 1–2; *The Jewish Criterion* (Pittsburgh), 27 July 1923, 4–5, 8, and 26–27; *The American Jewish World* (Saint Paul and Minneapolis), 3 August 1923, 1; 10 August 1923, 1 and 15.

90.   Louis Gautier-Vignal, "Hommage à Georges Cattaui" *Bulletin de la Société des Amis de Marcel Proust* 25 (1975): 192–95, at 194.

91.   Cattaui, *L'amitié de Proust*, 10.

92.   Cattaui, *L'amitié de Proust*, 184. See this letter-inscription sent with a copy of *À l'ombre des jeunes filles en fleur*, July 1919, *Correspondance*, 18:337–38.

93.   Georges Cattaui Papers, Bibliothèque de Genève, Ms. fr. 5158, f. 120–22.

94.   Ludmila Savitzky and André Spire, *Une amitié tenace: Correspondance, 1919–1957*, ed. Marie-Brunette Spire (Paris: Les Belles Lettres, 2010), 437.

95.   Savitzky and Spire, *Une amitié tenace*, 437.

96.   Savitzky and Spire, *Une amitié tenace*, letter of 1 August 1923, 440.

2. MENORAH

1.   *L'univers israélite* 39, no. 3 (6 October 1905): 68.

2.   "Élections consistoriales de Paris," *Archives israélites* 11 (August 1850): 401–4, at 403; *Archives israélites* 11 (September 1850): 449–54, at 449.

3.   *Archives israélites* 10 (October 1849): 498n1.

4.   G. Weil, "Défunt Ben-Lévi!" *Archives israélites* 11 (August 1850): 436–42, at 437.

5.   An allusion to the famous case of false cashmeres heard by the magistrates' court of Paris in June and July 1846: Cuthbert, owner of the fabric shop Le Grand Colbert, Rue Vivienne, had summoned for libel Laurent Biétry and company, of the Compagnie Biétry Père & Fils, suppliers of cashmere shawls and fabrics, following letters in the newspapers denouncing his counterfeits; Biétry brought Cuthbert before the same court for deception on the nature of the merchandise sold; the court dismissed their complaints. *Gazette des tribunaux* (Paris), 3 July 1846, 1171.

6.   Isidore Cahen, "Chronique du mois," *Archives israélites* 15 (January 1854): 21–22; see W., "La tour Saint-Jacques la Boucherie" and "La niche" in the same issue, 35–36 and 46–49.

7.   W., "L'égalité des cultes en France," *Archives israélites* 16 (September 1855): 515–16.

8. W. and S. Cahen, "Attaque contre la liberté des cultes," *Archives israélites* 19 (February 1858): 100–101; G. Weil, "Lettre," *Archives israélites* 19 (July 1858): 397–400.

9. G. Weil, "Bibliographie," *Archives israélites* 20 (November 1859): 657–62.

10. Ben Lévi (G. Weil), "Letter à son éminence le cardinal de Bonnechose," *Archives israélites* 26, no. 7 (1 April 1865): 293–99.

11. Ben Lévi (G. Weil), "Letter à son éminence le cardinal de Bonnechose," *Archives israélites* 26, no. 9 (1 May 1865): 409.

12. At the death of Hippolyte Prague (1856–1935), administrator and editor-in-chief, the *Archives israélites* was absorbed by *Le journal juif*. See Heidi Knörzer, "Hippolyte Prague, rédacteur en chef des *Archives israélites*," *Archives juives* 43, no. 1 (2010): 140–43; see also Joseph Voignac, "La communauté juive française et le sionisme dans les années 1930 à travers *L'univers israélite*," *Archives juives* 51, no. 1 (2018): 113–25; Ariel Danan, "Les français israélites et l'accession au pouvoir de Léon Blum, à travers *L'univers israélite*," *Archives juives* 37, no. 1 (2004): 97–110.

13. *L'illustration juive* became *Menorah* beginning with issue 3 (October 1922) until issue 183 (August 1933). See Nadia Malinovich, "Une expression du 'Réveil juif' des années vingt: La revue *Menorah* (1922–1933)," *Archives juives* 37, no. 1 (2004): 86–96.

14. *Menorah* 5 (10 November 1922): 66–69, and 6 (24 November 1922): 82–85; the article was later collected in André Spire, *Quelques juifs et demi-juifs* (Paris: Grasset, 1928), 2:65–91.

15. Anne de Lacretelle, *Tout un monde: Jacques de Lacretelle et ses amis* (Paris: Éditions de Fallois, 2019), 51; Jacques de Lacretelle, *Silbermann* (Paris: Gallimard, 1946), 36.

16. Émile Cahen, "*Silbermann*," *Archives israélites* 83, no. 48 (30 November 1922): 190–91, at 190.

17. "Un grave incident," *Menorah* 8 (22 December 1922): 115 and 118. The obituary by Cattaui appears on pages 116–18.

18. "Une petite affaire Silbermann," *L'univers israélite* 78, no. 17 (12 January 1923): 395.

19. "Un proviseur de lycée outrage les Français," *La vieille France*, 312 (18–25 January 1923): 18–19; "Au lycée de Besançon," *La vieille France* 313 (25 January–1 February 1923): 17; see "Les lycées 'français,'" *La vieille France* 318 (1–8 March 1923): 16.

20. "Sous le signe de l'Union sacrée, M. le Grand Rabbin de France rend hommage à un prêtre catholique," *L'univers israélite* 94, no. 44 (21 July 1939): 790, and 45 (28 July 1939): 807.

21. Joseph Ball, ed., *L'abbé Flory (1886–1949)* (Lantenne-Vertière: J. Garneret, 1978).

22. Alsaticus, "À propos de 'Silbermann,'" *L'univers israélite* 78, no. 18 (19 January 1923): 413–14, at 414.

23. *The Canadian Jewish Chronicle* (Montreal), 6 April 1923, 1 (document provided by M.-B. Spire); *The Reform Advocate* (Chicago), 7 April 1923, 292–93; *The Sentinel* (Chicago), 13 April 1923, 6 and 30; *The American Jewish World* (Saint Paul and Minneapolis), 27 April 1923, 7 and 16–17; *The Detroit Jewish Chronicle*, 18 May 1923, 4.

24. Georges Cattaui, "Marcel Proust," *Menorah* 8 (22 December 1922): 116–18.

25. Marcel Proust, Letter to Paul Souday, [January 1921], *Correspondance*, ed. Philip Kolb (Paris: Plon, 1970–1993), 20:71.

26. Robert Dreyfus, "Proust l'invisible," *Le Temps* (Paris), 16 February 1938, 3; collected in *De Monsieur Thiers à Marcel Proust* (Paris: Plon, 1939), 3–11, at 7.

27.   2 Samuel 1:26.

28.   Marcel Proust, *Contre Sainte-Beuve*, ed. Pierre Clarac and Yves Sandre (Paris: Gallimard, 1971), 186.

29.   Cattaui, "Marcel Proust," 116–17.

30.   Cattaui, "Marcel Proust," 117–18. In fact, Barrès had quickly retracted this claim ("all that reveals a foreigner who does not have our prejudices.... Montaigne's temperament is, basically, that of Heinrich Heine"), present in the first edition of his book, M. Barrès and Paul Lafond, *Le Greco* (Paris: H. Floury 1911), 67–68, explaining that it had been made "too lightly in an earlier edition": "All these assertions are too rash. Herein lies an issue that I am not entitled to resolve regarding a great French writer." *Greco ou le secret de Tolède* (Paris: Émile-Paul, 1912), 187. The note was prompted by a remark on the "great intellectuals of Israel" in Toledo who "criticized the ideas of Christians." Barrès and Lafond, *Le Greco*, 109–10.

31.   Cattaui, "Marcel Proust," 118.

32.   Cattaui, "Marcel Proust," 118.

33.   *Menorah* 13 (2 March 1923): 201 (issues no. 11 and 12, February 1923, are missing in the BNF); *Menorah* 9 (15 May 1924): 129; see Marie-Brunette Spire, "Gustave Kahn et la revue *Menorah*," in *Gustave Kahn (1859–1936)*, ed. Sophie Basch (Paris: Classiques Garnier, 2009), 483–505; *Menorah* 30 (9 December 1923): 491–93.

34.   The first paragraph from the *Jewish Chronicle* article is omitted (a biographical and bibliographical note for non-French readers unfamiliar with Proust).

35.   *Menorah* 30 (9 December 1923): 492.

36.   See the numerous references to Cattaui in the letters of Savitzky and Spire, *Un amitié tenace: Correspondance, 1910–1957*, ed. Marie-Brunette Spire (Paris: Les Belles Lettres, 2010). Spire's letters to Cattaui are held in the Bibliothèque Littéraire Jacques Doucet and the Bibliothèque Publique et Universitaire de Genève, Papiers Georges Cattaui. One letter from Ludmila Savitzky to Cattaui, dated 27 April 1923, is found in the Bibliothèque Littéraire Jacques Doucet, Ms Ms 35399 (28).

37.   J.-Y. Tadié, ed., *Proust et ses amis* (Paris: Gallimard, 2010); J.-Y. Tadié, ed., *Le cercle de Marcel Proust*, 3 vols. (Paris: Honoré Champion, 2013–2021).

38.   Spire, *Quelques juifs et demi-juifs*, 2:47.

39.   See Catherine Fhima, "Aux sources d'un renouveau identitaire juif en France: André Spire et Edmond Fleg," *Mil neuf cent: Revue d'histoire intellectuelle* (*Cahiers Georges Sorel*) 13 (1995): 171–89.

40.   Reissued in 2019 in the Albin Michel "Présences du judaïsme" series.

41.   *La libre parole* (Paris), 9 January 1895, 1, and 13 January 1895, 1; see André Spire, *Souvenirs à bâtons rompus* (Paris: Albin Michel, 1961), 54–58.

42.   "Les Dreyfus intellectuels," *La libre parole* (Paris), 23 February 1898, 2. The citation was identified by Yuji Marakami, "L'affaire Dreyfus dans l'oeuvre de Proust" (graduate thesis, Université Paris IV-Sorbonne, 2012), 135.

43.   *La libre parole* (Paris), 27 April 1899, 2.

44.   Marcel Proust, Letter to Daniel Halévy, [December 1913], *Correspondance*, 14:348.

45.   André Spire wrote to his mother on 28 January 1914: "I am dining at the Halévys.'" See Daniel and Marianne Halévy, André Spire, *Correspondance, 1899–1961*, ed. Marie-Brunette Spire-Uran (Paris: Honoré Champion, 2020), 636.

46. Marcel Proust, Letter to Daniel Halévy, [February 1914], *Correspondance*, 14:350.

47. Israel Zangwill, "*Chad Gadya!*," trans. Mathilde Salomon, *Cahiers de la quinzaine* 6, no. 3 (25 October 1904): 10, 12. The story appears last in Zangwill's collection *Dreamers of the Ghetto* (London: W. Heinemann, 1898).

48. André Spire, "Israel Zangwill," *Cahiers de la quinzaine* 11, no. 5 (19 December 1909): 12.

49. Spire, *Souvenirs*, 101. Lévy was secretary general of Louise Weiss's *L'Europe nouvelle* (1918–1934); Vernes was an eminent figure in Protestantism and former member of the Société des Études Juives; Zadoc-Kahn (1870–1943), son of France's chief rabbi Zadoc-Kahn, was head doctor of the Rothschild Hospital and president of the central committee of Keren Hayessod France.

50. See Catherine Nicault, *La France et le sionisme, 1897–1948: Une rencontre manquée?* (Paris: Calmann-Lévy, 1992), 111–13; C. Nicault, "L'acculturation des israélites français au sionisme après la Grande Guerre," *Archives juives* 39, no. 1 (2006): 9–28; Nadia Malinovich, *French and Jewish: Culture and the Politics of Identity in Early Twentieth-Century France* (Oxford: Littman Library of Jewish Civilization, 2008), French translation, *Heureux comme un juif en France: Intégration, identité, culture, 1900–1932* (Paris: Honoré Champion, 2010).

51. *Palestine* 1, no. 1 (October 1927); 3, nos. 10–12 (December 1930–February 1931).

52. *La vieille France* 342 (23–30 August 1923): 11–12; cited by Bernard Brun, "Brouillon et brouillages: Proust et l'antisémitisme," *Littérature* 70 (1988): 110–28, at 113.

53. Spire, *Quelques juifs et demi-juifs*, 2:54.

54. Spire, *Quelques juifs et demi-juifs*, 2:48–51.

55. Spire, *Quelques juifs et demi-juifs*, 2:53.

56. Hannah Arendt, *The Origins of Totalitarianism* (New York: Harcourt Brace, 1951; 2nd ed. New York: Meridian, 1958), 83; *Les origines du totalitarisme*, "Première partie: L'antisémitisme," trans. Micheline Pouteau and Hélène Frappat (Paris: Gallimard, 2002), 314–25, at 318.

57. Spire, *Quelques juifs et demi-juifs*, 2:54.

58. Spire, *Quelques juifs et demi-juifs*, 2:54, 2:56.

59. Spire, *Quelques juifs et demi-juifs*, 2:56.

60. See, for example, Juliette Hassine, *Marranisme et hébraïsme dans l'oeuvre de Proust* (Paris: Minard, 1994); Elaine Marks, *Marrano as Metaphor: The Jewish Presence in French Writing* (New York: Columbia University Press, 1995); Perrine Simon-Nahum, "Marcel Proust et la vocation du narrateur: Un marranisme littéraire," in *Les marranismes: De la religiosité cachée à la société ouverte*, ed. Jacques Ehrenfreund and Jean-Philippe Schreiber (Paris: Demopolis, 2014), 229–51.

61. Spire, *Quelques juifs et demi-juifs*, 2:57.

62. André Benhaïm, *Panim: Visages de Proust* (Lille: Presses Universitaires du Septentrion, 2006), 264; Marcel Proust, *Sodome et Gomorrhe II*, in *À la recherche du temps perdu*, ed. Jean-Yves Tadié (Paris: Gallimard, 1987–1989), 2:103; *Sodom and Gomorrah*, trans. John Sturrock (New York: Penguin, 2004), 106. This emblematic sentence appeared as an epigraph at the bottom of page 498 of *Menorah* 30 (9 December 1923); it was already cited a few pages earlier, in an article by Spire for the first anniversary of Proust's death in *Menorah* 30 (9 December 1923): 493.

63. Spire, *Quelques juifs et demi-juifs*, 2:57; see Proust, *Sodome et Gomorrhe II*, 2:103; *Sodom and Gomorrah*, 106.

64. Spire, *Quelques juifs et demi-juifs*, 2:60.

65. Spire, *Quelques juifs et demi-juifs*, note on 2:47.

66. Abel Bonnard, "Au jour le jour: Marcel Proust," *Journal des débats* (Paris), 14 January 1927, 1.

3. A POINTLESS QUESTION?

1. *Les nouvelles littéraires* (Paris), 20 June 1925, 5, and 27 June 1925, 5; see the review by Edmond Jaloux in *Les nouvelles littéraires* (Paris), 29 August 1925, 3.

2. Léon Pierre-Quint, *Marcel Proust: Sa vie, son oeuvre* (Paris: Éditions du Sagittaire, 1925), 19.

3. Léon Pierre-Quint, letter to Proust, BNF, 14 March 1919, NAF 27352, fol. 121 r°–122 r°; Pyra Wise, "Quatorze lettres inédites adressées à Proust," *Bulletin d'informations proustiennes* 41 (2011): 7–19, at 17; Léon Pierre-Quint, "Simplification amoureuse," *Mercure de France*, 15 April and 15 May 1921.

4. Léon Pierre-Quint, *Marcel Proust: Sa vie, son oeuvre*, rev ed. (Paris: Sagittaire, 1976).

5. Léon Pierre-Quint, *Déchéances aimables* (Paris: Éditions du Sagittaire, 1924); *La revue juive* 4 (July 1925): 498–99.

6. Léon Pierre-Quint, "Carl Sternheim," *La revue juive* 6 (November 1925): 733–41.

7. Pierre-Quint, *Marcel Proust* (1925), 218–20, 230; (1976), 163–64, 171.

8. *Archives israélites* 85, no. 22 (29 May 1924): 1.

9. Heidi Knörzer, "Isidore Cahen, directeur des *Archives israélites*," *Archives juives* 51, no. 1 (2018): 126–31.

10. See Jean-Baptiste Amadieu, "Jacques Baillès, évêque, censeur et critique littéraire," *La Vendée littéraire* (April 2013): 117–46.

11. Both were in the eighth grade in 1884–1885; Proust was absent the entire third trimester, while René Cahen was often named in the awards ceremonies. *Le Figaro* (Paris), 5 August 1885, 5.

12. *Le Figaro* (Paris), 27 February 1902, and *Journal des débats* (Paris), 28 February 1902, announced the marriage of René Cahen, senior stockbroker, and Marguerite Hayem at the Rue de la Victoire temple before many witnesses, including Henri Bergson.

13. Marcel Proust, Letter to Lucien Daudet, [16 December 1897], *Correspondance*, ed. Philip Kolb (Paris: Plon, 1970–1993), 21:585–86. See Véronique Long, "Les collectionneurs juif parisiens sous la Troisième République (1870–1940)," *Archives juives* 42, no. 1 (2009): 84–104. The drawing by Degas, *Soirée* (Mme Charles Hayem, Barbey d'Aurevilly, and Adolphe Franck), now at the Getty Museum, was the property of Ludovic Halévy. Theodore Reff, *Degas: The Artist's Mind* (New York: Metropolitan Museum of Art, 1976), 159.

14. *Le Figaro* (Paris), 24 March 1903, announced the marriage of Fernand Gregh and Harlette Hayem at the Eighth Arrondissement city hall, Rue d'Anjou, before many witnesses.

15. Fernand Gregh, *L'âge de fer: Souvenirs, 1925–1955* (Paris: Grasset, 1956), 192.

16. Doctor Georges Hayem and Amélie Weil née Oulman had the same great-grandfather, Isaïe Isaïe Oulman (1746–1822), who was born and died in Metz; the grandmother of Georges Hayem, Sara Hayem née Oulman, and the grandfather of Amélie Weil, Cerf Oulman (1775–1847), were born in Metz and died in Paris (information provided by François Heilbronn).

17. Proust, Letter to Madame de Brantes, 1 September 1897, *Correspondance*, 2:212–13.

18. *La vie parisienne*, 6 March 1897, 142.

19. Léon Blum, "Comment ont été faites les lois scélérates," *La revue blanche*, 1 July 1898, 338–52, see 346; Léon Blum, *Les lois scélérates de 1893–1894* (Paris: Éditions de la Revue Blanche, 1899), 20–21.

20. Marie-Louise Cahen-Hayem, "L'an prochain à Jérusalem," *Archives israélites* 85, no. 29 (17 July 1924): 114–15.

21. Marie-Louise Cahen-Hayem, "La psychologie et le roman," *Archives israélites* 86, no. 52(24 December 1925): 206.

22. Sigmund Freud, *Le rêve et son interprétation*, trans. Hélène Legros (Paris: Gallimard, 1925).

23. Pierre-Quint, *Marcel Proust* (1925), 131–39; (1976), 99–105; see "Le style de Marcel Proust," *Les nouvelles littéraires* (Paris), 6 June 1925, 6, which gives an excerpt from this chapter.

24. *La revue juive* 6 (November 1925): 792–95 ("Les revues").

25. See Nicole Racine, "Benjamin Crémieux et le Pen Club français," Collège de France, 28 November 2009.

26. Benjamin Crémieux, *Essai sur l'évolution littéraire de l'Italie de 1870 à not jour* (Paris: Kra, 1928); also published under the title *Littérature italienne* in the "Panorama des littératures contemporaines" series. His complementary thesis on Pirandello was *Henri IV et la dramaturgie de Luigi Pirandello* (Paris: Gallimard, 1928).

27. Jérémie Dubois, *L'enseignement de l'italien en France (1880–1940)* (Grenoble: UGA Éditions, 2015), 256.

28. Proust, Letter to Jacques Boulenger, [29 November 1921], *Correspondance*, 20:543.

29. Proust, Letter to Benjamin Crémieux, [15 January 1922], *Correspondance*, 21:34–35.

30. Paul Morand, letter to Proust, 6 May 1922, *Correspondance*, 21:172.

31. Proust, Letter to Benjamin Crémieux, [15 June 1922], *Correspondance*, 21:271.

32. Benjamin Crémieux, *XXᵉ siècle: Première série* (Paris: Éditions de la NRF, 1924), 9–98; *XXᵉ siècle: Première série*, ed. Catherine Helbert (Paris: Gallimard, 23–102.

33. Benjamin Crémieux, "La composition dans l'oeuvre de Marcel Proust," *Les nouvelles littéraires* (Paris), 31 May 1925, 5; Benjamin Crémieux, "La psychologie de Marcel Proust," *La revue de Paris* 31, vol. 5 (15 October 1924): 838–61.

34. Crémieux, *XXᵉ siècle* (1924), 51; (2010), 61.

35. Proust, *À l'ombre des jeunes filles en fleurs*, in *À la recherche du temps perdu*, ed. Jean-Yves Tadié (Paris: Gallimard, 1987–1989), 2:98; *In the Shadow of Young Girls in Flower*, trans. James Grieve (New York: Penguin, 2005), 319.

36. Crémieux, *XXᵉ siècle* (1924), 50; (2010), 60.

37. See "Judaïsme et littérature" in "Revue de presse," *Menorah* 20 (1 November 1925): 327; *La revue juive* 6 (November 1925): 804.

38. Benjamin Crémieux, "Judaïsme et littérature," *Les nouvelles littéraires* (Paris), 10 October 1925, 5.

39.   Crémieux, "Judaïsme et littérature," 5.

40.   On the reception of these books, perceived as pro-Jewish at the time of publication and now considered ambivalent to say the least, see Michel Leymarie, "Les frères Tharaud: de l'ambiguïté du 'filon juif' dans la littérature française des années vingt," *Archives juives* 39, no. 1 (2006): 89–109; Susan Ruben Suleiman, "Foreigners and Strangers: Jews in French Society and Literature Between the Two World Wars," in *Revisioning French Culture*, ed. Andrew Sobanet (Liverpool: Liverpool University Press, 2019), 89–99.

41.   André Maurois, *Les silences du colonel Bramble* (Paris: Grasset, 1918) and *Les discours du docteur O'Grady* (Paris: Grasset, 1922); see also: "Un livre gai./ André Maurois, l'auteur des *Silences du colonel Bramble*, vient de publier un nouveau roman: *Les Discours du docteur O'Grady*, qui sont un miracle de drôlerie, d'humour et de grâce enjouée," *L'Action française* (Paris), 23 March 1922, 1.

42.   Benjamin Crémieux, "Proust et les juifs," in *Du côté de Marcel Proust* (Paris: Lemarget, 1929), 95–126; repr. Tusson: Du Lérot, 2011.

43.   Armand Lunel, "*XXᵉ siècle*, par Benjamin Crémieux," *La revue juive* 6 (November 1925): 750–52.

44.   *La revue juive* 6 (November 1925): 804.

45.   The Savitzky collection is housed at IMEC, 388SVZ/1-388SVZ/38, 1898–1960.

46.   See Hervé Joly, *À Polytechnique: X 1901* (Paris: Flammarion, 2021), 355–56.

47.   See Pierre Abraham, *Les trois frères* (Paris: Les Éditeurs Français Réunis, 1971).

48.   See Leonid Livak, "'A Thankless Occupation': James Joyce and His Translator Ludmila Savitzky," *Joyce Studies Annual* (2013): 33–61. We are awaiting the French translation of Leonid Livak's biography of Savitzky, published in Moscow in 2019, *Ludmila Savitzky, portrait d'une traductrice* (Paris: Éditions des Archives contemporaines, 2024).

49.   Savitzky and Spire, *Une amitié tenace*, 362, note 292.

50.   Georges Cattaui, *La promesse accomplie: France-Égypte-Judée* (Paris: Camille Bloch, 1922); Ludmila Savitzky and André Spire, *Une amitié tenace: Correspondance, 1910–1957*, ed. Marie-Brunette Spire (Paris: Les Belles Lettres, 2010), 364–65, 367, 369, 370.

51.   Savitzky and Spire, *Une amitié tenace*, 380, 382.

52.   *Menorah* 9–10 (January 1923): 139–40.

53.   "Aube," *Menorah* 22 (15 December 1923): 325–26.

54.   *Menorah* 17 (15 September 1925): 274.

55.   Ludmila Savitzky, "*Marcel Proust, sa vie, son oeuvre*, par Léon Pierre-Quint," *Menorah* 20 (1 November 1925): 322.

56.   Savitzky, "*Marcel Proust*," 322.

57.   Savitzky, "*Marcel Proust*," 322.

58.   Savitzky, "*Marcel Proust*," 322.

4. "THE SAME DEGREE OF HEREDITY AS MONTAIGNE"

1.   Albert Thibaudet, "Marcel Proust et la tradition française," *La nouvelle revue française* (January 1923): 130–39; Antoine Compagnon and Christopher Pradeau, eds., *Réflexions sur la littérature* (Paris: Gallimard, 2007), 733–42.

2.   Georges Cattaui, "Marcel Proust," *Menorah* 8 (22 December 1922): 117.

3.   Théophile Malvezin, *Michel de Montaigne, son origine, sa famille* (Paris: Dentu, 1874).

4.   Théophile Malvezin, *Histoire des juifs à Bordeaux* (Bordeaux: Ch. Lefebvre, 1875).

5.   Maurice Barrès, *Greco ou le secret de Tolède* (Paris: Émile-Paul, 1912), 187.

6.   Marcel Proust, Letter to Daniel Halévy, [c. autumn 1888], *Correspondance*, ed. Philip Kolb (Paris: Plon, 1970-1993), 1:124.

7.   Henri Ghéon, *"Du côté de chez Swann," La nouvelle revue française* (1 January 1914): 139-43, at 139 and 142; see the first chapter of Paul J. Smith, "Réécrire l'homosexualité: Proust lecteur de Montaigne," *Réécrire la Renaissance, de Marcel Proust à Michel Tournier: Exercices de lecture rapprochée* (Amsterdam: Rodopi, 2009), 13-25.

8.   Charles Maurras, "La politique," *L'action française* (Paris), 23 June 1944, 1.

9.   Marcel Proust, Letter to Henri Ghéon, [2 January 1914], *Correspondance*, 13:23.

10. Marcel Proust, Letter to Henri Ghéon, [6 January 1914], *Correspondance*, 13:38.

11. See especially Jean de Pierrefeu, *Plutarque a menti* (Paris: Grasset, 1923).

12. Jean de Pierrefeu, "La vie littéraire: Le cas de M. Proust," *Journal des débats* (Paris), 2 January 1920, 3 (after an initial article, 12 December 1919, "Au jour le jour: Le prix Goncourt," 1, to which Boulenger responded in *L'Opinion*, 20 December 1919, under the title "Marcel Proust").

13. Jacques Boulenger, *Entretien avec Frédéric Lefèvre* (Paris: Le Divan, 1926), 46.

14. Jacques Boulenger, *Le sang français* (Paris: Denoël, 1943).

15. Jacques Boulenger, "Sur Marcel Proust," *L'Opinion* (Paris), 10 January 1920; *Mais l'art est difficile!* (Paris: Plon, 1921), 1:100.

16. André Beaunier, "Sésame," *Le Figaro* (Paris), 14 June 1906, 1.

17. André Beaunier, *Pour la défense française*, vol. 1, *Contre la réforme de l'orthographe* (Paris: Plon, 1909), and vol. 2, *Les plus détestables bonshommes* (Paris: Plon, 1912).

18. Léon Daudet, "André Beaunier," *L'action française* (Paris), 12 December 1925, 1.

19. Marcel Proust, Letter to Robert de Montesquiou, [15 May 1907], *Correspondance*, 7:157.

20. Marcel Cruppi, "Au Mercure: *Sésame et les lys*, par John Ruskin," *Le mouvement, revue mensuelle, artistique et sociale* 1, no. 4 (July 1906: 60); cited in Proust, *Correspondance*, 6:147.

21. Marcel Proust, Letter to Marcel Cruppi, [July 1906], *Correspondance*, 6:146-47.

22. Jean Bonnerot, "Impressions d'enfance," *La revue idéaliste*, 15 September 1907: 277-81, at 278, and 1 October 1907: 293-96, cited in Marcel Proust, *Contre Sainte-Beuve*, ed. Pierre Clarac and Yves Sandre (Paris: Gallimard, 1971), 789.

23. Marcel Proust, Letter to Jean Bonnerot, [June or July 1907], *Correspondance*, 7:165.

24. Célestin Bouglé and André Beaunier, *Choix de moralistes français des XVIIIᵉ et XIXᵉ siècles* (Paris: Delagrave, 1897).

25. Albert Thibaudet, *Histoire de la littérature française de 1789 à nos jours* (Paris: Stock, 1936), 358.

26. Albert Thibaudet, "Marcel Proust et la tradition française," in Compagnon and Pradeau, *Réflexions sur la littérature*, 736.

27. André Spire, *Quelques juifs et demi-juifs* (Paris: Grasset, 1928), 50-51.

28. André Gide, "Nationalisme et littérature," *La nouvelle revue française*, June 1909; *Essais critiques*, ed. Pierre Masson (Paris: Gallimard, 1999), 178.

29. See Albert Thibaudet, "Pour la géographie littéraire," *La nouvelle revue française*, April 1929; Thibaudet, *Réflexions sur la littérature*, 1277; André Gide, "Montaigne,"

Commerce 18 (Winter 1928), and "Suivant Montaigne," *La nouvelle revue française*, 1 June 1929, collected in *Essai sur Montaigne* (Paris: Gallimard, 1929); Gide, *Essais critiques*, 664–703.

30. André Gide, *Journal*, vol. 1, *1887–1925*, ed. Éric Marty (Paris: Gallimard, 1996), 1124–25.

31. André Gide, "Billet à Angèle," *La nouvelle revue française* (May 1921): 586–91; Gide, *Essais critiques*, 178.

32. Marcel Proust, Letter to Jacques Rivière, [6 February 1914], *Correspondance*, 13:98.

33. Maria van Rysselberghe, *Les cahiers de la petite dame* (Paris: Gallimard, 1973), 1:72 (7 April 1921); cited in Gide, *Essais critiques*, 1066n7).

34. Gide, *Journal*, 763–64 (24 January 1914).

35. Thibaudet, *Réflexions sur la littérature*, 739–40.

36. Albert Thibaudet, "Le roman de Montaigne," *La revue universelle*, vol. 60, no. 24 (15 March 1935): 655–77.

37. Thibaudet, *Réflexions sur la littérature*, 740.

38. Thibaudet, *Réflexions sur la littérature*, 740–41.

39. Thibaudet, *Réflexions sur la littérature*, 741–42.

40. Gérard Valbert, *Conversations avec Albert Cohen* (Lausanne: L'Âge d'Homme, 2006), 124.

41. Albert Cohen, "Les chroniques nationales: Israël–Vue d'ensemble sur la question juive et le sionisme," *La revue de Genève* 10 (April 1921): 598–608.

42. Albert Cohen, "Les chroniques nationales: Israël–Le juif et les romanciers français," *La revue de Genève* 33 (March 1923): 340–51, at 350.

43. Jacques de Lacretelle, *Silbermann* (Paris: Éditions de la NRF, 1922), 26; Marcel Proust, *Du côté de chez Swann*, in *À la recherche du temps perdu*, ed. Jean-Yves Tadié (Paris: Gallimard, 1987–1989), 1:89; *Swann's Way*, trans. Lydia Davis (New York: Penguin, 2004), 92.

44. Cohen, "Le juif et les romanciers français," 345.

45. Jacques Rivière, "Marcel Proust et l'esprit positif," *La nouvelle revue française* (January 1923): 179–87, at 184; Rivière, *Nouvelles études* (Paris: Gallimard, 1947), 207.

46. Cohen, "Le juif et les romanciers français," 347.

47. Henri Bergson, *Durée et simultanéité: À propos de la théorie d'Einstein* (Paris: Alcan, 1922), 5.

48. Cohen, "Le juif et les romanciers français," 348.

49. Cohen, "Le juif et les romanciers français," 348n1.

50. Alain Schaffner, "L'échec de *La Revue juive* d'Albert Cohen," *Mémoires du livre/Studies in Book Culture* 4, no. 1 (Autumn 2012), https://www.erudit.org/fr/revues/memoires/2012-v4-n1-memoires0385/1013324ar/.

51. Patrick Mimouni, *Les mémoires maudites: Juifs et homosexuels dans l'oeuvre et la vie de Marcel Proust* (Paris: Grasset, 2018), 12.

52. Albert Cohen, "Projections ou après-minuit à Genève," *La nouvelle revue française* (October 1922): 414–46; "Mort de Charlot," *La nouvelle revue française* (June 1923): 883–89; Valbert, *Conversations avec Albert Cohen*, 127.

53. *La revue juive* 2 (15 March 1925): 296.

54. Albert Cohen, *Belle du seigneur*, ed. Christel Peyrefitte and Bella Cohen (Paris: Gallimard, 1986), 878.

55. *Lettres à la comtesse de Noailles, 1901–1919, Correspondance générale de Marcel Proust*, ed. Robert Proust and Paul Brach(Paris: Plon, 1931), vol. 2.

56. Cohen, "Le juif et les romanciers français," 341.

57. Cohen, "Le juif et les romanciers français," 351.

58. Jacques de Lacretelle, *Le retour de Silbermann* (Paris: Éditions du Capitole, 1929), 179; *Silbermann*, 187.

5. *LA REVUE JUIVE*

1. http://www.revues-litteraires.com/articles.php?pg=1787.

2. See Richard L. Admussen, *Les petites revues littéraires, 1914–1939: Répertoire descriptif* (St. Louis, MO: Washington University Press, 1970), 108–9; Jean-Claude Kuperminc, "Le tour des revues juives," *La revue des revues* 6 (1988): 40–50; Catherine Fhima, "Au coeur de la 'renaissance juive' des années 20: Littérature et judéité," *Archives juives* 39, no. 1 (2006) ("Le 'Réveil juif' des années 20"): 29–45; Alain Schaffner, "L'échec de *La Revue juive*," *Mémoires du livre/Studies in Book Culture* 4, no. 1 (Autumn 2012), https://www.erudit.org/fr/revues/memoires/2012-v4-n1-memoires0385/1013324ar/.

3. Gérard Valbert, *Conversations avec Albert Cohen* (Lausanne: L'Âge d'Homme, 2006), 126.

4. Henry Bernstein, *Israël* (Paris: Fasquelle, 1909). This play was familiar to Proust, to whom Bernstein turned for information about the names of aristocrats. Marcel Proust, *Correspondance*, ed. Philip Kolb (Paris: Plon, 1970–1993), 7:174, 184, 186n7.

5. Jacques de Lacretelle, "Commentaires: *Silbermann*," *La revue juive* 1 (15 January 1925): 64–69, at 66.

6. Lacratelle, "Commentaires," 66n1.

7. Jaime de Beslou, *Idéologues* (Paris: Éditions du Sagittaire, 1923).

8. See Esther Benbassa and Aron Rodrigue, *Une vie judéo-espagnole à l'Est: Gabriel Arié (1863–1939), autobiographie, journal et correspondance* (Paris: Éditions du Cerf, 1992).

9. Gabriel Arié, *Histoire juive depuis les origines jusqu'à nos jours* (Paris: Durlacher et Léon Kaan, 1923). See Nicole Abravenel, "L'historicité en milieu sépharade ou le primat de la spatialité," *Vingtième siècle: Revue d'histoire* 117, no. 1 (2013): 183–97.

10. *Revue des études juives* 79 (1924): 80. See Heinrich Graetz, *Geschichte der Juden von den ältesten Zeiten bis auf die Gegenwart* (Leipzig: Leiner, 1853–1875), 11 vols.; Narcisse Leven, *Cinquante ans d'histoire: L'Alliance Israélite Universelle (1860–1910)*, (Paris: Alcan, 1911–1920), 2 vols.

11. Arié, *Histoire juive*, 365.

12. See the advertisement at the beginning of *La revue juive* 2 (15 March 1925).

13. *Le droit de vivre* (Paris), 20 June 1936, 5.

14. Emmanuel Arié, "*Idéologues (Les systèmes du Baron T'Phlex)*, par Jaime de Beslou," *La revue juive* 1 (15 January 1925): 96–98\.

15. Arié, "*Idéologues*," 97, 98.

16. Marcel Proust, "Lettres," *La revue juive* 4 (July 1925): 463–72; see *Correspondance*, 3:1932.

17. Emmanuel Arié, "*Poésie*, par Jean Cocteau," *La revue juive* 5 (September 1925): 606–8, at 606.

18. Arié, "*Poésie*," 607. See Jean Cocteau, *Le secret professionnel* (Paris: Stock, 1922), 42–43.

19. Arié, "*Poésie*," 608. See Anna de Noailles, "Souvenirs du coeur," *La nouvelle revue française* (1 January 1923): 19.

20. Charles Péguy, *Oeuvres complètes*, vol. 9, *Oeuvres posthumes* (Paris: Éditions de la NRF, 1924).

21. Georges Cattaui, "*Note conjointe sur M. Descartes, précédé de la note sur M. Bergson*, par Charles Péguy," *La revue juive* 1 (15 January 1925): 99–103, at 100, 101.

22. "Israël et les nations: La France et le sionisme," *La revue juive* 2 (March 1925): 235–49, at 243.

23. See Daniel Teysseire, "De l'usage historico-politique de race entre 1680 et 1820 et de sa transformation," *Mots: Les langages du politique* 33 (1992): 43–52.

24. "Israël et les nations," 248.

25. See Cécile Chombard Gaudin, *L'Orient dévoilé: Sur les traces de Myriam Harry* (Levallois-Perret: Éditions Turquoise, 2019).

26. Marcel Proust, Letter to Reynaldo Hahn, 30 August 1914, *Correspondance*, 13:296–98.

27. André Spire, "*Les Amants de Sion*, par Myriam Harry," *La revue juive* 3 (15 May 1925): 391–93, at 393.

28. Georges Cattaui, "Digressions: Un monument à Marcel Proust," *La revue juive* 5 (September 1925): 609–10, at 610.

29. Jean Ernest-Charles, "Pas de statue," *L'ère nouvelle*, 14 October 1925, 1; quoted in *La revue juive* 6 (November 1925): 804–5.

30. Marcel Proust, "Mademoiselle de Forcheville," *La revue juive* 6 (November 1925): 702–25; see Proust, *Albertine disparue*, in *À la recherche du temps perdu*, ed. Jean-Yves Tadié (Paris: Gallimard, 1987–1989), 4:153–72; *The Fugitive*, trans. Peter Collier (New York: Penguin, 2021), 153–225. The publication date of *Albertine disparue* was 30 November 1925.

31. *La revue juive* 6 (November 1925): 704; see Proust, *Albertine disparue*, 4:155; *The Fugitive*, 171.

32. *La revue juive* 6 (November 1925): 704; Proust, *Albertine disparue*, 4:161; *The Fugitive*, 177.

33. Marcel Proust, Letter to Robert de Montesquiou, [May 1896], *Correspondance*, 2:66.

34. *La revue juive* 6 (November 1925): 716; see Proust, *Albertine disparue*, 4:165; *The Fugitive*, 182.

35. *La revue juive* 6 (November 1925): 725; Proust, *Albertine disparue*, 171–72; *The Fugitive*, 190.

36. Armand Lunel, "*XXᵉ siècle*, par Benjamin Crémieux," *La revue juive* 6 (November 1925): 750–52, at 751.

37. Lunel, "*XXᵉ siècle*."

38. BNF, NAF 18359, Fonds Léon Pierre-Quint, fol. 183–196, see fol. 189, fol. 192 (transcription by Jessica Desclaux for this letter and the following ones).

39. BNF, NAF 18359, fol. 193.

40. Léon Pierre-Quint, "Carl Sternheim," *La revue juive* 6 (November 1925): 733–41.

41. BNF, NAF 18359, fol. 195.

42. The piece by Desnos does not seem to have been published elsewhere, since it is not mentioned by Douglas Alden in *Marcel Proust and His French Critics* (Los Angeles: Lymanhouse, 1940). See *La révolution surréaliste* (January 1925): 25.

43. See Michel Dousse and Jean-Michel Roessli, eds., *Jean de Menasce (1902–1973)* (Fribourg: Bibliothèque Cantonale et Universitaire, 1998); Jean-Michel Roessli, "Jean de Menasce (1902–1973), historien des religions, théologien et philosophe," *Revue des sciences philosophiques et théologiques* 101, no. 4 (2017): 611–54 (which, at 617, dates Menasce's conversion to May 1926 and that of his cousin Cattaui to 1928); Philippe Chenaux, "Du judaïsme au catholicisme: Réseaux de conversion dans l'entre-deux-guerres," in *La conversion aux XIXᵉ*

et XXᵉ siècles, ed. Nadine-Josette Chaline and Jean-Dominique Durant (Arras: Artois Presses Université, 1996), 95-106; Joël Sebban, "Être juif et chrétien: La question juive et les intellectuels catholiques français issus de judaïsme (1898-1940)," *Archives juives* 44, no. 1 (2011): 106-22.

44. Catherine Nicault, "Albert Cohen et les sionistes," in *Albert Cohen dans son siècle: Actes du colloque de Cerisy-la-Salle, septembre 2003*, ed. Alain Schaffner and Philippe Zard (Paris: Éditions Le Manuscrit, 2005), 101n3.

45. Philippe Chenaux, *Entre Maurras et Maritain, une génération intellectuelle catholique (1920–1930)* (Paris: Éditions du Cerf, 1999), 179.

46. Jean de Menasce, "Regards: *Ulysses*, par James Joyce," *La revue juive* 6 (November 1925): 761.

47. Adolph Hitler, *Mon combat*, trans. J. Gaudefroy-Demombynes and A. Calmetters (Paris: Nouvelles Éditions Latine, 1934), 540 (chap. 11, "Le peuple et la race"); *Mein Kampf*, trans. Ralph Manheim (New York: Houghton Mifflin, 1943), 307 (chap. 11, "Nation and Race").

48. Jean-Jacques Bernard, *Le camp de la mort lente: Compiègne 1941–1942* (Paris: Albin Michel, 1944), 87.

49. Jean de Menasce, "Antisémitisme: Hilaire Belloc, Hans Blüher et René Groos," *La revue juive* 4 (July 1925): 473-78, at 473.

50. *L'action française* (Paris), 28 October 1918, 1.

51. See Catherine Nicault, "Les 'Français israélites' et la ligue d'Action Française," in *L'Action Française: Culture, société, politique*, ed. Michel Leymarie and Jacques Prévotat (Lille: Presses Universitaires du Septentrion, 2008), 185-202; Romain Dupré, "René Groos, dit Pierre Herbel, homme de lettre et professeur," *Archives juives* 47, no. 2 (2014): 131-42.

52. Charles Maurras, "La question juive: Un schéma," *L'action française* (Paris), 27 September 1920; reproduced as an appendix in René Groos, *Enquête sur le problème juif* (Paris: Nouvelle Librairie Nationale, 1923), 253.

53. Groos, *Enquête sur le problème juif*, 18-19; quoted in part by Annick Duraffour and Pierre-André Taguieff, *Céline, la race, le juif: Légende littéraire et vérité historique* (Paris: Fayard, 2017), 143.

54. Groos, *Enquête sur le problème juif*, 85, 58.

55. Menasce, "Antisémitisme," 477.

56. Groos, *Enquête sur le problème juif*, 170; quoted by Dupré, "René Groos, dit Pierre Herbel," 131-42.

57. Menasce, "Antisémitisme," 478.

58. Crémieux, *Du côté de Marcel Proust*, 119; "Maurice Barrès," *L'univers israélite* 79, no. 14 (14 December 1923): 332.

59. René Groos, "Marcel Proust et le judaïsme," *Marcel Proust* (Paris: Éditions de la Revue Le Capitole, 1926), 65-72; Groos, *Esquisses: Charles Maurras, poète, Marcel Proust, Bernard Shaw* (Paris: Maison du Livre Français, 1928), 25-35.

60. *Charles Maurras* (Paris: Éditions de la Revue Le Capitole, 1925); *Jacques Bainville* (Paris: Éditions de la Revue Le Capitole, 1927); see *L'action française* (Paris), 2 December 1928, 4; 8 December 1929, 4; 12 November 1930, 6.

61. Menasce, "Antisémitisme," 473.

62. George D. Painter, *Marcel Proust*, 2 vols., trans. G. Cattaui and R.-P. Vial (Paris: Mercure de France, 1966).

63. "Assemblée générale du 23 juin 1966. Allocution du président Jacques de Lacretelle," *Bulletin de la Société des Amis de Marcel Proust* 17 (1967): 606. Roger Peyrefitte reports that Gaston Gallimard supposedly retorted to an intermediary proposal to erect a monument to Proust on the Champs-Élysées: "A monument? But there already is one, there's a urinal!" *Propos secrets*, with Claude Chevreuil (Paris: Albin Michel, 1977), 1:229.

64. "Adolphe Cattaui Bey," *Menorah* 14 (15 July 1925): 223-25. On the Cattaui family, see Kurt Grunwald, "On Cairo's Lombard Street," *Tradition: Zeitschrift für Firmengeshichte und Unternehmerbiographie* 17, no. 1 (January-February 1972): 8-22.

65. Bibliothèque littéraire Jacques Doucet, Alpha Ms 1983 (transcription by Jessica Desclaux).

66. Letter from Jacques Chevalier to Georges Cattaui, 13 November 1927, Georges Cattaui Papers, Bibliothèque de Genève, cited by Chenaux, *Entre Maurras et Maritain*, 183.

67. Henri Bergson, *Correspondances*, ed. André Robinet (Paris: PUF, 2002), 1670.

68. Cited by Chenaux, *Entre Maurras et Maritain*, 183; see also Daniel Lançon, "Georges Cattaui ou la France participée," *Entre Nil et sable: Écrivains d'Égypte d'expression française, 1920–1960*, ed. Marc Kober, Irène Fenoglio, and Daniel Lançon (Paris: Centre National de Documentation Pédagogique, 1999), 87-103.

69. Georges Cattaui, *La promesse accomplie* (Paris: Camille Bloch, 1922). See Dario Miccoli, "A Fragile Cradle: Writing Jewishness, Nationhood, and Modernity in Cairo, 1920-1940," *Jewish Social Studies* 21, no. 3 (Spring-Summer 2016): 1-30.

70. Pierre Benoit, "*Le puits de Jacob*," *La revue juive* 1 (15 January 1925): 69-73. A letter from Barrès to Cattaui is found in the Bibliothèque Littéraire Jacques Doucet, Ms Ms 22590.

71. Cattaui, *La promesse accomplie*, 77.

72. Maurice Barrès, *Le diverses familles spirituelles de la France* (Paris: Émile-Paul, 1917), 69; *Le diverses familles spirituelles de la France*, ed. Denis Pernot and Vital Rambaud (Paris: Classiques Garnier, 2017), 62.

73. See Cattaui's prepublication review of *Une enquête au pays du Levant* (*Revue des deux mondes*, 15 February 1923 and 1 March 1923): "Barrès aux Pays du Levant," *Menorah* 14 (16 March 1923): 220-22, and 15 (30 March 1923): 235-37, signed H. G. C.

74. André Berge, "Autour d'une trouvaille: Confession," *Les cahiers du mois* 7 (December 1924): 5-18; Marcel Proust, *Contre Sainte-Beuve*, ed. Pierre Clarac and Yves Sandre (Paris: Gallimard, 1971), 335-36. See Évelyne Bloch-Dano, *Une jeunesse de Marcel Proust* (Paris: Stock, 2017).

75. André Desson and André Harlaire, "Le sionisme, essai de renaissance juive," *Les cahiers du mois* 9-10 (February-March 1925): 364; quoted in part by *La revue juive* 3 (15 May 1925): 409-10.

76. André Harlaire (1905-1986), André Brottier or Louis Gardet, disciple of Maritain, Thomist, Catholic convert on Christmas 1926, would enter the Dominican order, like Jean de Menasce; he contributed to *Menorah* 11, 15 June 1924: 162 ("Émile Zola et l'antisémitisme"). See Dominique Avon, *Les frères prêcheurs en Orient: Les dominicains du Caire (années 1910–années 1960)* (Paris: Éditions du Cerf, 2005), 145-47.

77.   André Harlaire, *"La promesse accomplie,* par Georges Cattaui," *La revue juive* 6 (November 1925): 752–53.

78.   Georges Cattaui, "Barrès et les juifs," *La revue juive* 6 (November 1925): 726–33.

79.   Georges Cattaui, "Barrès et les juifs," *Critique art philosophie: Bulletin mensuel d'art et de littérature* 2 (May-June 1924): 11–12.

80.   Cattaui, "Barrès et les juifs," *La revue juive*, 727. See also H. G. C., "Blaise Pascal: L'influence de la pensée juive sur les lettres françaises," *Menorah* 21 (24 June 1923): 338–340, and 22 (8 July 1923): 357–58.

81.   Charles Péguy, *Oeuvres complètes*, vol. 2, *Oeuvres de prose* (Paris: Éditions de la NRF, 1920).

82.   Cattaui, "Barrès et les juifs," *La revue juive*, 731.

83.   "Maurice Barrès," *L'univers israélite* 79, no. 14 (14 December 1923): 332.

84.   André Spire, "Quelques souvenirs sur Maurice Barrès," *Le pays lorrain* 16, no. 3 (March 1924): 112–17.

85.   André Spire, *Quelques juifs et demi-juifs* (Paris: Grasset, 1928), 2:175, 177, 178.

86.   Spire, *Quelques juifs et demi-juifs*, 2:181. In *Le pays lorrain*, Cattaui is not named but presented as "an Egyptian poet" ("Quelques souvenirs sur Maurice Barrès," 117).

87.   Benjamin Crémieux, "La littérature juive française," *La revue juive de Genève* 5, no. 45 (February 1937): 196.

88.   André Spire, *Versets: Et vous riez—Poèmes juifs* (Paris: Mercure de France, 1908), BNF, Z Barrès 26145.

89.   André Spire, letter to Georges Cattaui, 10 January 1926, Bibliothèque de Genève, Georges Cattaui Papers, Ms. fr. 4968, f. 115-36 (transcription by Marie-Brunette Spire).

90.   Émile Cahen, *"Silbermann,"* *Archives israélites* 83, no. 48 (30 November 1922): 190.

6. "THE STYLE OF THE RABBI"

1.   Denis Saurat, "Le judaïsme de Proust," *Les Marges*, 15 October 1925, 83–87; see *La revue juive* 6 (November 1925): 792–95. Saurat would include his article in *Tendances* (Paris: Éditions du Monde Moderne, 1928), 154–60.

2.   Denis Saurat, *La pensée de Milton* (Paris: Alcan, 1920).

3.   Denis Saurat, *Blake and Milton* (Bordeaux: Imprimerie de l'Université, 1920).

4.   Saurat, "Le judaïsme de Proust," 83; *La revue juive* 6 (November 1925): 792.

5.   *La revue juive* 6 (November 1925): 792; quoting Saurat, "Le judaïsme de Proust," 84.

6.   It is the book that Saurat cites, not the advance pages published in *Les nouvelles littéraires*, 6 June 1925, under the title "Le style de Marcel Proust."

7.   *La revue juive* 6 (November 1925): 792–93; quoting Saurat, "Le judaïsme de Proust," 84–85. Proust quote is from *Swann's Way*, trans. Lydia Davis (New York: Penguin, 2004), 242.

8.   Léon Pierre-Quint, *Marcel Proust: Sa vie, son oeuvre* (Paris: Éditions du Sagittaire, 1925), 133.

9.   *La revue juive* 6 (November 1925): 793; quoting Saurat, "Le judaïsme de Proust," 85.

10.   Saurat, *La pensée de Milton*, 231.

11.   Denis Saurat, "Milton and the *Zohar*," *Studies in Philology* 19, no. 2 (April 1922): 136. Before publication in this American review from the University of North Carolina, the article

had appeared in an esoteric London monthly, *The Quest* 13 (January 1922): 145-65. Two publications by Saurat in French had preceded it, "La Cabal et la philosophie de Milton," *Revue des études juives* 73, no. 145 (1921): 1-13, and "Milton et le *Zohar*," *Revue germanique* 13 (January 1922): 1-19.

12. Denis Saurat, *Milton, Man and Thinker* (New York: Dial Press, 1925), 280. Saurat demonstrated more caution when writing in French in 1922: "I am only claiming here to propose and to try and prove the hypothesis that Milton made use of the *Zohar* and other kabbalistic writings that he could have known, that he found in them confirmation of his general ideas, that he drew from them most of the ideas in his work that seem at first either novel or singular" (Saurat, "Milton et le *Zohar*," 2).

13. See Kitty Cohen, *The Throne and the Chariot: Studies in Milton's Hebraism* (The Hague: Mouton, 1975), 3. See also Douglas A. Brooks, ed., *Milton and the Jews* (Cambridge: Cambridge University Press, 2008), in particular, Douglas Trevor, "Milton and Solomonic Education," 83-104, and Matthew Biberman, "T. S. Eliot, Anti-Semitism and the Milton Controversy," 105-27.

14. Jeffrey Shoulson, "Man and Thinker: Denis Saurat, and the Old New Milton Criticism," *The New Milton Criticism*, Peter C. Herman and Elizabeth Sauer, eds. (Cambridge: Cambridge University Press, 2012), 196 and 194; according to Shoulson, who sees Saurat was one of the first critics to be interested in Milton's thinking, his insistence on the influence of Jewish mysticism overshadows the other more valuable contributions of his study.

15. Denis Saurat, *Blake and Modern Thought* (London: Constable, 1929), 102. See Sheila Spector, "Kabbalistic Sources: Blake's and His Critics,'" *Blake: An Illustrated Quarterly* 17, no. 3 (Winter 1983-1984): 84-101.

16. Saurat, "Le judaïsme de Proust," 85, 87; *Tendances* (Paris: Éditions du Monde Moderne, 1928), 154.

17. Denis Saurat, "Proust et Joyce," *Les Marges*, 15 December 1924, 244.

18. *La revue juive* 6 (November 1925): 794; quoting Saurat, "Le judaïsme de Proust," 86.

19. *La revue juive* 6 (November 1925): 795; quoting Saurat, "Le judaïsme de Proust," 87.

20. Saurat, *Tendances*, 154-60.

21. Denis Saurat, "Propos: Le génie malade—Proust," *Les Marges*, 15 November 1925, 198-205, see 205; *Tendances*, 161-70.

22. *La revue juive* 6 (November 1925): 795; quoting Saurat, "Le judaïsme de Proust," 87.

23. Denis Saurat, "Proust," *Marsyas* 6, no. 61 (January 1926): 292-93; 62 (February 1926): 300-301; 63 (March 1926): 305-6; 64 (April 1926): 308; 65 (May 1926): 317-18; 66 (June 1926): 324-26; 67 (July 1926): 329-30; 68 (August 1926): 332-34.

24. Denis Saurat, "Meredith et Proust," *Marsyas* 5, no. 60 (December 1925): 284-85, note.

25. Denis Saurat, "*Le temps retrouvé*," *Marsyas* 8, no. 85 (January 1928): 401-2.

26. Saurat, *Tendances*, 181-82, 186-87 ("Proust").

27. Marcel Proust, *Sodome et Gomorrhe II*, in *À la recherche du temps perdu*, ed. Jean-Yves Tadié (Paris: Gallimard, 1987-1989), 3:332-33. *Sodom and Gomorrah*, trans. John Sturrock (New York: Penguin, 2005), 332.

28. Saurat, *Tendances*, 200-201, 221. Arnaud Dandieu takes up this idea: "It is through this disdain for the system that Proust is, in effect, the French response to Freud." *Marcel Proust: Sa révélation psychologique* (Paris: Éditions Firmin-Didot, 1930), 38.

29. Denis Saurat, "L'après-guerre: Le style 'moderne,' " *La nouvelle revue française* (1 November 1931): 800; Benjamin Crémieux, *Inquiétude et reconstruction: Essai sur la littérature d'après-guerre* (Paris: Corrêa, 1931); *Inquiétude et reconstruction: Essai sur la littérature d'après-guerre*, ed. Catherine Helbert (Paris: Gallimard, 2011).

30. Denis Saurat, *Modernes* (Paris: Denoël et Steele, 1935), 16.

31. Denis Saurat, "Victor Hugo et la Cabale," *Marsyas* 6, no. 71 (November 1926): 343; 72 (December 1926), 349-50; "Victor Hugo: Le panthéisme mystique," *Marsyas* 7, no. 73 (January 1927): 353-54; "Propos: Occultisme et sensualité—Alexandre Weill et Victor Hugo," *Les Marges*, 15 December 1926, 294-300; *La religion de Victor Hugo* (Paris: Hachette, 1929), chap, 2, "L'occultiste: Hugo et la Cabale." See *Mystères de la création*, trans. Alexandre Weill (Paris: Dentu, 1855).

32. Denis Saurat, "La nuit d'Idumée et la Cabale," *La nouvelle revue française*, 1 December 1931, 920-22.

33. Denis Saurat, "Baudelaire, Rimbaud, la Cabale," *La nouvelle revue française*, 1 February 1936, 258, 261.

34. Denis Saurat, "Le grand maître du moderne: Marcel Proust," *Les Marges*, Spring 1930, 123-44.

35. Cahier 5, BNF, NAF 16645, fol. 53 v°.

36. Carnet 1, BNF, NAF 16637, fol. 41 v°.

37. Juliette Hassine, *Ésotérisme et écriture dans l'oeuvre de Proust* (Paris: Minard, 1990), 89, note 31.

38. *Sepher ha-Zohar (Le livre de la splendeur), doctrine ésotérique des Israélites*, 6 vols., trans. Jean de Pauly (Paris: E. Leroux, 1906-1911).

39. Hassine, *Ésotérisme et écriture*, 7. See Plotinus, *Les Ennéades*, 3 vols., trans. Marie-Nicolas Bouillet (Paris: Hachette, 1857-1861), vol. 1, 374-77.

40. Patrick Mimouni, *Les mémoires maudites: Juifs et homosexuels dans l'oeuvre et la vie de Marcel Proust* (Paris: Grasset, 2018), 13 and 45.

41. Julia Kristeva, *Le temps sensible: Proust et l'experience littéraire* (Paris: Gallimard, 1994), 186-87.

42. Jean Milly, *Les pastiches de Proust* (Paris: Armand Colin, 1970).

43. Juliette Hassine, *Ésotérisme et écriture dans l'oeuvre de Proust* (Paris: Minard, 1990), 5.

44. Kristeva, *Le temps sensible*, 194, 190.

45. Letter from Jean de Pauly to Émile Lafuma-Giraud, 25 June 1900, quoted by Dominique Bourel, "Notes sur la première traduction française du *Zohar*," *Jüdisches Denken in einer Welt ohne Gott: Festschrift für Stéphane Mosès*, ed. J. Mattern, G. Motzkin, and S. Sandbank (Berlin: Vorwerk 8, 2000), 125.

46. "Le Zohar," *Le Temps* (Paris), 8 November 1908, 2.

47. Barrès owned all six volumes of the *Sepher ha-Zohar* translation by Jean de Pauly, probably sent to him by Émile Lafuma-Giraud (BNF, Z Barrès 9411-9416). His Nancy classmate, the occultist poet Stanislas de Guaita (1861-1897), a close friend of Joséphin Péladan, refers to the Zohar in *Au seuil du mystère* (Paris: Carré, 1886), a book for which Barrès wrote a preface in a posthumous edition (Paris: Derville, 1915).

48. *Le livre du Zohar* (Paris: Rieder, 1925), 7; *Le livre de la splendeur: Pages du "Livre de Zohar" choisies par Edmond Fleg* (Paris: J.-C. Lattès, 1980).

49. Adolphe Franck, *La Kabbale, ou la philosophie religieuse des Hébreux* (Paris: Hachette, 1843), 244–47; 3rd ed. (1892), 183–85. See Charles Mopsik, "Quelques remarques sur Adolphe Franck, philosophe français et pionnier de l'étude de la cabale au XIXᵉ siècle," *Pardès* 19–20 (1994): 239–44; Paul B. Fenton, "La contribution d'Adolphe Franck à l'étude historico-critique de la Kabbale," in *Adolphe Franck, philosophe juif, spiritualiste et libéral dans la France du XIXᵉ siècle*, ed. Jean-Pierre Rothschild and Jérome Grondeux (Turnhout: Brepols, 2012), 81–97.

50. Paul Vulliaud, *La Kabbale juive, histoire et doctrine: Essai critique*, 2 vols. (Paris: Nourry, 1923), 2:394–96, note on 394.

51. Jules Michelet, *Histoire de France*, vol. 7, *Réforme* (Paris: Chamerot, 1855), 21.

52. Other contemporary publications on the Zohar can be ruled out: Siméon bar Yohay, *Le Zohar*, trans. Henri Château (Paris: Chameul, 1895); Samuel Karppe, *Étude sur les origines et la nature du Zohar, précédée d'une étude sur l'histoire de la Kabbale* (Paris: Alcan, 1901 (thesis defended at the Sorbonne by a student of Renan and of James Darmesteter); Albert Jounet (Jhouney), *La clef du Zohar: Éclaircissement et unification des mystères de la Kabbale* (Paris: Charcornac, 1909).

53. Louis-Ferdinand Céline, *Bagatelles pour un massacre* (Paris: Denoël, 1937), 169 (with thanks to A. Kaplan for the translation); Céline, letter to Lucien Combelle, *Révolution nationale* (20 February 1943); *Cahiers Céline 7* (Paris: Gallimard, 1986), 180.

54. The correspondence between Bloch and Saurat is in the BNF's Jean-Richard Bloch Collection, NAF 28222 (184), vol. 42, fol. 361–439. Saurat's letters also appear in the Léon Pierre-Quint Collection, NAF 18363, vol. 12.

55. Jean-Richard Bloch and André Spire, *Correspondance, 1912–1947: "Sommes-nous d'accord?,"* ed. Marie-Brunette Spire (Paris: Éditions Claire Paulhan, 2011), 126n328.

56. See Roland Lardinois, "Sociologie d'un espace familial: Sylvain Lévi dans sa parentèle," in *Sylvain Lévi (1863–1935): Études indiennes, histoire social*, ed. Lyne Bansat-Boudon and Roland Lardinois (Turnhout: Brepols, 2007), 267–88; Denis Saurat, *La littérature et l'occultisme: Études sur la poésie philosophique moderne* (Paris: Rieder, 1929).

57. Denis Saurat, "Conversations avec Jean-Richard Bloch," *Europe* 135–136 (March–April 1957): 37–40, see 38–39.

58. Gershom Scholem, *Major Trends in Jewish Mysticism* (Jerusalem: Schocken, 1941), 2; *Les grands courants de la mystique juive*, trans. Marie-Madeleine Davy (Paris: Payot, 1950, 2014).

59. Gershom Scholem, *Von Berlin nach Jerusalem: Jugenderinnerungen* (Frankfurt: Suhrkamp, 1977); *De Berlin à Jérusalem: Souvenirs de jeunesse*, trans. Sabine Bollack (Paris: Albin Michel, 1984), 174, quoted by Bourel, "Notes sur la première traduction,"120.

60. André Spire, "Israel Zangwill humoriste," *L'univers israélite* 84, no. 17 (4 January 1929): 517.

61. Spire, "Israel Zangwill humoriste."

62. Denis Saurat, "Jean-Richard Bloch," *La nouvelle revue française*, 1 May 1932, 873, 877.

63. Letter from André Spire to Georges Cattaui, 16 October 1932, Bloch and Spire, *Correspondance*, 132n392.

64. Denis Saurat, *Watch Over Africa* (London: Dent, 1941).

65. Antoine Prost and Jay Winter, *René Cassin et les droits de l'homme: Le projet d'une génération* (Paris: Fayard, 2011), 264.

66. Jean-Richard Bloch, letter to Denis Saurat, 31 January 1946, BNF, NAF 28222 (184), vol. 42, fol. 439; quoted by Rachel Mazuy, "Jean-Richard Bloch–Denis Saurat: Une amitié littéraire (1925–1946)," 2017, https://cturss.hypotheses.org/88.

67. Denis Saurat, *L'expérience de l'au-delà* (La Colombe: Éditions du Vieux-Colombier, 1951); *L'Atlantide* (Paris: Denoël, 1954; Paris: J'ai Lu, 1968, 1986); *La religion des géants et la civilisation des insectes* (Paris: Denoël, 1955; Paris: J'ai Lu, 1969).

68. According to Robert Lafont quoted by Jean-François Courouau in his introduction to *Encaminament catar*, ed. and trans. J.-F. Courouau (Toulouse: Presses Universitaires du Mirail, 2010), 9, 10.

69. Jean Paulhan, "Denis Saurat," *La nouvelle nouvelle revue française*, July 1958, 172.

70. See John Robert Colombo, *O rare Denis Saurat: An Appreciation* (Toronto, C & C, 2003); Denis Saurat, *The Denis Saurat Reader*, ed. John Robert Colombo (Toronto: C & C, 2004).

7. "MAKING A NICHE FOR THEMSELVES IN THE FRENCH BOURGEOISIE"

1. Catherine Nicault, "Albert Cohen et les sionistes," in *Albert Cohen dans son siècle: Actes du colloque de Cerisy-la-Salle, septembre 2003*, ed. Alain Schaffner and Philippe Zard (Paris: Éditions Le Manuscrit, 2005), 101n5.

2. Bibliothèque de Genève, Georges Cattaui Papers, Ms. fr. 4968, fol. 115–136: Spire, André 15 letters and cards signed to Georges Cattaui, 19 March 1920–25 February 1936; Bibliothèque littéraire Jacques Doucet, Alpha 8524 (47–54), 8 letters, 5 July 1922–4 December 1935; Alpha Ms 2014–Alpha Ms 2022, Alpha Ms 5654, 10 letters . . .–8 September 1959.

3. Information provided by Marie-Brunette Spire.

4. Bibliothèque littéraire Jacques Doucet, Alpha Ms 7140, letter of 12 August 1968 (transcription by Jessica Desclaux).

5. Mélanie Fabre, *Dick May, une femme à l'avant-garde d'un nouveau siècle, 1859–1925* (Rennes: Presses Universitaires de Rennes, 2019).

6. [Judaeus], "La renaissance juive en France d'après M. André Spire," *L'univers israélite* 82, no. 16 (24 December 1926): 486.

7. *La tribune juive* 52 (31 December 1926): 809–10.

8. Robert Sommer, "Bibliographie des travaux du grand rabbin Maurice Liber (1884–1956)," *Revue des études juives* 68, no. 1 (1959): 111.

9. Maurice Liber, *Rashi* (London: Macmillan and Jewish Historical Society of England, 1906).

10. Judaeus, "Les paradoxes de M. Spire," *L'univers israélite* 82, no. 17 (31 December 1926): 519.

11. "Qu'est-ce que le judaïsme," *La Palestine nouvelle* 8 (1 May 1921): 21; quoted by Jean-Richard Bloch and André Spire in *Correspondance, 1912–1947: "Sommes-nous d'accord?"* ed. Marie-Brunette Spire (Paris: Éditions Claire Paulhan, 2011), 51.

12. Judaeus, "Les paradoxes," 519.

13. "Une lettre de M. Spire," *L'univers israélite* 82, no. 18 (7 January 1927): 552; see Proust, *Le côté de Guermantes I*, in *À la recherche du temps perdu*, ed. Jean-Yves Tadié (Paris: Gallimard, 1987–1989), 2:544; *The Guermantes Way*, trans. Mark Treharne (New York: Penguin, 2004), 241.

14.   Bloch and Spire, *Correspondance*, 355. See Georges Weill, "'Entre l'Orient et l'Occident': Sylvain Lévi président de l'Alliance Israélite Universelle," in *Sylvain Lévi (1863–1935): Études indiennes, histoire sociale*, ed. Lyne Bansat-Boudon and Roland Lardinois (Turnhout: Brepols, 2007), 391–420.

15.   Robert Dreyfus wrote that Proust had known Jacques Bizet "from early childhood at the Pape-Carpentier [*sic*] nursery school where my mother used to take me as well," but not that he himself had known Proust at that time. See his *Souvenirs sur Marcel Proust* (Paris: Grasset, 1926), 340; quoted by George D. Painter, *Marcel Proust*, trans. G. Cattaui and R.-P. Vial (Paris: Mercure de France, 1966), 1:77. Certain biographies add Daniel Halévy and Henri de Rothschild. See William C. Carter, *Marcel Proust: A Life* (New Haven, CT: Yale University Press, 2000), 40, which gives no source; Patrick Mimouni, *Les mémoires maudites: Juifs et homosexuels dans l'oeuvre et la vie de Marcel Proust* (Paris: Grasset, 2018), 390, which adds Élie Halévy and locates the Pape-Carpantier school on Rue de Surène (where there was a girls' elementary school). There is no further trace of this nursery school that would have followed the teaching methods of Marie Pape-Carpantier (1815–1878), school inspector of the Seine's *salles d'asile*, called *écoles maternelles* beginning in 1881. See also Robert Dreyfus, *Marcel Proust à dix-septs ans, avec des lettres inédites de Marcel Proust* (Paris: Kra, 1926).

16.   Marcel Proust, Letter to Daniel Halévy, [January 1908], *Correspondance*, ed. Philip Kolb (Paris: Plon, 1970–1993), 21:632.

17.   Dreyfus, *Souvenirs sur Marcel Proust*, 340; letter to Robert Dreyfus, [30 September 1920], *Correspondance*, 19:496.

18.   Jean Bourdariat, "Quinze ans avant le scandale de Panama, l'affaire du chemin de fer transocéanique de Honduras," *Revue d'histoire des chemins de fer* 44 (2013): 165–82.

19.   Mimouni, *Les mémoires maudites*, 390.

20.   Adolphe Dreyfus and Martin Scheyer became partners in 1858, first with Mardochée Fernandez Dias Sourdis (1819–1873), originally from Bordeaux, under the corporate name Sourdis et Cie, all at the address 28 Rue Bergère, where Robert Dreyfus was born in 1873. *Gazette des tribunaux* (Paris), 14 August 1859, 788; 30 July 1862, 738.

21.   *Archives israélites* 34, no. 10 (15 May 1873): 317.

22.   *Le Figaro* (Paris), 31 October 1875, 1.

23.   *Le Figaro* (Paris), 2 November 1875, 1.

24.   *Gazette des tribunaux* (Paris), 1 September 1876, 853–54. AN, Léonore database, L2479034.

25.   Court of Appeal of Paris, fourth chamber, 26 February 1880, *Le Droit* (Paris), 3 March 1880, 1–2; Court of Appeal of Paris, fourth chamber, 20 May 1881, *Le Droit* (Paris), 9 June 1881, 1–2; *Journal des sociétés civiles et commerciales* (Paris), 1884, 99–103. See Auguste Chirac, "L'agiotage de 1870 à 1894," *La revue socialiste* 3, no. 17 (May 1886): 397–99.

26.   Édouard Drumont, *La France juive*, 2 vols. (Paris: Marpon and Flammarion, 1886), 1:viii.

27.   Following the Paris Court of Appeals decision in the Honduras affair in 1881, which acquitted him, Raphaël Bischoffsheim, recently elected representative, sued *Le progrès de Nice* for libel and won; this was one of the first court cases resulting from the Press Law of 29 July 1881. See *Le Droit* (Paris), 12 December 1881, 2–3; 30 April 1882, 2.

28. Édouard Drumont, *La fin d'un monde: Étude psychologique et sociale* (Paris: Savine, 1889), 37.

29. Édouard Drumont, *La dernière bataille: Nouvelle étude psychologique et sociale* (Paris: Dentu, 1890), 75.

30. *La libre parole* (Paris), 29 November 1894, 1; 18 November 1895, 1; 7 April 1919, 1.

31. "The suspension of payments is announced for the National Credit Bank, Dreyfus-Scheyer et Cie, head office at Rue de la Chaussée d'Antin, in Paris. The loss is significant (10 million)," *Les tablettes des Deux-Charentes* (Rochefort), 3 November 1878, 2.

32. AD, Belfort, Births, 1826, no. 78, 1 E 10 N 34, view 584/620; AP, Deaths, Ninth Arrondissement, 1878, no. 1437, V4E 3561, view 20/27.

33. *Denver Daily Tribune*, 10 February 1878, 4. See *Colorado State Business Directory and Annual Register* (Denver: Blake, 1878), 48; *The Colorado Directory of Mines* (Denver: Rocky Mountain News, 1879), 70 and 193.

34. AP, Deaths, Ninth Arrondissement, 1880, no. 121-122, V4E 3584, view 17/33.

35. The naming of a liquidator for the Dreyfus, Scheyer et Cie and Sourdis et Cie banks was announced in the *Journal des sociétés civiles et commerciales*, 1880, on page 70.

36. *L'univers israélite* 80, no. 20 (6 February 1925): 466. AP Death, Seventeenth Arrondissement, 1925, no. 297, 17D 231, view 28/31.

37. Marcel Proust, Letters to Robert Dreyfus, [23 August 1909], *Correspondance*, 9:169; [September 1909], 9:182; [8 October 1910], 10:182.

38. *La petite république* (Paris), 8 November 1910, 4; *Le petit parisien* (Paris), 8 November 1910, 3; *Le Figaro* (Paris), 8 November 1910, 2. AP Death Seventeenth Arrondissement, 1910, no. 2510, 17D 173, view 22/31.

39. Marcel Proust, Letter to Robert Dreyfus, [March 1910], *Correspondance*, 9:69.

40. Marcel Proust, Letter to Robert Dreyfus, [10 November 1910], *Correspondance*, 10:207-8; *Le Figaro* (Paris), 10 November 1910, 3.

41. Marcel Proust, Letter to Robert Dreyfus, [November 1910], *Correspondance*, 10:211.

42. *Le Figaro* (Paris), 2 August 1884, 3; 31 July 1889, 5; 6 August 1890, 5.

43. *Le Figaro* (Paris), 5 August 1890, 2.

44. *Journal des débats* (Paris), 19 June 1939, 2.

45. "Robert Dreyfus," *L'univers israélite* 94, no. 42 (6 July 1939): 755.

46. AN, Léonore database, c-349133. See Augustin Hamon and X. Y. Z., *Les maîtres de la France*, 3 vols. (Paris: Éditions Sociales Internationales, 1936–1938) vol. 3, *La féodalité financière dans les transports ferroviaires, routiers, aériens, maritimes, dans les ports, canaux, entreprises coloniales*, 79.

47. AP, Deaths, Eighth Arrondissement, 1939, no. 438, 8D 219, view 15/31.

48. See also Robert Dreyfus, *Monsieur Thiers contre l'Empire, la guerre, la Commune, 1869–1871* (Paris: Grasset, 1928), and *La république de Monsieur Thiers, 1871–1873* (Paris: Gallimard, 1930).

49. Dreyfus, *Souvenirs sur Marcel Proust*, 274.

50. Proust, *Sodome et Gomorrhe II*, in *À la recherche du temps perdu*, 3:25-26; *Sodom and Gomorrah*, trans. John Sturrock (New York: Penguin, 2005), 25.

51. Marcel Proust, *Jean Santeuil*, preceded by *Les plaisirs et les jours*, ed. Pierre Clarac and Yves Sandre (Paris: Gallimard, 1971), 584; *Jean Santeuil*, trans. Gerard Hopkins (New York: Simon & Schuster, 1956), 314.

52.   Proust, *À l'ombre des jeunes filles en fleurs*, in *À la recherche du temps perdu*, 2:588–89. *In the Shadow of Young Girls in Flower*, trans. James Grieve (New York: Penguin, 2005), 174.

53.   Marcel Proust, Letter to Madame Scheikévitch, [November 1915], *Correspondance*, 14:280.

54.   Brunschwig exhibited "Chemises, caleçons, gilets, etc." at the 1878 Paris Exposition Universelle Internationale, *Catalogue officiel* (Paris: Imprimerie Nationale, 1878), 2:331.

55.   Bartholo [pseudonym of Robert Dreyfus], "Une rentrée littéraire," *Le Figaro* (Paris), 7 July 1919, 1.

56.   Frédéric Nietzsche, *Le cas Wagner: Un problème musical*, trans. Daniel Halévy and Robert Dreyfus (Paris: A. Schultz, 1893); Robert Dreyfus, "La vie et les prophéties du comte de Gobineau," *Cahiers de la quinzaine* 16 (9 May 1905) (talks given at the École des Hautes Études Sociales, winter 1904-1905); *La vie et les prophéties du comte de Gobineau* (Paris: Calmann-Lévy, 1905).

57.   Robert Dreyfus, "Vies des hommes obscurs: Alexandre Weill, ou le prophète du faubourg Saint-Honoré, 1811-1899," *Cahiers de la quinzaine* 9 (29 January 1908) (Lecture given at the Société des Études Juives, 23 March 1907); *Revue des études juives* 53 (1907): 46–75.

58.   Dreyfus, "Vies des hommes obscurs," 26–27.

59.   He had married Jeanne Bernheim (1853-1944), half-sister of Isabelle and Palmyre Bernheim.

60.   AP, Births, Ninth Arrondissement, 1873, no. 507, V4E 3495, view 4/31.

61.   Alfred Neymarck, *Le Honduras, son chemin de fer, son avenir industriel et commercial* (Paris: Dentu, 1872) (excerpt from *Le Rentier*).

62.   Paul Leroy-Beaulieu, "Le Honduras," *L'économiste français* (Paris), 14 August 1875, 193–95.

63.   AN, Léonore database, LH/1984/30.

64.   "Robert Dreyfus," *L'univers israélite*, 755.

65.   Daniel Halévy, "Correspondance," *La revue juive de Genève* 5, no. 50 (July 1937): 470.

66.   Marie-Louise Cahen-Hayem, "Romans et romanciers," *Archives israélites* 88, no. 10 (10 March 1927): 89.

67.   Lucien Herr, "À M. Maurice Barrès," *La revue blanche* 15, no. 113 (15 February 1898): 241–45.

68.   See the copy with dedication signed to Barrès by Robert Dreyfus, BNF, Z Barrès 18779.

69.   Marcel Proust, Letter to Robert Dreyfus, [May 1905], *Correspondance*, 5:148.

70.   Dreyfus, *La vie et les Prophéties*, 158, 159, 161.

71.   Robert Dreyfus, letter to Marcel Proust, [25 May 1905], BNF, NAF 27352, fol. 78 v°-79 r°; see Pyra Wise, "Quatorze lettres inédites adressées à Proust," *Bulletin d'informations proustiennes* 41 (2011): 9.

72.   Dreyfus, *Souvenirs sur Marcel Proust*, 176; Marcel Proust, letter to Robert Dreyfus, [29 May 1905], *Correspondance*, 5:180–81.

73.   Marcel Proust, Letter to Robert Dreyfus, [July 1905], *Correspondance*, 5:288.

74.   Marcel Proust, Letter to Robert Dreyfus, [16 December 1904], *Correspondance*, 4:393.

75.   Dreyfus, *Souvenirs sur Marcel Proust*, 176; Proust, letter to Robert Dreyfus, [29 May 1905].

76.   Marcel Proust, Letter to Robert de Montesquiou, [May 1896], *Correspondance*, 2:66.

77.   *La tribune juive* 47 (25 November 1927): 721.

78. *La tribune juive* 48 (27 November 1937): 725-26 (review of Léon Berman's *Histoire des juifs de France des origines à nos jours* (Paris: Lipschutz, 1937).

79. *La tribune juive* 22 (28 May 1937): 329; see also 24 (11 June 1937): 363; study by Siegfried van Praag, "Marcel Proust, témoin du judaïsme déjudaïsé," *La revue juive de Genève* 48 (May 1937): 338-47; 49 (June 1937): 388-93; 50 (July 1937): 446-54.

80. "Le charmant chroniqueur Robert Dreyfus, ou À la place d'un kaddiche," *La tribune juive* 28 (14 July 1939): 433. See *Journal des débats* (Paris), 21 June 1939, 6; *Le Figaro* (Paris), 21 June 1939, 2.

81. Dreyfus's tomb no longer exists: nothing remains at his former grave site (division 3/i line 18 no. 3 right rear). It was probably reclaimed by administrative authorities long ago due to its dilapidation.

8. THE ZOHAR OR *L'ASTRÉE?*

1. Georges Cattaui, *Léon Bloy* (Paris: Éditions Universitaires, 1954); *T. S. Eliot* (Paris: Éditions Universitaires, 1957); *Constantin Cavafy* (Paris: Seghers, 1964); *Péguy, témoin du temporel chrétien* (Paris: Éditions du Centurion, 1964); *Claudel: Le cycle des Coúfontaine et le mystere d'Israël* (Paris: Desclée de Brouwer, 1968).

2. Georges Cattaui, *Charles de Gaulle* (Thonon: Société d'Édition Savoyarde, 1944).

3. Georges Cattaui and Philip Kolb, eds., *Entretiens sur Marcel Proust: Centre culturel international de Cerisy-la-Salle, 17–25 juillet 1962* (The Hague: Mouton, 1966).

4. Georges Cattaui, "Proust et le juifs," *Palestine* 5 (February 1928): 196-205.

5. See Philippe Boukara, "Justin Godart et le sionisme: Autour de France-Palestine," in *Justin Godart, un homme dans son siècle (1871–1956)*, ed. Annette Wieviorka (Paris: CNRS Éditions, 2004), 199-220.

6. Paul-Boncour, Moutet, and Godart would be among the eighty who would vote against granting Pétain full power in July 1940. Herriot abstained.

7. *Palestine* ceased publication in early 1931 with volume 6, nos. 10-12 (December 1930-February 1931).

8. Georges Cattaui, *L'amitié de Proust* (Paris: Gallimard, 1935), 87-109 (chapters 5 and 6, "Hérédité" and "Proust et les juifs").

9. Its publication date was 22 September 1927, and it went on sale 18 November 1927.

10. Cattaui, "Proust et les juifs," 201.

11. Jacques-Émile Blanche, *Cahiers d'un artiste*, 6 vols. (Paris: Éditions de la NRF; Paris: Émile-Paul, 1915-1920).

12. Georges Cattaui, "The Vestal of Friendship," *Adam International Review* 29, no. 299 (1962): 46. See also, in the same issue, André Spire, "Hommage à une cadette," 25, and George D. Painter, "How Proust Met Miss Barney," 28-30.

13. Edmée de La Rochefoucauld, *Courts métrages II* (Paris: Grasset, 1980), 31-36, see 32-33 and 35 ("Georges Cattaui et Proust," 6 July 1976, Comédie-Française).

14. Cattaui, "Proust et les juifs," 196, 197. See Proust, *Le côté de Guermantes I*, in *À la recherche du temps perdu*, ed. Jean-Yves Tadié (Paris: Gallimard, 1987-1989), 2:488; *The Guermantes Way*, trans. Mark Treharne (New York: Penguin, 2005), 184. "On le sentait juif de corps, malade et peu normal" (He seems Jewish physically, ill, and abnormal). So wrote

Bernard Faÿ in *Panorama de la littérature contemporaine* (Paris: Éditions du Sagittaire, Simon Kra, 1925), 161. See Cattaui, *L'amitié de Proust*, 90 (where Faÿ is no longer cited, replaced by Paul Desjardins).

15. Cattaui, "Proust et les juifs," 199.

16. Cattaui, *L'amitié de Proust*, 93.

17. Cattaui, "Proust et les juifs," 202.

18. Cattaui, "Proust et les juifs," 202, 203.

19. Cattaui, "Proust et les juifs," 203, 205.

20. Cattaui, *L'amitié de Proust*, 92–93.

21. Crémieux, *Du côté de Marcel Proust*. According to Douglas Alden, this is the only unpublished text in the volume. Alden, *Marcel Proust and His French Critics* (Los Angeles: Lymanhouse, 1940), 231.

22. See again René Lalou, "Marcel Proust et l'esprit juif," *Menorah* 10 (April–June 1931): 84–85.

23. See chapter 3 herein.

24. Crémieux, *Du côté du Marcel Proust*, 95, 118, 119; see Groos, "Marcel Proust et le judaïsme," in *Marcel Proust* (Paris: Éditions de la Revue Le Capitole, 1926), 71n1.

25. Eugène Montfort, "L'art et la politique," *Les Marges* (1 September 1919): 66–67.

26. Groos, "Marcel Proust et le judaïsme," 67, 68.

27. "Le judaïsme et le style," *Menorah* 20 (1 November 1925): 313.

28. Ludmila Savitzky, "*Marcel Proust, sa vie, son oeuvre*, par Léon Pierre-Quint," *Menorah* 20 (1 November 1925): 322.

29. "Revue de presse," *Menorah* 20 (1 November 1925): 327.

30. Groos, "Marcel Proust et le judaïsme," 68.

31. See René Groos, "Romantisme et judaïsme," *Cours et conférences de l'Institut d'Action Française* 3, no. 1 (June 1925): 63–120; "Romantisme et judaïsme," *La revue du siècle* 1, no. 4 (1 June 1925): 404–12; 8 (1 November 1925): 409–18; 9 (1 December 1925): 70–77.

32. Groos, "Marcel Proust et le judaïsme," 72.

33. Crémieux, *Du côté de Marcel Proust*, 119.

34. Groos, "Marcel Proust et le judaïsme," 71n1.

35. Crémieux, *Du côté de Marcel Proust*, 119–21; see André Spire, *Quelques juifs et demi-juifs* (Paris: Grasset, 1928), 2:52.

36. Crémieux, *Du côté de Marcel Proust*, 121–22.

37. Crémieux, *Du côté de Marcel Proust*, 123–26.

38. Robert Le Masle, *Le Professeur Adrien Proust (1834–1903)* (Paris: Lipschutz, 1935), 54.

39. Crémieux, *Du côté de Marcel Proust*, 126.

40. Hannah Arendt, *The Origins of Totalitarianism* (New York: Harcourt Brace, 1951), 80, 85; Arendt quotes the 1937 study by van Praag, "Marcel Proust, témoin de judaïsme déjudaïsé," *La revue juive de Genève* 5, no. 48 (May 1937): 338–47; 49 (June 1937): 388–93; 50 (July 1937): 446–54.

41. Crémieux, *Du côté de Marcel Proust*, 127.

42. *L'univers israélite* 82, no. 26 (4 March 1927): 824.

43. *La tribune juive* 9 (4 March 1927): 138.

44. See Nadège Forestier, *Henri de Rothschild: Un humanitaire avant l'heure* (Paris: Cherche Midi, 2018).

45. William C. Carter, *Marcel Proust: A Life* (New Haven, CT: Yale University Press, 2000), 40.

46. "Chose d'Orient," *Littérature et critique* 3 (25 May 1892); Marcel Proust, *Contre Saint-Beuve*, ed. Pierre Clarac and Yves Sandre (Paris: Gallimard, 1971), 350–54.

47. See Nadia Malinovich, "Affirming Difference, Confirming Integration: New Forms of Sociability Among French Jews in the 1920s," in *The Jews of Modern France: Images and Identities*, ed. N. Malinovich and Zvi Jonathan Kaplan (Leiden: Brill, 2016), 122.

48. Pierre Paraf, "Israël dans les démocraties contemporaines: Une conférence de M. André Siegfried au 'Cercle d'études juives,'" *L'univers israélite* 85, no. 34 (23 May 1930): 203–4.

49. For another perspective on André Siegfried and Judaism, see Pierre Birnbaum, *La France aux français: Histoire des haines nationalistes* (Paris: Éditions du Seuil, 1993), 145–86 ("André Siegfried, la géographie des races").

50. "Au Cercle d'Études Juives: Conférence de M. René Lalou sur André Spire," *L'univers israélite* 87, no. 30 (1 April 1932): 938–39.

51. Lily Jean-Javal, *Noémi: Roman d'une jeune fille juive en pays basque* (Paris: Plon, 1925); *L'Inquiète* (Paris: Plon, 1927). See Nadia Malinovich, "Littérature populaire et romans juifs dans la France des années 1920," *Archives juives* 39, no. 1 (2006): 46–62, and *Heureux comme un juif: Intégration, identité, culture, 1900–1932* (Paris: Honoré Champion, 2010), 200.

52. Roger Lévy, "*Noémi*, par Lily Jean-Javal," *La revue juive* 2 (15 March 1925): 259–61.

53. Marie-Louise Cahen-Hayem, "Quelques livres nouveaux," *Archives israélites* 86, no. 9 (26 February 1925): 35; "Nouveautés," *Archives israélites* 88, no. 52 (29 December 1927): 211.

54. Lily Jean-Javal, "Les juifs dans la littérature française d'aujourd'hui: Conference faite par M. Benjamin Crémieux au Cercle d'Études Juives," *L'univers israélite*, year 86, no. 14, 19 December 1930: 430–32, see 431.

55. Proust, *Sodome et Gomorrhe II*, in *À la recherche du temps perdu*, 3:89; *Sodom and Gomorrah*, trans. John Sturrock (New York: Penguin, 2005), 92.

56. Jean-Javal, "Les juifs dans la littérature," 430, 432.

9. THE END OF THE POSTWAR ERA

1. Hannah Arendt, *The Origins of Totalitarianism* (New York: Harcourt Brace, 1951), 79–88.

2. Chanan Lehrmann, *L'élément juif dans la littérature française*, 2nd ed. (Paris: Albin Michel, 1960–1961), 2:134–41.

3. Robert Brasillach, "Causerie littéraire," *L'action française* (Paris), 11 June 1931, 3.

4. André Spire, "Israel Zangwill et le Congrès Juif Mondial," *La revue juive de Genève* 1, no. 1 (October 1932): 9–16.

5. Ludmila Savitzky, "*L'humanisme juif*, par Hans Kohn," *La revue juive de Genève* 1, no. 1 (October 1932): 40–41.

6. Hans Kohn, *The Idea of Nationalism: A Study in Its Origins and Background* (New York: Macmillan, 1944). See his memoir *Living in a World Revolution: My Encounters with History* (New York: Simon & Schuster, 1964), and Adi Gordon, *Toward Nationalism's End: An Intellectual Biography of Hans Kohn* (Waltham, MA: Brandeis University Press, 2017).

7. Benjamin Crémieux, "Le juif dans la littérature française," *La revue juive de Genève* 5, no. 44 (January 1937): 156-60; Benjamin Crémieux, "La littérature juive française," *La revue juive de Genève* 5, no. 45 (February 1937): 196.

8. Siegfried Emanuel van Praag, *Persoonlijkheden in het Koninkrijk der Nederlanden in woord en beeld* (Amsterdam: VanHolkema and Warendorf, 1938), 1178. See letter to Champfleury, November-December 1854, *Correspondance de Courbet*, ed. Petra ten-Doesschate Chu (Paris: Flammarion, 1996), 122.

9. Siegfried van Praag, "Der Jude im Roman," *Der Jude: Eine Monatsschrift* 6, no. 12 (1921-1922): 758-63. See Eleonore Lappin, *Der Jude 1916–1928: Jüdische Moderne zwischen Universalismus und Partikularismus* (Tübingen: Mohr Siebeck, 2000).

10. Julien Benda, *L'ordination: Cahiers de la quinzaine* (Paris: Émile-Paul, 1913).

11. Hans Kohn, "Henri Franck," *Der Jude* 6, no. 6 (1921-1922): 359-67; "André Spire," *Der Jude* 6, no. 8 (1921-1922): 506-9, and no. 9, 559-72; "Französische Juden," *Der Jude* 8, no. 10 (1924): 601-8; "*La Nuit kurde*," *Der Jude* 9, no. 1 (1925-1927): 133-36.

12. Siegfried van Praag, "Alexandre Weill (1811-1899)," *Der Jude* 7, no. 12 (1923): 681-91.

13. Siegfried van Praag, *De West-Joden en hun letterkunde sinds 1860* (Amsterdam: Elsevier, 1926).

14. http://www.historisches-unterfranken.uni-wuerzburg.de/juf/.

15. Chanan Lehrmann, *Das Humanitätsideal der sozialistisch-romantischen Epoche Frankreichs und seine Beziehung zur Judenfrage* (Wertheim am Main: Bechstein, 1932).

16. See also, by Lehrmann, *Bergsonisme et judaïsme, cours professé à l'université de Lausanne* (Geneva: Éditions Union, 1937), and *L'élément juif dans la pensée européenne* (Paris: Éditions du Chant Nouveau et Migdal, 1947).

17. Crémieux, "La littérature juive française," 198.

18. Benjamin Crémieux, "Autres réflexions sur Proust," *Les nouvelles littéraires* (Paris), 11 September 1926, 1-2; Benjamin Crémieux, "Un débat avec M. Louis de Robert sur la composition chez Proust," *Du côté de Marcel Proust*, 65-94, see 83.

19. Siegfried van Praag, "Marcel Proust, témoin du judaïsme déjudaïsé," *La revue juive de Genève* 5, no. 48 (May 1937): 338-40.

20. van Praag, "Marcel Proust, témoin du judaïsme déjudaïsé," 346, 347.

21. Siegfried van Praag, "Marcel Proust, témoin du judaïsme (II)," *La revue juive de Genève* 5, no. 49 (June 1937): 389.

22. Siegfried van Praag, "Marcel Proust, témoin du judaïsme déjudaïsé (III)," *La revue juive de Genève* 50 (July 1937): 449.

23. Robert Dreyfus, "Vies des hommes obscurs: Alexandre Weill, ou le prophète du faubourg Saint-Honoré, 1811-1899," *Cahiers de la quinzaine* 9 (26 January 1908). See also the obituary by Isadore Cahen, "Alexandre Weill," *Archives israélites* 60, no. 17 (23 April 1899): 133-35; Joë Friedemann, *Alexandre Weill, écrivain contestataire et historien engagé, 1811–1899* (Strasbourg: Istra, 1980).

24. van Praag, "Marcel Proust, témoin du judaïsme déjudaïsé (II)," 393.

25. Dreyfus, *Alexandre Weill*, 54n2. See Alexandre Weill, *Lois et mystères de la création conformes à la science la plus absolue* (Paris: Sauvaitre, 1896).

26. *L'univers israélite* 24, no. 1 (October 1868): 40.

27. Letter to Jean Lazard, [October 1896], *Correspondance*, 6:349-50; letter to his mother, [October 1896], *Correspondance*, 2:144, 2:330. See Didier Lazard, *La famille Lazard*, vol. 9,

Destins inattendus: Les descendants du fondateur de la banque Lazard (Neuilly: privately published, 1992); Guy de Rougemont, *Lazard Frères: Banquiers des deux mondes (1848–1939)* (Paris: Fayard, 2011).

28. Letter to Robert Dreyfus, [29 January 1908], *Correspondance*, 8:36–37.

29. van Praag, "Marcel Proust, témoin du judaïsme déjudaïsé (II)," 393.

30. van Praag, "Marcel Proust, témoin du judaïsme déjudaïsé (III)," 454.

31. Lehrmann, *L'élément juif*, 1941, 234; 1961, 135.

32. Lehrmann, *L'élément juif*, 1941, 234–236; 1961, 136, 137.

33. Lehrmann, *L'élément juif*, 1941, 237–38.

34. van Praag, "Marcel Proust, témoin du judaïsme (III)," 452.

35. Lehrmann, *L'élément juif*, 1961, 140.

36. See Laurent Moyse, *Du rejet à l'intégration: Histoire des juifs du Luxembourg des origines à nos jours* (Luxembourg: Éditions Saint-Paul, 2011), which talks about the president of the consistory, Edmond Marx, slapping the chief rabbi in the face during a discussion in 1957, shortly before Lehrmann left to teach at Bar-Ilan from 1958 to 1960.

37. Lehrmann, *L'élément juif*, 1961, 166. See Institut für Zeitgeschichte, Munich, and Research Foundation for Jewish Immigration, New York, *Biographisches Handbuch der deutschsprachigen Emigration nach 1933–1945*, vol. 1, *Politik, Wirtschaft, Öffenliches Leben*, ed. Werner Röder and Herbert A. Strauss (Munich: K. G. Saur, 1980), 426.

38. http://www.stolpersteine-stuttgart.de/index.php?docid=617&mid=30.

39. Robert Dreyfus, "À propos de Marcel Proust et de ses personnages juifs," *La revue juive de Genève* 5, no. 49 (June 1937): 419–20, see 419.

40. Robert Dreyfus, "Madame Straus et Marcel Proust," *La revue de Paris* 43, vol. 5 (October 1936): 803–14; Robert Dreyfus, *De Monsieur Thiers à Marcel Proust* (Paris: Grasset, 1926), 13–36; Robert Dryefus, "Lettres à Madame Straus," *La revue de Paris* 43, vol. 5 (October 1936): 815–47.

41. Dreyfus, "À propos de Marcel Proust," 420.

42. Dreyfus, *Souvenirs sur Marcel Proust*, 91. See "Un livre contre l'élégance: *Sens dessus dessous*," *Le Banquet* 2, April 1892; Marcel Proust, *Contre Sainte-Beuve*, ed. Pierre Clarac and Yves Sandre (Paris: Gallimard, 1971), 346–47.

43. Dreyfus, *De Monsieur Thiers à Marcel Proust*, 32.

44. Daniel Halévy, "Correspondance," *La revue juive de Genève* 5, no. 50 (July 1937): 470.

45. Proust, *Sodome et Gomorrhe II*, in *À la recherche du temps perdu*, ed. Jean-Yves Tadié (Paris: Gallimard, 1987–1989), 3:68; *Sodom and Gomorrah*, 4:71.

46. Halévy, "Correspondance," 470.

47. Spire visited Halévy at Quai de l'Horloge in January 1962, two weeks before Halévy died. Daniel Halévy, Marianne Halévy, and André Spire, *Correspondance, 1899–1961*, ed. Marie-Brunette Spire-Uran (Paris: Honoré Champion, 2020), 178.

48. Rachel Bespaloff, "Letter à M. Daniel Halévy," *La revue juive de Genève* 6, no. 59 (June 1938): 391–98, at 391.

49. "Réponse de M. Daniel Halévy," *La revue juive de Genève*, year 6, no. 59 (June 1938): 398.

50. See E. G. Benfey and Karen Remmler, eds., *Artists, Intellectuals, and World War II: The Pontigny Encounters at Mount Holyoke College, 1942–1944* (Amherst: University of

Massachusetts Press, 2006); Olivier Salazar-Ferrer, "Bespaloff," in *Dictionnaire Albert Camus*, ed. Jeanyves Guérin (Paris: Robert Laffont, 2009), 86–87.

51. Rachel Bespaloff, "Lettre sur Heidegger à M. Daniel Halévy," *Revue philosophique de la France et de l'étranger* 66, nos. 11–12 (November–December 1933): 321–39; *Sur Heidegger (Lettre à Daniel Halévy)* (Trocy-en-Multien: Éditions de la Revue Conférence, 2009).

52. Rachel Bespaloff, *Cheminements et carrefours* (Paris: Vrin, 1938), 116–17.

53. Rachel Bespaloff, "Le monde du condamné à mort," *Esprit* 163 (January 1950): 1–26.

54. Rachel Bespaloff, *Lettres à Jean Wahl, 1937–1947*, ed. Monique Jutrin (Paris: Éditions Claire Paulhan, 2003).

55. Rachel Bespaloff, *De l'Iliade* (New York: Brentano's, 1943); introduction by Monique Jutrin (Paris: Éditions Allia, 2004); *On the Iliad*, trans. Mary McCarthy (New York: Pantheon Books, 1947).

56. *Cahiers du Sud* 27, no. 230 (December 1940): 561–74; 28, no. 239 (January 1941): 21–34.

57. Hermann Broch, "Le style de l'âge mythique," in *Creation littéraire et connaissance*, ed. Hannah Arendt, trans. Albert Kohn (Paris: Gallimard, 1966, 2007), 257–75.

58. Monique Jutrin, "Bespaloff, Chestov, Fondane," in *The Tragic Discourse: Shestov and Fondane's Existential Thought*, ed. Ramona Fotiade (Berne: Peter Lang, 2006), 237–48, at 239.

59. Benfey, "A Tale of Two Iliads," *Artists, Intellectuals, and World War II*, 207–19, at 217.

60. Jean Cocteau, *Le passé défini: Journal*, ed. Pierre Chanel (Paris: Gallimard, 1983), 1:289.

61. See Seth L. Wolitz, *The Proustian Community* (New York: New York University Press, 1971), 143–209; see also Henri Raczymow, "Proust et la judéité: Les destins croisés de Swann et de Bloch," *Pardès* 21 (1995): 209–22, collected in *Ruse et déni: Cinq essais de littérature* (Paris: PUF, 2011), 65–95, at 67.

62. Albert Sonnenfeld, "Marcel Proust: Antisemite? I," *French Review* 62, no. 1 (October 1988): 25–40, at 38; "Marcel Proust: Antisemite? II," *French Review* 62, no. 2 (December 1988): 275–82.

63. Proust, *À l'ombre des jeunes filles en fleurs*, in *À la recherche du temps perdu*, 2:97; *In the Shadow of Young Girls in Flower*, trans. James Grieve, 318.

10. THE BARUCH TOMB

1. See, again, Georges Cattaui, who uses it as an epigraph for the chapter "Proust et les juifs" in *L'amitié de Proust* (Paris: Gallimard, 1935), 104; Benjamin Crémieux, *Du côté de Marcel Proust* (Paris: Lemarget, 1929), 116; Siegfried van Praag, "Marcel Proust, témoin de judaïsme déjudaïsé (II)," *La revue juive de Genève* 5, no. 49 (June 1937): 388.

2. Marcel Proust, Letter to Laure Hayman, [12 May 1896], *Correspondance*, ed. Philip Kolb (Paris: Plon, 1970–1993), 2:63.

3. Marcel Proust, Letter to Reynaldo Hahn, [26 August 1906], *Correspondance*, 6:196.

4. Marcel Proust, *Les plaisirs et les jours*, preceded by *Les plaisirs et les jours*, ed. Pierre Clarac and Yves Sandre (Paris: Gallimard, 1971), 122; *Pleasures and Days*, trans. Andrew Brown (London: Hesperus Classics, 2004), 128.

5. CAP 122.037: Baruch Weil (1780–1828), Godchaux Weil (1806–1878) and Frédérique Zunz (1823–1897), widow Godchaux Weil, Maurice Cohen (1826–1183), Nathé Weil (1814–1896) and Adèle Weil née Berncastell (1824–1890), Louis Weil (1816–1896) and Émilie

Weil née Oppenheim (1821–1870), Adélaïde Weil (1818–1892), widow Joseph Lazarus, and her son Paul Lazarus (1847–1870), Alphonse Weil (1822–1886). Georges Weil (1847–1906), the older brother of Jeanne Proust, and his wife, née Amélie Oulman (1853–1920) were buried in another plot located in the old Jewish section (CAP 120-1906).

6. AP, Burial registry, Père-Lachaise cemetery, 1 May 1854, general no. 122.037, Third Arrondissement, no. 530, 70 years, CPL_RJ18541854_01, view 24/31. The former Third Arrondissement corresponds to the Faubourg Poissonière neighborhood; the death of Marguerite Nathan does not appear in the reconstructed registry files.

7. AP, Burial registry, Père-Lachaise cemetery, CPL_RJ18711871_01, view 9/31; AP, Deaths, Ninth Arrondissement, no. 2009, V4E 1071, view 8/17; AP, Deaths, Tenth Arrondissement, no. 7127, view 18/31. At his birth on 22 February 1847 the name was Barruch Paul Lazarus; AP reconstructed registry files, V3E/N 1329, view 20/50.

8. Du Camp, *Paris, ses organes, ses fonctions et sa vie*, vol. 6, 95 ("L'état civil").

9. Stéphanie Sauget, "Enterrer les mort pendant le double siège de Paris (1870–1871)," *Revue historique* 317, no. 3 (July 2015): 557–855.

10. Du Camp, *Paris, ses organes, ses fonctions et sa vie*, vol. 6, 99.

11. AP, Burial registry, Père-Lachaise cemetery, 10 June 1878, CPL_RJ18771978_02, view 7/13; AP, Deaths, Tenth Arrondissement, 9 June 1878, no. 2296, V4E 3757, view 5/31.

12. AP, Burial registry, Père-Lachaise cemetery, 19 December 1883, coming from Cahors (Lot), CPL_RJ18831884_02, view 9/31.

13. AP, Burial registry, Père-Lachaise cemetery, 12 December 1886, CPL_RJ188861887_01, view 22/31; AP, Deaths, Sixteenth Arrondissement, 11 December 1886, no. 1311, V4E 7325, view 6/15.

14. AP, Burial registry, Père-Lachaise cemetery, 5 January 1890, CPL_RJ18891890_01, view 29/31; AP, Deaths, Tenth Arrondissement, 4 January 1890, no. 120, V4E 6456, view 23/31; Georges Weil, still living at 40a Rue du Faubourge-Poissonnière, registered the death of his mother.

15. AP, Burial registry, Père-Lachaise cemetery, 23 June 1892, CPL_RJ18911892_01, view 27/31; AP, Deaths, Sixteenth Arrondissement, 22 June 1892, no. 753, V4E 7336, view 9/31. Her residence is 80 Rue de la Tour. Her granddaughter, Louise Neuburger, married Henri Bergson on 7 January 1892.

16. AP, Burial registry, Père-Lachaise cemetery, 12 May 1896, CPL_RJ18951896_01, view 25/31; AP, Deaths, Eighth Arrondissement, 11 May 1896, no. 860, V4E 8723, view 1/25.

17. AP, Burial registry, Père-Lachaise cemetery, 2 July 1896, CPL_RJ18951896_01, view 22/31; AP, Deaths, Tenth Arrondissement, 1 July 1896, no. 2721, V4E 8983, view 21/31.

18. AP, Burial registry, Père-Lachaise cemetery, 17 January 1897, CPL_RJ18961897_01, view 12/31; AP, Deaths, Tenth Arrondissement, 16 January 1897, no. 262, V4E 9002 view 6/31.

19. AP, Deaths, Tenth Arrondissement, 29 January 1874, no.387, V4E 3678 view 22/31.

20. Alexandre Nerson, born in Bischheim (Bas-Rhin) on 25 January 1833, died at his residence, 42 Rue Damrémont, on 11 October 1910 at the age of seventy-seven (AP, Deaths, Eighteenth Arrondissement, no. 4194, 18D 241, view 16/31). He was buried in the Montparnasse cemetery on 12 October 1910 beside his wife, Nanette Weill, who died in 1903 (AP, Burial registry, no. 231, MTP_RJ19101912_01, view 13/31); *L'univers israélite* 66, no. 6

(21 October 1910): 163. His death was registered by Nepthalie Lévi, employee, 43 Rue de la Victoire (thus an agent of the Schneeberg Funeral Home).

21. AP, Deaths, Seventeenth Arrondissement, 24 August 1906, no. 2118, 17D 156, view 12/31; Édouard Schneeberg and Maurice Weill would give as their residence 43 Rue de la Victoire. Certain Proust biographers make Maurice Weil, thirty years old, an employee, 43 Avenue Trudaine, who registered the death of Frédérique Zunz in 1897, a son of Godchaux Weil and of Frédérique Zunz, born in 1867; but his name is written as Weill, not Weil, in 1906, and he accompanied Schneeberg. Moreover, his name appears again at the death of Daniel Mayer, first cousin of Jeanne Weil; he was then living on Boulevard Edgar-Quinet, across from the Montparnasse cemetery (AP, Deaths, Eighth Arrondissement, 18 March 1903, no. 496, 8D 108, view 6/31). The death certificate of Jeanne Weil, signed by Georges Weil and Robert Proust, does not indicate if Schneeberg was called (AP, Deaths, Eighth Arrondissement, 27 September 1905, no. 1838, 8D 117, view 14/31); the same two had signed for the death of Adrien Proust (AP, Deaths, Eighth Arrondissement, 27 November 1903, no. 2089, 8D 111, view 7/31).

22. AD, Lot, Death, 1883, 4 November 1883, no. 366 4 E 783, view 93/117.

23. La Dépêche (Cahors), 7 November 1883, 3.

24. Le Moliériste 5 (January 1884): 293-95.

25. Le Figaro (Paris), 20 April 1884, 4.

26. Léonce Cohen, École du musicien, ou solfège théorique et pratique avec accompagnement de piano (Paris: Éditions Margueritat, 1862).

27. Le Temps (Paris), 27 November 1881, 3.

28. Archives israélites 58, no. 48 (1 December 1881): 402.

29. Edmond About, "Charles Sellier: Trente ans de peinture," Le XIXᵉ siècle (Paris), 12 December 1883, 2.

30. Le Figaro (Paris), 28 June 1897, 4.

31. AP, Deaths, Sixth Arrondissement, no. 366 (the same number as for his brother in Cahors in 1883), V4E 8593, view 23/31; AP, Burial registry, Père-Lachaise cemetery, 28 February 1901, no. 1954, CPL_RJ19001901_01, view 14/31.

32. We might think of Proust's letter of August 1922 to Lacretelle in which Proust responds to reading the advance pages of Silbermann in La nouvelle revue française, a letter that has not come down to us intact. see Correspondance, 21:417-18.

33. Marcel Proust, Letter to his mother, [18-19 March 1903], Correspondance, 3:275.

34. Marcel Proust, Sodome et Gomorrhe I, in À la recherche du temps perdu, ed. Jean-Yves Tadié (Paris: Gallimard, 1987-1989), 3:33; Sodom and Gomorrah, trans. John Sturrock (New York: Penguin, 2005), 33.

35. Proust, Sodome et Gomorrhe I, 3:22; Sodom and Gomorrah, 22.

36. Marcel Proust, À l'ombre des jeunes filles en fleurs, in À la recherche du temps perdu, 2:245; In the Shadow of Young Girls in Flower, trans. James Grieve (New York: Penguin, 2005), 470.

37. Marcel Proust, "Mondanité de Bouvard et Pécuchet," La revue blanche 5, nos. 21-22 (July-August 1893): 67-68; Les plaisirs et les jours, 62; Pleasures and Days, 64.

38. Proust, "Mondanité," 62; Les plaisirs et les jours, 57; Pleasures and Days, 59.

39. Laurent Dispot, "Marcel Proust-Weil et Titi Tiszelman, face à Maurras et au mot 'race,'" La règle du jeu 40 (May 2009): 249.

40. André Spire, *Quelques juifs et demi-juifs* (Paris: Grasset, 1928), 2:56; Crémieux, *Du côté de Marcel Proust*, 97.

41. David Ewen (1907–1985), born in Lemberg, in Galicia in central Europe, at that time part of Austria-Hungary, today Lviv in Ukraine, emigrated as a child to the United States and subsequently wrote a biography of Schubert (1931) and numerous works on musicology.

42. *The Reform Advocate* (Chicago), 27 April 1929, 319–20; *The Sentinel* (Chicago), 5 July 1929, 28 and 31.

43. Fernand Gregh, *Mon amitié avec Marcel Proust* (Paris: Grasset, 1958), 55.

44. The note is considered "anti-Semitic—or rather, self-hating" by Maurice Samuels. See *Inventing the Israelite: Jewish Fiction in Nineteenth-Century France* (Stanford, CA: Stanford University Press, 2010), 245.

45. Marcel Proust, Letters to Gabriel Astruc, [December 1913], *Correspondance*, 12:383–84 and 385–92.

46. Léon Brunschvicg, "Le moment historique de Montaigne," *La revue juive* 4 (July 1925): 423.

47. Julien Benda, *Belphégor: Essai sur l'esthétique de la présente société française* (Paris: Émile-Paul, 1918); Julien Benda, "L'éternelle idole," *Le Figaro* (Paris), 9 March 1920, 1, regarding the new edition of *Romantisme français: Essai sur la révolution dans les sentiments et dans les idées au XIXᵉ siècle* by Pierre Lasserre (Paris: Classiques Garnier, 1919).

48. Marcel Proust, Letter to Jacques Boulenger, [29 November 1921], *Correspondance*, 20:542.

49. Julien Benda, *La France byzantine, ou le Triomphe de la littérature pure: Mallarmé, Gide, Proust, Valéry, Alain Giraudoux, Suarès, les surréalistes, essai d'une psychologie originelle du littérateur* (Paris: Gallimard, 1945).

50. Julien Benda, *La trahison des clercs* (Paris: Grasset, 1927), 298.

51. Pierre Abraham, *Proust: Recherches sur la création intellectuelle* (Paris: Rieder, 1930), 66, 68; see Marie-Louise Cahen-Hayem, "Proses," *Archives israélites* 92, no. 2 (8 January 1931): 7.

52. Emmanuel Berl, *Sylvia* (Paris: Gallimard, 1972), 131.

53. Emmanuel Berl, "Chronique philosophique: Freud et Proust," *Les nouvelles littéraires* (Paris), 7 July 1923, 3.

54. See the Mémorial de la Shoah website and http://proustien.over-blog.com/pages/Lassassinat_de_la_cousine_de_Marcel_PROUST_et_de_son_mari_par_les_nazis-650676.html.

55. Marcel Proust, Letter to Antoine Bibesco, [August 1902], *Correspondance*, 3:102–03.

56. Proust, *Du côté de chez Swann*, in *À la recherche du temps perdu*, 1:395; *Swann's Way*, trans. Lydia Davis (New York: Penguin, 2004), 418.

57. See Anne Sinclair, *La rafle des notables* (Paris: Grasset, 2020).

58. David Rousset, *L'univers concentrationnaire* (Éditions de Minuit, 1965), 71–75.

59. "Arrêté du 6 octobre 1987 relatif à l'apposition de la mention 'Mort en déportation' sur les actes ou jugements déclaratifs de décès," *Journal officiel*, 13 November 1987, 13231.

60. *Le Droit* (Paris), 31 July 1873, 736.

61. *L'univers israélite* 69, no. 27 (3 April 1914): 15; *Le Temps* (Paris), 10 February 1934, 5; *L'univers israélite* 81, no. 41 (2 July 1926): 10; *Le Temps* (Paris), 27 May 1932, 3. See Johanna Lehr, "Les sociétés de pompes funèbres 'israélites' à Paris sous l'Occupation à l'épreuve des

persécutions allemandes et vichystes," *Revue d'histoire moderne et contemporaine* 67, no. 4 (2020): 94–118.

62.   André Arnyvelde, "À propos d'un livre récent," in *Textes retrouvés*, ed. P. Kolb (Paris: Gallimard, 1971), 292–95.

63.   Claude Carras, "Ceux qu'ils ont tués: André Arnyvelde," *Gavroche* (Paris), 8 February 1945, 3.

64.   Michel Pinault, *Frédéric Joliot-Curie* (Paris: Odile Jacob, 2000), 236 ("Allocution prononcées aux obsèques d'André Arnyvelde").

65.   Fernand Gregh, *L'âge de fer: Souvenirs, 1925–1955* (Paris: Grasset, 1956), 190.

66.   "Arrêté du 6 octobre 1987."

67.   René Cahen, "Le théâtre," *Archives israélites* 93, no. 41 (13 October 1932): 163.

11. MANUSCRIPTS REGAINED

1.   Collection Family of Marcel Proust. We would like to thank the Marcel Proust rights holders for giving us permission to publish these pages.

2.   Antoine Compagnon, "'Le long de la rue du Repos': Brouillon d'une letter à Daniel Halévy (1908)," *Bulletin d'informations proustiennes* 50 (2020): 13–32.

3.   AP, Annual index of burials, Père-Lachaise cemetery, 1895-1899, CPL_RA18951899_01, view 16/21; AP, Daily index of burials, 2 July 1896, no. 2940, CPL_RJ18951896_01, view 22/31.

4.   *Revue d'hygiène et de police sanitaire* 19, no. 6 (June 1897): 574–75; report of the *Bulletin de la Société pour la propagation de l'incinération* 16, no. 16 May 1897).

5.   *Annuaire statistique de la ville de Paris, XVIIᵉ année, 1896* (Paris: Masson, 1898), 176.

6.   Adrien Proust, "La conférence sanitaire internationale de Venise de 1897," *Revue d'hygiène et de police sanitaire* 19, no. 7 (July 1897): 577–89.

7.   See Paul Pasteur, "Les débuts de la crémation moderne en France," *Le mouvement social* 179 (April-June 1997): 59–80.

8.   *L'univers israélite* 41, no. 7 (16 December 1885): 215.

9.   Michel A. Weill, "De la crémation envisagée au point du vue de la doctrine et des traditions du judaïsme," *L'univers israélite* 43, no. 5 (16 November 1887): 143–45; no. 6 (1 December 1887): 176–78; no. 7 (16 December 1887): 208–10; no. 8 (1 January 1888): 232–34; no. 9 (16 January 1888): 266–68; no. 10 (1 February 1888): 304–6; no. 12 (1 March 1888): 335–37.

10.   Weill, "De la crémation," no. 12, 335–37.

11.   Hippolyte Prague, "Un cérémonie crématoire israélite," *Archives israélites* 49, no. 17 (26 April 1888): 131.

12.   Marcel Proust, *Jean Santeuil*, preceded by *Les plaisirs et les jours*, ed. Pierre Clarac and Yves Sandre (Paris: Gallimard, 1971), 244–45; *Jean Santeuil*, trans. Gerard Hopkins (New York: Simon & Schuster, 1956), 67.

13.   Marcel Proust, Letter to Paul Morand, [16 June 1922], *Correspondance*, ed. Philip Kolb (Paris: Plon, 1970–1993), 21:288.

14.   Marcel Proust, Letter to his mother, [6 July 1896], *Correspondance*, 2:92.

15.   Marcel Proust, *La prisonnière*, in *À la recherche du temps perdu*, ed. Jean-Yves Tadié (Paris: Gallimard, 1987–1989), 3:693; *The Prisoner*, trans. Carol Clark (New York: Penguin, 2019), 174.

16. Adrien Proust, *Traité d'hygiène publique et privée* (Paris: Masson, 1877), 610–11; 2nd ed. (Paris: Masson, 1881), 654.

17. Adrien Proust, *Traité d'hygiène publique et privée*, 3rd ed. (Paris: Masson, 1903), 956–57.

18. Maxime Du Camp, "Les cimetières de Paris," *Revue des Deux Mondes*, 15 April 1874, 812–51; Du Camp, *Paris, ses organes, ses fonctions et sa vie dans la seconde moitié du XIXe siècle* (Paris: Hachette, 1875), 6:165–66.

19. See André Combes, *Adolphe Crémieux, 1796–1880: Le grand-maître du rite écossais, l'avocat et l'homme politique, le président de l'Alliance israélite universelle* (Paris: Éditions Maçonniques de France, 2003, 2013); Jean-Philippe Schreiber, "Les élites politiques juives et la franc-maçonnerie dans la France du XIXᵉ siècle," *Archives juives* 43, no. 2 (2010): 58–69.

20. Fichier Bossu 319, BNF.

21. *L'Orient, revue universelle de la franc-maçonnerie* (1844–1845): 277, 211.

22. Suprême Conseil pour la France et Ses Dépendances, *Fête de l'Ordre au solstice d'hiver* (Paris: Ordre de Paris, 1846), 55, 42; Suprême Conseil pour la France et Ses Dépendances, *Fête de l'Ordre au solstice d'hiver* (Paris: Ordre de Paris, 1847), 73, 41, 58.

23. *Almanach royal* (Paris: Guyot et Scribe, 1842), 903.

24. It remained so in the *Almanach impérial* (1853), before switching back to 59 Boulevard Saint-Martin (from 1854 to 1860), then to 50 Rue Meslay (1861), and then to 29 Boulevard Saint-Martin and 20 Rue Meslay (beginning in 1865); G. Weil sat in the Chambre de Discipline des Huissiers Parisiens from 1855 to 1857.

25. *Almanach-Bottin du commerce de Paris* (1842), 390.

26. *Archives israélites* 2 (September 1841): 586.

27. *Annuaire-almanach du commerce, de l'industrie, de la magistrature et de l'administration* (Paris: Firmin Didot et Bottin, 1876), 1105; *Annuaire-almanach du commerce, de l'industrie, de la magistrature et de l'administration* (Paris: Firmin Didot et Bottin, 1877), 1108. According to this annual directory, his address changed in 1864 from 59 Boulevard Saint-Martin and 50 Rue Meslay to 13 Boulevard Saint-Martin and 20 Rue Meslay, variations that could have resulted from opening of the Place de la République. *Le Droit*, a weekly law journal, published notices from his practice between 1842 and 1873.

28. "Du rôle des israélites dans la franc-maçonnerie," *Archives israélites* 5 (June 1844): 423–29.

29. "Les loges allemandes et les maçons israélites," *L'Orient* 1 (1844): 11–16 and passim.

30. Pierre Benet, *Le Mont-Sinaï, 1816–2016* (N.p.: Privately published, 2016), 44–45; see Pierre Noël, "Le général de Fernig, officier et franc-maçon," *Ordo ab chao*, Supplément to no. 46, 2nd semester 2002 ("Bicentenaire de la création du Suprême Conseil pour les îles françaises de l'Amérique du Vent et Sous-le-Vent").

31. "De la position des francs-maçons israélites en Prusse," article signed W . . ., Vénérable de la loge le Mont Sinaï, Orient de Paris, *Archives israélites* 5 (September 1844): 644–49.

32. "Élections consistoriales du collège des notables de Paris," *Archives israélites* 6 (October 1845): 782–87; "Élection de M. Crémieux," *Archives israélites* 6 (November 1845): 838–42.

33. "Élections consistoriales de Paris," *Archives israélites* 11 (August 1850): 401–4, at 403; 12 (September 1850): 449–52, at 449.

34. AP, Deaths, Tenth Arrondissement, 9 June 1878, no. 2296, V4E 3757, view 5/31. Edmond Revel was the son of Jacques Revel, deceased in 1848, and of Frédérique née Zunz,

remarried to Godchaux Weil, 30 September 1849 (AP, Reconstructed registry, V3E/M 1019, view 48/51).

35.   AP, Marriages, Tenth Arrondissement, 25 April 1881, no. 447, V4E 3809, view 29/31.

36.   AP, Marriages, Tenth Arrondissement, 5 June 1882, no. 751, V4E 3832, view 18/31. The mother of Aline Aron, née Rachel Lazard (1829–1894), was the sister of the founders of the Lazard Frères banking house; their daughter, Germaine Revel (1888–1975), would marry Pierre Wertheimer (1888–1965), founder, with his brother Paul and Coco Chanel, of Chanel Perfumes.

37.   AP, Marriages, Tenth Arrondissement, 6 September 1871, no. 475, V4E 3614, view 27/31 (Joseph Lazarus supposedly died in 1849, according to his widow, not in 1850, as in the reconstructed registry).

38.   AP, Marriages, Tenth Arrondissement, 10 April 1877, no. 370, V4E 3731, view 25/31; 20 September 1882, no. 1216, V4E 3834, view 11/31

39.   AD, Oise, NMD, no. 5, 3 January 1870, 2MI/ECA 057 R5, views 197–198/609; AD, Oise, NME, no. 574, August 1872, 2MI/ECA 057 R7, views 126–127/635; AD, Oise, NMD, no. 920, 12 December 1872, 2MI/ECA 057 R7, views 275–76/635.

40.   AP, Births, Sixteenth Arrondissement, 13 July 1871, no. 456, V4E 4643, view 8/11.

41.   Charles Nathan (1830–1915), trade broker, was the son of Abraham Nathan (1794–1871), glove maker, younger brother of Marguerite Nathan, the second wife of Baruch Weil. He signed as witness, with Nathé Weil, the death certificate of Émilie Oppenheim, the wife of Louis Weil, in November 1870. Nathé Weil would be witness for his marriage, 14 February 1874, in the Ninth Arrondissement, and Jean Weil would remain very close to Charles Nathan and his wife Laura Rodrigues-Ely (1849–1932), whom she called "les Greffülhe" after the name of their street. *Correspondance*, 1:143 and 3:397. AP, Marriages, Tenth Arrondissement, 30 March 1887, no. 312, V4E 6371, view 22/31.

42.   Proust, *Du côté de chez Swann*, in *À la recherche du temps perdu*, 1:72; *Swann's Way*, trans. Lydia Davis (New York: Penguin, 2004), 74–75.

43.   AP, Marriages, Sixteenth Arrondissement, 22 February 1894, no. 127, V4E 10002, view 6/31.

44.   See Jacques Simon, *Histoire du rite écossais ancien et accepté en France*, vol. 1, *Des origines à 1900* (Paris: Dervy, 2019); Jean-Marie Mayeur and Arlette Schweitz, *Les parlementaires de la Seine sous la Troisième République*, vol. 1 (Paris: Publications de la Sorbonne, 2001), 551.

45.   Benet, *Le Mont-Sinaï*, 374. In the list of dignitaries of the Grande Loge de France published following the law of 11 August 1941 regarding secret societies, he appears as Freemason of the 33rd degree, Worshipful Master of the lodge of La Nouvelle Jérusalem, Aréopage Lutetia (*Journal officiel*, 19 August 1941, 293a); arrested 10 September 1941 (as a Freemason or following denunciation by a non-Jewish competitor), he was interned at Drancy, transferred in December to Compiègne-Royallieu with the victims of the "roundup of the notables," and freed on an unknown date; he was arrested again on 20 March 1942, incarcerated at Fresnes, then at La Santé, transferred to Drancy on 12 April 1943, and deported to Auschwitz by convoy no. 58, 31 July 1943.

46.   *La vielle France* 342 (23–30 August 1923): 12.

47. Proust, *Sodome et Gomorrhe I*, in *À la recherche du temps perdu*, 3:17–19; *Sodom and Gomor-rah*, trans. John Sturrock (New York: Penguin, 2005), 17–18.

48. Marcel Proust, Letter to Daniel Halévy, [c. autumn 1888], *Correspondance*, 1:123.

49. Daniel Halévy, letter to Marcel Proust, 31 March [1904], *Correspondance*, 6:102.

50. Robert Dreyfus, "Madame Straus et Marcel Proust," *De Monsieur Thiers à Marcel Proust* (Paris: Plon, 1939), 31.

51. Daniel Halévy, *Journal*, BNF, NAP 28147 (154), Cahier 1924, 101=08.

52. Léon Halévy, *F. Halévy: Sa vie et ses oeuvres* (Paris: Heugel, 1863), 16. See Sébastien Lau-rent, *Daniel Halévy: Du libéralisme au traditionalisme* (Paris: Grasset, 2001); Diana R. Hall-man, *Opera, Liberalism, and Antisemitism in Nineteenth-Century France: The Politics of Halévy's La Juive* (Cambridge: Cambridge University Press, 2002). Élie Halévy was buried in tomb no. 204, plot 1843.

53. *Archives israélites* 39, no. 13 (1 July 1878): 407.

54. E[mmanuel]. D[upaty]., "Nécrologie," *L'Opinion* (Paris), 6 November 1826, 1–2.

55. Sainte-Beuve, letter to Albert Collignon, 29 July 1869, *Correspondance générale* (Toulouse: Privat, 1983), 19:189.

56. Anne Borrel and Jean-Pierre Halévy, eds., *Correspondance avec Daniel Halévy* (Paris: Édi-tions de Fallois, 1992), 115–20, at 228 (note 72 for page 115).

57. BNF, Fonds Halévy, NAF 28147 (46).

58. Marcel Proust, Letter to Daniel Halévy, [December 1907], *Correspondance*, 21:626–27.

59. Quoted by Robert Dreyfus, *Souvenirs sur Marcel Proust* (Paris: Grasset, 1926), 202.

60. Marcel Proust, Letter to Reynaldo Hahn, [8 February 1907], *Correspondance*, 7:74.

61. Marcel Proust, Letter to Madame Straus, [10 May 1908], *Correspondance*, 8:116; "La vie de Paris: Une grand-mère," *Le Figaro* (Paris), 23 July 1907, 2.

62. Marcel Proust, Letter to Daniel Halévy, [January 1908], *Correspondance*, 21:632 (Kolb reads "Grace" for "Greece," but "Greece" is more plausible).

63. Marcel Proust, *Le côté de Guermantes I*, in *À la recherche du temps perdu*, 2:505; *The Guer-mantes Way*, trans. Mark Treharne (New York: Penguin, 2005).

64. See the "Albums photographiques" of Ludovic Halévy in the superb auction catalogue *Proust-Degas*, Beaussant Lefèvre, Drouot, 10 July 2019, lot 57, https://www.beaussant -lefevre.com/catalogue/99622.

65. Marcel Proust, Letter to Daniel Halévy, [19 July 1919], *Correspondance*, 18:334–35.

66. Marcel Proust, Letter to Madame Straus, *Correspondance*, 8:116.

67. Sainte-Beuve, *Nouveaux lundis* (Paris: Michel Lévy, 1864), 2:226–45.

68. If he was slow to send Madame Straus Sainte-Beuve's article on her father, perhaps it was because he had wanted to "precede it with a short study of my own," which remained unwritten. Letter to Madame Straus, [8 or 9 October 1912], *Correspondance*, 11:222.

69. Marcel Proust, Letter to Robert Dreyfus, [10 May 1908], *Correspondance*, 8:117.

70. Robert Dreyfus, "Ludovic Halévy," *Pages libres*, year 8, no. 385, 16 May 1908: 554–56, see 556.

71. Marcel Proust, "Préface," *Contre Sainte-Beuve*, ed. Pierre Clarac and Yves Sandre (Paris: Gallimard, 1971), 610.

72. Daniel Halévy, "Sur la critique de Sainte-Beuve," *La Minerve française* (Paris), 1 Febru-ary 1920, 291–96.

73. Daniel Halévy, "Apologie pour notre passé," *Cahiers de la quinzaine* 10 (10 April 1910); Péguy, "Notre jeunesse," *Cahiers de la quinzaine* 12 (17 July 1910).

74. Marcel Proust, Letter to Daniel Halévy, [January 1908], *Correspondance*, 21:631.

75. Marcel Proust, Letter to Robert Dreyfus, [10 May 1908], *Correspondance*, 8:118.

76. Marcel Proust, Letter to Daniel Halévy, [May or June 1908], *Correspondance*, 18:584–85.

77. Flavien Bonnett-Roy, *Ferdinand-Philippe, duc d'Orléans, prince royal, 1810–1842* (Paris: Société d'Éditions Françaises et Internationales, 1947), 48.

78. Marcel Proust, Letter to André Gide, [October 1917], *Correspondance*, 16:238; letter to Robert de Billy, October 1919, *Correspondance*, 18:447; letter to Daniel Halévy, [December 1921], *Correspondance*, 21:681.

79. André Spire, *Quelques juifs et demi-juifs* (Paris: Grasset, 1928), 2:55.

80. Proust, *Du côté de chez Swann*, 1:90–91. *Swann's Way*, 93–94.

81. *La Dépêche* (Cahors), 7 November 1883, 3.

82. Proust, *Du côté de chez Swann*, 1:395–96. *Swann's Way*, 419.

83. Marcel Proust, Letter to Daniel Halévy, [December 1913], *Correspondance*, 14:348.

84. See the letters from Spire to Halévy, BNF, Fonds Halévy, NAF 28147 (193).

85. Marcel Proust, *Le temps retrouvé*, in *À la recherche du temps perdu*, 4:482; *Finding Time Again*, trans. Ian Patterson (New York: Penguin, 2023), 232.

86. "Marcel Proust du côté de la mère," exposition, Paris, Musée d'Art et d'Histoire du Judaïsme (MAHJ), 14 April–28 August 2022.

87. Collection of Bernard Malle, brother of filmmaker Louis Malle, catalogue published on the occasion of the exhibit "Fine Arts Paris et La Biennale 2022," https://deproyart .com/litterature/fiction/sentiments-filiaux-d-un-parricide.

88. Daniel Halévy, letter to Marcel Proust, [ca. 18 December 1907], *Correspondance* 7:321.

89. *Correspondance*, 18:584–85.

90. Collection of Family of Marcel Proust. See Nathalie Mauriac Dyer, "'Sentiments filiaux d'un parricide': Les brouillons de l'article 'sans brouillon' (1907) et de l'envoi à Daniel Halévy (1908)," *Bulletin d'informations proustiennes* 53 (2023): 41-59.

POSTSCRIPT

1. Antoine Compagnon, "Israël avant Israël," in *Les intellectuels français et Israël*, ed. Denis Charbit (Paris: Éditions de l'Éclat, 2009), 9-27.

2. Antoine Compagnon, "Le 'profil assyrien' ou l'antisémitisme qui n'ose pas dire son nom: Les libéraux dans l'affaire Dreyfus," *Études de langue et littérature françaises* (Kyoto) 28 (1997); *Nichifutsu Bunka* (Tokyo), 63 (1998).

3. Jeanne Bem, "Le juif et l'homosexuel dans *À la recherche du temps perdu*: Fonctionnements textuels," *Littérature* 37 (February 1980): 100-12.

4. See Naomi Diamant, "Judaism, Homosexuality, and Other Sign Systems in *À la recherche du temps perdu*," *Romanic Review* 82, no. 2 (1991): 179-92; Jonathan Freedman, "Coming out of the Jewish Closet," in *Queer Theory and the Jewish Question*, ed. Daniel Boyarin, Daniel Itzkovitz and Ann Pellegrin (New York: Columbia University Press, 2003), 334-64.

5. Marcel Proust, Letter to Paul Souday, [17 December 1919], *Correspondance*, ed. Philip Kolb (Paris: Plon, 1970-1993), 18:535-36.

6. Proust, *Le temps retrouvé*, in *À la recherche du temps perdu*, ed. Jean-Yves Tadié (Paris: Gallimard, 1987–1989), 4:458.

7. Alexandre Weill, *Ma jeunesse (Mon enfance, Mon adolescence, Réginèle mon premier amour)* (Paris: Dentu, 1870).

8. Robert Dreyfus, "Vies des hommes obscurs: Alexandre Weill, ou le prophète du faubourg Saint-Honoré, 1811–1899," *Cahiers de la quinzaine* 9 (26 January 1908): 26–27.

Bibliography

CONTEMPORARY SOURCES

Abraham, Pierre. *Les trois frères*. Paris: Les Éditeurs Français Réunis, 1971.

——. *Proust: Recherches sur la création intellectuelle*. Paris: Rieder, 1930.

Arié, Emmanuel. *"Idéologues (Les systèmes du Baron T'Phlex), par Jaime de Beslou." La revue juive* 1 (January 15, 1925): 96–98.

——. *"Poésie, par Jean Cocteau." La revue juive* 5 (September 1925): 606–8.

Arié, Gabriel. *Histoire juive depuis les origines jusqu'à nos jours*. Paris: Durlacher et Léon Kaan, 1923.

——. *Histoire juive depuis les origines jusqu'à nos jours*. Paris: Éditions du Monde Moderne, 1926.

——. *Histoire juive depuis les origines jusqu'à nos jours*. 2nd ed. Paris: Éditions du Monde Moderne, 1928.

Barrès, Maurice. *Greco ou le secret de Tolède*. Paris: Émile-Paul, 1912.

——. *Les diverses familles spirituelles de la France*. Paris: Émile-Paul, 1917.

——. *Les diverses familles spirituelles de la France*. Ed. Denis Pernot and Vital Rambaud. Paris: Classiques Garnier, 2017.

Baruch-Weil, Godecheaux. *Réflexions d'un jeune israélite français, sur les deux brochures de M. Tsarphati*. Paris: Sétier, 1821.

Beaunier, André. *Pour la défense française*, vol. 1, *Contre la réforme de l'orthographe*. Paris: Plon, 1909.

——. *Pour la défense française*, vol. 2, *Les plus détestables bonshommes*. Paris: Plon, 1912.

——. *"Sésame." Le Figaro*, 14 June 1906.

Bell, Clive. *Proust*. London: The Hogarth Press, 1928.

Benda, Julien. *Belphégor: Essai sur l'esthétique de la présente société française*. Paris: Émile-Paul, 1918.

——. *La France byzantine, ou le Triomphe de la littérature pure: Mallarmé, Gide, Proust, Valéry, Alain Giraudoux, Suarès, les Surréalistes, essai d'une psychologie originelle du littérateur*. Paris: Gallimard, 1945.

——. *La trahison des clercs*. Paris: Grasset, 1927.

——. *"L'éternelle idole." Le Figaro*, March 9, 1920.

——. *L'ordination: Cahiers de la quinzaine*. Paris: Émile-Paul, 1913.

Benoit, Pierre. *"Commentaires: Le puits de Jacob." La revue juive* 1 (15 January 1925): 69–73.

——. *Le puits de Jacob*. Paris: Albin Michel, 1925.

Berge, André. *"Autour d'une trouvaille: Confession." Les cahiers du mois* 7 (December 1924): 5–18.

Bergson, Henri. *Correspondances.* Ed. André Robinet. Paris: PUF, 2002.

——. *Durée et simultanéité: À propos de la théorie d'Einstein.* Paris: Alcan, 1922.

Berl, Emmanuel. "Chronique philosophique: Freud et Proust." *Les nouvelles littéraires* (July 7, 1923): 3.

——. *Sylvia.* 1952. Paris: Gallimard, 1972.

Beslou, Jaime de. *Idéologues.* Paris: Éditions du Sagittaire, 1923.

——. *Propos de peintre.* Paris: Émile-Paul, 1919.

Bespaloff, Rachel. *Cheminements et carrefours.* 1938. Paris: Vrin, 2004.

——. *De l'Iliade.* Paris: Éditions Allia, 2004.

——. "Lettre à M. Daniel Halévy." *La revue juive de Genève* 6, no. 59 (June 1938): 391–98.

——. "Lettre sur Heidegger à M. Daniel Halévy." *Revue philosophique de la France et de l'étranger* 66, nos. 11–12 (November–December 1933): 321–39.

——. *On the Iliad.* Trans. Mary McCarthy. New York: Pantheon, 1947.

——. *Sur Heidegger (Lettre à Daniel Halévy).* Trocy-en-Multien: Éditions de la Revue Conférence, 2009.

Blanche, Jacques-Émile. *Cahiers d'un artiste.* 6 vols. Paris: Éditions de la NRF; Paris: Émile-Paul, 1915–1920.

Bloch, Jean-Richard. *Lévy.* Paris: Éditions de la NRF, 1912.

[Blum, Léon]. "Comment ont été faites les lois scélérates." *La revue blanche,* 1 July 1898, 338–52.

——. *Les lois scélérates de 1893–1894.* Paris: Éditions de la Revue Blanche, 1899.

Bonnard, Abel. "Au jour le jour: Marcel Proust." *Journal des débats,* 14 January 1927, 1.

Bonnerot, Jean. "Impressions d'enfance." *La revue idéaliste,* 15 September 1907, 277–81; October 1, 1907, 293–96.

Bouglé, Célestin, and André Beaunier. *Choix de moralistes français des XVIIIe et XIXe siècles.* Paris: Delagrave, 1897.

Boulenger, Jacques. *Entretien avec Frédéric Lefèvre.* Paris: Le Divan, 1926.

——. *Mais l'art est difficile!* 2 vols. Paris: Plon, 1921.

——. "Sur Marcel Proust." *L'Opinion* (Paris), 20 December 1919 and 10 January 1920.

Brasillach, Robert. "Causerie littéraire." *L'action française* (Paris), 11 June 1931.

Brunschvicg, Léon. "Le moment historique de Montaigne." *La revue juive* 4 (July 1925): 417–35.

Cahen, Émile. "*Silbermann.*" *Archives israélites* 83, no. 48 (30 November 1922): 190–91.

Cahen, René. "Le théâtre." *Archives israélites* 93, no. 41 (13 October 1932): 163.

Cahen-Hayem, Marie-Louise. "L'an prochain à Jérusalem." *Archives israélites* 85, no. 29 (17 July 1924): 114–15.

——. "La psychologie et le roman." *Archives israélites* 86, no. 52 (24 December 1925): 206.

——. "Nouveautés." *Archives israélites* 88, no. 52 (29 December 1927): 211.

——. "Proses." *Archives israélites* 92, no. 2 (8 January 1931): 7.

——. "Quelques livres nouveaux." *Archives israélites* 86, no. 9 (26 February 1925): 35.

——. "Romans et romanciers." *Archives israélites* 88, no. 10 (10 March 1927): 89.

Carras, Claude. "Ceux qu'ils ont tués: André Arnyvelde." *Gavroche* (Paris), 8 February 1945, 3.

Cattaui, Georges. "Barrès aux pays du Levant." *Menorah* 14 (16 March 1923): 220–22; 15 (30 March 1923): 235–37.

——. "Barrès et les juifs." *Critique art philosophie: Bulletin mensuel d'art et de littérature* 2 (May–June 1924): 11–12.

——. "Barrès et les juifs." *La revue juive* 6 (November 1925): 726–33.

——. "Blaise Pascal: L'influence de la pensée juive sur les lettres françaises." *Menorah* 21 (14 June 1923): 338-40; 22 (8 July 1923): 357-58.

——. *Charles de Gaulle.* Thonon: Société d'Édition Savoyarde, 1944.

——. *Claudel: Le cycle des Coûfontaine et le mystere d'Israël.* Paris: Desclée de Brouwer, 1968.

——. *Constantin Cavafy.* Paris: Seghers, 1964.

——. "Digressions: Un monument à Marcel Proust." *La revue juive* 5 (September 1925): 609-10.

——. *La promesse accomplie: France-Égypte-Judée.* Paris: Camille Bloch, 1922.

——. *L'amitié de Proust.* Paris: Gallimard, 1935.

——. *Léon Bloy.* Paris: Éditions Universitaires, 1954.

——. "Marcel Proust." *Menorah* 8 (22 December 1922): 116-18.

——. *Marcel Proust.* Paris: Éditions Universitaires, 1958.

——. *Marcel Proust: Documents iconographiques.* Geneva: Pierre Cailler, 1956.

——. *Marcel Proust: Proust et son temps, Proust et le temps.* Paris: Julliard, 1952.

——. "*Note conjointe sur M. Descartes, précédée de la note sur M. Bergson*, par Charles Péguy." *La revue juive* 1 (15 January 1925): 99-103.

——. *Péguy, témoin du temporel chrétien.* Paris: Éditions du Centurion, 1964.

——. "Proust et les juifs." *Palestine* 5 (February 1928): 196-205.

——. *Proust et ses métamorphoses.* Paris: Nizet, 1972.

——. *Proust perdu et retrouvé.* Paris: Plon, 1963.

——. *T. S. Eliot.* Paris: Éditions Universitaires, 1957.

——. "The Vestal of Friendship." *Adam International Review* 29, no. 299 (1962): 46-48.

Céline, Louis-Ferdinand. *Bagatelles pour un massacre.* Paris: Denoël, 1937.

Cocteau, Jean. *Le passé défini: Journal*, vol. 1, *1951–1952.* Ed. Pierre Chanel. Paris: Gallimard, 1983.

——. *Le secret professionnel.* Paris: Stock, 1922.

——. *Poésie, 1916–1923.* Paris: Éditions de la NRF, 1924).

Cohen, Albert. *Belle du seigneur.* 1968. Ed. Christel Peyrefitte and Bella Cohen. Paris: Gallimard, 1986.

——. "Les chroniques nationales: Israël—Le juif et les romanciers français." *La revue de Genève* (March 1923): 340-51.

——. "Les chroniques nationales: Israël—Vue d'ensemble sur la question juive et le sionisme." *La revue de Genève* 10 (April 1921): 598-608.

——. "Mort de Charlot." *La nouvelle revue française*, June 1923, 883-89.

——. *Paroles juives.* Paris: Crès et Kundig, 1921.

——. "Projections ou après-minuit à Genève." *La nouvelle revue française*, October 1922, 414-46.

Cohen, Léonce. *École du musicien, ou solfège théorique et pratique avec accompagnement de piano.* Paris: Éditions Margueritat, 1862.

Crémieux, Benjamin. "Autres réflexions sur Proust," *Les nouvelles littéraires* (Paris), 11 September 1926, 1-2.

——. *Du côté de Marcel Proust.* Paris: Lemarget, 1929.

——. *Du côté de Marcel Proust.* Tusson: Du Lérot, 2011.

——. *Essai sur l'évolution littéraire de l'Italie de 1870 à not jour.* Paris: Kra, 1928.

——. *Henri IV et la dramaturgie de Luigi Pirandello.* Paris: Gallimard, 1928.

——. *Inquiétude et reconstruction: Essai sur la littérature d'après-guerre.* 1931. Ed. Catherine Helbert. Paris: Gallimard, 2011.

——. "Judaïsme et littérature." *Les nouvelles littéraires* (10 October 1925): 5.

——. "La composition dans l'oeuvre de Marcel Proust." *Les nouvelles littéraires* (31 May 1924): 5.

——. "La littérature juive française." *La revue juive de Genève* 5, no. 45 (February 1937): 196–200.

——. "La psychologie de Marcel Proust." *La revue de Paris* 5 (15 October 1924): 838–61.

——. "Le juif dans la littérature française." *La revue juive de Genève* 5, no. 44 (January 1937): 156–60.

——. *Le premier de la classe.* Paris: Grasset, 1921.

——. *XXᵉ siècle: Première série.* Paris: Éditions de la NRF, 1924.

——. *XXᵉ siècle: Première série.* Ed. Catherine Helbert. Paris: Gallimard, 2010.

[Cruppi, Marcel]. "Au Mercure: *Sésame et les lys,* par John Ruskin." *Le mouvement, revue mensuelle, artistique et sociale* 2, no. 4 (July 1906): 60.

Dandieu, Arnaud. *Marcel Proust: Sa révélation psychologique.* Paris: Firmin-Didot, 1930.

Daudet, Léon. "André Beaunier." *L'action française* (Paris), 12 December 1925.

Desson, André, and André Harlaire. "Le sionisme, essai de renaissance juive." *Les cahiers du mois* 9–10 (February–March 1925): 362–65.

Drach, Chevalier. *De l'harmonie entre l'Église et la synagogue.* Paris: Mellier, 1844.

Dreyfus, Robert. "À propos de Marcel Proust et de ses personnages juifs." *La revue juive de Genève* 5, no. 49 (June 1937): 419–20.

——. *De Monsieur Thiers à Marcel Proust.* Paris: Plon, 1939.

——. *La république de Monsieur Thiers, 1871–1873.* Paris: Gallimard, 1930.

——. *La vie et les prophéties du comte de Gobineau.* Paris: Calmann-Lévy, 1905.

——. "Lettres à Madame Straus." *La revue de Paris* 43, vol. 5 (October 1936): 815–47.

——. "Ludovic Halévy." *Pages libres* 8, no. 385 (16 May 1908): 554–56.

——. "Madame Straus et Marcel Proust." *La revue de Paris* 43, vol. 5 (October 1936): 803–14.

——. *Marcel Proust à dix-septs ans, avec des lettres inédites de Marcel Proust.* Paris: Kra, 1926.

——. *Monsieur Thiers contre l'Empire, la guerre, la Commune, 1869–1871.* Paris: Grasset, 1928.

——. *Souvenirs sur Marcel Proust.* Paris: Grasset, 1926.

——. "Vies des hommes obscurs: Alexandre Weill, ou le prophète du faubourg Saint-Honoré, 1811–1899." *Cahiers de la quinzaine* 9 (26 January 1908).

Drumont, Édouard. *La dernière bataille: Nouvelle étude psychologique et sociale.* Paris: Dentu, 1890.

——. *La fin d'un monde: Étude psychologique et sociale.* Paris: Savine, 1889.

——. *La France juive.* 2 vols. Paris: Marpon and Flammarion, 1886.

Du Camp, Maxime. *Paris, ses organes, ses fonctions et sa vie dans la seconde moitié du XIXᵉ siècle.* 6 vols. Paris: Hachette, 1875.

Ernest-Charles, Jean. "Pas de statue." *L'ère nouvelle,* 14 October 1925.

Faÿ, Bernard. *Panorama de la littérature contemporaine.* Paris: Éditions du Sagittaire, Simon Kra, 1925.

Franck, Adolphe. *La Kabbale, ou la philosophie religieuse des Hébreux.* 1843. 3rd ed. Paris: Hachette, 1892.

Freud, Sigmund. *Le rêve et son interprétation.* Trans. Hélène Legros. Paris: Gallimard, 1925.

Ghéon, Henri. "*Du côté de chez Swann.*" *La nouvelle revue française,* January 1, 1914, 139–43.

Gide, André. "Billet à Angèle." *La nouvelle revue française,* 1 May 1921, 586–91.

——. *Essai sur Montaigne.* Paris: Gallimard, 1929.

——. *Essais critiques.* Ed. Pierre Masson. Paris: Gallimard, 1999.

—. *Journal*, vol. 1, *1887–1925*. Ed. Éric Marty. Paris: Gallimard, 1996.

—. "Nationalisme et littérature." *La nouvelle revue française*, 1 June 1909, 429–34.

Graetz, Heinrich. *Geschichte der Juden von den ältesten Zeiten bis auf die Gegenwart*. 11 vols. Leipzig: Leiner, 1853–1875.

Gregh, Fernand. *L'âge de fer: Souvenirs, 1925–1955*. Paris: Grasset, 1956.

—. *Mon amitié avec Marcel Proust*. Paris: Grasset, 1958.

Groos, René. *Enquête sur le problème juif*. Paris: Nouvelle Librairie Nationale, 1923.

—. *Esquisses: Charles Maurras, poète; Marcel Proust, Bernard Shaw*. Paris: Maison du Livre Français, 1928.

—. *Marcel Proust*. Paris: Éditions de la Revue le Capitole, 1926.

—. "Romantisme et judaïsme." *Cours et conférences de l'Institut d'Action Française* 3, no. 1 (June 1925): 63–120.

—. "Romantisme et judaïsme." *La revue du siècle* 1, no. 4 (1 June 1925): 404–12; 8 (1 November 1925): 409–18; 9 (1 December 1925): 70–77.

Guillebon, Régine de Plinval de. *Bibliographie analytiques des expositions industrielles et commerciales en France depuis l'origine jusqu'à 1867*. Dijon: L'Échelle de Jacob, 2006.

—. *Faïence et porcelaine de Paris, XVIIIe–XIXe siècles*. Dijon: Faton, 1995.

—. *La porcelaine à Paris sous le Consultat et l'Empire: Fabrication, commerce, étude topographiques des immeubles ayant abrité des manufactures de porcelaine*. Geneva: Droz, 1985.

Halévy, Daniel. "Apologie pour notre passé." *Cahiers de la quinzaine* 10 (10 April 1910):

—. "Correspondance." *La revue juive de Genève* 5, no. 50 (July 1937): 470.

Halévy, Daniel, Marianne Halévy, and André Spire. *Correspondance, 1899–1961*. Ed. Marie-Brunette Spire-Uran. Paris: Honoré Champion, 2020.

Halévy, Léon. *F. Halévy: Sa vie et ses oeuvres*. Paris: Heugel, 1863.

Harlaire, André. " Émile Zola et l'antisémitisme." *Menorah* 11 (15 June 1924): 162.

—. "*La promesse accomplie*, par Georges Cattaui." *La revue juive* 6 (November 1925): 752–53.

Harry, Myriam. *Les amants de Sion*. Paris: Fayard, 1923.

Hertz, Henri. "Regards: *Déchéances aimables*, par Léon Pierre-Quint." *La revue juive* 4 (July 1925): 498–99.

Jean-Javal, Lily. *L'inquiète*. Paris: Plon, 1927.

—. *Noémi: Roman d'une jeune fille juive en pays basque*. Paris: Plon, 1925.

Judaeus [Maurice Liber]. "La renaissance juive en France d'après M. André Spire." *L'univers israélite* 82, no. 16 (24 December 1926): 485–87.

—. "Les paradoxes de M. Spire." *L'univers israélite* 82, no. 17 (December 31, 1926): 517–19.

[Kahn, Gustave]. "Le judaïsme et le style." *Menorah* 4 (1 November 1925): 313.

Kahn, Léon. *Histoire de la communauté israélite de Paris*, vol. 1, *Histoire des écoles communales et consistoriales israélites de Paris (1809–1884)*. Paris: Durlacher, 1884.

—. *Histoire de la communauté israélite de Paris*, vol. 3, *Le Comité de Bienfaisance, l'hôpital, l'orphelinat, les cimetières*. Paris: Durlacher, 1886.

—. *Histoire de la communauté israélite de Paris*, vol. 4, *Les sociétés de secours mutuels, philanthropiques et de prévoyance*. Paris: Durlacher, 1887.

—. *Histoire de la communauté israélite de Paris*, vol. 5, *Les juifs à Paris depuis le VIᵉ siècle*. Paris: Durlacher, 1889.

Lacretelle, Jacques de. "Commentaires: *Silbermann*." *La revue juive* 1 (15 January 1925): 64–69.

——. *Le retour de Silbermann.* 1929. Paris: Gallimard, 1930.

——. *Silbermann.* Paris: Éditions de la NRF, 1922.

Lalou, René. "Marcel Proust et l'esprit juif." *Menorah* 10 (April-June 1931): 84-85.

Le livre du Zohar. Trans. Jean de Pauly. Ed. Edmond Fleg. Paris: Rieder, 1925.

Le Masle, Robert. *Le Professeur Adrien Proust (1834–1903).* Paris: Lipschutz, 1935.

Lehrmann, Chanan (Charles Cuno). *Bergsonisme et judaïsme, cours professé à l'université de Lausanne.* Geneva: Éditions Union, 1937.

——. *Das Humanitätsideal der sozialistisch-romantischen Epoche Frankreichs und seine Beziehung zur Judenfrage.* Wertheim am Main: Bechstein, 1932.

——. *L'élément juif dans la littérature française.* 2 vols. Paris: Albin Michel, 1941.

——. *L'élément juif dans la littérature française.* 2nd ed. 2 vols. Paris: Albin Michel, 1961.

——. *L'élément juif dans la pensée européenne.* Paris: Éditions du Chant Nouveau and Migdal, 1947.

Leven, Narcisse. *Cinquante ans d'histoire: L'Alliance Israélite Universelle (1860–1910).* 2 vols. Paris: Alcan, 1911-1920.

Lévi, Ben [Godchaux Weil]. "Cimetières israélites de Paris." *Archives israélites de France* 2 (May 1841): 323-33.

——. "Défunt Ben-Lévi!" *Archives israélites* 11 (August 1850): 436-42.

——. *Les matinées du samedi: Livre d'éducation morale et religieuse à l'usage de la jeunesse israélite.* 2 vols. 3rd ed. Paris: Bureau des Archives Israélites de France, 1859.

——. *Les matinées du samedi: Livre d'éducation morale et religieuse à l'usage de la jeunesse israélite.* 2 vols. 4th ed. Paris: Bureau des Archives Israélites de France, 1897.

——. "Les poissons et les miettes de pain." *Archives israélites* 7 (October 1846): 630-38.

——. "Mémoires d'un colporteur juif, écrits par lui-même." *Archives israélites de France* 2 (November 1841): 686-91, and 3 (August 1842): 459-66.

——. "Première lettre d'un humoriste: Les trois générations." *Archives israélites de France* 1 (October 1840): 527-30.

——. "Samuel Cahen." *Archives israélites* 23, no. 2 (1 February 1862): 81-87.

Lévy, Roger. "*Noémi,* par Lily Jean-Javal." *La revue juive* 2 (15 March 1925): 259-61.

Liber, Maurice. *Rashi.* London: Macmillan and Jewish Historical Society of England, 1906.

Lunel, Armand. "Marcel Proust, sa mère et les juifs." *Europe* 49, nos. 502-3 (February-March 1971): 64-67.

——. "*XXᵉ siècle,* par Benjamin Crémieux." *La revue juive* 6 (November 1925): 750-52.

Malvezin, Théophile. *Histoire des juifs à Bordeaux.* Bordeaux: Ch. Lefebvre, 1875.

——. *Michel de Montaigne, son origine, sa famille.* Paris: Dentu, 1874.

Maurras, Charles. *Enquête sur la monarchie.* Paris: Nouvelle Librairie Nationale, 1909.

——. "La politique." *L'action française* (Paris), 23 June 1944.

Menasce, Jean de. "Antisémitisme: Hilaire Belloc, Hans Blüher et René Groos." *La revue juive* 4 (July 1925): 473-78.

——. "Regards: *Ulysses,* par James Joyce." *La revue juive* 6 (November 1925): 756-62.

Neymarck, Alfred. *Le Honduras, son chemin de fer, son avenir industriel et commercial.* Paris: Dentu, 1872.

——. *Que doit-on faire de son argent? Notions et conseils practical sur les valeurs mobilières, placements et operations.* Paris: Marchal et Godde, 1913.

Paraf, Pierre. "Israël dans les démocraties contemporaines: Une conférence de M. André Siegfried au 'Cercle d'études juives.'" *L'univers israélite* 85, no. 34 (23 May 1930): 203-4.

[Paulhan, Jean]. "Denis Saurat." *La nouvelle nouvelle revue française*, July 1958, 171–73.

Péguy, Charles. "Notre jeunesse." *Cahiers de la quinzaine* 12 (17 July 1910):

——. *Oeuvres complètes*, vol. 2, *Oeuvres de prose*. Paris: Éditions de la NRF, 1920.

Pierrefeu, Jean de. "Au jour le jour: Le prix Goncourt." *Journal des débats*, 12 December 1919, 1.

——. "La vie littéraire: Le cas de M. Proust." *Journal des débats*, 2 January 1920, 3.

——. *Plutarque a menti*. Paris: Grasset, 1923.

Pierre-Quint, Léon. *Après le temps retrouvé: Le comique et le mystère chez Proust*. Paris: Simon Kra, 1928.

——. "Carl Sternheim." *La revue juive* 6 (November 1925): 733–41.

——. *Comment parut "Du côté de chez Swann."* Paris: Simon Kra, 1930.

——. *Comment travaillait Proust: Bibliographie, variantes, lettres de Proust*. Paris: Éditions des Cahiers Libres, 1928.

——. *Déchéances aimables*. Paris: Éditions du Sagittaire, Simon Kra, 1924.

——. *Le combat de Marcel Proust*. Paris: Le Club Français du Livre, 1955.

——. "Le style de Marcel Proust." *Les nouvelles littéraires*, 6 June 1925, 6.

——. *Marcel Proust: Sa vie, son oeuvre*. Paris: Éditions du Sagittaire, Simon Kra, 1925.

——. *Marcel Proust, sa vie, son oeuvre*. Rev. ed. Paris: Simon Kra, 1929.

——. *Marcel Proust, sa vie, son oeuvre*. Rev. ed. Paris: Sagittaire, 1976.

——. *Proust et la stratégie littéraire, avec des lettres de Marcel Proust à René Blum, Bernard Grasset et Louis Brun*. Paris: Corrêa, 1954.

——. "Simplification amoureuse." *Mercure de France*, 15 April and 15 May 1921.

——. *Une nouvelle lecture de Marcel Proust dix ans plus tard, suivi de Proust et la jeunesse d'aujourd'hui*. Paris: Sagittaire, 1935.

Plotinus. *Les Ennéades*. Trans. Marie-Nicolas Bouillet. 3 vols. Paris: Hachette, 1857–1861.

Praag, Siegfried van. "Alexandre Weill (1811–1899)." *Der Jude: Eine Monatsschrift* 7, no. 12 (1923): 681–91.

——. *De West-Joden en hun letterkunde sinds 1860*. Amsterdam: Elsevier, 1926.

——. "Der Jude im Roman." *Der Jude: Eine Monatsschrift* 6, no. 12 (1921–1922): 758–63.

——. "Marcel Proust, témoin du judaïsme déjudaïsé." *La revue juive de Genève* 5, no. 48 (May 1937): 338–47; 49 (June 1937): 388–93; 50 (July 1937): 446–54.

——. *Persoonlijkheden in het Koninkrijk der Nederlanden in woord en beeld*. Amsterdam: VanHolkema and Warendorf, 1938.

Prague, Hippolyte. "Un cérémonie crématoire israélite." *Archives israélites* 49, no. 17 (26 April 1888): 131.

Proust, Adrien. "La conférence sanitaire internationale de Venise de 1897." *Revue d'hygiène et de police sanitaire* 19, no. 7 (July 1897): 577–89.

——. *Traité d'hygiène publique et privée*. Paris: Masson, 1877.

——. *Traité d'hygiène publique et privée*. 2nd ed. Paris: Masson, 1881.

——. *Traité d'hygiène publique et privée*. 3rd ed. Paris: Masson, 1903.

Proust, Marcel. *À la recherche du temps perdu*. Ed. Jean-Yves Tadié. 4 vols. Paris: Gallimard, 1987–1989.

——. *Contre Sainte-Beuve*. Ed. Pierre Clarac and Yves Sandre. Paris: Gallimard, 1971.

——. *Correspondance*. Ed. Philip Kolb. 21 vols. Paris: Plon, 1970–1993.

——. *Correspondance avec Daniel Halévy*. Ed. Anne Borrel and Jean-Pierre Halévy. Paris: Éditions de Fallois, 1992.

——. *Finding Time Again.* Trans. Ian Patterson. New York: Penguin, 2023.

——. *The Fugitive.* Trans. Peter Collier. New York: Penguin, 2021.

——. *The Guermantes Way.* Trans. Mark Treharne. New York: Penguin, 2005.

——. *In the Shadow of Young Girls in Flower.* Trans. James Grieve. New York: Penguin, 2005.

——. *Jean Santeuil, preceded by Les plaisirs et les jours.* Ed. Pierre Clarac and Yves Sandre. Paris: Gallimard, 1971.

——. *Jean Santeuil.* Trans. Gerard Hopkins. New York: Simon & Schuster, 1956.

——. "Lettres." *La revue juive* 4 (July 1925): 463–72.

——. "Mademoiselle de Forcheville." *La revue juive* 6 (November 1925): 702–25.

——. "Mondanité de Bouvard et Pécuchet." *La revue blanche* 5, nos. 21–22 (July–August 1893): 67–68.

——. *Pleasures and Days.* Trans. Andrew Brown. London: Hesperus Classics, 2004.

——. *The Prisoner.* Trans. Carol Clark. New York: Penguin, 2019.

——. *Sodom and Gomorrah.* Trans. John Sturrock. New York: Penguin, 2005.

——. *Swann's Way.* Trans. Lydia Davis. New York: Penguin, 2004.

——. *Textes retrouvés.* Ed. Philip Kolb. Paris: Gallimard, 1971.

Rivière, Jacques. "Marcel Proust et l'esprit positif." *La nouvelle revue française*, January 1923, 179–87.

——. *Nouvelles études.* Paris: Gallimard, 1947.

Sainte-Beuve, Charles Augustin. *Nouveaux lundis.* Paris: Michel Lévy, 1864.

Saurat, Denis. "Baudelaire, Rimbaud, la Cabale." *La nouvelle revue française*, 1 February 1936, 258–61.

——. *Blake and Milton.* Bordeaux: Imprimerie de l'Université, 1920.

——. *Blake and Modern Thought.* London: Constable, 1929.

——. "Conversations avec Jean-Richard Bloch." *Europe* 135–136 (March–April 1957): 37–40.

——. *The Denis Saurat Reader.* Ed. John Robert Colombo. Toronto: C & C, 2004.

——. *Encaminament catar.* Toulouse: Oc, 1955.

——. *Encaminament catar.* Toulouse: Oc, 1960.

——. *Encaminament catar.* Trans. and ed. Jean-François Courouau. Toulouse: Presses Universitaires du Mirail, 2010.

——. "Jean-Richard Bloch." *La nouvelle revue française*, 1 May 1932, 873–87.

——. "La Cabale et la philosophie de Milton." *Revue des études juives* 73, no. 145 (1921): 1–13.

——. *La littérature et l'occultisme: Études sur la poésie philosophique moderne.* Paris: Rieder, 1929.

——. "La nuit d'Idumée: Mallarmé et la Cabale." *La nouvelle revue française*, 1 December 1931, 920–22.

——. *La pensée de Milton.* Paris: Alcan, 1920.

——. *La religion de Victor Hugo.* Paris: Hachette, 1929.

——. *La religion des géants et la civilisation des insectes.* Paris: Denoël, 1955.

——. *La religion des géants et la civilisation des insectes.* Paris: J'ai Lu, 1969.

——. "L'après-guerre: Le style 'moderne.'" *La nouvelle revue française*, 1 November 1931, 793–800.

——. *L'Atlantide.* Paris: Denoël, 1954.

——. *L'Atlantide.* Paris: J'ai Lu, 1986.

——. "Le grand maître du moderne: Marcel Proust." *Les Marges*, Spring 1930, 123–44.

——. "Le judaïsme de Proust." *Les Marges*, 15 October 1925, 83–87.

——. "Le temps retrouvé." *Marsyas* 8 (January 1928): 401–2.

——. *L'expérience de l'au-delà*. La Colombe: Éd. du Vieux-Colombier, 1951.

——. "Milton and the Zohar." *The Quest* 13 (January 1922): 145–65.

——. "Milton and the Zohar." *Studies in Philology* 19, no. 2 (April 1922): 136–51.

——. "Milton et le Zohar." *Revue germanique* 13 (January 1922): 1–19.

——. *Milton, Man and Thinker*. New York: Dial Press, 1925.

——. *Modernes*. Paris: Denoël et Steele, 1935.

——. "Propos: Le génie malade—Proust." *Les Marges*, 15 November 1925, 198–205.

——. "Propos: Occultisme et sensualité—Alexandre Weill et Victor Hugo." *Les Marges*, 15 December 1926, 294–300.

——. "Proust." *Marsyas* 6, no. 61 (January 1926): 292–93; 6, no. 62 (February 1926): 300–301; 6, no. 63 (March 1926): 305–6; 6, no. 64 (April 1926): 308; 6, no. 65 (May 1926): 317–18; 6, no. 66 (June 1926): 324–26; 6, no. 67 (July 1926): 329–30; 6, no. 68 (August 1926): 332–34.

——. "Proust et Joyce." *Les Marges*, 15 December 1924, 244–46.

——. *Tendances*. Paris: Éditions du Monde Moderne, 1928.

——. *Tendances*. La Colombe: Éditions du Vieux-Colombier, 1946.

——. "Victor Hugo: Le panthéisme mystique." *Marsyas* 7, no. 73 (January 1927): 353–54.

——. "Victor Hugo et la Cabale." *Marsyas* 6, no. 71 (November 1926): 343; 6, no. 72 (December 1926): 349–50.

——. *Watch Over Africa*. London: Dent, 1941.

Savitzky, Ludmila. "*Marcel Proust, sa vie, son oeuvre*, par Léon Pierre-Quint." *Menorah* 20 (1 November 1925): 322.

Savitzky, Ludmila, and André Spire. *Une amitié tenace: Correspondance, 1910–1957*. Ed. Marie-Brunette Spire. Paris: Les Belles Lettres, 2010.

Scholem, Gershom. *De Berlin à Jérusalem: Souvenirs de jeunesse*. Trans. Sabine Bollack. Paris: Albin Michel, 1984.

——. *Les grands courants de la mystique juive*. Trans. Marie-Madeleine Davy. 1950. Paris: Payot et Rivages, 2014.

——. *Major Trends in Jewish Mysticism*. Jerusalem: Schocken, 1941.

——. *Von Berlin nach Jerusalem: Jugenderinnerungen*. Frankfurt: Suhrkamp, 1977.

Sepher ha-Zohar (Le livre de la splendeur), doctrine ésotérique des Israélites. 6 vols. Trans. Jean de Pauly. Ed. Émile Lafuma-Giraud. Paris: E. Leroux, 1906–1911.

Shapira, Maria Rosette. *La conquête de Jérusalem*. Paris: Calmann-Lévy, 1904.

Spire, André. "Du côté de chez Swann: Marcel Proust et les juifs." *Les nouvelles littéraires* (28 July 1923): 1.

——. "Hommage à une cadette." *Adam International Review* 29, no. 299 (1962): 25.

——. "Israel Zangwill et le Congrès juif mondial." *La revue juive de Genève* 1, no. 1 (October 1932): 9–16.

——. "Israel Zangwill humoriste." *L'univers israélite* 84, no. 17 (4 January 1929): 517–19.

——. *Le secret*. Paris: Èditions de la NRF, 1919.

——. "*Les amants de Sion*, par Myriam Harry." *La revue juive* 3 (15 May 1925): 391–93.

——. "Marcel Proust." *The Jewish Chronicle Supplement* 29 (25 May 1923): 6–7.

——. "Marcel Proust." *Menorah* 30 (9 December 1923): 491–93.

——. *Plaisir poétique et plaisir musculaire: Essai sur l'évolution des techniques poétiques*. Paris: Corti, 1949.

——. *Poèmes de Loire*. Paris: Grasset, 1929.

——. *Poèmes juifs*. Paris: Mercure de France, 1908.

——. *Poèmes juifs*. Paris: Albin Michel, 2019.

——. *Quelques juifs*. Paris: Mercure de France, 1913.

——. *Quelques juifs et demi-juifs*. 2 vols. Paris: Grasset, 1928.

——. "Quelques souvenirs sur Maurice Barrès." *Le pays lorrain* 16, no. 3 (March 1924): 112-17.

——. "Romans judéo-français." *Menorah* 5 (10 November 1922): 66-69; 6 (24 November 1922): 82-85.

——. *Souvenirs à bâtons rompus*. Paris: Albin Michel, 1961.

——. "Une lettre de M. Spire." *L'univers israélite* 82, no. 18 (7 January 1927): 551-54.

Tharaud, Jean, and Jérôme Tharaud. *L'an prochain à Jérusalem!* Paris: Plon, 1924.

——. *L'ombre de la croix*. Paris: Émile-Paul, 1917.

Thibaudet, Albert. *Histoire de la littérature française de 1789 à nos jours*. Paris: Stock, 1936.

——. "Le roman de Montaigne." *La revue universelle* 60, no. 24 (15 March 1935): 655-77.

——. "Marcel Proust et la tradition français." *La nouvelle revue française*, 1 January 1923, 130-39.

——. "Pour la géographie littéraire." *La nouvelle revue française*, April 1929.

——. *Réflexions sur la littérature*. Ed. Antoine Compagnon and Christopher Pradeau. Paris: Gallimard, 2007.

Tsarsphati. *Première lettre d'un Israélite français à ses coreligionnaires, sur l'urgente nécessité de célébrer l'office en français le jour de dimanche, à l'usage des Israélites qui ne peuvent assister à l'office asiatique de la veille, comme unique moyen de rendre désormais l'éducation religieuse possible en France*. Paris: Bachelier, 1820.

——. *Projet de règlement concernant la circoncision, suivi d'observations sur une lettre pastorale du grand rabbin de Metz et sur un écrit de M. Lazare (aîné)*. Paris: A. Béraud, 1821.

Weill, Alexandre. *Lois et mystères de la création conformes à la science la plus absolue*. Paris: Sauvaitre, 1896.

——. *Ma jeunesse (Mon enfance, Mon adolescence, Réginéle mon premier amour)*. Paris: Dentu, 1870.

——. *Mystères de la création*. Trans. A. Weill. Paris: Dentu, 1855.

Weill, Michel A. "De la crémation envisagée au point du vue de la doctrine et des traditions du judaïsme." *L'univers israélite* 43, no. 5 (16 November 1887): 143-45; no. 6 (1 December 1887): 176-78; no. 7 (16 December 1887): 208-10; no. 8 (1 January 1888): 232-34; no. 9 (16 January 1888): 266-68; no. 10 (1 February 1888): 304-6; no. 12 (1 March 1888): 335-37.

SECONDARY SOURCES

Abraham, Pierre. *Les trois frères*. Paris: Les Éditeurs Français Réunis, 1971.

Abravanel, Nicole. "L'historicité en milieu sépharade ou le primat de la spatialité." *Vingtième siècle: Revue d'histoire* 117, no. 1 (2013): 183-97.

Alden, Douglas. *Marcel Proust and His French Critics*. Los Angeles: Lymanhouse, 1940.

Alexandre, Rosine. *Fontainbleau, naissance d'une communauté juive à l'époque de la Révolution, 1788–1808*. N.p.: Privately published, 1991.

Amadieu, Jean-Baptiste. "Jacques Baillès, évêque, censeur et critique littéraire." *La Vendée littéraire* (April 2013): 117-46.

Arendt, Hannah. *Les origines du totalitarisme: Eichmann à Jérusalem.* Trans. Micheline Pouteau and Hélène Frappat. Ed. Pierre Bouretz. Paris: Gallimard, 2002.

——. *The Origins of Totalitarianism.* New York: Harcourt Brace, 1951.

——. *The Origins of Totalitarianism.* 2nd ed. New York: Harcourt, Brace, 1958.

Arnyvelde, André. *Textes retrouvés.* Ed. P. Kolb. Paris: Gallimard, 1971.

Avon, Dominique. *Les frères prêcheurs en Orient: Les dominicains du Caire (années 1910–années 1960).* Paris: Éditions du Cerf, 2005.

Ball, Joseph, ed. *L'abbé Flory (1886–1949).* Lantenne-Vertière: J. Garneret, 1978.

Bem, Jeanne. "Le juif et l'homosexuel dans À la recherche du temps perdu: Fonctionnements textuels." *Littérature* 37 (February 1980): 100–112.

Benbassa, Esther, and Aron Rodrigue. *Une vie judéo-espagnole à l'Est: Gabriel Arié (1863–1939), autobiographie, journal et correspondance.* Paris: Éditions du Cerf, 1992.

Benfey, Christopher E. G., and Karen Remmler, eds. *Artists, Intellectuals, and World War II: The Pontigny Encounters at Mount Holyoke College, 1942–1944.* Amherst: University of Massachusetts Press, 2006.

Benhaïm, André. *Panim: Visages de Proust.* Lille: Presses Universitaires du Septentrion, 2006.

Berkovitz, Jay R. *The Shaping of Jewish Identity in Nineteenth-Century France.* Detroit: Wayne State University Press, 1989.

Bernard, Jean-Jacques. *Le camp de la mort lente: Compiègne 1941–1942.* Paris: Albin Michel, 1944.

Birnbaum, Pierre. *La république et le cochon.* Paris: Éditions du Seuil, 2013.

——. *Un mythe politique: La "République juive," de Léon Blum à Pierre Mendès France.* Paris: Fayard, 1988.

Blamont, Claudie. "Mariages juifs à Paris de 1793 à 1802." *Revue du cercle de généalogie juive* 57 (Spring 1999): 2–8; 58 (Summer 1999): 2–14.

Bloch, Jean-Richard. and André Spire. *Correspondance, 1912–1947: "Sommes-nous d'accord?"* Ed. Marie-Brunette Spire. Paris: Éditions Claire Paulhan, 2011.

Bloch-Dano, Évelyne. *Madame Proust.* Paris: Le Livre de Poche, 2018.

——. *Madame Proust: A Biography.* Trans. Alice Kaplan. Chicago: University of Chicago Press, 2007.

——. *Une jeunesse de Marcel Proust.* Paris: Stock, 2017.

Bonnet-Roy, Flavien. *Ferdinand-Philippe, duc d'Orléans, prince royal, 1810–1842.* Paris: Société d'Éditions Françaises et Internationales, 1947.

Boukara, Philippe. "Justin Godart et le sionisme: Autour de France-Palestine." In *Justin Godart, un homme dans son siècle (1871–1956),* ed. Annette Wieviorka, 199–200. Paris: CNRS Éditions, 2004.

Bourdariat, Jean. "Quinze ans avant le scandale de Panama, l'affaire du chemin de fer transocéanique de Honduras." *Revue d'histoire des chemins de fer* 44 (2013): 165–82.

Bourel, Dominique. "Notes sur la première traduction française du *Zohar.*" In *Jüdisches Denken in einer Welt ohne Gott: Festschrift für Stéphane Mosès,* ed. J. Mattern, G. Motzkin, and S. Sandbank, 120–29. Berlin: Vorwerk 8, 2000.

Brami, Joseph. "Premières réceptions critiques 'juives' de *Swann,* 1923-1941." *Francofonia* 64 (Spring 2013): 141–59.

Broch, Hermann. "Le style de l'âge mythique." Trans. Albert Kohn. In *Création littéraire et connaissance,* ed. Hannah Arendt, 257–75. Paris: Gallimard, 1966, 2007.

Brooks, Douglas A., ed. *Milton and the Jews.* Cambridge: Cambridge University Press, 2008.

Brun, Bernard. "Brouillons et brouillages: Proust et l'antisémitisme." *Littérature* 70 (1988): 110–28.

——. "Les juifs dans *Sodome et Gomorrhe*." *Cahiers textuel* 23 (2001): 119–26.

——. "Sur quelques plaisanteries antisémites dans les manuscrits de rédaction de Proust." *La revue des lettres modernes: Marcel Proust 4* (2004): 41–53.

Cahiers Céline 7. Paris: Gallimard, 1986.

Carlson, Erin G. "Secret Dossiers: Sexuality, Race and Treason in Proust and the Dreyfus Affair." *Modern Fiction Studies* 48, no. 4 (2002): 937–68.

Carter, William C. *Marcel Proust: A Life*. New Haven, CT: Yale University Press, 2000.

——. *Marcel Proust: A Life*. 2nd ed. New Haven, CT: Yale University Press, 2013.

Cattaui, Georges, and Philip Kolb, eds. *Entretiens sur Marcel Proust: Centre culturel international de Cerisy-la-Salle, 17–25 juillet 1962*. 1966. Paris: Hermann, 2013.

Cesarani, David. *The Jewish Chronicle and Anglo-Jewry, 1841–1991*. Cambridge: Cambridge University Press, 1994.

Chaudier, Stéphane. "Proust, l'antisémitisme et le non-engagement." *La revue internationale des livres et des idées* 4 (March–April 2008): 43–46.

Chebahi, Malik, and Claudine Piaton. "Les architectes d'Alger, 1830–1940." In *Alger, architectures 1830–1940*, ed. B. Aïche, J. Hueber, T. Lochard, and C. Piaton, 30–49. Arles: Honoré Clair, 2016.

Chenaux, Philippe. "Du judaïsme au catholicisme: Réseaux de conversion dans l'entre-deux-guerres." In *La conversion aux XIXe et XXe siècles*, ed. Nadine-Josette Chaline and Jean-Dominique Durant, 95–106. Arras: Artois Presses Université, 1996.

——. *Entre Maurras et Maritain, une génération intellectuelle catholique (1920–1930)*. Paris: Éditions du Cerf, 1999.

Cohen, Kitty. *The Throne and the Chariot: Studies in Milton's Hebraism*. The Hague: Mouton, 1975.

Cohen Albert, Phyllis. *The Modernization of French Jewry: Consistory and Community in the Nineteenth Century*. Waltham, MA: Brandeis University Press, 1977.

Colombo, John Robert. *O rare Denis Saurat: An Appreciation*. Toronto: C & C, 2003.

Compagnon, Antoine. "Israël avant Israël." In *Les intellectuels français et Israël*, ed. Denis Charbit, 9–27. Paris: Éditions de l'Éclat, 2009.

——. "'Le long de la rue du Repos': Brouillon d'une lettre à Daniel Halévy (1908)." *Bulletin d'informations proustiennes* 50 (2020): 13–32.

——. "Le 'profil assyrien' ou l'antisémitisme qui n'ose pas dire son nom: Les libéraux dans l'affaire Dreyfus." *Études de langue et littérature françaises* (Kyoto) 28 (1997).

Danan, Ariel. "Les français israélites et l'accession au pouvoir de Léon Blum, à travers *L'univers israélite*." *Archives juives* 37, no. 1 (2004): 97–110.

Decout, Maxime. *Albert Cohen: Les fictions de la judéité*. Paris: Classiques Garnier, 2011.

——. *Écrire la judéité: Enquête sur un malaise dans la littérature française*. Seyssel: Champ Vallon, 2014.

Diamant, Naomi. "Judaism, Homosexuality, and Other Sign Systems in *À la recherche du temps perdu*." *Romanic Review* 82, no. 2 (1991): 179–92.

Dispot, Laurent. "Marcel Proust-Weil et Titi Tiszelman, face à Maurras et au mot 'race.'" *La règle du jeu* 40 (May 2009): 238–302.

Dousse, Michel, and Jean-Michel Roessli, eds. *Jean de Menasce (1902–1973)*. Fribourg: Bibliothèque Cantonale et Universitaire, 1998.

Dubois, Jérémie. *L'enseignement de l'italien en France (1880–1940)*. Grenoble: UGA Éditions, 2015.

Duchêne, Roger. "Un inédit proustien, le testament de 'L'Oncle Adolphe.'" *Revue d'histoire littéraire de la France* 104 (2004–2003).

Dupré, Romain. "René Groos, dit Pierre Herbel, homme de lettres et professeur." *Archives juives* 47, no. 2 (2014): 131–42.

Duraffour, Annick, and Pierre-André Taguieff. *Céline, la race, le juif: Légende littéraire et vérité historique*. Paris: Fayard, 2017.

Dyer, Nathalie Mauriac. "'Sentiments filiaux d'un parricide': Les brouillons de l'article 'sans brouillon' (1907) et de l'envoi à Daniel Halévy (1908)." *Bulletin d'informations proustiennes* 53 (2023): 41-59.

Fabre, Mélanie. *Dick May, une femme à l'avant-garde d'un nouveau siècle, 1859–1925*. Rennes: Presses Universitaires de Rennes, 2019.

Fenton, Paul B. "La contribution d'Adolphe Franck à l'étude historico-critique de la kabbale." In *Adolphe Franck, philosophe juif, spiritualiste et libéral dans la France du XIXe siècle*, ed. Jean-Pierre Rothschild Jérôme Grondeux, 81-97. Turnhout: Brepols, 2012.

Fhima, Catherine. "Au coeur de la 'renaissance juive' des années 20: Littérature et judéité." *Archives juives* 39, no. 1 (2006): 29-45.

——. "Aux sources d'un renouveau identitaire juif en France: André Spire et Edmond Fleg." *Mil neuf cent: Revue d'histoire intellectuelle (Cahiers Georges Sorel)* 13 (1995): 171-89.

Forestier, Nadège. *Henri de Rothschild: Un humanitaire avant l'heure*. Paris: Cherche Midi, 2018.

Fournier, Albert. "Du côté de chez Proust." *Europe* 48, nos. 496-97 (August-September 1970): 246-63.

Freedman, Jonathan. "Coming out of the Jewish Closet with Marcel Proust." In *Queer Theory and the Jewish Question*, ed. Daniel Boyarin, Daniel Itzkovitz and Ann Pellegrin, 334-64. New York: Columbia University Press, 2003.

Friedemann, Joë. *Alexandre Weill, écrivain contestataire et historien engagé, 1811–1899*. Strasbourg: Istra, 1980.

Gaudin, Cécile Chombard. *L'Orient dévoilé: Sur les traces de Myriam Harry*. Levallois-Perret: Éditions Turquoise, 2019.

Gautier-Vignal, Louis. "Hommage à Georges Cattaui." *Bulletin de la Société des Amis de Marcel Proust* 25 (1975): 192-95.

Gordon, Adi. *Toward Nationalism's End: An Intellectual Biography of Hans Kohn*. Waltham, MA: Brandeis University Press, 2017.

Gregh, Fernand. *L'âge de fer: Souvenirs, 1925–1955*. Paris: Grasset, 1956.

Grunwald, Kurt. "On Cairo's Lombard Street." *Tradition: Zeitschrift für Firmengeschichte und Unternehmerbiographie* 17, no. 1 (January-February 1972): 8-22.

Hallman, Diana R. *Opera, Liberalism, and Antisemitism in Nineteenth-Century France: The Politics of Halévy's La Juive*. Cambridge: Cambridge University Press, 2002.

Hamon, Augustin, and X. Y. Z. *Les maîtres de la France*, vol. 3, *La féodalité financière dans les transports ferroviaires, routiers, aériens, maritimes, dans les ports, canaux, entreprises coloniales*. Paris: Éditions Sociales Internationales, 1936-1938.

Hassine, Juliette. *Ésotérisme et écriture dans l'oeuvre de Proust*. Paris: Minard, 1990.

——. *Marranisme et hébraïsme dans l'oeuvre de Proust*. Paris: Minard, 1994.

Heumann, Claude. "Correspondance." *Europe* 49, nos. 502-3 (February-March 1971): 190-91.

Joly, Hervé. *À Polytechnique: X 1901*. Paris: Flammarion, 2021.

Jutrin, Monique. "Bespaloff, Chestov, Fondane." In *The Tragic Discourse: Shestov and Fondane's Existential Thought*, ed. Ramona Fotiade, 237-48. Berne: Peter Lang, 2006.

Knörzer, Heidi. "Hippolyte Prague, rédacteur en chef des *Archives israélites*." *Archives juives* 43, no. 1 (2010): 140-43.

——. "Isidore Cahen, directeur des *Archives israélites*." *Archives juives* 51, no. 1 (2018): 126-31.

Kohn, Hans. *The Idea of Nationalism: A Study in Its Origins and Background*. New York: Macmillan, 1944.

——. *Living in a World Revolution: My Encounters with History*. New York: Simon and & Schuster, 1964.

Kristeva, Julia. *Le temps sensible: Proust et l'expérience littéraire*. Paris: Gallimard, 1994.

Kuperminc, Jean-Claude. "Le tour des revues juives." *La revue des revues* 6 (1988): 40-50.

La Rochefoucauld, Edmée de. *Courts métrages II*. Paris: Grasset, 1980.

Lacretelle, Anne de. *Tout un monde: Jacques de Lacretelle et ses amis*. Paris: Éditions de Fallois, 2019.

Lançon, Daniel. "Georges Cattaui ou la France participée." In *Entre Nil et sable: Écrivains d'Égypte d'expression française, 1920–1960*, ed. Marc Kober, Irène Fenoglio, and Daniel Lançon, 87-103. Paris: Centre National de Documentation Pédagogique, 1999.

Lappin, Eleonore. *Der Jude 1916–1928: Jüdische Moderne zwischen Universalismus und Partikularismus*. Tübingen: Mohr Siebeck, 2000.

Lardinois, Roland. "Sociologie d'un espace familial: Sylvain Lévi dans sa parentèle." In *Sylvain Lévi (1863–1935): Études indiennes, histoire sociale*, ed. Lyne Bansat-Boudon and Roland Lardinois, 267-88. Turnhout: Brepols, 2007.

Laurent, Sébastien. *Daniel Halévy: Du libéralisme au traditionalisme*. Paris: Grasset, 2001.

Lazard, Didier. *La famille Lazard*. Neully: Privately published, 1992.

Lehr, Johanna. "Les sociétés de pompes funèbres 'israélites' à Paris sous l'Occupation à l'épreuve des persécutions allemandes et vichystes." *Revue d'histoire moderne et contemporaine* 67, no. 4 (2020): 94-118.

Leymarie, Michel. "Les frères Tharaud: De l'ambiguïté du 'filon juif' dans la littérature française des années vingt." *Archives juives* 39, no. 1 (2006): 89-109.

Livak, Leonid. "'A Thankless Occupation': James Joyce and His Translator Ludmila Savitzky." *Joyce Studies Annual* (2013): 33-61.

Long, Véronique. "Les collectionneurs juifs parisiens sous la Troisième République (1870-1940)." *Archives juives* 42, no. 1 (2009): 84-104.

Malinovich, Nadia. "Affirming Difference, Confirming Integration: New Forms of Sociability Among French Jews in the 1920s." In *The Jews of Modern France: Images and Identities*, ed. N. Malinovich and Zvi Jonathan Kaplan, 102-26. Leiden: Brill, 2016.

——. *French and Jewish: Culture and the Politics of Identity in Early Twentieth-Century France*. Oxford: Littman Library of Jewish Civilization, 2008.

——. *Heureux comme un juif en France: Intégration, identité, culture, 1900–1932*. Paris: Honoré Champion, 2010.

——. "Littérature populaire et romans juifs dans la France des années 1920." *Archives juives* 39, no. 1 (2006): 46-62.

——. "Une expression du 'Réveil juif' des années vingt: La revue *Menorah* (1922-1933)." *Archives juives* 37, no. 1 (2004): 86-96.

Marks, Elaine. *Marrano as Metaphor: The Jewish Presence in French Writing.* New York: Columbia University Press, 1995.

Maurois, André. *À la recherche de Marcel Proust.* 1949. Paris: Hachette, 1986.

Mayeur, Jean-Marie, and Arlette Schweitz. *Les parlementaires de la Seine sous la Troisième République.* Paris: Publications de la Sorbonne, 2001.

Mazuy, Rachel. "Jean-Richard Bloch–Denis Saurat: Une amitié littéraire (1925–1946)." 2017. https://cturss.hypotheses.org/88.

Mesnil-Amar, Jacqueline. "Jeanne Proust et son fils." *Les nouveaux cahiers* 28 (Spring 1972): 50–57.

——. "Proust, les juifs et le monde." *Les nouveaux cahiers* 19 (Autumn 1969): 35–45.

——. "Racisme et snobisme chez Proust." *La Nef* 19–20 (September–December 1964): 173–82.

Mesnil-Amar, Jacqueline, and André Amar. *Parcours d'écriture: Deux figures du judaïsme français d'après-guerre.* Ed. Michèle Bitton and Sylvie Jessua-Amar. Paris: Alliance Israélite Universelle, 2005.

Miccoli, Dario. "A Fragile Cradle: Writing Jewishness, Nationhood, and Modernity in Cairo, 1920–1940." *Jewish Social Studies* 21, no. 3 (Spring–Summer 2016): 1–30.

Milly, Jean. *Les pastiches de Proust.* Paris: Armand Colin, 1970.

Mimouni, Patrick. *Les mémoires maudites: Juifs et homosexuels dans l'oeuvre et la vie de Marcel Proust.* Paris: Grasset, 2018.

Mingelgrün, Albert. *Thèmes et structures bibliques dans l'oeuvre de Marcel Proust: Étude stylistique de quelques interférences.* Lausanne: L'Âge d'Homme, 1978.

Mopsik, Charles. "Quelques remarques sur Adolphe Franck, philosophe français et pionnier de l'étude de la Cabale au XIXe siècle." *Pardès* 19–20 (1994): 239–44.

Moyse, Laurent. *Du rejet à l'intégration: Histoire des juifs du Luxembourg des origines à nos jours.* Luxembourg: Éditions Saint-Paul, 2011.

Murakami, Yuji. "L'affaire Dreyfus dans l'oeuvre de Proust." Thesis, Université Paris IV-Sorbonne, 2012.

Nicault, Catherine. "Albert Cohen et les sionistes." In *Albert Cohen dans son siècle: Actes du colloque de Cerisy-la-Salle, septembre 2003,* ed. Alain Schaffner and Philippe Zard, 99–118. Paris: Éditions Le Manuscrit, 2005.

——. *La France et le sionisme, 1897–1948: Une rencontre manquée?* Paris: Calmann-Lévy, 1992.

——. "L'acculturation des israélites français au sionisme après la Grande Guerre." *Archives juives* 39, no. 1 (2006): 9–28.

——. "Les 'Français israélites' et la ligue d'Action Française." In *L'Action Française: Culture, société, politique,* ed. Michel Leymarie and Jacques Prévotat, 185–202. Lille: Presses Universitaires du Septentrion, 2008.

Painter, George D. *Marcel Proust.* 2 vols. Trans. G. Cattaui and R.-P. Vial. Paris: Mercure de France, 1966.

Pasteur, Paul. "Les débuts de la crémation moderne en France." *Le mouvement social* 179 (April–June 1997): 59–80.

Peyrefitte, Roger. *Propos secrets.* Paris: Albin Michel, 1977.

Pinault, Michel. *Frédéric Joliot-Curie.* Paris: Odile Jacob, 2000.

Piperno, Alessandro. *Proust antiebreo.* Milan: FrancoAngeli, 2000.

——. *Proust antijuif.* Trans. Fanchita Gonzalez Batlle. Paris: Liana Levi, 2007.

Plaut, Gilles. *Cimetière du Père-Lachaise: Division israélite.* Paris: Cercle de Généalogie Juive, 1999.

Polack, Emmanuelle. "À la fondation CASIP-COJASOR: Retrouvées, classées, enfin accessibles: Les Archives du Comité de bienfaisance israélite de Paris (CBIP)." *Archives juives* 36, no. 2 (2003): 131–38.

Prost, Antoine, and Jay Winter. *René Cassin et les droits de l'homme: Le projet d'une génération*. Paris: Fayard, 2011.

Raczymow, Henri. "Proust et la judéité: Les destins croisés de Swann et de Bloch." *Pardès* 21 (1995): 209–22.

—. *Ruse et déni: Cinq essais de littérature*. Paris: PUF, 2011.

Recanati, Jean. *Profils juifs de Marcel Proust*. Paris: Buchet-Chastel, 1979.

Reff, Theodore. *Degas: The Artist's Mind*. New York: Metropolitan Museum of Art, 1976.

Roessli, Jean-Michel. "Jean de Menasce (1902–1973), historien des religions, théologien et philosophe." *Revue des sciences philosophiques et théologiques* 101, no. 4 (2017): 611–54.

Rougemont, Guy de. *Lazard Frères: Banquiers des deux mondes (1848–1939)*. Paris: Fayard, 2011.

Rousset, David. *L'univers concentrationnaire*. 1946. Paris: Éditions de Minuit, 1965.

Rysselberghe, Maria van. *Les cahiers de la petite dame*. Paris: Gallimard, 1973.

Salazar-Ferrer, Olivier. "Bespaloff." In *Dictionnaire Albert Camus*, ed. Jeanyves Guérin, 86–87. Paris: Robert Laffont, 2009.

Samuels, Maurice. *Inventing the Israelite: Jewish Fiction in Nineteenth-Century France*. Stanford, CA: Stanford University Press, 2010.

Sauget, Stéphanie. "Enterrer les mort pendant le double siège de Paris (1870–1871)." *Revue historique* 317, no. 3 (July 2015): 557–855.

Schaffner, Alain. "L'échec de *La revue juive* d'Albert Cohen." *Mémoires du livre/Studies in Book Culture* 4, no. 1 (Autumn 2012). https://www.erudit.org/fr/revues/memoires/2012-v4-n1-memoires 0385/1013324ar/.

Schreiber, Jean-Philippe. "Les élites politiques juives et la franc-maçonnerie dans la France du XIXᵉ siècle." *Archives juives* 43, no. 2 (2010): 58–69.

Sebban, Joël. "Être juif et chrétien: La question juive et les intellectuels catholiques français issus du judaïsme (1898–1940)." *Archives juives* 44, no. 1 (2011): 106–22.

Sedgwick, Eve Kosofsky. *Epistemology of the Closet*. Berkeley: University of California Press, 1990.

Shoulson, Jeffrey. "Man and Thinker: Denis Saurat, and the Old New Milton Criticism." In *The New Milton Criticism*, ed. Peter C. Herman and Elizabeth Sauer, 194–211. Cambridge: Cambridge University Press, 2012.

Simon, Jacques. *Histoire du rite écossais ancien et accepté en France*, vol. 1, *Des origines à 1900*. Paris: Dervy, 2019.

Simon-Nahum, Perrine. "Marcel Proust et la vocation du narrateur: Un marranisme littéraire." In *Les marranismes: De la religiosité cachée à la société ouverte*, ed. Jacques Ehrenfreund and Jean-Philippe Schreiber, 229–51. Paris: Demopolis, 2014.

Sinclair, Anne. *La rafle des notables*. Paris: Grasset, 2020.

Smith, Paul J. *Réécrire la Renaissance, de Marcel Proust à Michel Tournier: Exercices de lecture rapprochée*. New York: Rodopi, 2009.

Sommer, Robert. "Bibliographie des travaux du grand rabbin Maurice Liber (1884–1956)." *Revue des études juives* 68, no. 1 (1959): 95–119.

Sonnenfeld, Albert. "Marcel Proust: Antisemite? I." *French Review* 62, no. 1 (October 1988): 25–40.

—. "Marcel Proust: Antisemite? II." *French Review* 62, no. 2 (December 1988): 275–82.

Spector, Sheila. "Kabbalistic Sources: Blake's and His Critics.'" *Blake: An Illustrated Quarterly* 17, no. 3 (Winter 1983–1984): 84–101.

Spire, Marie-Brunette. "Gustave Kahn et la revue *Menorah*." In *Gustave Kahn (1859–1936)*, ed. Sophie Basch, 483–505. Paris: Classiques Garnier, 2009.

Suleiman, Susan Rubin. "Foreigners and Strangers: Jews in French Society and Literature between the Two World Wars." In *Revisioning French Culture*, ed. Andrew Sobanet, 88–89. Liverpool: Liverpool University Press, 2019.

Tadié, Jean-Yves. *Le cercle de Marcel Proust*. 3 vols. Ed. J.-Y. Tadié. Paris: Honoré Champion, 2013–2021.

—. *Marcel Proust*. Paris: Gallimard, 1996.

—. *Proust et ses amis*. Ed. J.-Y. Tadié. Paris: Gallimard, 2010.

Teysseire, Daniel. "De l'usage historico-politique de race entre 1680 et 1820 et de sa transformation." *Mots: Les langages du politique* 33 (1992): 43–52.

Valbert, Gérard. *Conversations avec Albert Cohen*. Lausanne: L'Âge d'Homme, 2006.

Viey, Frédéric. "Historique du carré israélite du cimetière du Père-Lachaise." www.judaicultures.info, 2010.

—. "Les porcelainiers juifs à Fontainebleau." www.judaicultures.info, 2012.

Voignac, Joseph. "La communauté juive française et le sionisme dans les années 1930 à travers *L'univers israélite*." *Archives juives* 51, no. 1 (2018): 113–25.

Weill, Georges. "'Entre l'Orient et l'Occident': Sylvain Lévi président de l'Alliance Israélite Universelle." In *Sylvain Lévi (1863–1935): Études indiennes, histoire sociale*, ed. Lyne Bansat-Boudon and Roland Lardinois, 391–420. Turnhout: Brepols, 2007.

Wise, Pyra. "Quatorze lettres inédites adressées à Proust." *Bulletin d'informations proustiennes* 41 (2011): 7–19.

Wolitz, Seth L. *The Proustian Community*. New York: New York University Press, 1971.

Index